Unlocking Mallarmé

Unlocking Mallarmé

Graham Robb

Yale University Press
New Haven and London
1996

Set in Goudy by Best-set Typesetter Ltd, Hong Kong
Printed and bound in Great Britain by
Biddles Ltd, Guildford and Kings Lynn

Library of Congress Cataloging-in-Publication Data

Robb. Graham.
Unlocking Mallarmé/Graham Robb.
Includes index.
ISBN 0–300–06486–1 (C: alk.paper)
1. Mallarmé, Stéphane, 1842–1898 – Criticism and interpretation.
I. Title.
PQ2344.Z5R63   1996
841′, 8 – dc20   95–46661
                                                           CIP

A catalogue record for this book is available from the British Library.

'le principe qui n'est – que le Vers!'

Contents

Foreword

'*Toute méthode est une fiction*'[1]

The object of this study is to provide the reader of Mallarmé's verse poetry with a key. Not, of course, a key which gives access to some essential treasure-trove of definitive meanings; rather, a guiding principle which makes it possible to pass from one part of the labyrinth to the next without losing the thread or uprooting the hedges.

Once we have read a Mallarmé poem several times, looked up all the words in Littré, applied auxiliary etymological meanings, explained grammatical oddities or ambiguities, detected a theme, attached the poem to a field of general human interest, responded to its moods and images, compared our impressions with the opinions of a critic and, finally, assumed that when he claimed his poetry was not obscure, Mallarmé was either teasing or in error, there is probably no quick and easy way to acquire a deeper understanding (or an illusion of it), or even a conviction that deeper understanding is on offer. In fact, the most pleasurable or painful lesson of this poetry is perhaps the realization that the reward for solving one puzzle is the revelation of countless other, previously unsuspected puzzles. However, since the majority of his poems were written in accordance with a set of rules which changed very little in thirty years, strategies can be developed and insights gained into the poet's methods. Sometimes, a seemingly local observation can illuminate a whole area of his verse. The present book had its origin in such an obser-vation. Hopefully it will convey some of the excitement I felt when I saw a new path of partial understanding opening up.

The original discovery, which will be described in detail in Part I, but which should be given credit at the outset, was this: Jacques Heugel's *Dictionnaire des rimes françaises* (1941) contains a list of French words that rhyme with only a few or with no other words. The list appeared to include a large number of words frequently used by Mallarmé. This seemed a curious fact. Why would a poet who so obviously enjoys producing rich rhymes use so many unrhymable words?

This discovery then led to the following, conventional idea – so conventional that one is surprised and (to be honest) delighted to see that it has never been properly exploited: the very process of producing rhyming verse constitutes for Mallarmé an allegorical drama. The writing of the poem represents a victory over the arbitrary nature of language, and the poem itself, apart from its ostensible function as a homage, a toast, a *tableau* or the address on an envelope, tells the story of how this victory was won or the battle lost. Most of the verse poems written by Mallarmé from about 1868 on act out this allegorical drama. Sometimes the drama is performed in all its miraculous, mechanical detail; sometimes it emerges episodically in the background, but even then exercises an influence over the poem as a whole. Once abstracted from the poetry, then reapplied in a fresh reading, the drama of verse has the effect of elucidating several aspects of Mallarmé's most obscure and complex pieces. In this, it might be compared – and is in fact directly analogous to – the *drame solaire* which Gardner Davies has traced in many of Mallarmé's poems. The *drame du vers*, though, is the mother of all the other dramas and the only one that actually takes place. The rising and setting of the sun is not indispensable to the writing of the poem; verse is.

This will all become clearer in the following pages. For the time being, it may be useful to say what this book will *not* be about since a possible confusion exists.

The 'reflexivity' or 'auto-referentiality' of Mallarmé's verse – the idea that the poem 'writes itself', according to a needlessly distracting phrase – has for a long time now been the social addiction of Mallarmé criticism. Sometimes it represents an attempt to show how Mallarmé's poetry offers a vivid illustration of certain general linguistic principles. In this case, the reader looking for a peculiarly Mallarmean thrill of enlightenment might protest that something which can be said of *all* poetry tells us very little about a particular poet; we may even feel that we have been fobbed off with the truism that no text can be reduced to a single meaning.

An alternative reflexive approach usually makes its appearance in discussions of the *sonnet en yx* ('Ses purs ongles . . .'). Mallarmé didactically entitled the first version of the sonnet *Sonnet allégorique de lui-même*. The idea of a sonnet which is its own allegorical representation has been explored in various ways, often with disappointing results. The present author, for example, suggested that the vesperal dreams which are consumed in the flames of the Phoenix might be viewed in the light of Boileau's famous description of the sonnet form in his consistently defeatist *Art poétique*:

> Un sonnet sans défauts vaut seul un long poème.
> Mais en vain mille auteurs y pensent arriver;
> Et cet heureux phénix est encore à trouver.

Thus, the poem is 'consumed' by the impossible ideal of itself; or, in more conventional Romantic terms, the dreaming poet is devoured by his own hopeless desire for perfection.[2] Unfortunately, efforts to extrapolate a general principle from this one 'allegorical' sonnet have very quickly reached an unprofitable degree of generality. One could, for instance, point to the rhymes on *yx* which stand out like sore thumbs – or like pure onyx fingernails – at the end of four verses and conclude that Mallarmé draws attention to the technical aspects of verse. But what then? Does this not simply provide us with an example of Mallarmé's reflections on language – the keys to the city which, traditionally, open no door? Most poets of the period wrote poems which have poetry as their subject, and any poem written in verse can be said to refer to itself as a poem.

Where this study hopes to differ is in its demonstration that the auto-referential character of Mallarmé's poetry is not confined to consciously literary themes (as in *Don du poème*), nor to the definition of a dilemma to which the writing of the poem is more or less explicitly said to be a possible answer (in much the same way that *A la recherche du temps perdu* ends with the narrator's decision to write it), nor to a prosodic bag of tricks – an amusing rhyme, an impertinent *rejet*, an evocative alliteration or a stunning series of conceits. It will also be seen that the *sonnet en yx* is not the only poem that can be read as a prosodic allegory of itself. Most of the poems written from 1868 on might have carried a similar subtitle, but the comment had become superfluous. Mallarmé had discovered his own poetry, 'une doctrine en même temps qu'une contrée',[3] though it was to be several years before he colonized it completely.

One might ask in any case: what do we know of Mallarmé's poetic technique? Despite the wide-ranging excavations of Albert Thibaudet, Émilie Noulet and Jean-Pierre Richard, the building still lacks foundations, while the electricians, decorators and even the demolition crew have already arrived and started work. More recently, critics have studied the evidence in Mallarmé's poetry of more fundamental structures – the bedrock of mind and language. There have also been some brilliant exegeses of particular poems, to which I am clearly indebted. But the Mallarmean verse itself, that intricate product of a few rules and tools, has usually been inspected in a flighty, fragmentary fashion. Is it, for instance, really helpful if the critic simply catalogues the different types of rhyme which Mallarmé likes, or points out an *audace* here, a timid conformity to classical norm there?[4] One intended side-effect of this book, therefore, is to provide some procedures and materials which might be used in the building of these foundations, or to suggest where digging might begin.

The first part of the book (Chapters 1–5) is meant to establish the fact that Mallarmé's poems derive certain values or connotations from the prosodic tradition in which he places his work. This historical-prosodic perspective is one which has been: a) largely ignored, perhaps because much of this poetry is now well over a century old, and deviations from forgotten norms are unlikely to be considered significant; b) converted to a thousand peepholes through which the 'vieil ébat triomphal' of source studies is practised with a grim, obsessive pleasure; c) used as a pretext for glib generalizations of a historical nature based on a tiny number of texts.

Chapters 6–10 will consist of selective analyses in which poems are treated as manifestations of a prosody which, far from hiding behind the subject, constantly pushes to the front of the stage. These analyses will be complemented by a comparative study of different texts, in verse and in prose. Mallarmé's repeated use of certain words reveals groups of images to which he attaches a particular significance and which are almost always renovations of well-worn clichés or of facts that seemed too self-evident to be worth mentioning. This use of concentric allegories or metaphors, each dependent on the other, is well attested. What has not been sufficiently emphasized is the extent to which these images refer to specific, verifiable and retrospectively obvious prosodic realities.

Bringing key words together in a sort of narrative concordance is not always a guarantee of rewarding results. It may, on the other hand, be convenient to cultivate an equally suspicious attitude to the sort of approach that sets out in the other direction. Mallarmé has always attracted critics who sit down in his texts with the confidence of people who can rely on their weight to remould the armchair. For example: the word 'gisement', in the Vasco da Gama sonnet ('Au seul souci de voyager . . .'), is interpreted either as 'bearing' or as 'deposit' (see p. 105):

> [Un oiseau]
> Qui criait monotonement
> Sans que la barre ne varie
> Un inutile gisement
> Nuit, désespoir et pierrerie

Several critics, passing up an excellent opportunity to practise Negative Capability, have issued statements like this: 'X is mistaken in her commentary: *gisement* is a nautical/mineralogical term.' One is reminded here of the argument which takes place in the engine-yard between Gordon, Duck and an engine from the Other Railway: they have all been to London, but on different lines, and so they all know the name of London station.[5]

A moment's relaxation would reveal that we have not been called upon to cast our vote for one sense or the other. Mallarmé uses the word 'gisement' in such a way as to emphasize, in a clear and unequivocal fashion, its ambiguity – whatever additional doubts he may create. In line 10, he attaches it in advance to the tiller ('barre') of the ship; in line 12, to precious stones ('pierrerie'). There are many such examples in his poetry of what is apparently known as parisology: the deliberate pursuit of ambiguity in one's use of language.[6] Similarly – but worse – a general term like 'oiseau' may be taken to refer to a particular member of the group. No one now tries to identify the 'sister' of *Prose pour des Esseintes* or 'Pulchérie' as particular individuals, but bets are still being taken for the unnamed bird of *Petit Air II*; the 'bouquin' (ignoring the plural) 'closed on the name of Paphos' has been identified several times; and then of course there is the *ptyx* . . .[7] Mallarmé's poems are a wonderful testing-ground for extreme forms of reading, but they also provide a structure in which very different strategies can be combined experimentally. They do not, it seems to me, simply open poetry up to 'la compréhension multiple'[8] so that it can be locked away in a hermetic cell, its secret, absent meanings unglimpsed by rare visitors through the fourteen bars of the sonnet. But then neither do they have a single official meaning, nor even a single form of meaning.

They might be read with greater profit if they were viewed, for example, as complex developments of the Baroque *metafora di decettione*. The 'deception' normally consists in preventing the reader from deciding which term of the comparison is supposed to be dominant. The hierarchy of subject and image dissolves; the 'tenor' is indistinguishable from the 'vehicle'. In the twenty-fourth *Fleur du Mal*, for instance, the 'subject' may be identified either as the Moon compared to a woman, or as a woman compared to the Moon.[9] Perhaps it was the Song of Solomon that suggested the provocative power of the device to Baudelaire. With Mallarmé, the poem itself becomes a metaphor for the apparent subject, or rather, the subject loses its traditional importance and becomes a metaphor, one might almost say an excuse, for the poem. For this reason, it is possible to give a thematic reading of the formal aspects of Mallarmé's verse.

The structure of this rhetorical device obviously appealed to Mallarmé. He talks – using an image which is now common currency – of different layers ('couches') of meaning, referring not simply to the use of ambiguous words or to the reader's wandering mind, but to the poem in its entirety, the poem as a skilful entanglement of themes, like *L'Après-midi d'un faune* – 'une sorte de *fugue* littéraire', according to Valéry, in which 'toutes les ressources de la poétique s'emploient à soutenir un triple développement d'images et d'idées'.[10] To borrow an image that Mallarmé borrowed from Baudelaire: the drama of verse allows us to trace the meandering of one of the spirals that form the thyrsus. Once identified and followed, one spiral reveals the relative position of all the others.

The principal motif or organizer of these poetic *tours de force* is invariably verse itself. In saying this, my intention is not to ensure that every poem stays firmly on the page and talks shop. Anyone who likes to see the dramatic preoccupations of human existence loom large in poetry might feel, however, that this is a self-defeating inversion of the normal arrangement. Who but the most fanatical cryptophile would wish to see the poignant stoicism of 'Le vierge, le vivace et le bel aujourd'hui . . .' turned into an image of the words which express it? In fact, this inversion opens up far wider and more surprising perspectives. Seen as a recorded expedition into itself, Mallarmé's poetry is perhaps even more rewarding than it is when read simply as description

made difficult. For him, the word *verse* does not refer exclusively to versification; it alludes also to primordial structures which are common to all
human expression. *Le vers* therefore also exists in prose, but, as Mallarmé puts
it, its rhymes are concealed (*dissimulées*).[11] The organization of the poem
around this 'principle' – the starting point and end of all expression – thus
reflects and develops a particular conception of the world. *Vers* and *univers* –
both the words and the things – have the same origin. (This point is dealt
with at length in Chapter 3.) In other words, the prosodic reading will be
both partial (because it deals primarily with the actual components of
verse) and global (because verse is taken by Mallarmé to be a microcosmic
structure). Let it be said with all due modesty: if Mallarmé was right, then
the person who investigates his verse is performing a scientific function
far superior to that of the most powerful telescope or the largest particle
accelerator.

The philosophical significance of prosodic 'constraints' in Mallarmé's
poetry, and, especially, the influential role he and French verse assign to
rhyme ('la primauté dans l'enchantement donnée à la rime')[12] will inevitably
remain obscure or tediously abstract if the frills of prosody are seen as mere
ornaments or servile complements of theme. To say that Mallarmé accepts –
with a vengeance – the rules of French versification is not to say that his
poetry is just a glorified word-game. It certainly is that; but it is also an
original way of expounding a philosophy – or, more appropriately, an original
use of philosophy. For someone who believes that verse corresponds to a
primordial 'instinct', the struggle will necessarily reside, not in the manipulation of logical propositions, but in the arrangement of syllables and rhymes.
The impression may at first be one of trivial obsession – Mallarmé himself was
aware of this – but it is partly the doubts raised in the mind of the reader (is
the poem a magical, metaphysical revelation or the useless result of tinkering
with an outmoded machine?) that make our reading of these poems a drama
in itself, full of discouragements and discoveries.

One might then quite cheerfully reverse the normal order of perception:
the *drame solaire*, the waving of a fan, kissing, eating, sailing, drowning or any
other theme can be appreciated as images of the prosodic drama. Mallarmé
actually says this on several different occasions: the 'sacred rules' of poetry,
highlighted 'on every page of the book', form a thrilling 'intellectual spectacle', whereas 'l'autre, tiré de l'affabulation ou le prétexte, lui est comparable'. Heads of hair, fans, pieces of lace, idle compliments, even the grand old
abstractions, all contribute to the 'ciel métaphorique qui se propage à l'entour
de la foudre du vers'.[13] Mallarmé's 'philosophy' was simply (for the poet) 'une
sorte d'armature sur laquelle il *modelait* son poème, une corde sonore où il le
modulait'.[14] The 'theme', in the traditional sense, is just one motif among
many, 'le motif général qu'on appelle à tort sujet'.[15] Or, to recall one of those
charming insults which, provisionally at least, we must assume are directed at

someone else: all texts should offer 'un sens même indifférent', because then the idle browser will pass on happily, thinking that there is nothing there of interest.[16]

The internal logic of the drama has determined my presentation of the facts. For this reason, though it was written several years before most of the other poems discussed, I have left *Prose pour des Esseintes* until close to the end because it seems to sum up the drama as a whole and to provoke the most spectacular showdown between poetry and reality.

Some of Mallarmé's most important 'serious' poems occupy a secondary place in this book. There are two reasons for this. First, I thought it useful to comment on poems which are rarely analysed or even mentioned. Readers who have explored the quieter resorts of Mallarmé's poetry may be pleased to find opinions expressed which they can share or contradict. Second, the drama is acted out most vividly in the poems written in short verses. The effect, it must be said, is diluted in many of the more complex alexandrine sonnets. However, readers may wish to apply the findings of this study to other poems: some suggestions are made in the Conclusion. The main aim of this book is to present an idea which can, of course, be refined, developed or dismissed.

A penultimate word before setting the scene. The approach adopted in this study has as its corollary the following, conventional supposition: that there is inherent in Mallarmé's later poems a perceptible unity, both philosophical and methodological, which can be formulated and then used as a point of reference in the exegesis of any one of those poems. This determining unity is revealed in part by the historical state of French poetry in the aftermath of *Les Fleurs du Mal*, partly by the rules of versification, and partly by the avowed intentions of the poet. No claim is made here that only the explicit statements of the poet himself have the power to deliver into our hands some irrefutable, final reading. Every reader, as we know, recreates the text in reading. But recreation, like restoration, is often an impoverishment – a fact of which every reader of Mallarmé is made painfully aware at almost every step. Though readers who erect their critical scaffolding on the face of a literary monument are in no way obliged, in order to complete their task, to know everything that the original builders had to know – the plastic and aesthetic qualities of the material or the nature of the tools used to fashion it – such knowledge can nevertheless be a source of interest and enhance the quality of the restoration. It also helps to uncover new or old hypotheses and allows us to become, momentarily, in reading, unlike ourselves.

The other supposition is that, with patience, Mallarmé pays back our mental investment (for example, in a fund designed to meet our burial costs) at a much higher rate of interest than almost any other poet. I mention this here because it may not seem to be implied by what follows. We may (to

change the metaphor) have to weigh ourselves down with compasses, sex-
tants and other distracting, useful pieces of equipment and survive for a time
on tasteless, dehydrated food; but when we reach the Pole, there will be more
than just a geographical satisfaction. The other, considerable satisfactions
may even have to console us for a suspicion, when we find no other flag, that
our instruments have malfunctioned. With that possibility in mind – though
not for that reason – verifiable observations have been made along the way so
that the scientific results will in any case justify the hypothetical funding –
and, it is hoped, the reader's patience.

I should like to thank the following for theirs: Malcolm Bowie and Jim
Hiddleston (who read the manuscript), Gregory Hutchinson, Bertrand
Marchal, Geoffrey Neate, Claude Pichois, Raymond Poggenburg and
Stephen Roberts. Thanks also to Robert Baldock, Candida Brazil and Fiona
Screen.

Part I
Rehearsals

1

Poetry on the Production Line

'. . . des rythmes uniformes et convenus là où l'on prétend, au contraire, nous intéresser à l'essentielle variété des sentiments humains!'[1]

When Mallarmé began writing poems in the 1850s, French poetry, for all its scope and ambitions, was still remarkable for its uniformity and conformity. Rhyme, metre, stanzaic form, vocabulary and theme were all governed by certain conventions, the most important of which could be summed up in a few pages. Worse still, it was all so obvious. A modern reader, confronted for the first time with the poetry of Chénier, Lamartine or Vigny, can hardly fail to be struck by this regularity. At first sight, the similarities between the poems of these three poets are considerably more impressive than any differences. Even poetry dating from the latter half of the century is likely to disappoint or reassure the uninitiated. Anyone who opens an edition of Rimbaud after hearing about his systematic flouting of rules and conventions might be forgiven for not immediately recognizing the 'mystique à l'état sauvage' in the tidy ranks of his *Poésies*.

The superficial homogeneity of French poetry is apparent not only in each of the constituent elements of a poem, but also in the various groupings of these elements. A certain metre frequently accompanies a particular form or even a particular subject, as if everything were conveniently preordained. In addition, certain word-combinations recur so insistently that it would be relatively easy to reconstitute most of *Les Fleurs du Mal* by cutting and pasting phrases from the poetry of thirty or so poets of the same period, say from 1800 to 1850. This is what the source-seekers of this century inadvertently demonstrated when they found that almost any line of poetry could be attached to a giant family tree whose size was limited only by the critic's erudition. One trembles to think how much poetry was read merely as a source of spare parts for the big machines. So, when Baudelaire boasted in one of the prefaces he planned for *Les Fleurs du Mal* that he could teach us all to become poets in twenty lessons, he was pulling our leg with one hand and pointing something out with the other. The sarcasm consists not so much in the idea itself as in the fact that he thought of inserting this inflammatory remark in a 'serious' book of poetry.

There are also several external signs of this systematization of poetry which placed poetic 'creation' within the reach of any literate person. Sonnets, elegies, even epic poems were manufactured by people who were not primarily poets. Typesetters seem to have been especially prolific, access to the production line apparently being a large part of poetic ability. Even without conducting any research into the rhyming habits of nineteenth-century metromaniacs, one can find evidence of the fossilized state of French poetry quite close to home. A modern reader with a knowledge of the rules of versification and some experience of regular French verse should be able to construct a sonnet that would at least be technically entitled to be called a sonnet. The system which had remained in force since the Renaissance provides the pseudo-poet not only with themes and phrases but also with hundreds of masculine and feminine rhymes in groups of four – some of which must have had a considerable influence on what poets actually decided to say. A brief experiment with these poetic building-blocks would show that the idea that the sonnet is the most difficult form in French poetry calls for some qualification. Furthermore, the longer the tradition lasts, the more productive it becomes: some major developments and influences in French poetry can be explained by analogy with Tupperware parties. Sales increase pyramidally, while the inherent quality of the merchandise is not necessarily important, still less its contents.

The evidence of professional versifiers leads to the same conclusion. Almost every prominent poet of the mid-nineteenth century was able to improvise poems in regular, rhyming verse with what now seems astonishing ease. Impromptus were not the prerogative of musicians. Even Mallarmé, whose pen we imagine hovering so hesitantly over the whiteness of the page, appears to have enjoyed the ability to write without thinking too hard, before subsequently extracting the poem from the initial draft 'par *élimination*'. The rapidity and relative ease of the preliminary work are suggested in this rhythmical phrase in a letter to Eugène Lefébure:

> je me suis dit, aux heures de synthèse nécessaire 'je vais travailler du coeur' et je sens mon coeur (sans doute que toute ma vie s'y porte), et le reste de mon corps oublié, sauf la main qui écrit et ce coeur qui vit, mon ébauche se fait.[2]

The final action is intransitive. Perhaps, a few decades later, Mallarmé might have hired apprentices to prepare his *ébauches*.

Confirmation of this unMallarmean facility can be found in his collection of juvenilia, *Entre quatre murs*, which contains four 'improvised' poems dated 1859,[3] and also in the memoirs of Léopold Dauphin, who remembers

Mallarmé improvising verses in the manner of several different modern poets.[4]

Despite attempts by Baudelaire and other champions of Poe's *Philosophy of Composition* to discredit the Romantic cliché, 'inspiration' seems in any case to have had a very distant relationship with 'disorder'. This is what the inventors of automatic writing discovered when they tried to write automatically. The pen so naturally runs in ancient ruts that a whole machinery of tricks and stratagems must be called upon in order to push it off the road. The Surrealist experiment occurs in less drastic forms throughout the history of French Romantic verse. Long before the end of the nineteenth century, poets were trying to galvanize classical verse by developing forms like the dithyramb. In this dishevelled type of ode, lines and stanzas of different length are combined (though the verses themselves are still regular) with the aim of expressing the 'fièvre inspirée' of the poet.[5] 'Fièvre inspirée' is not a phrase that springs to mind when one reads most dithyrambs of the period. The conventions still in force tended to guarantee the coherence and unity of the text and to swamp the most energetic outburst in a reassuring tide of familiarity and insignificance. No doubt this explains why so many lyrical poems took the form of lullabies, and why a journalist writing for *Le Voleur* was able to report in 1848 that dentists were reciting Lamartine to their patients before pulling their teeth.[6]

For Mallarmé, this superficial coherence becomes a starting-point for something new. The deliberate difficulty of his poems and the resulting impression of complex, unusual significance increases with each revision. We shall see this not as a revolt against restrictive norms, but as an exploitation of the possibilities they support.

An important corollary of this system constantly reinforced by successive poets is the following, seemingly esoteric phenomenon: the 'meaning' of a poem is to a large extent a function of prosodic norms. To give just one example for the moment: in the 1830s and 1840s, lyric poets who frequently write in verses of five syllables or less can be said to be proclaiming their allegiance to the author of *Les Orientales*. One can immediately infer from the shortness of their lines, with a fair chance of being correct, that they share with Victor Hugo the notion that 'pure poetry' is essentially 'useless'. One might even formulate the following axiom (excluding collections of political songs): the lower the average number of syllables in a line of poetry, the less interested the poet is in current affairs. Such sweeping claims can normally be confirmed with other evidence: themes, titles, epigraphs and prefaces.

Like many poets after Baudelaire who continued to use regular verse forms, Mallarmé exploits the relationship between the formal and semantic elements of poetic language. A vivid example is his brief experiment with the *sonnet libertin* (or *licencieux*) in two early sonnets: *Renouveau* and *Angoisse* (originally entitled *Vere novo* and *À une putain*). In the *sonnet libertin*, the two quatrains are constructed on three or four different rhymes (e.g. ABBA

CDDC or ABAB CDCD instead of the usual ABBA ABBA or ABAB ABAB). In the course of a study of *Les Fleurs du Mal* and French poetry in the 1840s, it emerged that the four-rhyme *sonnet libertin* was extremely rare in the first half of the nineteenth century. Out of several hundred sonnets, excluding Baudelaire's, I found only seventeen (by ten poets) with four different rhymes in the quatrains. Moreover, most of these sonnets have other unusual features, such as the use of more than one metre or the repetition of rhymes in the tercets, which tend to soften the impact of the irregularity: they act as distractions or excuses for the poet's licence. Baudelaire, on the other hand, uses the *sonnet libertin* very frequently, though most of his sonnets appear quite regular in other respects. Out of a total of seventy-six sonnets,[7] forty-one are *sonnets libertins*, many of them written in the 1840s.

Because of the extreme rarity of this form, the absence of the expected rhymes in the second quatrain was immediately apparent to a reader of the time. Its effect might be compared to a discord in an otherwise harmonious piece of music. And because of its obviousness, the deviation could acquire a particular significance in relation to the context. A *sonnet libertin* by Arsène Houssaye demonstrates its potential beyond any reasonable doubt:

> Pour chanter sous le ciel ce que j'ai dans le coeur,
> Je demandais un luth à la muse amoureuse,
> Quand ma jeune beauté vint, fraîche et savoureuse,
> S'asseoir sur mes genoux avec un air moqueur.
>
> – Pour accorder ainsi la raison et la rime,
> Ah! que de temps perdu dans les jours précieux;
> C'est chercher le soleil quand la nuit est aux cieux:
> Crois-moi, ne lasse pas ton coeur à cette escrime.[8]

The unexpected arrival of different rhymes in the second quatrain (underlined by the fact that the deviation is introduced by the word *rime*) corresponds to the muse's desire to distract the poet from his futile effort to marry rhyme and reason. This is a *sonnet libertin* inspired by a libertine muse – a mocking muse who proves her point by trotting out the cliché, *rime-escrime* (though it may be unfair to blame the muse for this).

Whatever the specific, contextual reasons for Mallarmé's flirtation with the *sonnet libertin* – graphic evidence of what the sonnets themselves call 'impuissance' and 'stérilité'? – it can be considered as a hitherto unrecognized aspect of his youthful homage to Baudelaire. Some poets, like Gautier and Banville, found Baudelaire's habit of implicitly pointing out the rule he persistently refused to obey perverse, irritating or incomprehensible: why deliberately produce a sonnet that 'limps'?[9] Others, like Verlaine and Mallarmé, saw that the negative connotations of this deviant form could be made to complement the explicit theme of the poem. The disequilibrium of the quatrains had a historically determined value to which Mallarmé alluded when he described *Renouveau* in a letter to Henri Cazalis as a pathetic runt – 'un pauvre sonnet éclos, ces jours-ci, triste et laid. . . . Cela pourrait s'appeler *Spleen printanier*.'[10]

The sentence used as an epigraph for this chapter is intended as a reminder that the rules and norms that governed French poetry produced in some poets a reaction which stick-in-the-muds liked to describe as cynical. As Baudelaire's provocative *sonnets libertins* suggest, this reaction is seen to full advantage in the use of rhyme. Rhyme is especially revealing for several reasons. First because Mallarmé and his favourite poets tend to treat it with unusual respect. In Mallarmé's poetry, the rhyming word is often the corner-stone or 'final seed'[11] of the entire verse: the rhyme-scheme precedes the poem. Second, rhyme is subject to a greater number of rules than any other element of versification – rules which govern the sound, gender and even spelling of the rhyming word. Its (mis)behaviour therefore has many possible connotations. Third, in addition to the values conferred on them by the poet's procedures and by the rules of versification, rhymes can also be coloured by the use other poets have made of them. This point is worth developing because it leads to observations which might otherwise seem far-fetched or naive.

Lyre-délire or *encensoir-soir* are instantly recognizable in the nineteenth century as clichéd rhymes. A rapid survey of a few randomly selected books of poetry from the first half of the century should turn up at least one occurrence of each rhyme, and all readers of French poetry could easily draw up a list of other noticeably common rhymes. Even the supposedly recherché *caravane-savane* is very prevalent, part of a mini-repertoire which supplies the needs of 'exotic' poets: *more-sycomore, dromadaire-bayadère, sultane-platane-mahométane*, or, recrossing the Mediterranean, *Andalouse-pelouse-jalouse, Castille-Séville-mantille, Grenade-sérénade-embuscade-alcade*, etc. Some poets who try to make their rhymes as rich as possible seem to have found the *caravane-savane* combination so tempting that they often force *savane* to mean 'desert' so that a *caravane* can be driven through it. One poet with a finer sense of geography gets round the difficulty with an awkward periphrasis, evoking 'l'Amérique aux immenses savanes', and its rivers, 'Qui jamais sur [leurs] bords n'[ont] vu les caravanes'.[12] Lines like these have the merit of enhancing one's pleasure in reading Baudelaire's 'Sed non satiata', with its four perfectly justified rhymes on *avane*.

In the days before Baudelaire offered up-to-date proof that serious poetry could be self-consciously ironic, the 'cynical' poet would often direct his attack against one part of the system of norms but without calling the whole system into question. According to Sainte-Beuve, Alfred de Musset deliber-ately weakened the first masculine rhyme of his ballad, 'L'Andalouse':[13] the name 'Améoni', forming a *rime suffisante* with 'bruni' (because two phonemes are identical), was changed to 'Amaëgui'. The resulting rhyme, in which only the final phoneme corresponds, is a *rime pauvre*.[14] Implicit in this change was Musset's antipathy for Hugolian poets who were allegedly prepared to sacrifice almost anything in order to obtain a *rime riche*. Such is the value, in certain contexts, of a single phoneme. Similarly, but conversely, when Banville brags about the richness of his rhymes, he implicitly declares his historical allegiance to Hugo's Grand Cénacle. For connected reasons, during most of the nineteenth century, the number of identical phonemes in a poet's average rhyme (like the length of his lines) is a fairly accurate guide to voting intentions (assuming eligibility). Poor rhymes tend to be a sign of socialist sympathies, rich rhymes of conservatism or political indifference.

In the second half of the century, as the frontiers between poetic genres began to fade, these tacit allusions sometimes formed part of an attack on the system as a whole or on French poetry's excessive reliance on convention. In one of his earliest sonnets, Baudelaire uses the hackneyed rhymes *ange*, *étrange*, *sans mélange*, *fange*, underlining the word *ange*. The rhymes of the sonnet illustrate the theme: a denunciation of Romantic poets who ask these tired old harmonies to tart up the most tawdry or mercenary little girlfriend and present her to the reader as yet another Virgin Mary from the icon factory. Towards the end of his life, Baudelaire was still being sarcastic in his choice of rhymes, hinting, as he does in his criticism, that mere convention is usually a mask for crass stupidity. In 'L'Examen de minuit', for the first and only time, he brings out the old chestnut, *lyre-délire*:

> Enfin, nous avons, pour noyer
> Le vertige dans le délire,
> Nous, prêtre orgueilleux de la Lyre,
> . . .
> Bu sans soif et mangé sans faim!

Here, the rhyme is prevented from performing its traditional function. For Baudelaire, lyricism and delirium are incompatible, and their chance phonetic similarity little more than a sad irony. Words cannot be trusted to arrange themselves in truthful patterns; natural harmonies are vicious unless modified. The *délire* in 'L'Examen de minuit' is not the prophetic frenzy of a Sibyl, but a purely material, brutish drunkenness.

In Corbière's *Amours jaunes*, which appeared six years after Baudelaire's death, there are far more flagrant instances of this masochistic devalorization of poetic language. In 'I Sonnet, avec la manière de s'en servir', the unusual rhyme, 'chloroforme', is stuck at the end of a line, not because the poem has to do with scientific progress, but because the poet was looking for any old word that might satisfy the rules of rhyme. (He may also, of course, have been thinking of the anaesthetic virtues of French verse.)

> A chaque pieu, la rime – exemple: *chloroforme*.
> – Chaque vers est un fil, et la rime un jalon.

Appropriately, the sonnet ends, just before the poet runs out of syllables, with the line: '"O lyre! O délire! O . . ." – Sonnet – Attention!'*

Corbière's do-it-yourself sonnet is sarcastic partly because it compares a venerable cultural item to something as recent and banal as a telegraph, but also because all the rules are scrupulously followed – all, that is, except the unwritten rule that forbids any direct reference to the rules.

Such uncouth behaviour on the part of poets is conventionally cited as an example of a revolution in Western literature and described in heroic, negative terms as a subversion or demolition of the old system. However, if one adopts the point of view of the poet, running his software on the mainframe of the sonnet, it might just as well be described in positive terms. The currency of generally accepted norms provided poets with a reliable mechanism which allowed them to take advantage of the reader's expectations when calculating their effects. Every deviation from the norm is suggestive or, in the terms of a famous theory, carries more information. If the normal link is missing, the reader's mind is activated and will attempt to fill whatever gaps the poet has created. Baudelaire's 'Yankee' images, admired by Laforgue and the Surrealists – a woman's chest compared to a wardrobe, kisses to watermelons and so on[15] – are, in terms of convention, 'errors'. For most critics of the time, they were just that. Interestingly, some of the most curious images of mediocre collections of poetry can often be found on the *errata* page: sometimes the 'corrections' are unusual images which might have been judged eccentric but which the poet was unwilling to sacrifice.

Some poets, including Mallarmé, turned this phenomenon into a precept. The process might be seen as a methodical development of the classical idea of a *beau désordre*, a *désordre* produced in a deliberate and organized fashion. This is surely the sense of Verlaine's bizarre advice to poets in his 'Art poétique': 'Il faut aussi que tu n'ailles point / Choisir tes mots sans quelque méprise' (the *méprise* being an error from the pedant's point of view). And in the later 'L'Art poétique *ad hoc*' in *Invectives*, he warns any reader who may still not have realized how poetic a deliberate mistake can be: 'Surtout n'excusez pas les fautes de l'auteur!'

The preceding remarks would ideally be refined and qualified by a historical study which would consider more than just a few exceptional poets. For the time being, I hope to have established the plausibility of the idea that the constraints of a still classical prosody were assimilated and neutralized by certain poets, then made to serve a new type of poetry. Devices were developed which chipped away at the classical block, but which also made it

---

* The same joke occurred to Mallarmé in 1859, in the penultimate line of *Sonnet* ('Quand sous votre corps nu . . .'): '– Quoi! J'ai tant bavardé! plus qu'un vers pour te dire / Mon voeu'.

possible to clamber over it in new ways. Significantly, a great many of these
devices were already active in satirical poetry. The technically amusing tricks
and conceits of poets like Banville were incorporated into serious poetry.
Once abstracted from their original contexts, these tricks become less prominent and lose the traces of their parodic origins. They also acquire an
extraordinary power of suggestion.

The following example, which ends this chapter, is intended to highlight
both the poetic value of these conventions and the point of view which
Mallarmé came to adopt.

An old favourite of satirical poets is a type of rhyme which might be called
the *rime-fantôme*. To start with a typically coy example, here are two lines
from one of Banville's chronicles of Parisian life:

> Lesbienne rêveuse, éprise de Phyllis,
> Tu n'as pas, il est vrai, célébré S . . . .[16]

The fact that the second rhyme word (the title of a poem by Barthélemy) is
missing only serves to draw attention to it and, once the giggles have sub-
sided, invites us to share the poet's pleasure in finding a nice rich rhyme. The
same device is the principal attraction of Banville's *rondeaux*, republished in
the *Odes funambulesques*. In some of the *rondeaux*, an individual's name can
be heard at the rhyme long before the individual is actually named in the text
(a type of antonomasia): 'où c'est' stands for Houssaye, 'quel air!' for Keller,
and so on. Coincidentally, perhaps, it was in a *rondeau* that Mallarmé borrowed Banville's medical joke in 1862 – the *rondeau* of the *Six Phyllis*, which
has unfortunately disappeared. There is a similar example in *Faust, Part One*
(*Walpurgisnacht*, vv. 4138–9), which makes one suspect that censorship
– self-imposed or not – may be at the origin of the *rime-fantôme*.
Mephistopheles happily recalls his smutty dream about a forked tree with a
huge hole in it: *ungeheures Loch* (omitted) rhymes with *gefiel mir's doch*.
Rhymes also fail to appear, in a more subtle fashion, in some infantile ditties
in which a 'naughty' word is implied by the rhyme but given a respectable
substitute which does not rhyme. A curiously unforgettable example runs:
'Up in the loft where the lamplight flickers, / I lost my heart and she lost her
parasol.' Which effectively makes the point that definitions often fail to give
a true impression of the thing itself.

When the same trick is used in serious poetry, it can create some equally
suggestive silences. The difference is that the serious poet tends to play, not
on the repertoire of all possible rhymes, but on the smaller repertoire which
has been established by years of use or abuse. Both Mallarmé and Rimbaud,
for instance, tacitly allude to the Romantic *encensoir* – Rimbaud in the first
stanza of 'Ce qu'on dit au poète à propos de fleurs' (ironically aimed at
Banville, Mallarmé and other Parnassians), Mallarmé in the fourth verse of
'Tout Orgueil fume-t-il du soir . . .':

Tout Orgueil fume-t-il du soir,
Torche dans un branle étouffée
Sans que l'immortelle bouffée
Ne puisse à l'aban*don surseoir*!

The rhyme on *soir*, the hint of a religious ceremony, the puff of smoke, all lead us to expect the seemingly inevitable *encensoir*. And it almost does appear in the almost identical phonemes: āsāswar/ɔ̃syrswar. Here, the ghostly presence of the ceremonial object might be said to correspond to the inefficacy or unreality of the 'immortelle bouffée' – the fumes that ought to issue from the censer.

An equally satisfying specimen of a *rime-fantôme* can be found lurking in the sonnet sent to the Egyptologist, Gaston Maspero, on the fourth anniversary of his wife's death. In an elegy whose subject is mourning and which uses four rhymes on œj (*seuil, orgueil, oeil, fauteuil*), one might reasonably expect to hear the word Mallarmé himself had used in his letter of condolence: 'J'envisage ce *deuil* comme une tristesse . . . personnelle.'[17] The fact that the obvious rhyme does not appear lends subtle emphasis to the idea that Ettie still returns to visit her husband and should be celebrated instead of mourned.

Perhaps the most convincing example of an absent rhyme is this splendid subtlety in another sonnet of Corbière's *Amours jaunes*. The *rime-fantôme* in this case is the well-known Romantic rhyme which Banville in particular uses dozens of times – *apothéose-rose*:[18]

Tu parais! c'est l'apothéose!!! . . .
Et l'on te jette quelque chose:
– Fleur en papier, ou saleté. –

When the actress makes her impressive entrance as a goddess, she should, of course, be greeted with something like a rose. But because this is a cheap and nasty little theatre, the only object thrown from the audience is an unspecified *chose*. The reader, like the actress, is, so to speak, disappointed when she finds at the end of the poem, in place of a rose, a paper flower, or even something worse.[19]

The magnetic quality of time-honoured (or dishonoured) rhymes allows them to act as a source of ideas. Rhymes exist in pools of varying size in the poet's memory. Dipping into the pool for one word, the poet inevitably picks up some of the others. As a result, even if the putative rhyme-word disappears entirely, it may still have deposited its meaning somewhere in the poem before it was rejected. There is an example of this in Baudelaire's 'Sed non satiata': 'puits' is the only singular rhyme for the masculine singular 'nuits' (the wine). Instead, Baudelaire chose 'ennuis'. And yet the 'puits' still comes to the surface in the 'citerne' of line 8: 'Tes yeux sont la citerne où boivent mes ennuis.'

The variants of Mallarmé's poems show this taking place in what might be considered an obvious fashion. In a draft of the *Prélude* of *Les Noces d'Hérodiade*, 'foison' and 'pâmoison', placed at the rhyme, are closely followed by 'venaison'.[20] In the *Ouverture*, the rhyme *pensée-encensée* seems to have summoned up the 'ostensoirs' of the following line. The unicorn of the *sonnet en yx* may have been conjured up by the unused rhyme, 'oryx'.[21] One might also tentatively point to still fainter traces of these rhyme-groups. In Romantic and pre-Romantic poetry, the rhyme *confus-touffus* is surprisingly common. Because of the sense of 'touffus', 'confus' is almost always attached to the noun 'amas'. This, then, may be the origin of the image in verse 4 of *L'Après-midi d'un faune*:

Assoupi de sommeils *touffus*.

Aimai-je un rêve?

Mon doute, *amas* de nuit ancienne, s'achève

Perhaps more convincingly, in *Le Tombeau de Charles Baudelaire* ('Le temple enseveli . . .'), the overused *arbre-marbre* combination (which is the only possible rhyme on that ending) produces 'Quel *feuillage* . . . pourra . . . se rasseoir / Contre le *marbre* vainement de Baudelaire'. The same rhyme-based association occurred to Mallarmé when he thanked Léon Dierx for the first volume of his *Oeuvres complètes* (the letter dates from the same period as the *Tombeau*): 'ce petit livre ou temple', 'un bien chaste *marbre* . . . ; mais en sa blancheur . . . resplendit la souffrance éparse et glorieuse d'une entière forêt de maux' – a whole forest instead of an *arbre*.[22]

Our doubts, unlike those of the Faun, must continue. These are the sort of imponderable questions which may leave us grasping after proofs where none exist. Fortunately, Mallarmé provides us with several persuasive testimonies which will be examined in Chapter 3. These satirical devices, wherever one decides to detect them, have in themselves a certain significance which is related to his view of the universe. Mallarmé's metaphysical system is expressed not only in abstract speculations but also in prosody itself. Prosody, in Mallarmé's verse, is the visible manifestation of abstract or spiritual realities. But the precise significance of its various elements can be understood only if we first have some sense, as his contemporaries did, of its historical connotations.

Before going on to describe this philosophy of versification, it may be helpful to sum up. The word 'poetry' has two principal meanings: the art itself and the qualities it is supposed to evoke – beauty, nobility, suggestiveness, etc. Unfortunately, one does not necessarily produce the other. Prose may be more 'poetic' than verse, the subject of a poem more 'poetic' than the poem itself. Printed or recited poetry nevertheless has the power to evoke this other, ideal poetry by means of linguistic tricks – what Mallarmé calls 'supercheries'. Poets like Corbière or Laforgue draw attention to these tricks, perhaps to the detriment of the poem's emotional charge; but, by so doing, they highlight the gap between mere words and some inaccessible, perhaps nonexistent reality. The artificiality and inadequacy of poetic language can be used to summon up an absent Beauty, while the poem plays the role of the Beast.

Sometimes, Mallarmé, like Baudelaire, is deemed less modern than Corbière or Laforgue because of his apparent respect for form and convention. The prejudice of progressive disintegration – an inverted form of the belief in Progress – might account for this opinion. In practice, he seems far closer to our time: prosody, like a computer language, is just a tool, but a tool which may turn out to be far more interesting than the products that are supposed to transcend it. Or, as Mallarmé says, reversing, as usual, the normal order of the equation (rhyming is just a game, but a game which has the power to reveal a superior reality):

> je vénère comment, par une supercherie, on projette, à quelque élévation
> défendue et de foudre! le conscient manque chez nous de ce qui là-haut éclate.
>   À quoi sert cela –
>   À un jeu.[23]

2

The Rules of the Game

'poète, . . . serviteur, par avance, de rythmes –'[1]

Faced with the rules of poetry, the most courageously obsequious poet in the history of French literature generally behaves with extreme courtesy and even prudishness. In *Crise de vers* in 1895, Mallarmé remembered his initial reaction to the emergence of free verse fifteen years before: 'le pédant, que nous demeurions, exaspéré, comme devant quelque sacrilège ignare!'[2] Growing tolerant in his old age, he nevertheless remains suspicious of the brash intruder. The *vers libre*, he asserts, is acceptable so long as it pays tribute to convention and contains some 'réminiscence du vers strict'. If it does hark back to regular verse, then its deviations become a challenge rather than an insult: 'des infractions volontaires ou de savantes dissonances en appellent à notre délicatesse.' But subversive behaviour can go too far; the sensitive reader must be able to recognize the rules the poet has decided to break, to hear the rhythmical patterns that have been altered or dissolved. These 'games' will be entirely without 'profit' if no vestige of the classical norms survives.

Why, then, did so many poets choose to rebel against classical prosody? The reason, says Mallarmé, is boredom and impatience, a 'lassitude par abus de la cadence nationale'. The twelve-syllable alexandrine, the 'national cadence', had been overused when it should have remained 'exceptional'. Like a Sunday suit, it should be brought out only 'dans les occasions amples' or, as he says elsewhere, 'dans les grandes occasions'.[3]

Luckily for anyone who tries to understand his poetry by reading his critical texts, Mallarmé invariably follows his own precepts. Alexandrines appear in only about half the poems written from 1868 on (without counting the *Vers de circonstance*). And when he does bring the alexandrine out of the classical wardrobe, its starched form is often loosened up, as in *L'Après-midi d'un faune*, with multiple enjambments and by an unignorable use of assonance and alliteration.[4] The rules, however, are still scrupulously observed. Mere 'lassitude', it seems, is no excuse for abandoning regular verse altogether.

It would be wrong to see Mallarmé as a latter-day Boileau, waving his ferule at a class of blithering young poets. The alexandrine, that 'compteur factice',[5] is not the object of some unreasoning fetish. It would be more accurate to say that, in his advice to fellow producers, Mallarmé retains two broad criteria from classical verse, each dependent on the other. First, there must be some repetition or regularity in the sounds and rhythms of the poem. Second, the poet must have the reader's 'consent': in other words, through the necessary fragmentation, the reader must be able to perceive at least the remnants of the classical verse and, through that, the deeper, underlying harmony of 'le vers'.[6] (Exactly what he means by 'le vers' is the subject of the next chapter.)

Mallarmé's benevolently dictatorial tone is in any case consciously ironic, since the *ars poetica* he proposes is an entirely personal rearrangement and interpretation of classical rules. But in his own verse he *is* a tyrant. The art that he expounds with remarkable consistency in so many texts is based on a small set of principles which must be learnt if we want to follow the 'games' that form the drama of verse.

Mention has been made now several times of that shadowy figure known as 'the reader'. Since this figure plays an important role in the drama, a brief character-sketch is necessary before we go any further. Mallarmé has a very particular conception of the reader – so particular that, without wishful thinking, we may not always be able to recognize ourselves in the entity referred to as 'le lecteur' (as opposed to those inferior beings, 'l'oisif', 'le passant', 'le vulgaire' or even 'un être d'une intelligence moyenne, et d'une préparation littéraire insuffisante').[7] For Mallarmé, the ideal reader is a person steeped in French poetry and familiar with its most arcane and rarely applied rules and categories. In short, a reader who is practically a writer of verse. Mallarmé's first readers were in fact poets, and some of the remarks he makes about his own work suggest that poets were his intended audience. When he tells Henri Cazalis in July 1865 about the first version of *L'Après-midi d'un faune* with its 'vers originaux . . . et dignes, dans leurs suprêmes mystères, de réjouir l'âme d'un poète!',[8] we should infer not only that these 'mysteries' are worthy of delighting a poet's soul, but also that they will probably be unintelligible to anyone who is not a poet or who fails to look at words and verses with a poet's eye.

During his 'Baudelairean' period, Mallarmé may have derived a certain pleasure from being privy to his own secret prosody. He might also be accused of being actively indifferent to his audience (a schoolmaster's relaxation?) or even of harbouring the opinion that the beauty of a work of art exists whether or not it succeeds in communicating itself to any but its creator (a schoolmaster's conviction?). A more cheerful view would be that Mallarmé's remarks on prosody are an invitation to watch for those relations and connotations that only players of the game would normally perceive. By contrasting himself with the *vers-libristes*, Mallarmé emphasizes his own courtesy towards the reader. This may seem a strange thing to say about a poet who answered complaints that his poetry was obscure by hinting that the only texts his contemporaries were capable of deciphering were newspapers. Being courteous means providing us with a way of understanding. And even if our literary training is inadequate, there is hope: the prosody invented by 'le génie classique' is there, says Mallarmé, to give us access to the arcana of verse and universe. This information is readily available.

Armed with optimism and a sense of imminent revelation, we can begin now to consider some of these poetic games. The following examples are meant to introduce some of the elements which go to make up the drama of verse. Once incorporated into the drama, their poetic value will be seen to be more than merely technical. Mallarmé's seemingly decorative conceits should be considered, metaphorically, as fragments of existence – anecdotes, observations, objects – which, in spite of their triviality, are given a role to play in a coherent work of fiction.

Circumstantial verse occupies about one-third of the Barbier-Millan edition of Mallarmé's poetry. The metaphysical concerns of the 'serious' poems are accompanied – some might say undermined – by an almost ridiculous proliferation of addresses, birthday greetings, visiting-cards, inscriptions and captions, including graffiti on a toilet wall. At first, the role of ideal reader was filled by poets, and now, it seems, by friends, relatives and postmen. The discrepancy gives pause for thought. Perhaps there is more to the *Vers de circonstance* than meets the eye, or perhaps, after all, the major poems are simply idle amusements. Let us hope that they are not, and instead take the word 'metaphysical' in its English sense: like the Metaphysical Poets, Mallarmé shows in *all* his poems how any word or object, no matter how banal, can give rise to complicated and revealing comparisons.

It would be interesting, though futile in the present context, to categorize all the different devices which Mallarmé uses in his *Vers de circonstance*. The most prevalent device (and a convenient focus for these remarks) is the pun on a person's name: allusions to the 'bonté' of Mlle Labonté; a certain 'Dubois dont on fait les maris'; Cazalis split into what the poet imagines are his two constituent flowers – 'azalée' and 'lis' – and his wife, Alice, attached to a 'calice'.[9] Sometimes the puns take the form of conundrums:

> Ce que votre sourire avec grâce rêva
> Vous l'avez dans Willy ainsi que dans Éva.

This distich, inscribed on a visiting-card for Mme Ponsot, presumably contains a personal allusion which now renders it indecipherable. There is a clue, perhaps, in the fact that the original in Mallarmé's own hand misspells 'Willy' as 'Willie' (it was corrected by Mallarmé's daughter, Geneviève). What is both in *Willie* and in *Éva*? Solutions will be gratefully received . . .

Other, more limpid verses are like little portraits or silhouettes traced in words instead of lines. The Christian name of Julie Manet, the painter's niece, inspires a quatrain based on the fact that *Julie* is almost identical to *Jolie*:

> Ici même l'humble greffier
> Atteste la mélancolie
> Qui le prend d'orthographier
> Julie autrement que Jolie.[10]

Even that most un-Gallic name, Whistler, can be assimilated by French verse, though it may sometimes have to be stretched out to three syllables:

> Tu peux, Faune, oui c'est l'air
> Le jouer à Whistler

> Mai dont le rayon ne dure
> Pour qu'il éblouisse l'air
> Mêle l'art à sa verdure
> Et joint au printemps Whistler.[11]

Few of these verses are as rewarding as Mallarmé's major poems, and to say that they have certain elements in common is not to say that all of Mallarmé's poetry should be presented to the unsuspecting reader as a uniform masterpiece. Nevertheless, some of the rhymed addresses do reward a little probing: 'J'exprime . . . à Monsieur Degas / La satisfaction qu'il rime / Avec la fleur des syringas.'[12] The unusual rhyme, of course, creates a pleasant surprise; but, as usual, Mallarmé was also thinking etymologically. His 'satisfaction' comes from the fact that *syringa* (or *seringat*) is a derivative of *syrinx*, meaning, as it does in *L'Après-midi d'un faune*, a flute or panpipes. A mere phonetic coincidence – or rather, a linguistic 'mystery' – is made to highlight the close relationship of the two arts practised by Mallarmé and Degas: a flowering plant that is also a musical instrument.

If the *Vers de circonstance* can be said to have a general theme, it is, quite simply, the poet's virtuosity, his 'satisfaction' at finding unexpected associations by means of rhyme and, by implication, the 'genius' of language. A five-line stanza is addressed to Mallarmé's second cousin, the poet Victor Margueritte, 'qui disait qu'il n'existait pas de rimes en "or"'. Rhymes were clearly not Victor's strong point. There are actually about sixty rhymes on *or* – four of which are used in the *sonnet en yx* – and far more if one also counts words like *effort*, *corps*, *fiord*, *Oxford*, etc. Mallarmé predictably accepts the challenge by making it more difficult and pulls some quite spectacular rabbits out of the hat. Victor's name gives rise to four rhymes, not just on *or* but on *tor*: *alligator*, *butor*, *castor*, *stentor*.[13] (It is touching to note that once Victor had learnt his lesson there was no stopping him: of the 138 poems in his collection *Au fil de l'heure*, no fewer than twenty contain rhymes on *or*, including *encor*, *essor*, *trésor*, *cor*, *décor* and *Conquistador*.)[14]

The family resemblances between the serious and circumstantial verse – as well as all the features that separate them – can best be appreciated by seeing how a name game is played out in one of the longer poems. (This involves raising the curtain for a quick preview of the drama before the actors are ready, but it might give a greater sense of purpose to the rehearsals.)

In the sonnet, 'Mes bouquins refermés sur le nom de Paphos . . .', a *rime-fantôme* is seen (or not seen) in action. In the quatrains, four words rhyme on fo, each spelt differently: *Paphos*, *triomphaux*, *faulx*, *faux*. Only six other rhymes on fo remain,[15] one of which – the most obviously poetic – haunts the sonnet. *Sappho* not only rhymes with *Paphos* but is also an exact anagram. The graphic and prosodic similarity of the two words is reinforced by their semantic proximity. In 'Lesbos', Baudelaire compared Paphos with the island of Sappho, and apparently the word *Paphos* is likely in any case to make 'the cultivated reader' think of Aphrodite, Lesbos, Sappho and the Amazons.[16] Is this just a coincidence? No, because, after the sequence of rhymes on o, the theme of the sonnet is absence and a form of illicit love:

> Ma faim qui d'aucuns fruits ici ne se régale
> Trouve en leur docte manque une saveur égale:
> Qu'un éclate de chair humain et parfumant!
>
> Le pied sur quelque guivre où notre amour tisonne,
> Je pense plus longtemps peut-être éperdûment
> À l'autre, au sein brûlé d'une antique amazone.

The absent fruits the poet does not savour include a fruit of 'human flesh' that corresponds to the Amazon of the last verse. The 'autre' of the last line can therefore be attached (for example) to 'amour' or to the implied woman and the poet supposed to be thinking, like most of his contemporaries after Baudelaire's *femmes damnées* – and, inevitably, 'éperdûment' – of another type of love: the love represented by Sappho, which, here, dares not speak its name; or perhaps the love of poetry, contrasted, as in many of his poems, with the love of Aphrodite. (For the connection with Orpheus and the position of the sonnet at the end of *Poésies*, see pp. 22 and 192.) This would explain why 'amazone' has a small *a* in all versions of the sonnet.

Discussing absent words is always risky and, in this case, may be thought to depend on a very specialized sort of knowledge (though a category of knowledge that is far easier to obtain than historical erudition). The difference with the *rimes-fantômes* discussed in Chapter 1 is that Mallarmé's absent rhyme is implied, not by a familiar group of clichéd rhymes, but by the words themselves – as words – and by the prosodic system as a whole. The poem itself does warn us that this is a *learned* absence, a '*docte* manque'. Besides which, the Sappho interpretation would show that what seems to be an untypically awkward resolution of the sonnet – dependent on the knowledge that the city of Paphos may have been founded by Amazons – actually confirms the subtle, prosodic circularity that characterizes Mallarmé's other sonnets. As Cohn points out in another context, 'Mallarmé is not at all apt to draw on the historically specific in his poems'.[17] Attempts have been made nonetheless to identify the book itself – *Les Fleurs du Mal*, a poem by Banville or an archaeological study written in English[18] – as if Mallarmé could never have described the action if he had not performed it himself. Moreover, the opening line – 'Mes bouquins *refermés* sur le *nom* de Paphos' – is a reminder of his observation that poems do not contain any material reality, for example stones, 'sur quoi les pages se refermeraient mal': the *name* or *noun*, Paphos, not Paphos itself.

It is interesting to see that, without detecting the Paphos-Sappho correlation, some critics have noticed the 'necessary' structure it imparts to the sonnet, and, in order to account for this, have had to resort to the unsatisfactory hypothesis of a historical, anecdotal allusion (which could hardly be described as 'necessary'). Émilie Noulet, without reading the poem in prosodic terms, notes on two occasions that 'le poème finit sur une rime annoncée par la première rime':[19] 'La qualité extraordinaire, dans ce sonnet, . . . c'est l'agencement de ses parties et leur rattachement à un centre invisible mais existant, comme si le premier mot, dernier mot, rimes, métaphores se déroulaient d'un fuseau de tout temps préparé. De cet appel mutuel des mots, l'exemple le plus frappant est *Paphos* à quoi répond, après des détours que l'on croit d'abord capricieux et qui se révèlent prémédités, le nom nécessaire d'*amazone*.'[20] One could hardly be closer to the door without walking through it.

'Mes bouquins refermés . . .' is not just an impressionistic reverie tracing chance ideas conjured up by Paphos, but, as Mallarmé so often leads us to suspect, another poetic game. The end of the sonnet is not just one possible conclusion out of many, but the single necessary, poetic product of the initiating word, *Paphos*.

Similar name games, sometimes based on still more tenuous links, are played out in other texts – even when the poet is 'off duty', in his letters. The following are some representative examples which show Mallarmé making use of practically every type of hidden reference – graphic, phonetic, anagrammatical, etymological and semantic. They therefore have disturbing implications for anyone who takes all his critical writings at face value!

A preface to the *Iconographie de Laurent Tailhade* begins, 'À ceux ici par un aigu crayon, le portrait, en phrases, joint de Laurent Tailhade' (from 'tailler un crayon').[21]

Whistler's 'discrétion' 'éclate en le vital sarcasme qu'aggrave l'habit noir ici au miroitement de linge comme siffle le rire'.[22]

Dujardin is congratulated on becoming, in his poetry, 'un primitif, du vrai jardin'.[23]

Banville is presented with an etymological, anagrammatical and phonetic *blason*: 'l'élu est cet homme au nom prédestiné [*Théodore* means 'gift of God'], harmonieux comme un poème [*ode*] et charmant comme un décor [*Théodore* – *décor(e)*]' – all this rendered still more subtle by the fact that Banville's Christian name is never mentioned.[24]

Those who saw Verlaine as a ne'er-do-well are chided for the '*vaine* vision' that misled them on the 'sens extérieur' of '*Verlaine*'.[25]

Coppée – or rather, *Coppée* – receives the same treatment. Cohn notes that 'Mallarmé usually takes his key tone from the name of the celebrated one' (for example the eighteen *b*'s of *Le Tombeau de Charles Baudelaire*) and quotes as evidence the following sentence from a letter:

> Votre vraie confraternité serait avec Mendès, si vous n'étiez parfaitement Coppée, dont les vers s'amalgament si bien, de loin, pour moi, avec la figure de camée, et avec le nom qui s'inscrirait sur une lame d'épée, et plierait avec elle.[26]

Voltaire seems to be treated more impressionistically: 'Jeu (avec miracle, n'est-ce pas?) résumé, départ de flèche et vibration de corde, dans le nom idéal de – *Voltaire*'. But he also appears anagrammatically and semantically (and perhaps with his real name, Arouet, phonetically): 'comme archer dévoré par la joie et l'ire du trait qu'il perd'.[27]

In one of the *Loisirs de la Poste*, Mallarmé manages to pack into a twenty-eight-syllable address a hidden word, a double etymological pun, an anagram and an allusion to a synonym:

> Quarante-neuf rue Ampère
> Madame, Madame Allys
> Arsel, une qui tempère
> Le diamant par des lys.[28]

The Latin etymon of 'diamond' – *adamas* – is tempered (literally, 'mingled') with lilies, first because the constituent letters are interrupted by *lys*, second because 'Madame Allys Arsel' contains an anagram of *amaryllis* (minus the *i*), which is also known as the 'lys Saint-Jacques'.

Finally, one to try at home (because I haven't been able to solve it myself): Berthe Morisot, 'un Nom . . . pour lui-même prononcé . . . , évoque une figure de race, dans la vie et de personnelle élégance extrêmes'. ('Extrêmes' may refer to the extremities of the two words, which supply the two phonemes of 'beau'.) The presence of conundrums is indicated by the phrase 'pour lui-même prononcé' and by the beginning of the article:

BERTHE MORISOT
bɛʀt   ʀizo

Tant de clairs tableaux irisés, ici, exacts, primesautiers,
ɛ ʀ t b o   ʀiz   ʀimso

More spectacular than any of these is an unforgettable cryptographer's orgy in 'Tennyson vu d'ici' – which, in view of its biographical vagueness, might have been entitled '*Tennyson* vu d'ici' (i.e. the word seen by a French speaker). The passage in question is an extraordinary linguistic *tour de force* which has always been passed by on the outside as an evocation of Tennyson's posthumous image, but which can also be entered and explored internally – a deluxe crossword puzzle whose clues, even unsolved, form a satisfactory narrative.

First, 'ce chaste agencement de syllabes, *Tennyson*' is pronounced 'avec solennité', rhyming anagrammatically on *s*, *o*, *e*, *n*, *i/y* and *t*. Then, 'cette fois: *Lord Tennyson*', again italicized to indicate that the words, not the human being, are in play. *Lord Tennyson* is said to awaken in the mind, 'à travers le malentendu même d'idiome à idiome', the following:

> hautaine [*tenn*] et tendre [anagram of lo*rd* *tennyson*] figure, volontaire [partial anagram and echoes of *tenir*, *tenace*?] mais surtout retirée [*laure*, homophone of *lord*, a monastery] et avare aussi de tout dû [*l'or* + *tenir* + *son*], par noblesse [*lord*], en une manière seigneuriale apportée dans l'esprit, ingénue [*tennyson* → *innocent*], taciturne [*ni son*]: et presque j'ajouterai que le décès serein [*lord* rhymes with *mort*] y installe quelque chose d'isolé ['something of *isolé*' in tennyson] ou complète, pour la foule, le retrait fier de la physionomie.

This verbal coronet is in turn supposed to be a partial analysis of that single, ideal word formed of the poet's name and all the words of his work – 'celui-là, significatif, résumé de toute l'âme, la communiquant au passant', who may or may not perceive it consciously.[29]

Passages like these are important: first, because they prove that most phonetic coincidences in Mallarmé's work are deliberate conceits and – more portentously – sustained, determined attempts to show that signifiers, even if they belong to a different tongue, can be made to stick, essentially, to their signifieds; second, because they illustrate the devices Mallarmé uses to nullify the arbitrariness of proper nouns. Names are treated, even in prose, according to their rhyming potential; or else they may be broken down into their constituent elements, like *Voltaire* or *Tennyson*. They can then be reconstituted poetically and their supposedly inherent figurative potential realized, in much the same way that significant, prophetic anagrams were extracted from famous names (e.g. Napoléon) – except that, in Mallarmé's case, the omens are realized in the act itself.

One can of course say perfectly intelligent and illuminating things about these texts without noticing the lower layer of the palimpsest; in fact, by not noticing it, we probably appreciate Mallarmé's achievement more fully. The actual production of the homage text follows the same trend as its message: very little of specific value is said about the subject's work. The tendency is to the general, the typical and not the individual, the subject as example or, as Banville noticed, 'pretext'.[30] The manipulation of Tennyson's name is not meant to suggest that names have a determining influence on their owners, as Balzac would claim. The idea of mystical affinities is simply alluded to as a symbolic illustration of the main point: that language forms its own structures and systems quite independently of any object or human being.

To take a final example from *Poésies*: 'Tout Orgueil fume-t-il du soir . . .' contains the scattered remnants of *Orphée*. Reading the sonnet as a *Tombeau* for an unnamed predecessor, critics have identified the 'il' of line eight as 'the hero', 'the revered poet-master representing a true tradition' – Villiers, Baudelaire or Poe.[31] The poet has failed to keep up the inherited domain: the room would be unheated if the master returned – the 'hoir' (from *heres*, 'heir' and *herus*, 'master').

For a poet who sees his 'duty' as 'l'explication orphique de la Terre'[32] and himself as the inadequate representative of the lost tradition of Orphic poetry,[33] 'il' could also be Orpheus, 'notre aïeul Orphée',[34] the son and heir of Apollo – which, incidentally, also fits the 'drame solaire' reading: 'Son nom est le même, Orpheus, que l'indien Ribhu, appellation qui paraît avoir été, à une époque très primitive, donnée au soleil' (*Les Dieux antiques*):

> Tout Orgueil fume-t-il du soir,
> Torche dans un branle étouffée
> Sans que l'immortelle bouffée
> Ne puisse à l'abandon surseoir!
>
> La chambre ancienne de l'hoir
> De maint riche mais chu trophée
> Ne serait pas même chauffée
> S'il survenait par le couloir.

Orphée is present (that is to say, absent), first, in the rhymes – étouf*fée*, bouf*fée*, tro*phée*, chauf*fée*, with the corresponding *o* and *r* in the masculine rhymes; second, in *trophée*, which is especially redolent of *Orphée* because of the anagram and because *trophée*, for a poet, inevitably conjures up *Orphée* since there are only eight other nouns which rhyme on *fe* and only five on 'phée';[35] third, in lines 2 and 3, in a manner reminiscent of the dislocated 'Dujardin':

>Torche dans un branle étouffée
>Sans que l'immortelle bouffée

Fourth, in the 'Or' of 'Orgueil', with its significant capital 'O' – the only capitalized word not at the beginning of a line.[36] Orphée himself – like the 'encensoir' – does not appear, except in the poet's mind and, more importantly, his syllables. Absence is not just a theme but, as it were, a physical presence.

The poetic lesson – before we wander too far behind the scenes – seems to be this: the principal function of nearly all the *Vers de circonstance*, very few of which are longer than eight syllables, is to lead up to a rhyme. Often, the rhyme is deduced from a name, which implicitly makes a linguistic point with philosophical connotations: names which seem at first immune to the poet's interference can after all be incorporated into verse. The rhyme which makes this assimilation possible therefore comes to represent a poetic victory. Like awkwardly shaped gems to be set by a skilful craftsman, they turn up on his tray as irreducible, unmanageable realities, exceptions in the language which offer a challenge to the poet: 'Mêlés encore à la Langue, leur sens [that of proper nouns] tient l'imagination en éveil; autrement, incompréhensibles ou anciens, c'est par leur aspect presque bizarre'.[37]

The rhymes, as we saw, may be anagrams or internal rhymes, not just end-rhymes – 'Semble *l'âme de Madeleine*'[38] – or miscellaneous echoes, as in Verlaine's *Tombeau*: 'Verlaine / A ne . . . naïvement d'accord / La lèvre . . . haleine', in which the poet's name 'accords' with other elements in the poem. In *Toast funèbre*, the older form of Gautier's name is referred to in the rhyme *altier-Gautier*, of which the succeeding rhyme – *taire* – is a partial anagram, while, earlier in the same poem, his name is announced in a rhyme on the same four letters:

>Que ce *beau* monument l'enferme tout en*tier*.
>Si ce n'est que la gloire *a*rdente *du* mé*tier*,

Appropriately, the preceding line affirms that the purpose of the celebration is to 'chanter l'absence du poëte'. And when, ten lines further on, Mallarmé refers to his own verse, he does so in a similar fashion, with a discreet, phonetic signature at the end: 'Quand, sourd même à mon vers sacré qui ne l'alarme'.[39]

Without the evidence of the later poems and critical texts, the *Vers de circonstance* would have to be described in much simpler, less philosophical terms. They show, for example, that Mallarmé likes to invent rhymes which are either extremely rare or unique: *album-Atchum!*; *Léopold-kobold*; *réussi-Debussy*.[40] He also tries to find new partners for words which are normally attached to others: *célèbre* rhymes, not as it usually does, with *funèbre* or *vertèbre*, but with *zèbre*; *onze* is coupled with *gonze* and not, as it is in the work

of other poets, with *bronze* or *bonze*.[41] As a result, the *Vers de circonstance*
probably have the highest percentage of previously unused rhymes of any
collection in the history of French poetry – all of which, no doubt, is
interesting in its own way. However, in relation to the rest of his work, the
Vers de circonstance can be seen as the marginal calculations that eventually
produce the longer, more complex equations of the serious poems.

The *Hommage* to Puvis de Chavannes and other poems discussed in Chapter 6 will show that these witticisms have a metaphorical significance. Even
in the flimsiest verse, there are hints of something more intellectually satisfying than a pun. The 'vertical axis' of these poems is unusually prominent
because of the shortness of the lines and the richness or ingenuity of the
rhymes, many of which are *rimes complexes*.[42] The deliberate imbalance –
normally termed frivolity – suggests that, along with the 'horizontal axis'
which carries the conventional sense, there is another reality, more purely
poetic, more coherent, and which appears in its own little universe to be not
entirely subject to chance.

The other, perhaps unexpected lesson to be drawn from Mallarmé's rhymes
is that this foregrounding of technical aspects is not simply a subjective
impression to be ignored for the benefit of the poet or emphasized to the
detriment of his intentions. Mallarmé deliberately and self-consciously creates direct correspondences between sense and prosody which might be
construed as another source of pleasure. The puns and anagrams not only say
something about the 'remunerative' power of poetic language, as they do in
the prose texts; they also confirm, sometimes quite directly, the essential
correlation that exists between words and the prosodic structures that contain them. For example, the following quatrain was inscribed in the copy of
L'Après-midi d'un faune sent to Édouard Dujardin:

> Faune, qui dans une éclaircie
> Vas te glisser tout en dormant,
> Avec quatre vers remercie
> Dujardin, ton frère normand.[43]

The rich end-rhymes are complemented by the five internal rhymes on ɛʀ.
The joke here is that, just as Dujardin is described as the Faun's 'frère
normand', the rhymes themselves, including 'glisser' (of which the final *r* can
be pronounced), are so-called *rimes normandes*. As usual, a historical pre-
cedent can be found for Mallarmé's variations. Clément Marot also placed his
rimes normandes in the middle of the verse:

> Quand Neptunus, puissant dieu de la *mer*,
> Cessa d'ar*mer* caraques et galées,
> Les Gallicans bien le durent ai*mer*
> Et récla*mer* ses grandes ondes salées.[44]

The difference in Mallarmé's poem is that the rhymes and the subject refer to each other. The technical aspects of the verse are entwined with the theme.

A similar conceit brightens up this quatrain from *Albums*:

> Un beau nom est l'essentiel
> Comme dans la glace on s'y mire
> Céline reflète du ciel
> Juste autant qu'il faut pour sourire.[45]

Céline in this case is two things: the person and the word. The word contains an anagram of 'ciel'; it also contains the first letters of 'céleste' and is an abbreviation of 'Célestine'. Seen, so to speak, 'dans la glace', *Céline* reflects 'le ciel' just enough to put a smile on the poet's face ('Juste autant qu'il faut pour sourire'). The 'sourire' which signals a successful rhyme will reappear several times in later chapters.

These technical games in which formal elements usurp some of the function of theme and draw attention to the conditions of the poem's production are also played out in some of the longer poems dating from the period in which the drama of verse was still being developed. *Le Faune, intermède héroïque* – the first version of *L'Après-midi d'un faune* – contains some of the earliest traces of this self-conscious, reflexive language which we considered briefly in Chapter 1. In *Le Faune*, as in the poetry of Corbière or Verlaine, semantic values are attached to elements that would normally occupy a secondary place. This redistribution of significance in the poem tends to disturb the conventional order of tenor and vehicle, but at the same time it creates the possibility of exploiting new poetic devices, or devices which were previously confined to frivolous genres:

> Le remords sur sa lèvre amènera, fatal
> Les stériles lambeaux du poème natal.
> Et la voix part des joncs unis, que nous n'osâmes
> Briser, pour demander le reste de nos âmes.[46]

Two points can be made about these lines. First, the enjambment 'n'osâmes / Briser' creates an obvious correspondence between structure and theme. The verb 'briser' reports the presence of a *vers brisé*. This use of enjambment is perhaps the commonest of such conceits, and writers of *explications de texte* are traditionally encouraged to look out for them. Usually, the correspondence involves two elements: form and theme. In the 1875 *Improvisation d'un faune*:

> Mon doute, loin ici | de finir, se prolonge
> En de mornes rameaux;[47]

where the idea of prolongation is also conveyed by the displaced caesura. Or, in *Les Fleurs*:

> Des avalanches d'or du vieil azur, au jour
> Premier

Less conventionally, three elements are brought into play: form, theme and the technical term(s) for the formal feature. A fine pre-Mallarmean example is the opening of Baudelaire's 'Le Flacon':

> Il est de forts parfums pour qui toute matière
> Est poreuse. On dirait qu'ils pénètrent le verre.

Strong perfumes pass through solid matter just as the sentence extends beyond the end of the verse. Baudelaire underlines the conceit with a nice pun: 'les parfums pénètrent le *verre*' just as meaning penetrates the confines of the *vers*. Mallarmé often resorts to the same and similar ambiguities, referring here to the *coupe* of the verse: 'Fée, au parfum subtil de foin / *Coupé*'; 'A vous dont un regard me *coupe* / La louange'. Or, alluding also to the 'verse' which seems to have no subject but itself:

> Rien, cette écume, vierge vers
> A ne désigner que la coupe;

where 'coupe' is both the cup and the enjambment. (The aural ambiguity of 'vers' is hinted at in Mallarmé's bibliographical notes: '*Salut*: ce Sonnet, en levant le verre, récemment, à un Banquet de *la Plume*, avec l'honneur d'y présider.' In fact, the intricacies of this particular conceit are too numerous to be described in detail here: see p. 191.)

Another subtle allusion to trade terms occurs in one of the early fragments of *Hérodiade* (shortly after *Le Faune*). A well-attested though rarely used device is the *vers léonin*.[48] A *vers léonin* is a verse in which the hemistich rhymes with the hemistich of the following verse. Typically, the rhyme takes the form of two matching vowels separated by an unmatching consonant. (An example from Banville's *Le Forgeron* is quoted on p. 65.) In *Hérodiade*, the device is implicated in the theme; both are, so to speak, 'léonins', just as Dujardin and the rhymes of his quatrain were 'normands':

> Sous la lourde prison de pierres et de fer
> Où de mes vieux lions traînent les siècles fauves

No specialist knowledge is necessary for understanding the verse, and the pleasure of discovering the conceit may even act as a distraction or induce the reader to revel in the putative ignorance of 'le vulgaire'. The thematic integrity of the poem may be undermined by the inclusion of secret allusions, like the sort of isolated, specific references which are usually enough to give a film cult status. The unity of theme, form and/or prosodic terms is fleetingly established at the expense (if noticed) of the unity of the whole text. In later poems, Mallarmé succeeds in maintaining both unities concurrently: the prosodic conceits are coextensive with the poem, and the theme itself may even be more effectively concealed than the 'secret' allusions.

The second point to be made about the verses from *Le Faune* is that not all these allusions are clearly labelled with a reference to the technical term. The rich and unusual feminine rhyme refers implicitly to the fact that *nos âmes* is a disintegration of *n'osâmes*: like the twin rhymes, the 'joncs | unis' of the pipes – contradictorily divided by the caesura – can be separated and the primordial unity of the 'poème natal' lost, scattered in 'lambeaux'. This may be an inconspicuous device, but it is a device that is there to be noticed. The same significant operation occurs, in reverse, in *Prose pour des Esseintes*. As Malcolm Bowie points out, the enormous rhymes re-enact the formation of syntheses, the second rhyme uniting in a single word the phonemes of the first: *de visions → devisions; de voir → devoir; par chemins → parchemins*, etc.[49]

When Mallarmé enthuses about the 'suprêmes mystères' of *Le Faune* in his letter to Cazalis, he uses the adjective in the older sense of 'final', with connotations of solemnity. These delightful 'mysteries' refer, not to some vague aura of transcendence but to something precise, the mysteries of the 'final seed' of every line of poetry: rhyme.

A later draft of *Le Faune* provides another example of these self-conscious *divertissements*. In the *Monologue* sent to Philippe Burty in 1873 or 1874 (though it was probably written in 1866), a curious rhyme coincides with the moment of greatest confusion:

> Je ne sais pas, moi! Tout, sur la terre, est obscur:
> Et ceci mieux que tout encor: car les preuves
> D'une femme, où faut-il, mon sein, que tu les treuves?[50]

'Treuves' is probably a temporary stopgap, a *cheville*, and the *Monologue* itself a rough draft, hastily corrected or completed when 'le tyrannique Burty' asked him for a copy.[51] 'Treuves' in any case is a flagrant archaism which was expunged from the definitive version.[52] And yet, for a *cheville*, it fits the context perfectly. The lack of any 'preuves' corresponds to the absence of any satisfying rhyme. 'Preuve', moreover (to anticipate the next chapter and remarks below), is a word that Mallarmé applies to rhyme.[53] Here, as elsewhere, the 'explication orphique de la Terre' is also 'le jeu littéraire par excellence', a game at which the musical Faun is not always entirely successful.[54]

A detailed study of Mallarmé's verse at this turning point of his poetic career would throw up many similar conceits. One simultaneously discreet and spectacular variety should be mentioned, last of all, because it marks an important date in the history of French verse. The prosodic referent in this case is not rhyme but the metrical structure of the alexandrine.

The 'césure *enjambante*', in which a single word straddles the caesura at the sixth syllable, is so rare in French poetry that Frédéric Deloffre claims that it simply ceased to exist between the latter half of the fifteenth century and the beginning of the twentieth when it was revived by Apollinaire.[55] Mallarmé's verse, which is so correct and punctual in most respects, in fact contains twelve specimens of this *rarissima avis*, six of them in the various versions of *Hérodiade*. Not surprisingly, many of these verses contain subtle allusions to their prosodic sin.*

Mallarmé's earliest 'césure enjambante' is in the second verse of *L'Azur*:

> De l'éternel Azur la sereine ironie
> Accable, belle indo | lemment comme les fleurs,
> Le poète impuissant qui maudit son génie
> A travers le désert stérile des Douleurs. (1864 version)

The 'indolence' of the natural world overwhelms the 'impotent' poet, who is apparently incapable even of constructing an orderly alexandrine. A few years later, in *Hérodiade*, a similar connection between form and theme is established – with a similar adverb (the same verse recurs in later versions): 'A me peigner noncha | lamment dans un miroir.'[56] An adolescent princess obsessed with herself may very well neglect, nonchalantly, to put the caesura in the right place.

Twice, the 'transgression' is associated, appropriately, with a 'disaster' ('Toujours plus souriant . . .', v. 2 and the *Finale* of *Hérodiade*, v. 17); else-where, with the idea of dissolution, evaporation, flight or loss. In *Le Faune* (chronologically, this is the second example):

> D'une enfance qui s'enfuyait avec de longs
> Fleuves

A different version, in which a thirteen-syllable line was corrected (so, presumably, a later version), prudently divides the offending verb in two: 's'en fuyait'.[57] Nonetheless, the effect, emphasized by the enjambment, 'longs

---

* A wider-ranging study might show that prosodic innovations are often 'justified' in their infancy by thematic references. It might also show that the thematic reference is often to some kind of unacceptable behaviour. Banville's 'Érinna' (1861) in *Les Exilés* is written exclusively in feminine rhymes (still a noticeable naughtiness at the time) 'Pour que l'impression en restât plus poignante', he says, but also, clearly, because the subject is Lesbos and its 'jeunes poëtesses'. Similarly, the feminine rhymes of the fourth 'Ariette oubliée' of Verlaine's *Romances sans paroles* (1874) are a not-so-subtle allusion to the 'âmes sœurs', one of whom would normally be male: 'Soyons deux enfants, soyons deux jeunes filles.' All the rhymes of the six 'Amies' in *Parallèlement* are also feminine.

/ Fleuves', was certainly calculated. Twenty-eight years later, the same conceit resurfaces in *Remémoration d'amis belges* to suggest the dematerialization of the city through the mists of time. The blocks that make up the poem lose their rigid contours and the verse dissolves:

> je sens
> Que se dévêt pli se | lon pli la pierre veuve
>
> Flotte ou semble par soi n'apporter une preuve

In Mallarmé's special prosodic vocabulary, 'floating' and the absence of 'preuves' (as in *Le Faune*) are allusions to what, at the time, was the very obvious decomposition of the regular verse.[58]*

Mallarmé's unfinished *Faune* and other 'faulty' texts serve as reminders, first, that poetic creation for him, as for Baudelaire, is in large part a reworking of existing texts; second, that the writer who works on a text that has already been written will come to see it in an increasingly objective light. The continual polishing of the poem fosters that 'reflexivity' which became more and more prominent in French poetry. The principal variations on a theme, the paths and diversions of an intellectual adventure, have already been explored and charted; the emphasis shifts and the adventure or point of interest is now the search for the perfect expression. The real drama is performed inside the text, while the outside becomes ever more insignificant and can happily explode into the ephemeral fireworks of the *Vers de circonstance*, some of whose sparks land in the parched garden of serious verse.

As we saw – and as many critics have said before – from the mid-nineteenth century, prosodic conventions acted, first as an incitement to parody, and then as the basis of experiments which no longer seem to have much to do with parody. Like any cautious satirical poet, Mallarmé adopts a mask or 'disappears', not in order to escape the censor but, as he puts it in a famous phrase, to 'céder l'initiative aux mots'.[59] The irony of satirical poets who distance themselves from the language they nevertheless continue to use establishes a second layer of meaning, as in Corbière's sonnets. In Mallarmé's poetry, this self-consciousness of the text survives and is aggravated by successive rewritings. The irony, however, is no longer directed against 'other people's' poetry but against poetry itself – against the illusion of some global meaning inhabiting the world outside the text and which is eventually supposed to be expressed, with greater or lesser efficiency, by the poem. Rhyme plays a particularly important part in this reorganization. The richer it is, the more it reminds us that language is riddled with arbitrary or spurious

---

* One might add that even Mallarmé's ellipses are self-referential. He uses two full-stops instead of the usual three. Thus, part of the omission is omitted and the *points de suspension* are left in suspense.

connections, coincidental harmonies which, like Victor with his alligators, beavers and bitterns, have no essential sense beyond themselves. Yet rhyme still seems to postulate the Romantic integrity of meaning which it calls into question.* Poets like Laforgue or Eliot might associate this irony with a metaphysical nostalgia or panic. For Mallarmé the pre-Postmodernist, it represents a liberation of language from its crude, conventional functions. The 'cynical' use of self-referential language is seen, not as iconoclasm, but as practically the opposite: a process of purification and a search for fundamental, abstract patterns.

Rhyme is the most perceptible manifestation or parallel of these patterns or 'rhythms'. For this reason, Mallarmé often uses *rime* as a synonym of *vers* – just as *rimes* can be used as a synonym of *poésies*. Since the word *vers* can be applied, according to him, to any form of organized expression – prose, music, painting – rhyme becomes one of the main distinguishing features of poetry. If *le vers* is the *principe* of poetry, rhyme is the principle, in a literal sense, of verse. The drama of verse begins and ends with rhyme.

It is all too easy to get carried away with rhyme. The coincidence of sense and consonance gives rhymes the mysterious appeal of slogans and allows us to pretend that any further reflection would be a waste of time. It may, of course, be rewarding, sometimes, to speculate on the connotations of a particular rhyme in isolation and then to draw conclusions which can be applied to the whole poem. Once again, this is a habit encouraged by the traditional *explication de texte*. If practised too often, it causes critical blindness. There is only so much one can usefully say about the fact that *mal* rhymes with *animal*, *femme* with *infâme*, *homme* with *consomme* or, for that matter, *pleurnichons* richly with *cornichons* but only weakly with *oignons*.[60]

Mallarmé's poetry provides a more fertile outlet for the rhyme mania of which the *Vers de circonstance* are informative symptoms. In his poems, rhyme *qua* rhyme has special connotations that are present in different contexts; it has a metaphorical, metaphysical value to which each poem alludes. His poetry, in other words, is organized according to a 'local' prosody which is a development of the 'national' prosody that produced it. The 'meaning' of the poem is a function, not only of time-honoured rules – whether they are

---

* Mallarmé's best-known description of the reparative function of verse is the passage on the 'perversity' of language, 'conférant à *jour* comme à *nuit*, contradictoirement, des timbres obscur ici, là clair' (OC, 364). The passage has been used to demonstrate Mallarmé's supposedly rather cranky and subjective mysticism; but his ideological intention was to stress the necessity of verse, which '*philosophically*' makes up the shortfall of language. The example itself is a reference to Genesis 1:5 and a rhetorical blasphemy: 'Il donna à la lumière le nom de Jour, et aux ténèbres le nom de Nuit'. The poet improves on God's original. Bertrand Marchal underlines the rhetorical nature of the example by replacing the passage in the context of the archetypal drama of day and night (*La Religion de Mallarmé* [Corti, 1988], 492). Individual sensibility should not be discounted altogether: see 'Quand l'ombre menaça . . .', where 'ébloui' rhymes internally with 'nuit', or *Hérodiade*: 'Nuit blanche de glaçons et de neige cruelle!'

observed or not – but also of the peculiar, personal set of conventions which only a reading of Mallarmé's poems and critical texts can reveal.

It is possible, then, to give a reductive reading of this poetry, to reduce it to a philosophy or an aesthetics; this will be the subject of the next chapter. Mallarmé himself invites us to do so. But there would be little point in pursuing this reading if it failed to open the poems up to multiple interpretations – multiple but (one should hasten to add) complementary.

3

The Metaphysics of Rhyme

'la loi mystérieuse de la Rime'[1]

For all its metaphysical ramifications, Mallarmé's conception of rhyme is not as fantastic as it first appears. There is, as far as I know, no real trace of any Baroque arithmology, no code that might reveal precise correlations between numbers and letters and imbue the slightest detail with a secret, cabbalistic meaning. It is true that whenever he talks about the technical elements of verse, Mallarmé uses analogies which impart a transcendent value to those elements. Verse is placed in a symbolic relation to *the* subject of literature (according to him) – 'l'antagonisme de rêve chez l'homme avec les fatalités à son existence départies par le malheur'.[2] It then comes to represent a victory or at least the hope that a synthesis will be achieved. In fact, Mallarmé appears to view the completion of a verse or the construction of a rhyme as literal victories, as if verse, '[qui] n'est doué que de faible pouvoir dehors',[3] were actually fighting real battles in a different dimension. Nonetheless, his descriptions of rhyme are based, initially, on its real and evident characteristics, features which are immediately obvious to anyone who gives the matter any thought and which may even seem too obvious to merit much reflection. If rhyme is first considered from a purely formal point of view, most of Mallarmé's remarks on the subject become instantly comprehensible. The metaphysical 'triumph' which forms the subject of this chapter can be equated, simply, with the satisfaction one experiences when perceiving a harmonious combination of sounds, or with the poet's relief when he finds the rhyme he was looking for.

In more precise terms, rhyme undergoes a dual metaphorical transformation which is based on certain incontestable facts and common ideas. First, rhyme, like verse, is personified. The actions of personified rhymes are then incorporated into an allegorical drama – usually described with such concision that it is easily missed. In this drama, the poet's success is identified with that of rhyme itself. For example, discussing *Le Forgeron*, Mallarmé brings to life the enormous rhymes of Banville's play, in much the same way that musical notes are animated in Walt Disney's *Fantasia*:

> la rime ici extraordinaire parce qu'elle ne fait qu'un avec l'alexandrin qui [. . .] semble par elle dévoré tout entier comme si cette fulgurante cause de délice y triomphait jusqu'à l'initiale syllabe.[4]

As in his poetry, Mallarmé depicts, not the thing itself, but the effect it produces. Here, he explains exactly why Banville's rhymes are a 'cause de délice'. Whatever obstacles to understanding this method might be thought to create, the figure always refers back to recognizable realities. The referent of the image may be the fact that a rhyme is normally made up of two words, while the image itself may be an exaggeration or complication of an equally recognizable poetic cliché, for example the idea that a soaring bird is a symbol of joy and freedom. There is always some precise correlation between the two: in this case, rhymes have two words just as birds have two wings.

The second stage of the metaphorical transformation is slightly less obvious and requires a small philosophical leap. Mallarmé gives the word *vers* two main meanings, one conventional, the other peculiar to him. *Vers* refers to a line of poetry and to versified poetry in general; it also refers to any form of organized expression in which language is treated as language. The reasoning behind the second meaning is that the structures inherent in French verse are identical to the structures inherent in everything. Since structuralist anthropology and psycholinguistics, Mallarmé's fundamentalist view seems far less ambitious.[5] The alexandrine, for instance, is not an artificial construct but the natural product of the human mind or what we might now call the collective unconscious: 'l'alexandrin, que personne n'a inventé et qui a jailli tout seul de l'instrument de la langue';[6] 'né de l'âme populaire, il jaillit du sol d'autrefois'.[7] Claims similar to those Mallarmé makes for regular French verse have been made in this century for twelve-bar blues and reggae; and in his own time, several poets, including Mallarmé, hoped to rediscover these archetypal rhythms in folk music.[8] (Baudelaire refers to them in a tantalizing note as a 'prosodie mystérieuse et méconnue . . . dont les racines plongent plus avant dans l'âme humaine que ne l'indique aucune théorie classique'.)[9]*

Regular verse is simply the most recognizable and analysable manifestation of these primal structures, archetypes or 'rhythms' that are present in all

---

* Mallarmé's 'anthropological' view of versification is interestingly close to that of Émile Littré. In his 'Coup d'oeil sur l'histoire de la langue française' in volume I of his *Dictionnaire* (1873), he pooh-poohs Boileau's notion that the prosodic rules date from Villon: 'Villon n'eut rien à débrouiller; il ne fit, lui et ses successeurs, que se servir des créations d'un âge primordial'; 'Aussi la force spontanément créatrice qui . . . appartient à toute civilisation, fit son office'; 'si l'ère des mythologies n'avait pas été irrévocablement passée, l'imagination populaire aurait attribué à quelque Orphée des âges intermédiaires l'oeuvre de mélodie et de chant' (xliii–xlv).

things. More efficiently than any other form of expression, verse 'harmonizes' language with its 'origin',[10] reactivating those 'mysterious' aspects of words that are lost when they are used 'commercially', like coins, for the mere exchange of pre-established concepts. The idea is not that verse is a separate form of discourse with its own particular, mystical virtues;[11] verse is simply a more rarefied form of expression, a microscope instead of a naked eye. According to Mallarmé, the same potential can be discovered in other forms of expression: 'Le vers est partout dans la langue où il y a rythme'[12] – that is, whenever any attempt is made to organize the letters of the alphabet, seen as letters. 'Verse', therefore, also exists in prose, but its 'rhymes' are concealed: 'c'est pourquoi toute prose d'écrivain fastueux, soustraite à ce laisser-aller en usage, ornementale, vaut en tant qu'un vers rompu'.[13] 'Ornamental' prose is more likely to reveal the hidden structures, the 'primitives foudres de la logique',[14] because, to some extent, it frees words from their customary functions, treating them not as labels but as visible and audible entities in their own right. The additional value of verse is that, as well as treating language as an organic system with its own internal logic, it provides a parallel structure – prosody. This structure 'authenticates' the text, acts as a guarantee that the poet's verse is a miniature model of the universe.

The role of rhyme in these universal, immutable structures is, by the nature of things, constant. Rhyme is the cornerstone of verse, and it can be related to whatever occupies an analogous place in the human mind and in the universe as a whole. Which explains why the images Mallarmé applies to rhyme – birds, flowers, jewels, etc. – reappear in different contexts without any change occurring in the relationship between each image and its referent or between one image and another.

This is one of the most useful points to bear in mind when reading Mallarmé's criticism. His metaphors are not the product of a moment's inspiration; they belong to an orrery of ideas and images which has already been constructed and which models what Jean-Pierre Richard was the first to call Mallarmé's imaginary universe – a *symbolique*, or fixed system of images and referents, which seems to want to be treated as *symbolisme*, where signs function as symbols but without indicating a single or even any referent (to use L.J. Austin's distinction). One of the aims of this chapter is to introduce some of the images which Mallarmé applies to rhyme, images which, for him, imply the abstract patterns, not just of his own imaginary world but of the objective universe as a whole.

Perhaps it would be best to start by asking which of the several characteristics of rhyme Mallarmé chooses to emphasize. There are two in particular which recur in nearly all his remarks and which seem at first to produce an interesting contradiction.

1. Rhyme creates a perceptible unity out of different elements. This dynamic, dialectical unity is indicated, incidentally, by the word itself: *rime*

can mean both one rhyme-word or several rhyme-words. *Jour-amour* is one rhyme and two rhymes.

Sometimes, the only difference is in the meaning, as in the *rimes homonymes* which Mallarmé uses so frequently: *nuit* (verb)-*nuit* (noun), *gourde* (adjective)-*gourde* (noun), *lui* and *tu* (pronouns and past participles); and also *allée, brise, coupe, fin, joue, neuf, nue, pas, r/Racine, rose, rosée, rue, sourde, vagues* and *vins*. Normally, of course, there is also a phonetic difference which highlights the similarity of the rhyming phonemes: *langage-dégage, sanglots-flots, voulûtes-flûtes, rature-littérature*, etc.

Visual rhymes are also important in Mallarmé's poetry. The fact that two endings not only sound the same but also have the same spelling can reinforce the similarity and remind us that poems have a visual, concrete dimension. This may rank quite low on some readers' scale of poetic pleasure, but, for Mallarmé, it was one of the principal delights of reading a poem and he attached a particular significance to it. When two grammatically different words are seen to rhyme, the eye lingers pleasurably on the matching, unpronounced letters: 'l'oeil s'attardant parmi la parité des signes éteints'. Specifically, Mallarmé mentions the possibility of combining singular and plural in the same rhyme: '(je suppose l's du pluriel) et lui opposer une rime nette sur un son le même au singulier.'[15] In Baudelaire's 'Sed non satiata', *ennuis, nuits* and *minuits*, all in the plural, rhyme unexpectedly with the singular *nuits*. The example Mallarmé himself gives is the *s* 'qui s'ajoute à la seconde personne du singulier', in which case we might think of his sonnet, 'Victorieusement fui . . .' (where 'tu la poses' rhymes with 'des roses') or of *Autre éventail* (where 'rivages roses' rhymes with 'tu poses'). For Mallarmé, the coincidence of *s*'s reveals one of those mysterious connections that exist independently of any obviously logical system like etymology, semantics or grammar, 'à moins que celle-ci [la grammaire] ne soit une philosophie latente et particulière en même temps que l'armature de la langue'. (Any linguistician offering a logical explanation for the *s* will find that Mallarmé calls their effort a 'juvénile simplification'.)[16]

It would be untrue to say, however, that Mallarmé's rhymes are 'toujours pour l'oeil'.[17] Sometimes the visual difference serves to emphasize the aural similarity: *paresse-apparaisse, blasphème-j'aime, poind-point, oeuf-9, Qu'est-ce?-caisse*, and (with a little practice) *cueille-Bird's eye*. This contrasting device is used in what seems to be a systematic fashion in 'Mes bouquins refermés . . .'. The masculine rhymes of the quatrains have four different endings which nevertheless produce the same sound: P*aphos*, triom*phaux*, *faulx*, *faux*. I say 'systematic' because in 'Surgi de la croupe . . .' the disparity of the unpronounced letters (or the 'signes éteints') corresponds to the theme of the poem (see p. 91).

The unity produced by rhyme in these various ways contributes in turn to the unity of each stanza and, in a form like the regular sonnet in which rhymes recur, to the unity of the whole poem – a unity which Mallarmé often

highlights quite dramatically: all the rhymes of 'Le vierge, le vivace...'
rhyme on *i*, all the rhymes of the *sonnet en yx* on *or* and *ix*; in *Placet futile* and
Le Pitre châtié, the rhymes of the tercets continue those of the quatrains,
either phonetically or graphically.

Rhymes also create more complex syntheses by setting up assonantal and
alliterative echoes throughout the poem. But even then, for Mallarmé, these
phonetic connections begin and end with rhyme in the conventional
sense:

> Je crois... que la rime ne subira que peu de modification, quand on ne
> cherche pas à lui communiquer par l'emploi de l'assonance un charme
> mouvant et de lointain, *encore peut-être faudra-t-il avoir précédemment posé les
> rimes fermes*, dont elles opèrent la dégradation.[18]

An example of this might be the 'jeu courant' that Mallarmé added as a
'musical accompaniment' to the alexandrines of *L'Après-midi d'un faune*: in
almost every case, one or more of the rhyming phonemes are picked up in the
body of the following verse; or 'La chevelure vol...' in which the end-
rhymes are repeated internally, notably in the self-explanatory 'L'ignition du
feu toujours intérieur'.

2. The second important characteristic of the Mallarmean rhyme has more
disturbing connotations. The unusually noticeable rhymes encourage us to
dwell, willy-nilly, on the arbitrary nature of linguistic signs. The richer
the rhyme, the more the coupling of two words will appear to be due to
chance.

A reader who lacks the professional goodwill of the critic may well harbour
serious doubts about the rhymes of poems like *Prose pour des Esseintes*. If only
because of his vocabulary, Mallarmé gives a strong impression of wanting to
be more than just a writer of agreeable ditties; yet he also seems quite willing
to be led astray (in this case, quite literally down the garden path) by
coincidental harmonies and by his own desire to generate enormous
rhymes.

Anastase, to give just one example, is the only suitable rich rhyme for
extase, the other unlikely candidates being *épitase*, *pétase* and *protase*. Marshall
Olds, somewhat alarmingly for the present author, calls this sort of observation 'naive';[19] but no amount of sophistication can entirely drown out the
question, which we are invited to ask anyway (in fact, not asking it is also
naive): how can we expect a poem produced in accordance with such restrictive criteria to contain a satisfactory philosophical message? It is all very well
pretending that rhyme performs the divine function of creating order out of
chaos, but isn't this order a very artificial, shallow sort of synthesis? Even after
several readings of the poem, we are still left clutching at straws, some of
which only *sound* like straws. The coherence of *signifiés* has simply been

replaced by that of *signifiants*. The rhymes are as vivid as the meaning of the poem is obscure. If the themes of the poem are so subtle and complex, why was *Prose* not written in prose?

This unsettling aspect of rhyme is one of Mallarmé's favourite themes – a theme which he develops in an almost ludicrous fashion in the *sonnet en yx*. One of the *yx* rhymes is a word which, he hoped, had no meaning and which was apparently created by the constraints of prosody: the famous *ptyx*, to which we shall return. This is not a problem for which we should rush to find an emergency solution – because it *is* a problem and should be relished as such.

Rhyme, then, appears to produce its pleasing syntheses only to undermine them. According to the classical point of view, poets must negotiate a compromise with words if they want them to manufacture memorable harmonies and still say something sensible. This is the old dilemma of Rhyme and Reason or Having Your Cake and Eating It. The dilemma is formulated – or simplified – by Boileau in a suitably clumsy and (for once the image is appropriate) imperialistic fashion:

> Que toujours le bon sens s'accorde avec la rime:
> L'un l'autre vainement ils semblent se haïr;
> La rime est une esclave et ne doit qu'obéir.
> Lorsqu'à la bien chercher d'abord on s'évertue,
> L'esprit à la trouver aisément s'habitue;
> Au joug de la raison sans peine elle fléchit
> Et, loin de la gêner, la sert et l'enrichit.
> Mais lorsqu'on la néglige, elle devient rebelle;
> Et pour la rattraper le sens court après elle.
> Aimez donc la raison[20]

On a superficial level, this is the dilemma which several of Mallarmé's poems recount. Rhyme is always misbehaving – especially when 'le Maître' is out to lunch as in the *ptyx* sonnet – and must be held in check. Mallarmé's view, however, is entirely different from that of a classical poet. Someone who detects mysterious correlations between the structures of verse and universe and who believes that the world we perceive is mere appearance could hardly consider rhyme to be the 'slave' of human reason: hence the provocative nonsensicality of the *ptyx*. Rhymes may be just as capable – more capable – of revealing fundamental truths as any other form of human expression, though the answers they provide may be hard to decipher.

The alternative to Boileau's approach would normally be a retreat into 'musicality' and 'Verlainean' imprecision, and this is a temptation Mallarmé often alludes to in his poetry. The ploy here would be to make the rhymes so prominent and so pleasing that they would act as the spoonful of sugar which, as in popular songs, makes illogical statements, errors or even sheer nonsense quite acceptable. A variation on this theme emerges in the prose poem, *Le Démon de l'analogie*. The poet, tormented by the scraps ('lambeaux') of a 'phrase absurde' – 'La Pénultième est morte' – tries to rid his mind of the phrase by 'burying' it 'en l'amplification de la psalmodie' or by placing it at the end of a verse.[21] Rhyme in this case is just a trick, a veil drawn over the absurdity which persists, a ritual mumbling to conjure away the evil spirit, just as it was once thought that rhyme was capable of destroying rats.[22]

In reality, Mallarmé chooses neither approach. He starts, in fact, with a considerably less despondent view than Boileau. Instead of worrying from the outset about the difficulty of marrying rhyme and reason, he concentrates on the *formal* connections that rhyme establishes. This at least is solid ground, the realm of verifiable truths. On several occasions, he points out that rhyme dramatically brings together variable elements in a recognizable structure. Rhyme is the stable point towards which the drifting, multifarious components of the poem tend. It 'commands' the reader's attention 'à tel motif de sentiment, qui devient noeud capital':

> dans la multiple répétition de son jeu [i.e. the play of verse] seulement, je saisis l'ensemble métrique nécessaire. Ce tissu transformable et ondoyant pour que, sur tel point, afflue le luxe essentiel à la versification . . . convient à l'expression verbale en scène.[23]

The paradoxical 'luxe essentiel à la versification' – an echo of Voltaire's 'Le superflu, chose très nécessaire'? – designates rhyme, as does the word 'richesse' in another passage. The word 'luxe' is especially fitting, first because it refers to the idea of 'rich' rhymes; second because it contains the Latin word for 'light': *lux*. Mallarmé exploits the same etymological nuance in the second quatrain of 'Quand l'ombre menaça . . .', and in the sonnet, 'De l'orient passé des Temps . . .': the line '*Lumineux* en l'esprit font naître' was changed, revealingly, to 'Font *luxueusement* renaître'.[24] Baudelaire defined rhymes as lanterns lighting the path of the idea.[25] Here, we might also think of 'luxe' as the sparkle on the crest of a wave ('ondoyant', 'afflue') or as a jewel on a piece of material ('tissu', which has the same etymon as 'texte').

The notion of 'affluence' (in the sense of concourse as well as luxury) is also present in the idea of a 'motif' (cf. above, 'tel motif de sentiment'). The word recurs in a similar context in *Crise de vers*:

> l'acte poétique consiste à voir soudain qu'une idée se fractionne en un nombre de motifs égaux par valeur et à les grouper; ils riment: pour sceau extérieur, leur commune mesure qu'apparente le coup final.[26]

In another version of the same phrase, Mallarmé talks of grouping 'en un certain nombre de traits égaux ... telles pensées lointaines autrement et éparses; mais qui, cela éclate, riment ensemble, pour ainsi parler'.[27] Rhyme is both the figurative representation of a philosophical unity and the real, external sign or 'seal' of this unity.

This explains why rhymes are so dominant in Mallarmé's poetics. They stand for the visible synthesis of an idea that logical analysis can only suggest; they represent and in fact *are* an 'identité de deux fragments constitutifs'[28] – or, as he wrote in a letter, staying a little closer to the literal truth: 'identité *plus ou moins proche* de deux fragments'.

Such a highly formalized view of rhyme would do little to convince our hypothetical reader who suspects the rhyme-obsessed poet of trying to pull the wool over our eyes. Surely Mallarmé is simply evading the problem posed by Boileau. Regular verse, which could claim to abolish or pretend to abolish the gratuity and absurdity of existence by bringing a pre-established set of rules into play, is still 'un emploi extraordinaire de la parole'.[29] Poetry and Life are separate, and 'Un coup de dés [or the arranging of a few similar-sounding words] jamais n'abolira le hasard'.

This is the point at which we shall have to make the philosophical leap mentioned above – bearing in mind that, given 'eternal circumstances', we shall inevitably end up in the void. For Mallarmé, any verse is a microcosm. Like a molecule, it has a structure that exists in all things. The 'bonheur' created by rhyme, he insists, turns out to be an 'instinct'.[30] Seen in this light, all verse bears witness, however imperfectly, to an essential, primordial unity, like the unity of human language before the Tower of Babel, except that it has always existed.[31] Consequently, the formal and metaphorical qualities of rhyme are indissociable. Perhaps the richest example of this entanglement of rules and realities is the following passage, with its biblical echoes of shepherds, sheep and the Ark:

> les vers ne vont que par deux ou à plusieurs, en raison de leur accord final, soit la loi mystérieuse de la Rime, qui se révèle avec la fonction de gardienne et d'empêcher qu'entre tous, un usurpe, ou ne demeure péremptoirement: en quelle pensée fabriqué celui-là! peu m'importe, attendu que sa matière discutable aussitôt, gratuite, ne produirait de preuve à se tenir dans un équilibre momentané et double à la façon du vol, identité de deux fragments constitutifs remémorée extérieurement par une parité dans la consonance.[32]

Words, with all their multiple, contradictory meanings, their arbitrary sounds, are herded together by rhyme like sheep by a shepherd or like the animals ushered into the Ark two by two. The 'gardienne' creates a unity or an 'equilibrium' out of divergent elements. The same idea is then expressed by another comparison: the two verses united by rhyme are like the two wings of a bird. Either way, the primordial integrity of two or more fragments is revealed.

Being determined by the rules of prosody – rules which are actually a 'loi mystérieuse', like a DNA code – rhyme makes each verse the necessary part of a whole, not just the chance product of thought. Rhyme represents a 'proof' that a synthesis has taken place.

The same concept is expressed more subtly in the essay on Gautier in 1865. The phrase 'le souvenir du rythme antérieur' refers, first, to the notion of a former life, a *vie antérieure* or lost paradise, the memory of older 'rhythms'. These Romantic allusions should be treated in the same way as allusions to the Tower of Babel. Both are ironic: their original religious connotations are used for rhetorical and philosophical effect. The reference is not to a lost past but to a hidden present or rather a constant. This constant is then associated typically with a tangible truth. In this case, the 'souvenir' is associated with 'la science mystérieuse du Verbe'. 'Rythme' can then be taken as a reference to rhyme (which has the same etymon: *rhythmus*). In prosaic terms, the word that completes the rhyme harks back to an earlier word. Even here, the metaphorical or mystical power which Mallarmé attributes to rhyme corresponds to an obvious, mechanical reality.

Verse in this way 'philosophiquement rémunère le défaut des langues'.[33] Wandering about in the infinite spaces beyond the sheepfold of verse, words are arbitrary signs; or at least, without a poet to activate their occult connections, they seem to be arbitrary signs. Within verse, after being driven through the sheep-dip of poetic constraints, they regain their own, particular virtues, notably their phonetic and prosodic values. They join together, not in accordance with conventional logic, but according to the 'fatality' of versification. This is the sense of the conjunction *pour que* in the phrase 'Ce tissu transformable et ondoyant pour que, sur tel point, afflue le luxe essentiel à la versification'. The vagaries of words and images are seen retrospectively to have been eminently convenient. Instead of being mere labels, the words *are* what they represent; they establish a link between 'les spectacles du monde' and 'la parole chargée de les exprimer'.[34] The random activity of language, which gave so much trouble to Boileau and which cast doubts on the integrity of the author of *Prose pour des Esseintes*, becomes necessary and inevitable.

Of course, the victory has to be won over and over again. There is a constant battle, as in any rhymed poetry, between chance and the poet's skill. Verse denies chance, which nonetheless remains 'aux termes' (i.e. in the rhymes at the end of each verse), as Mallarmé says at the end of *Crise de vers*, 'malgré l'artifice de leur retrempe alternée en le sens [the horizontal axis] et la sonorité [the vertical axis]'.[35] The poet's 'artifice' in finding and arranging rhymes is obviously ineffective against randomness which, from a universal point of view, controls everything; and yet the 'incantatory', unitary nature of poetry allows us to glimpse some ideal 'mot total' – a summing-up, a simpli-fication, an impersonal structure. Chance, which rhymes 'naître' with 'n'être' and 'génie' with 'nénie', is made necessary: 'pour omettre l'auteur'. The irony, which is partly the subject of *Prose pour des Esseintes*, is that Mallarmé's words are still on one level the 'mots de la tribu'; they still have their 'commercial' meanings; their syntax and grammar are still recognizably human, and there is some doubt in Mallarmé's mind as to whether syntax and grammar partici-pate in the same collective structures as prosody and the letters of the alphabet.

Probably, this is as close as anyone can come to resolving the dilemma of Rhyme and Reason without resorting to magic. Rich rhymes seem to drain poetic discourse of its meaning. Words imply the absence of the object they designate, and then the objects as it were disappear a second time when those words form new phonetic and prosodic patterns. But as words organized in verse erode reality, they suggest a different order which lies beyond logic: some 'signe pur général qui doit marquer le vers'.[36] As Mallarmé told Vielé-Griffin, a *vers-libriste*: 'Tout le mystère est là: établir les identités secrètes par un deux à deux qui ronge et use les objets, au nom d'une centrale pureté.'[37]

Each of Mallarmé's rhymes could therefore be described by the following equation: $1 + (-1) = 0$, where zero is not just a hypothetical point between positive and negative, but another dimension, a dimension that eludes analy-sis, but which is suggested by the operation that precedes it.

Philosophically, Mallarmé transcends the old Rhyme-Reason dichotomy. Rhyme is not just an ornament which has to fit in with the rational discourse. Its value lies in the aural and visual pleasure it creates and in the very procedures that bring it into existence. Mallarmé himself sums up the whole process in the following passage, using once again the image of a 'seal' and the ideas of 'richness' and 'forging', which will lead us back eventually to Banville's play, *Le Forgeron*:

> le principe qui n'est – que le Vers! attire . . . les mille éléments de beauté pressés d'accourir et de s'ordonner dans leur valeur essentielle. Signe! au gouffre central . . . , le numérateur divin de notre apothéose, quelque suprême moule qui n'ayant pas lieu en tant que d'aucun objet qui existe: mais il emprunte, pour y aviver un sceau tous gisements épars, ignorés et flottants selon quelque richesse, et les forger.[38]

From a historical perspective, one could say that the negative connotations of the poetic games indulged in by Baudelaire, Corbière or Laforgue have been reversed. By devaluing the theme or the 'meaning' of the poem, by revalorizing classical prosody, and by endowing poetic techniques with a metaphorical value, Mallarmé shows that this antiquated, clanking vehicle has the unexpected power to annihilate the reality it uses as a pretext and to evoke the world of pure, essential ideas.

Perhaps for the time being it would be simpler to use Mallarmé's notion of a type of 'magic' based on analogies between words and things, or between words and ideas, which 'riment ensemble, pour ainsi parler':

> Le vers, trait incantatoire! et, on ne déniera au cercle que perpétuellement ferme, ouvre la rime une similitude avec les ronds, parmi l'herbe, de la fée ou du magicien.[39]

The image of rhymes like fairy-rings in the grass has an exact equivalent in a verse which itself forms a rhyming circle and, significantly, includes the phrase used in the passage just quoted – 'parmi l'herbe': 'Verlaine? Il est caché parmi l'herbe, Verlaine.'

In Mallarmé's poetry, Boileau's 'slave' becomes a conquering hero – virtually. Rhyme is itself the synthesis it conjures up and the perfect example – or cause – of that monumental rigidity and evanescence that makes Mallarmé's poetry so frustrating and rewarding.

One important image of rhyme mentioned only in passing is the thyrsus,[40] related etymologically to the 'tige' on which the rhyme-flower appears. As readers of Baudelaire's prose poems know, the thyrsus is the stick carried by Bacchus, with ivy or vine leaves wound around it and a pine-cone on top. Abstractly, it can be seen as an entanglement of motifs, organized around an essential centre that is invisible yet suggested by all the secondary, decorative elements. 'Et quel est, cependant,' asks Baudelaire in 'Le Thyrse', 'le mortel imprudent qui osera décider si les fleurs et les pampres ont été faits pour le bâton, ou si le bâton n'est que le prétexte pour montrer la beauté des pampres et des fleurs?' In other words, are the rhymes and verses there to give form to an essential idea, or is Mallarmé's idealism simply a pretext for playing with rhymes? – another reckless question we shall have to try hard not to answer.

4

Un poëte en quête de rimes:
Difficult Rhymes and Impossible Rhymes

'le mot intact et nul' [1]

We have just seen that, for Mallarmé, French verse and the universe are governed by the same laws, and that rhymed poetry enables the poet to offer virtual solutions to philosophical dilemmas. It follows that the dreary literary genre known as the *traité de versification* is actually, whether its author knows it or not, a philosophical and dramatic work of universal interest. It also follows that the little rhyme-games of Mallarmé's *Vers de circonstance* potentially have an unexpectedly profound significance. By endowing rhymes, however flippant, with a value that transcends prosody, Mallarmé incorporates them, both in his verse and in his criticism, into a drama in several different acts and with several different dénouements.

On its simplest level, the drama is that of the 'poëte en quête d'une rime'. Mallarmé applied this expression to himself when asking Lefébure for information on the word *ptyx*.[2] The fact that he placed it in inverted commas indicates its status as a cliché. In *La Peau de chagrin*, for instance, Balzac calls Raphaël de Valentin's dishevelled, absent-minded old schoolmaster the epitome of a 'Poète classique en quête d'une rime'.[3] Other avatars of this risible figure can be found in the work of most satirical or ironical poets: the thrusting, stumbling rhymester of Baudelaire's 'Le Soleil', 'Trébuchant sur les mots comme sur les pavés, / Heurtant parfois des vers depuis longtemps rêvés'; or, once again, Boileau with his eternal lamentations. Here, he envies Molière his infuriating ability always to find the perfect rhyme:

> Souvent j'ai beau rêver du matin jusqu'au soir,
> Quand je veux dire blanc, la quinteuse dit noir.
> Si je veux d'un galant dépeindre la figure,
> Ma plume pour rimer trouve l'abbé de Pure.[4]

(And, as Banville pointed out, when he wants to describe failure his verse becomes more nimble, especially in the last line, where the word 'rimer' itself

43

rhymes at the hemistich with 'rêver', is echoed in most of the other words and enclosed in the phonetic circle, *plume-Pure*.)

For most nineteenth-century writers who refuse to believe that poets enjoy a direct line to superior realities, the trivial pursuit of rhymes is what distinguishes poets from their fellow humans. A futile and vacuous activity which makes the rules of versification seem little more than a nuisance:

> Et quand sonnerait au cadran *suprême*
> Midi moins un quart,
> Avec probité je payerais mon *terme* (*ter.*)
> A monsieur Bernard.

– Diable, fit Schaunard en relisant sa composition, *terme* et *suprême*, voilà des rimes qui ne sont pas millionnaires, mais je n'ai point le temps de les enrichir.

Murger had a painfully low opinion of his own poetic capacity. As a result, his *Scènes de la Vie de Bohème* are full of these miserable, self-deprecating rhymes:

Marcel reprit:

> Ils virent arriver un' petit' soeur,
> Eur! eur! eur! eur!

– Si tu ne te tais pas, dit Schaunard, qui ressentait déjà des symptômes d'aliénation mentale, je vais t'exécuter l'allégro de ma symphonie sur *l'influence du bleu dans les arts*.[5]

Rhyme-games in Murger's *Scènes* are intended to trivialize the noble art of poetry and make us feel sorry for the young men who are forced to earn their living in such a degrading, unprofitable way. Because the irony *seems* to be directed against the author himself and his fellow Bohemians, the play adapted from the *Scènes* in 1849 was a huge success, as was Puccini's even more sentimental opera. Apparently, those young tearaways who helped to overturn the Government in 1848 were not such a menace after all.

In Mallarmé's poetry, where there is no such sardonic distance between the author and his text, these frivolous games have an entirely different purpose and point to an opposite conclusion. In his own search for rhymes, Mallarmé asserts that this trifling pastime has all the urgent interest of a philosophical investigation or a spiritual quest. The tedious search in which the writing of verse involves the poet becomes the adventure that forms the subject of the poem.

We have also encountered some of the images that will recur in the drama of verse. First, those figures which represent rhyme itself: 'luxe', 'preuve', 'sceau', 'gardienne', the 'deux à deux', above all the 'aile', which, in Mallarmé's concentric allegories, can represent not only rhyme but also the whole verse or a page or sheet of the book.[6] Second, words which refer to the 'topography' of the poem or to the place that rhymes occupy on the printed page: 'final', 'suprême', 'extrême' and 'termes', not in the sense in which Murger uses the word, but in the more literal sense it has in Verlaine's *Invectives* – 'Termes affreux! Rimes? Comment?'[7] Long before *Un coup de Dés*, Mallarmé was writing with one eye on the spatial dimensions of poetry, though his poems were still stuck fast, like the swan, in the frozen lake of fixed verse forms:

> La chevelure vol d'une flamme à l'extrême
> Occident

Finally, we have also had a preview of various images which refer to the disparate elements that rhyme brings together or completes: 'gisements', 'motifs', 'thyrse', and the 'tige' of the verse on which, it is hoped, the rhyme will blossom like a flower.

These images, to which several others will be added as we go along, seem at first to belong to a personal repertoire of private symbols; yet they all have perfectly familiar literary precedents. Just as Mallarmé teases unexpected nuances from everyday words, so he draws out the implications of all the hackneyed images normally applied to poetry or to aspects of poetic creation. When he talks of giving 'un sens plus pur aux mots de la tribu', 'mots' can be taken to mean not only individual words whose connotations and physical characteristics are reactivated in the poem, but also metaphorical expressions that seemed to have lost their figurative power. Images roused from a long sleep are not always recognizable when they reemerge. The comparison of rhymes to the two wings of a bird, for example, might be thought rather precious, especially when the comparison is not made explicit. But the wing belongs to that group of images which are based on an analogy of flight and inspiration. In Romantic poetry, verses are often 'ailés'; poets snatch rhymes out of the sky as they fly past;[8] Banville talks of 'deux vers jumeaux [qui] volent d'un même essor, / Attachés par la Rime avec des liens d'or';[9] and before Banville, Amédée Pommier observed that rhymes are 'Ce que sont dans l'oiseau les ailes accouplées'.[10] Poets are therefore like bird-catchers ('oiseleurs') stretching their nets (see p. 125); and, of course, poets are also birds – swans, swallows, skylarks, falcons, eagles, pelicans or albatrosses.

Now that we have a passing acquaintance with some of the actors, it is time to show in a more concrete fashion how the drama is acted out in Mallarmé's poetry. In short, a dress-rehearsal. To do this without too much premature complication I should like first to introduce a single protagonist – an actor who plays the same role in the drama of verse as the villain in a melodrama.

The remainder of this chapter is therefore devoted to an extreme case. It has the advantage of placing us in the best seat before the play begins. It will also serve to show how Mallarmé combines classical versification, modified by usage, with his own 'local' prosody.

One of the more exasperating *boutades* of Baudelaire's abortive prefaces for *Les Fleurs du Mal* is a short note on rhyme. Baudelaire claims that, before indifference and disgust overwhelmed him, he was intending to explain to us

> pourquoi tout poète qui ne sait pas au juste combien chaque mot comporte de rimes est incapable d'exprimer une idée quelconque.[11]

Baudelaire's axiom has, understandably enough, often been dismissed as a puerile attempt to mystify the reader. If I wanted to write a sonnet using the feminine rhymes of 'Sed non satiata' (*havane, savane, pavane, caravane*), why should I be incapable of expressing an idea if I have never heard of the word *paravane* (a device for protecting the hull of a ship from underwater mines)? After all, Baudelaire also tells us that anyone can become a poet in twenty lessons, and there is no suggestion that one of those lessons would consist of memorizing a rhyme dictionary. In fact, Baudelaire's axiom jabs a finger at an important aspect of poetic language as seen by a poet. People who write in rhyming verse can obviously not be expected to keep a constantly updated list of all possible rhymes in their head. Baudelaire himself, when correcting the proofs of *Les Fleurs du Mal*, asked his publisher for a rhyme dictionary: 'Je n'en ai jamais eu. – Mais ce doit être une chose excellente dans le cas d'épreuves.'[12] So much for rhyming omniscience.

A more reasonable interpretation might be this: when poets sit down to write their poems, they should not only have in mind a certain number of suitable rhymes but should also know whether or not a given word has a great many or very few possible rhymes. Baudelaire's peremptory remark is a provocative reminder that certain rhymes derive a particular value from the rules of versification. Rhymes, as we saw, belong to groups that are formed by years of use. This is sometimes what makes it possible to predict the rhymes of mediocre poems. But each rhyme also belongs to a hierarchy established by the rules alone. The value of a rhyme, at least for those who have tried to use it, may be determined in part by the difficulties it creates (or does not create) for the poet.

Like many poetic curios, this apparently insignificant fact first exerts an

influence in parodic verse. Banville, in his *Odes funambulesques* and elsewhere, frequently places a word at the end of a line which rhymes with only
one other word: *cintre-peintre*; *Kurde-absurde*; *Thècle-siècle*; *truffe-Tartuffe*;
etc.[13] If the rhyme is skilfully produced and the difficulty overcome, these are
rhymes which, Mallarmé would say, are worthy of delighting a poet's soul.
When Banville succeeds in combining *cintre* and *peintre* in the same context
without lapsing entirely into nonsense, any poet worth his salt – that is, any
poet who knows approximately how many rhymes there are for a given word
– should experience a pang of pleasure, intensified by the knowledge that
most other readers will have missed it.

Banville is so fond of using extremely rare rhymes that he goes to great
lengths in order to fit them in. He even 'cheats' in several ways. Sometimes
he alters the spelling of a word (*fenouil-verrouil*); sometimes he borrows words
from other languages (child-*Rothschild*), or forces us to pronounce the word
incorrectly (*holocauste-chaises de poste*).[14] Strictly speaking, these are false
rhymes. If, like Mallarmé, one observes the classical rules, which state that
both rhyme-words must be either masculine or feminine, then one must
believe that *fenouil*, *Rothschild* and *holocauste* have no rhymes.

A possible objection is that these unusual rhymes are an unavoidable
feature of Banville's 'chroniques rimées': proper nouns are inevitably very
common in satires of contemporary life. But the proper nouns that appear in
the rhyming position often seem to have very little to do with the actual
subject of the poem: the artist *Diéterle* crops up only because he rhymes with
perle, the lawyer *Chicoisneau* is unflatteringly stuck with *guano*, etc.[15] It would
be more appropriate to say that Banville indulged in satirical verse because he
liked the challenge of finding rhymes that are both rich and novel, and also
extremely difficult to use effectively. The humour, as Mallarmé observed, is
produced not so much by topical jokes as by French prosody: 'le comique
versifié ou issu de la prosodie, rimes et coupes'.[16]

In some poems, Banville takes his cheating one stage further. In 'Songe
d'une nuit d'hiver' in *Les Cariatides* (1842), he creates a kind of optical
illusion by 'rhyming' words that do not rhyme: *sculptes*, *cultes*, *abruptes*.
Though it rhymes aurally, *sculptes* is the only word in French with that
ending, and *abrupte* has no rhyme at all, either aurally or visually. Most
readers of the time would probably have noticed deliberate mistakes like
these and even, like a pernickety critic pontificating in the *Revue de Belgique*,
found them quite offensive.[17] A 'mistake' like *terme-suprême*, which betrays
the ineptitude of Schaunard in the *Scènes de la Vie de Bohème*, can serve as
proof of the poet's virtuosity. Banville's approximate, assonant rhymes
contributed (though it seems hardly credible today) to the image of an *enfant
terrible*.*

---

* The only example of an approximate end-rhyme in Mallarmé is a New Year's greeting on a box
of glacé fruits: *ensemble-exemple* (*P*, 586).

Difficult rhymes become increasingly common in French verse poetry throughout the second half of the century. They begin to appear not only in satires but also in poems that have no obvious parodic intentions: in Verlaine's 'Croquis parisien', for example (*zinc-cinq*,[18] *Phidias-gaz*), or in the majority of Mallarmé's poems. The exotic or arbitrary origins of these words (which often explains why they have few or no rhymes) gives the text a strange, picturesque appearance. It also draws attention to the difficult task that faced the poet. The usual term for this is 'foregrounding', perhaps more easily remembered in the present context as 'showing off'.

Clearly, words that are difficult to rhyme have no special, inherent quality. People have been using the word 'abrupte' for five centuries now without stopping to think what a lonely word it is. However, classical prosody imparts a value to these words which certain poets are unable to forget. Thus, when Verlaine wrote an epigram attacking that wingless bird, the *vers libre*, he exploited not only the sound and sense of the rhymes, but also their formal connotations:

> Il est vrai que je reste dans ce nombre
> Et dans la rime, un abus que je sais
> Combien il pèse et combien il encombre,
> Mais indispensable à notre art français.

The feminine rhymes are themselves an example of this 'encombrement' that the *vers-libristes* associate with rhyme. The *ombre* ending offers very few possibilities: hence the frequency of the rhyme *ombre-sombre*. The awkwardness of the quatrain – 'je reste . . . dans la rime', 'un abus que je sais . . . combien il encombre' – ironically illustrates the sacrifices that must be made for the sake of rhyme. It may be ugly and cumbersome, but at least it flies.

Difficult rhymes might be thought a nuisance; impossible rhymes are a depressingly immovable obstacle. In French, there are approximately one hundred words that rhyme with no other word (see Appendix I). Strangely, this zero degree of rhyme has been ignored or missed in all the recent studies of rhyme; and yet, for poets writing in regular verse, these echoless words have a particular significance. Once again, it would be absurd to pretend that the fact that 'Belge', for example, has no rhyme corresponds to something real. The significance is entirely dependent on the system of rules applied by the poet.

Like difficult rhymes, impossible rhymes sometimes play a role in satirical verse. We have already encountered some impossible rhymes in Banville's poetry. Another example is the 'Prologue' written by Baudelaire for the *Salon caricatural de 1846*, to which Banville also contributed:

> C'est moi, messieurs, qui suis le terrible Prologue,
> Cicérone effroyable, et taillé comme un ogre.

A note at the end of the first line instructs the reader, 'Prononcez *prologre*', the reason being that *ogre* is the only word that has this ending – unless one thinks (but who would?) of *dogre*, a type of fishing vessel that used to sail from Holland to Dogger Bank. Similarly, a note attached to a distich on the pianist Henri Herz invites us to pronounce *pervers* so that it rhymes with *Herz*: 'Prononcez *pervertz*.'[19] The humour comes, of course, not only from the mispronunciation of the rhyming word, but also from the self-conscious allusion to the rule and the suggestion that the poet was, on this occasion, unable to control Boileau's recalcitrant 'slave'.

Words like these are understandably fascinating to anyone who tries to use them as rhymes. They act as disturbing reminders that exceptions exist, that prosody has loopholes and can only ever be partially effective. In his *Prosodie de l'école moderne* (1844), Wilhem (*sic*) Ténint mentioned with some regret the existence of both types of word. First, those 'pour lesquels s'offrent si peu de rimes' 'qu'il faut bien . . . se départir de la règle [de la rime riche] à leur endroit':

> Nous ne parlons pas seulement des rimes tout à fait rares, comme *angle*, *ague*, *obe*, *ouque*, etc.; nous parlons aussi des rimes qu'en cherchant bien on pourrait trouver à faire riches, mais dans un cercle trop restreint, comme *or* et *ore* (*encore*, *honore*), *ude* (*étude*, *prude*), *ange* (*échange*, *louange*), *are* (*fanfare*, *avare*), etc.

(Curiously, the word *cercle*, which he uses, would have provided a better example since it rhymes only with *couvercle*.) Second – and worse – those troublesome rhymeless words: 'tous les mots d'une langue doivent servir à la rime, et . . . lorsqu'un mot vient naturellement à la fin d'un vers, il faut l'y laisser, à moins qu'il n'ait pas de rime, ce qui est un cas de force majeure.' Ténint offers no example of such a word, though his own Christian name would probably have been rhymeless if he had kept its second *l*.[20]

Ferdinand de Gramont was more thorough and gave a list of sixty-five words that, according to him, are rhymeless (though some, like 'épargne', are not). Poets should get to know these 'unsociable' words, he says, so as to avoid unnecessary disappointment – because, unfortunately, 'beaucoup de ces mots insociables sonnent très bien à l'oreille et seraient d'un excellent effet à la fin d'un vers'.[21]

Rhymeless words, which classical prosody is powerless to place with a mating partner in its Ark, present an important challenge, a challenge that must be faced if the integrity of the whole system is to be preserved. We have already seen how Banville tries to solve the problem by using assonance and visual similarity.* Aragon's answer to the problem was to create a new type of rhyme: the *rime enjambée* – a rhyme which is completed only when the first phoneme of the following verse is pronounced. (Actually, earlier poets sometimes use the same device so that *nus*, followed at the beginning of the next line by an *s*, rhymes aurally as well as visually with *Vénus*.) In 'J'attends sa lettre au crépuscule', he constructs three rhymes for *Ourcq*, which, according to him, counts among the hundred or so words that have no rhyme – though Jacques Heugel claims that it rhymes with *Bourg*:

> Que les heures tuées
> Guerre à Crouy-sur-*Ourcq*
> Meurent mal et tu es
> Mon âme et mon vaut*our*
> Camion de buées
> Mélancolique am*our*
> Qui suit l'avenue et
> Capitaine au long *cours*
> Quitte pour les nuées
> Les terres remuées

In his article on 'La Rime en 1940', Aragon offered this analysis of his poem: 'L'emploi simultané de la rime enjambée et de la rime complexe [a rhyme which straddles two or more words] permet l'emploi dans le vers français de tous les mots de la langue sans exception, même de ceux qui sont avérés sonorement impairs et que jamais personne n'a jusqu'ici mariés à d'autres mots avec l'anneau de la rime'.[22]

It is interesting to note that Banville, who goes out looking for problems to solve, managed to 'rhyme' the rhymeless word, *polke*, in a similar fashion, by using a *rime complexe* (though, as far as I know, without boasting about it):

---

* Lamartine's *La Chute d'un ange* (vv. 55–6) contains a rhymeless rhyme ('algue') which he rhymes in the same way:

> Comme au bleu d'une mer sans écume et sans algue
> Le vert des bois se fond en trempant dans la vague.

J. Heugel quotes this as an example of 'négligence'. Lamartine probably would have agreed since he changed the rhyme at the first opportunity:

> Comme au bleu d'une mer qui dort sous le rivage
> Le vert des bois se fond en doublant son image.

Faced with this 'mot du démon' at the end of a verse, Hugo wonders 'comment amener l'abbé de Salgues' (*Océan vers*, *Oeuvres complètes* [Laffont, 'Bouquins', 1986], IV, 965). He might have asked a pedantic parodist called Courtat, who rewrote some of Hugo's verse in classical form and also wrote poems using rhymeless words: see Albert de Bersaucourt, *Les Pamphlets contre Victor Hugo* (Mercure de France, 1912), 69.

> Si vous savez, à cha*que pas*,
> Murmurer: 'Je ne pol*ke pas*,'
> Landrirette,
> Vous allez gagner vos paris,
> Landriry.[23]

A more desperate strategy, mentioned by Gramont, is to make words up – preferably proper nouns since they are harder to check:

> Le jour de ce triomphe
> J'allai me réjouir chez mon ami *Panomphe.*

> Au sommet d'un coteau tout revêtu de pampre
> On voit se dessiner le château de *Belcampre.*

These experiments, says Gramont, met with too little success 'pour qu'on puisse sérieusement conseiller à personne de s'en servir' (which must mean Gramont himself was responsible).[24] Yet 'Panomphe' and 'Belcampre' surely have as much right to exist as 'ptyx'.

Half a century later, Apollinaire also made the attempt. In 'La Chanson du mal-aimé', he managed to supply the apparently rhymeless word, *holocauste*, with two rhymes: *pyraustes* (a mythical insect) and the adjective *faustes* (a neologism derived from the Latin, *faustus*).[25]

These insubordinate words exert such a strong fascination that they appear, with the same connotations, in other places – even in prose. Expressing his admiration for Gautier's *Émaux et Camées*, Baudelaire talks of 'la pourpre régulière et symétrique d'une rime plus qu'exacte'.[26] The critic Edmond Scherer found this peculiar use of the word 'pourpre' quite shocking: 'J'aime mieux des fautes de grammaire', he wrote in 1869, 'qu'un phébus comme la *pourpre symétrique d'une rime exacte*' (*sic*).[27] But when we know, as Baudelaire did, that *pourpre* is one of those rare words that have no rhyme, the phrase becomes a subtle evocation of the exquisite surprise created by 'une rime plus qu'exacte'. Baudelaire may even have been thinking of a specific poem of *Émaux et Camées*. In 'Carmen', Gautier supplies the same rhymeless word with several compensatory internal echoes:

> Et, parmi sa pâleur, éclate
>   p R   p   R
> Une bouche aux rires vainqueurs;
>   u   RR   R
> Piment rouge, fleur écarlate,
> p   RU   R   R
> Qui prend sa *pourpre* au sang des coeurs.
>   pR   puRpR   R

(Especially satisfying because the internal rhyme for 'pourpre' – 'rouge' – rhymes only with 'gouge' and 'bouge'.)[28]

Almost certainly for the same reason, Mallarmé often describes rhyme with rhymeless words like *luxe* and *thyrse*. It is certain in any case that he was acutely aware of this 'cas de force majeure', as Ténint calls it. As we saw earlier, the function of rhyme's 'mysterious law' for Mallarmé is to prevent anomalies: 'd'empêcher qu'entre tous, un [vers] usurpe, ou ne demeure péremptoirement'.[29] The adverb should be given its etymological sense (*perimere* = destroy): the exceptional word threatens to break up the synthesis created by rhyme or simply to show how arbitrary it all is, 'discutable' and 'gratuit'.[30] One might add that 'usurpe' also belongs to the select group of rhymeless words.

It should come as no surprise then that rhymeless words acquire a metaphysical sense in Mallarmé's figurative prosody. The sense is easy to guess. It can be deduced from this very Mallarmean passage in which Claudel celebrates the vital importance of rhyme:

> La parole humaine ne retentit pas dans le vide. Elle ne demeure pas stérile. Elle est une sommation du silence, elle appelle, elle provoque quelque chose d'égal ou de comparable à elle-même. Quand le poète a proféré le vers pareil à une formule incantatoire, il répond quelque chose dans le blanc.[31]

The rhymeless word, on the other hand, isolated by its inability to form a rhyme, is an exception that calls into question the laws of an optimistic science. It creates a nasty suspicion that the synthesis might fail to occur. The rhymeless word can be compared to an irreducible absolute, a particle that forms no bond. It denies the possibility of reestablishing, 'philosophically', the 'identity' of *signifiants* and *signifiés*; ominously, it presupposes silence. And in case this seems a gross exaggeration, the same mystical view of language is implicit in the everyday expression 'Cela ne rime à rien'.

Before applying these observations to Mallarmé's *Poésies*, it may be helpful to look briefly at one example of how he deals with a rhymeless word. The poem, 'L'aile s'évanouit . . .' – almost entirely neglected by critics – was never included in any list drawn up by Mallarmé for an edition of his poems, probably because it was too much like one of Banville's conjuring tricks or Baudelaire's illicit *prologre*:

A Méry Laurent

L'aile s'évanouit et fond
Des Cupidons vers d'autres nues
Que celles peintes au plafond,
Prends garde! quand tu éternues –

Ou que ce couple qui jouait
N'interrompe sa gymnastique
Pour te décerner le fouet
Sur quelque chose d'élastique

Si (moi-même je reconnais
Comme avec à propos on t'aime
Pâlie en de petits bonnets)
Jamais tu gazouilles ce thème

Ancien: Z'ai mal à la gorze –
Pendant l'an quatre-vingt-quatorze.

The word *quatorze* would normally be rhymeless. Mallarmé manages to provide it with a rhyme by transcribing Méry Laurent's faulty pronunciation of 'gorge', apparently due to a dose of flu (sneezing and a sore throat). Bearing in mind the significance of rhymeless words, one might say that this prosodic witticism is the aim or pretext of the whole poem, certainly its conclusion.

There are several other casual poems in which Mallarmé playfully contrasts some charming reality – a woman or a landscape – with the abstruse and sterile game of devising rhymes. In the sonnet to Méry Laurent, an involuntary action – a sneeze – threatens to interrupt the movement that begins in the first line. This movement (perhaps a feather floating down from the ceiling[32] which a sneeze would blow away) is related to the poetic 'game': the wing refers to one element of a pair and thus to one of the two words that form a rhyme. By its movement, it establishes or implies a link between one realm (the clouds – 'nues' – painted on the ceiling) and another ('nues' in the sense of nudes?). This is the function of rhyme: to confirm metaphorical relations between two distinct realities.

The second quatrain introduces the idea of a 'gymnastique' practised by a couple: perhaps figures forming part of the ceiling decoration. The image of gymnastics is commonly applied, not only by Mallarmé, to rhyme-games, and the connection is strengthened here by the fact that *two* people are engaged in it. ('Couple', in fact, by one of those linguistic ironies that delighted Mallarmé, rhymes with only one other word. Knowing that that word is 'souple' makes the rhyme 'élastique' appear as an illustration of its own meaning – a diversion from or over-extension of the game.) The game, we are told, could be interrupted, not only by a sneeze, but also if the woman for whom the poem is intended ever twitters the frivolous theme: 'Z'ai mal à la gorze – / Pendant l'an quatre-vingt-quatorze.' The poet apparently wants the elaborate game to continue, and fears that this 'thème ancien' will persuade the 'couple' to award the woman the 'fouet'. ('Fouet', in line with the first word of the poem, can refer to the tip of a wing.) In other words, the poetic game will end if this charming woman in her pretty little bonnets becomes a distraction from the serious task at hand. The curious, contradictory association of 'décerner', implying a reward, and 'fouet', implying punishment, brings to mind the mixture of reproach and congratulation with which good (i.e. bad) puns are usually greeted.

The 'quelque chose d'élastique', originally produced by the 'couple', would therefore refer to the rhyme at the end of the poem which is clearly too accommodating or 'elastic'. It can also refer to the masculine rhymes of the second and third quatrains (jou*ait*-fou*et*, reconn*ais*-bon*nets*). According to the strict rules that Mallarmé observes, rhymes like these (ɛ-e) are inadmissible (see p. 127). Significantly, the 'trick' rhyme, *gorze-quatorze*, which makes this poem an exception in Mallarmé's poetry, is not uttered by the poet himself, but by Méry Laurent. It represents the irruption into the poem of an external reality, one which the rules of prosody are unable to contain and organize. Even the over-fussy poet, however, is forced to acknowledge the satisfying charm of this friend who refuses to take his professional efforts seriously.

'L'aile s'évanouit . . .' can be read, if we see it as an allegory of itself (and in no other guise does it make sense anyway), as a superior dramatization of the *topos* exploited by Murger: the reaction of a poet whose poetic sensibility is offended by a silly song. It can also be read as a development of the theme treated by Houssaye in his *sonnet libertin*: even the most obsessively conscientious poet may be forced by his muse to admit that his rhymes are no match for natural elegance.

The last rhyme of the poem is a kind of victory – but one which takes place outside the game and, in a sense, doesn't count – over a word that seemed to be exceptional and thus 'peremptory'. Méry Laurent's 'thème ancien' manages, like the fan described in *Étalages* – but in a manner that is far too literal, direct and unrefined – to 'rapporter contre les lèvres une muette fleur peinte comme le mot intact et nul de la songerie par les battements approché'.[33] French verse was certainly capable of greater things than this.

After this brief and technically unsuccessful dress-rehearsal, we can now complete the preliminaries by making some general remarks about Mallarmé's later poetry: how precisely does he put his poetic principles into practice, and does he manage (to adapt the image from *Étalages*) to put his prosodic money where his philosophical mouth is?

5

Composing the Poem

'la pauvreté des rimes'[1]

Since writing a sonnet is easier than writing a poem with no predetermined form, it seems reasonable to assume that the more rules and limitations there are, the easier it is to write the poem. This easiness is usually referred to as 'difficulty'.

From 1868 or so, Mallarmé began to restrict his possibilities and to make things easier for himself by using words that offer very few rhymes. The first aim of this chapter is to show that this perverse practice is far more common in his poetry than guessing would suggest. The second is to show that these exceptional words – including those that have no rhymes at all – are also significantly prevalent in other parts of the poem. Even when a difficult word does not appear at the end of a line, it may still harbour the connotations which it derives from the rules of rhyme: Mallarmé's later poems are full of frustrated rhyme-words whose tensions affect the rest of the poem they inhabit. The third aim is to indicate in a very general fashion that this peculiarity has a thematic value. Every sequence of words tells a poetic story, which may or may not match the narrative. The composition of the poem then becomes a little drama in itself: will the unity demanded by the rules of prosody be produced or not? Because of the structure of rhyme, if the synthesis does take place, it will do so only *in extremis*, at the end of the stanza or at the end of the poem. Hence, on the most basic level, a certain abstract, intellectual excitement.

The overall point is one already made about other poets: by exacerbating constraints and by applying rules with extreme rigour, Mallarmé allows what he sees as the peculiar 'genius' of French verse to act out its mysteries. In terms of Sartre's quaint analogy, Mallarmé decides not to throw a bomb at French verse but to work the system from the inside. The end of this book will show whether or not he was acting as a double agent.

The most spectacular instances of this courting of the rules are Mallarmé's regular sonnets, the reason being that the quatrains of a regular sonnet call for two sets of four words that rhyme: usually ABBA ABBA ou ABAB ABAB. This means that by the time we reach the end of the second quatrain we have almost certainly been thinking about rhyme. We may even try to guess what the fourth masculine and feminine rhymes will be or look ahead to see what they are. The example that always springs to mind is the *sonnet en yx* and Mallarmé's seemingly indiscreet letter to Lefébure:

> comme il se pourrait toutefois que . . . je fisse un sonnet, et que je n'ai que trois rimes en *ix*, concertez-vous pour m'envoyer le sens réel du mot *ptyx*, ou m'assurer qu'il n'existe dans aucune langue, ce que je préférerais de beaucoup afin de me donner le charme de le créer par la magie de la rime.[2]

All that needs to be retained for the moment from Mallarmé's reference question is the implication that the rhymes come before or 'preside over' the poem, which is what we probably would have realized just by glancing at the sonnet. The likelihood of four etymologically unrelated words ending in *yx* occurring naturally to someone who wants to express a particular idea or tell a particular story must be very small indeed.

Something that is not immediately apparent is that the *sonnet en yx* is just the earliest of these *tours de force*: an exception only at the time it was written or for a few years afterwards. This simple, important fact has been obscured, and the culprit, one suspects, is what Mallarmé calls 'the magic of rhyme'. The *yx* rhymes have exerted such a powerful, hypnotic influence as to become a distraction from a general truth; the example is so memorable that it effectively obliterates the rule. The problem is that the *yx* rhymes *look* difficult – awkward, exotic endings which draw attention to their strangeness. Some treatises on versification even advise poets not to use *yx* rhymes at all. La Harpe and Dessiaux both consider *ix* an unpoetic and unconventional ending – not necessarily incompatible qualities at the time.[3]

Rather than gloating over its obvious eccentricity, it would be preferable to see the *sonnet en yx* as one example of an important principle. To immunize ourselves against the distraction, we might begin by observing that the *yx* rhymes do not present such a difficult challenge after all, at least not in comparison to Mallarmé's later poems. Even excluding the four rhymes on *yx* that are used in the sonnet – *onyx, Phoenix, ptyx, Styx* – there are still about thirteen others on *ix* or *yx*. Some of these had already been used by other poets. In 1858, Banville composed a sonnet with the rhymes *phénix, Styx, onyx, Alix*.[4] Four years earlier, Ferdinand de Gramont published an *yx* sonnet which has the interest of containing none of the rhymes of Mallarmé's sonnet: *X, Béatrix, Éryx, natrix*.[5] True, Mallarmé may simply not have been aware of these other words; but obviously he was aware that rhyme diction-aries existed and he could have asked Lefébure to look one up for him instead of digging about for what he hoped was the non-existent *ptyx*.

Predictably, Mallarmé outstrips his predecessors by introducing the feminine equivalent, *ixe*, in the tercets. Arithmetically, the feminine rhyme actually creates a greater challenge than the masculine, since there are only seven rhymes on *ixe*: *rixe*, *nixe* and *fixe* (all in the first version of the sonnet), plus the rather dull and unpromising *prolixe*, *pré-*, *anté-* and *suf-fixe*. The last three are redundant anyway because *fixe* has already been used, which means that Mallarmé recruited every possible rhyme but one for *ixe*.

Having as it were belittled Mallarmé's famous achievement in the *sonnet en yx*, we can now go on to be more confidently impressed by the larger picture.

It would be tedious to prove that many of Mallarmé's short poems after the *sonnet en yx* imply the same sort of challenge; and plenty of evidence will emerge as we go along. The following table offers just a few examples, which may be tedious anyway, but brief. The first column gives the title of the poem. The second column lists the 'difficult' rhymes of the poem in question. The third column shows the number of other words that share the same ending. In arriving at this number, I have taken into account two rules which Mallarmé always observes and which can best be remembered as a ban on promiscuity and incest: the rule which prohibits the coupling of a masculine rhyme with a feminine rhyme (i.e. a word ending with a mute *e*), and the rule which forbids the use of 'derivative' rhymes (e.g. *fixe*, *suffixe*, etc.). Thus, *vivre*, *survivre* and *revivre* count as one rhyme.

As elsewhere in this book, I have treated Jacques Heugel's *Dictionnaire des rimes françaises* as the ultimate authority. Other rhyme dictionaries would produce slightly different results. Most, if not all, would make Mallarmé's task look more difficult rather than easier. The idea is simply to give a flavour of his approach.

Title	Rhymes used	Number of other possible rhymes
'Au seul souci'	trouble, double	1 on *ouble*
'Mes bouquins refermés'	Paphos, triomphaux, faulx, faux	6 on *faut*
Placet futile	lèvres, Sèvres, mièvres, orfèvres	5 on *èvres*
'Quand l'ombre menaça'	vertèbres, funèbres, célèbres, ténèbres	4 on *èbres*
	moins, témoins	0 on *moins**
Remémoration d'amis belges	émeuve, veuve, preuve, neuve	4 on *euve*

* *Néanmoins* is excluded as a 'derivative' rhyme.

'Sur les bois oubliés'	sombre, s'encombre nombre, ombre	7 on *ombre*
	défunte, emprunte	0 on *unte*
'Victorieusement fui'	beau, tombeau, lambeau, flambeau	4 on *beau*
'Le vierge, le vivace'	aujourd'hui, fui, lui, ennui	8 on *ui*
	ivre, givre, délivre, vivre*	5 on *ivre*
	Cygne, assigne	3 on *signe*

The table confirms what we already know from other sources – René Ghil, Paul Valéry and Mallarmé himself: he liked to write his poems with the rhymes already in place;[6] and, as we know from the *sonnet en yx*, the set rhymes are often severely restrictive. They may even exhaust all the possibilities, as with *moins-témoins* or *défunte-emprunte*: a game of *bouts-rimés* played by a masochist. (A cynic might say that this explains Mallarmé's contorted syntax, just as some poets use what might be thought clumsy inversions to place the right word at the rhyme.)

But that's not all. Only the most obvious difficulty has been considered. Several other impediments should also be taken into account, some created by the rules of versification, some by the rule-hungry poet.

In order to be sensible rather than just statistically correct, most of the numbers in the third column should really be lower since many of the other possible rhymes would almost certainly be unusable. 'Mirabeau' and 'escabeau' have no apparent connection with anything in 'Victorieusement fui . . .'; and it is hard to imagine what Vasco da Gama might be doing with a 'rouble' in 'Au seul souci . . .'.

Another reason to lower the numbers is Mallarmé's tendency to observe all available rules, not just the indispensable rules of versification. In his later poems especially, he regularly imposes restrictions on himself that other poets apply only intermittently.

First, his poems have an unusually high proportion of 'rich' rhymes (rhymes on three or more phonemes).[7] In the quatrains of *Le Tombeau de Charles Baudelaire*, the masculine rhymes are *subis, pubis, Anubis* and *rubis*. There are twenty masculine rhymes for *bi*, but only five (including the four used by Mallarmé) for *ubi*. Similarly, in the *Hommage* to Wagner, every word ending in *moire* was used, except for *écumoire* (conceivably usable as a symbol of the poetic act: the poet skims the froth off the surface of things – 'Rien, cette écume, vierge vers'). Many other examples could be given, and the 'complex' rhymes of *Prose pour des Esseintes*, stretching over more than one

---

* The same four rhymes are used in *Éventail* ('De frigides roses pour vivre . . .').

word, could be construed as an amplification of the same rule. Apart from *de visions* and *devisions*, how many other rhymes are there on *devisions*? (Realistically, none.)

Second, Mallarmé also seems to observe, at least retrospectively, the principle of visual rhymes. According to this principle, the hypothetical fifth rhyme on *ubi* (*subit*) would have to be excluded since the other rhymes end in *is*, not in *it*. In 'Surgi de la croupe . . .', any word ending in *mère* or *maire* would be considered a perfectly good rhyme by a pedant; but since the feminine rhymes of the quatrains all end in *mère*, we can suppose that Mallarmé, with a more refined sort of pedantry, chose his four rhymes from a possible field of only eleven. In 'Victorieusement fui . . .', the same criterion for selection appears to have been applied to diacritics and thus to etymology. Once 'poëte' had been replaced with 'tempête', all the feminine rhymes of the quatrains sported a circumflex accent.

A third restrictive practice which gives the rhymes an appearance of greater uniformity is the occasional use of so-called 'isometric' rhymes (rhymes which share the same number of syllables) – though this is possibly not frequent enough to be significant. The masculine rhymes in the quatrains of 'Quand l'ombre menaça . . .' are all monosyllabic: *loi, moi, roi, foi*. If all other rhymes ending in *oi* with more than one syllable are rejected, only four remain.

The point is that even rhymes that would normally offer several possibilities are turned into difficult rhymes. They are, in other words, made as necessary and inevitable as possible. One effect of this is to allow the rules of versification to nag at us as we read the poem, thereby highlighting the challenge of composing the poem in the first place.

We come now to two remarkable facts which are the first steps of a staircase leading down to a sealed tomb. These 'difficult' rhymes crop up with surprising regularity in other parts of Mallarmé's verse, not just in the rhyming position. And so do several 'impossible' rhymes. Clearly, with the exception of *gorze-quatorze* (which is cheating anyway), 'impossible' rhymes would not occur at the end of a line. But they do appear in other places. Many of these words, as we shall see, play a key role in their respective poems, not just because they tend to look exotic, but above all because of their unusual prosodic status. Segregated from other words by the rules of versification, they take on a particular significance which, for Mallarmé, is simultaneously prosodic and metaphysical.

Some of these words will be old acquaintances by the end of this book. For now, all that needs to be said is that rhymeless words are common in Mallarmé's poetry: for example, *luxe, pourpre, sceptre, sépulcre, sylphe*, etc. To these can be added a larger contingent of words that rhyme with only one or two other words: *défunte* (rhymes only with *emprunte*), *hymne* (*médimne*), *nymphe* (*lymphe, paranymphe*), *ongle* (*jongle*), *siècle* (*Thècle*), *spectre* (*Électre*, *plectre*), etc. What this seems to suggest is that Mallarmé's fondness for difficult rhymes infects the whole verse with stubborn, obstructive words which would normally be left to moulder in the ghetto of the rhyme dictionary.

At this point, a reasonable, though uninformed, objection might be made. The last observation could be dismissed as the sort of anthropomorphic remark often induced by a fetishistic obsession with an isolated aspect of Mallarmé's verse. After all, a poet much possessed by death is quite likely to use words like *défunte*, *sépulcre* and *spectre*, while a preoccupation with mythology might be expected to generate the occasional *nymphe* or *sylphe*. This is true. However, improbability is one of the delights of Mallarmé's poetry, and, despite appearances, we have yet to stray from the realm of provable assertions. When Mallarmé's poems are compared to those of other poets, the frequency of these words turns out to be statistically significant.

As they do in so many other ways, Mallarmé's poems act as historical commentaries on French verse, teaching by example of the opposite. A by-product of the observation that Mallarmé favours difficult and impossible rhymes in all parts of the poem is the realization that his predecessors tend to use words (again, in all parts of the poem) that frequently occur in the rhyming position and rhyme with a great many other words. Rhyme is so important and attracts such a high proportion of the mental activity required by the whole poem that it easily extends its influence from the edge of the verse into the hinterland.

As an example, I have taken, more or less at random (though partly because its rhymes are often discussed), the quatrains of a regular sonnet by Baudelaire: 'Parfum exotique'. A more dramatic result would be achieved by analysing a poem by a more conventional Romantic like Lamartine; but since Baudelaire is generally recognized as someone who tried to be original, he might be thought to offer more persuasive proof of the phenomenon.

In the following quotation, I have underlined every word that a) provides dozens, even hundreds of rhymes, and b) *also* appears in the rhyming position in at least one other *Fleur du Mal* (of which there are only 126).

> Quand, les *deux yeux* fermés, en un *soir chaud* d'*automne*,
> Je *respire* l'*odeur* de ton *sein chaleureux*,
> Je vois* se dérouler des *rivages heureux*
> Qu'éblouissent* les *feux* d'un *soleil monotone*;
>
> Une *île* paresseuse* où la *nature donne*
> Des arbres *singuliers* et des fruits *savoureux*;
> Des *hommes* dont le *corps* est *mince* et *vigoureux*,
> Et des *femmes* dont l'*oeil* par sa franchise *étonne*.

* *Voient*, *éblouies*, *éblouissantes* and *paresse* are all used as rhymes.

Baudelaire's sonnet, in effect, is full of highly serviceable words, like potential substitutes or sections of scaffolding which can be placed on any part of the structure. With Mallarmé, the opposite is true: words that offer few rhymes and fit in less easily are far more frequent. This partly accounts for the 'strange' appearance of his poems on the page.

The first example is taken from *Le Tombeau de Charles Baudelaire*. To heighten the contrast, I have underlined not the easy rhymes – of which there are very few – but the difficult and impossible rhymes. The numbers in parentheses show how many other words rhyme on the ending underlined. Only those endings offering fewer than ten rhymes have been noted.

> Le *temple* (3) enseveli divu*lgue* (1) par la bouche
> Sépulcrale* d'é*gout* (6) bavant *boue* (0)[†] et r*ubis* (4)
>
> Abominablement que*lque* (0) i*dole* (5) An*ubis* (4)
> Tout le museau fl*ambé* (1) comme un *aboi* (3)[‡] farouche
>
> Ou que le *gaz* (3) récent torde la mèche louche
> Essuyeuse on le sait des opp*robres* (4) s*ubis* (4)
> Il allume ha*gard* (9) un immortel p*ubis* (4)
> Dont le vol selon le réverbère découche

By contrast with Baudelaire (as further examples would show), Mallarmé favours words that seldom or never act as rhymes. Baudelaire's words are like symmetrical bricks, Mallarmé's like rough pieces of granite with awkward edges and irregularities. His vocabulary seems to be ill-adapted to its prosodic environment.

A comparative analysis of poems written by Mallarmé before and after the late 1860s would produce similar results. To make the comparison as convincing as possible, I have compared early and late versions of the same poem. The two lists that follow are a rhyme analysis of both versions of *Le Pitre châtié*, the first (or earliest known) dating from 1864, the second from 1887. As before, only endings with fewer than ten rhymes are indicated.

> 1864: enj*ambé* (1), h*erbes* (7), m*embres* (7), s*uif* (1)
> 1887: s*imple* (0), *autre* (6), s*uie* (5), ign*oble* (2), j*ambe* (6), sép*ulcres* (0), v*ierge* (2), p*oings* (4 with this spelling), n*acre* / s*acre* (9)

To conclude so far: the *sonnet en yx*, which draws attention to the spokes Mallarmé throws in his own wheel (or carefully inserts in it), is not the

---

*   *Sépulcre* is a rhymeless word.
[†]   It seems unnecessarily pedantic to include *Topinamboue*.
[‡]   *Aboi* is the only word in French which ends in *boi*.

prosodic exception it seems; but it is important because of its place in the history of his poetry. Some of its undeservedly superior status can be attributed, as we saw, to the *yx* endings, but also to the explanatory title Mallarmé gave it in 1868: *Sonnet allégorique de lui-même*. Why, one might ask, is the 1887 version no longer said to be an allegory of itself? Because, by then, the *sonnet en yx* was not the only poem that fell into that category. When Mallarmé gave it its intriguing title in 1868 he was marking the discovery of a principle, not just describing an isolated antic. The *sonnet en yx* is a beginning, not an anomaly. From then on – though perhaps after a gap of several years, excepting *Hérodiade* and *Le Faune* – all of his poems are in varying degrees *allégoriques d'eux-mêmes*. Not just because their subject is poetry, but because they recount their own creation in an unexpectedly detailed fashion. He had, in short, marked out a large part of his poetic territory and solved once and for all the problem of finding a theme.

A very brief and summary preview of the drama might be extracted at this point from the *sonnet en yx*. This is not intended as a thorough analysis but as an introduction to the approach that will be adopted in the second part of this book.

Here is the first version of the sonnet, written between 3 May and 18 July, 1868:

SONNET
allégorique de lui-même

La Nuit approbatrice allume les onyx
De ses ongles au pur Crime, lampadophore,
Du Soir aboli par le vespéral Phoenix
De qui la cendre n'a de cinéraire amphore

Sur des consoles, en le noir Salon: nul ptyx,
Insolite vaisseau d'inanité sonore,
Car le Maître est allé puiser de l'eau du Styx
Avec tous ses objets dont le Rêve s'honore.

Et selon la croisée au Nord vacante, un or
Néfaste incite pour son beau cadre une rixe
Faite d'un dieu que croit emporter une nixe

En l'obscurcissement de la glace, décor
De l'absence, sinon que sur la glace encor
De scintillations le septuor se fixe.

Mallarmé explained the title of his sonnet in a letter to Cazalis: '[le sonnet] est inverse, je veux dire que le sens, s'il en a un (mais je me consolerais du contraire grâce à la dose de poësie qu'il renferme, ce me semble) est évoqué par un mirage interne des mots mêmes.'[8] The supposed absence of meaning seems to be concentrated or exemplified in the nonsensical word, *ptyx*. The part of the sonnet that is least comprehensible seems to offer the greatest hope of comprehension. Understand what the *ptyx* is or what its function is, we are led to hope, and we might understand the sonnet.

Several different meanings have been found for the *ptyx*,[9] none of which need concern us here.* When Mallarmé wrote the sonnet, he had already decided that, outside the poem, *ptyx* had no meaning. In the letter to Lefébure, he hopes to be able to congratulate himself on having brought it into being 'par la magie de la rime', though apparently suspecting it of having a 'sens réel'. And we might just as well accept the poet's explanation of his word since it corresponds so nicely to the context. When Leconte de Lisle asked him whether the *ptyx* might not be a piano (thinking presumably of that instrument's 'inanité sonore'; perhaps, too, of the theoretical possibility of using one as a bucket), Mallarmé told him it was not. The word *ptyx* was there for the simple reason that he needed a rhyme for *Styx*, and this is what the poem itself allegedly makes clear:

> or, c'est bien clair, le ptyx est insolite, puisqu'il n'y en a pas; il résonne bien, puisqu'il rime; et ce n'en est pas moins un vaisseau d'inanité, puisqu'il n'a jamais existé![10]

For the first time, the central paradox of Mallarmé's verse is presented. In general terms, the paradox is the use of a form (the sonnet) which is thought to lend itself to the development of a logical argument – a 'machine à penser', as Aragon called it – and the attempt to rid it of any 'meaning'. Specifically, the paradox is the use of a word (*ptyx*) which supposedly has no conventional meaning, but which, when used as a rhyme, acquires a sense in relation to the rules of versification, contributing as it does to the audible and visible unity of the sonnet.

Like *gorze-quatorze*, the absurd *ptyx-Styx* rhyme is not just an ornament but an element of the sonnet's theme: writing a sonnet creates nothing but a sonnet. Or, to enter into the spirit of the paradox, it is precisely because of its purely ornamental character that the rhyme becomes a significant element in this *sonnet allégorique de lui-même*. The *ptyx* makes a point about language that any word could be made to make, though far more laboriously: meaning is use, and language a system with its own internal logic.

---

*   Except one, pointed out to me by Geoffrey Neate, which is so satisfyingly Mallarmean that one wonders how unaware of it he was: the meaning of *ptyx* as a waxed wooden tablet used for writing is not widely known. But the meaning of *diptych* as a pair of such tablets (later applied to panels for painting or carving) is. (Mallarmé later grouped three sonnets under the title *Triptyque*.) The *ptyx* therefore belongs to that group of images, so prevalent in Mallarmé's poetry, designating isolated elements normally found in pairs – like a wing or a rhyme.

The same 'reflexivity' emerges in other parts of the *sonnet en yx*. The 'mirage' Mallarmé refers to can be taken in the sense of 'illusion', but also in the sense of 'reflection'. Objects are reflected (or not) in the darkness of the mirror, just as the masculine and feminine rhymes of the quatrains are inverted in the tercets: *ore* → *or*; *ix* → *ixe*.

The *sonnet en yx*, as dozens of commentators including Mallarmé have shown, has a meaning or a *décor* that can be abstracted from the poem. Yet it also proves that it is possible to base a poem on the rules and contrivances that produce it. Both 'meanings', or methods of producing meaning, are interrelated. The drama of versification corresponds in the *sonnet en yx* to a metaphysical drama which can be expressed in the following simplistic fashion: 1. Two rhymes (or objects) postulate a certain dual identity; 2. But the duality formed in this way is immediately called into question: not only is the fourth rhyme (*ptyx*) nonsensical, but there isn't even a *ptyx* in the room; 3. The apparent absurdity or nonexistence of the duality is necessary in order for a third, indefinable term to be suggested – or, to use the phrase that Mallarmé applies to verse, the poem's general subject is 'le conscient manque chez nous de ce qui là-haut éclate'.[11] In this case, the final, implicit subject would be represented by the 'septuor', the seven-starred constellation which 'là-haut éclate', or the seven rhymes of the sonnet, which are both gratuitous (in terms of the universe) and necessary (in terms of verse), appearing in the empty frame ('cadre', 'croisée vacante') or on the unencumbered 'consoles' of the sonnet.

In the first version of the *sonnet en yx*, the drama of verse is acted out in a relatively diffuse manner, as if Mallarmé were still exploring the possibilities of his idea. But the elements of the drama are already present, notably in the characteristic development of images commonly applied to verse. For instance, as we are about to see, precious stones often designate rhymes. Here, the word *onyx* is applied to finger-nails, referring to their colour and feeble translucence (*onyx* and *ongle* have the same etymon), but also to the rhyme-words themselves, positioned at the end of the finger of each verse. (Or, in view of the metrical meaning of 'foot', 'the toe' of each verse.)

From 1868, most of Mallarmé's poems enact a similar drama. As they describe their own production, they reveal a cosmogony that Mallarmé believes to be inherent in verse itself. However esoteric this conception of poetry might appear, its starting point is simply the phenomenon that Baudelaire and a few later poets were so painfully or playfully aware of: meaning is a function of verse, just as the poet, Mallarmé would add, is a function of the universe.

Before raising the curtain on the drama itself, I should confess to a slight misrepresentation. For the sake of clarity it has been convenient to refer mostly to end-rhymes, and there is an excellent excuse in the fact that Mallarmé himself gives them precedence over every other sort of rhyme. But the prosodic games he plays are actually more complex and varied (though the principle is just as simple). Like other poets who revived poetic forms that had fallen out of favour, Mallarmé gave a new lease of life to the different types of rhyme that had always been faithfully listed in treatises on versification, even though few poets were still using them.

Mallarmé's studiedly enthusiastic praise of Banville's rhymes in *Le Forgeron* serves as a reminder – as do the *Vers de circonstance* – that 'rhyme' does not always mean 'end-rhyme' and that, for an erudite poet, or anyone else who cares to pick up the information, all the other echoes which lie scattered through the verse can bear some of the thematic weight of the allegorical poem. This is especially true if these echoes constitute examples of particular types of rhyme. The fact that certain forms of rhyme already have a recognized, 'official' existence emphasizes their identity as prosodic elements. A pleasant medley of repetitions to the untutored ear; to the poet and to the suitably obsessed reader, actors in the drama of verse.

Here, again, is what Mallarmé says about *Le Forgeron*:

la rime ici extraordinaire parce qu'elle ne fait qu'un avec l'alexandrin qui, dans ses poses et la multiplicité de son jeu, semble par elle dévoré tout entier comme si cette fulgurante cause de délice y triomphait jusqu'à l'initiale syllabe.[12]

Mallarmé's description is often illustrated with examples from his own poetry, usually from *Prose pour des Esseintes*, in which several enormous rhymes begin half-way through the verse and might indeed be said to be 'devouring' the verse:

> Gloire du long *désir, Idées*

> La famille *des iridées*

Except of course that these are not alexandrines and half of each verse is left uneaten. The appropriateness of the eating image only becomes apparent when one looks at the verses Mallarmé was actually describing.

Banville's *Forgeron* does contain similar examples of *rimes complexes* – que *ton aire-le tonnerre*; caresse-*les-Bracelets* – but these represent only one variety of verse-devouring rhyme. Even a cursory reading of *Le Forgeron* reveals it to be a little jewel-case containing almost every type of rhyme for which French prosody has a name:

rime léonine

> Au-dessus de *Ténos* que le zéphyr effleure,
> Et de cette *Délos* qui flotta jusqu'à l'heure

rime batelée

mais enc*or*e,
Avec ce front qu'un *or* mystérieux déc*ore*

rime couronnée

La Force et la Victoire, en ce lieu souterrain,
L'ont enchaîné, captif en des li*ens* d'air*ain*.

Elsewhere, homophony spreads itself throughout the verse according to less definable but equally noticeable patterns:

La m*er* sur ses pieds nus *ver*sait de b*leus* sa*phirs*,
Et les *fleurs*, les forêts, les *lyres*, les zé*phyrs*
Acclamaient par leurs chants cette jeune immortelle.[13]

This is presumably why Mallarmé envisions the rhymes of *Le Forgeron* retrospectively gobbling up the entire verse, right back to 'the initial syllable'. From beginning to end, Banville's drama is awash with rhyme, providing an efficient conductor for the poetic charge which Mallarmé hoped would rid the *sonnet en yx* of any 'meaning': the foregrounding of the material aspects of words eats away at their capacity to refer to things.[14] And this is what he subtly indicates in his description. The phrase itself is an imitation in prose of Banville's technique:

la rime ici extraordinaire . . . dans ses poses et la
   i   isi   i   s
multiplicité de son jeu . . . comme si cette fulgurante cause
   i   isi   si s
de délice y triomphait jusqu'à l'initiale syllabe
   is   i   i   s   i isi   si

Like Banville, Mallarmé revels in these exorbitant rhymes and what we can now call their semiotic rhythms, especially in poems with lines of seven or eight syllables where such effects can hardly be missed. These conceits are not just phonetic decorations but expressions of an idea. They have an intellectual as well as a 'musical' value. Even in this respect, Banville can be counted as a predecessor. When Mallarmé enthused about the rhymes of *Le Forgeron*, he was not simply inserting the standard paragraph on the author's style; he was indicating in *Le Forgeron* an important example of his own approach and proving to the playwright that he understood his play.[15]

Le Forgeron was written as an allegory of poetry itself, or of Banville's type of poetry, in which the transcendent quality known as Beauty is dependent, paradoxically, if one wishes, on the tedious, mechanical work of the poet. The story is that Venus rejects all the handsome, self-important gods of Olympus and finally decides to take as her husband the hard-working, grubby god of the title, Vulcan. The reason she prefers Vulcan to all the others is that Vulcan is the god who forges jewels for her and is thus the only god who is able to enhance her beauty – the most precious gift of all, especially for the Goddess of Beauty. The clear implication is that Banville's verses are their own subject. The spectacular rhymes are the jewels forged in the heat of poetic creation, a '*fulgurante* cause de délice', as Mallarmé says, alluding etymologically to Vulcan, God of Thunder. At the time, the auto-allegorical character of *Le Forgeron* was more apparent than it is today: by treating the subject of jewellery, Banville was recycling the images that were commonly applied to his 'materialistic' poetry – *joyaux, pierreries, ciselures, orfèvrerie*, etc. – in order to create a personal and dramatic *art poétique*.

Mallarmé in turn talks of the poet 'forging' the 'precious stones' of verse into a work of art. He, too, likes to point out that the poet's labours, however otiose or abstract they might appear, are the condition of poetic beauty; or, as he says with a typical precision sweeping generalization: 'Que tout poème composé autrement qu'en vue d'obéir au vieux génie du vers, n'en est pas un'.[16] From which we might infer that any explication which fails to take into account the 'genius' of French verse is not an explication at all.

Part II
The Drama of Verse

Programme

The commentaries that form most of the second part of this book are not meant to be exhaustive interpretations but outlines of the various 'acts' that make up the drama of verse. These acts are not strung together in a linear plot. The situation they describe – the nature of verse and the universe – remains the same; but the poet's response to it varies. Different responses may coexist antagonistically within the same poem or lead to divergent conclusions. The poet who speaks in the first person may hold opinions which are not to be found in Mallarmé's critical texts or which are contradicted by the verse in which they are expressed. The poet may be an unauthoritative commentator on a more impersonal drama whose protagonists are letters, phonemes, words and prosodic functions; and this drama in turn, though it may enact a poetic victory, will be seen eventually in metaphysical terms as a failure. Because, in the end, what difference does it make, except to hammer the nail into the empty coffin and 'authentiquer le silence'?

Between these different levels there are structural similarities which make it possible to present the evidence according to a very general, overall scenario. In view of the concentric nature of the drama, it seemed likely, as I said in the introduction, that a strictly chronological order would only muddy the waters and involve a great deal of repetition. By deriving the order of the second part of this book from the poetic drama itself, I do not mean to suggest that this is the only way to read the poetry prosodically, though it does correspond to a pattern that turns up again and again in Mallarmé's work – here described as an archetypal structure commonly found in music, but which, since it comes from the 'répertoire de la nature et du ciel', should really be common property:

> On peut . . . commencer d'un éclat triomphal trop brusque pour durer; invitant que se groupe, en retards, libérés par l'écho, la surprise.

> L'inverse: sont, en un reploiement noir soucieux d'attester l'état d'esprit sur un point, foulés et épaissis des doutes pour que sorte une splendeur définitive simple.[1]

71

These two complementary scenarios can be treated as maps of most of Mallarmé's poems and of the drama as a whole, or at least as sources of useful analogies. Very roughly, the sequence of aspects emphasized in the following chapters corresponds to the first scenario: a quick and facile triumph, then uncertainty, and finally – or penultimately – new hope or the wisdom of despair. The grand finale comes in Chapter 9 with *Prose pour des Esseintes*, followed by some caveats and remarks on how the prosodic approach might be extended to other poems. An epilogue on *Un coup de Dés* takes the drama to its logical conclusion and shows that, all along, it implied its own destruction.

By chance (I think), this is a good order in which to read the poems. It has the incidental merit of placing the more difficult poems towards the end, and the inherent virtue of proving that Mallarmé's poetry is far richer than any systematic reading can demonstrate – except, of course, by its conspicuous failure to account for everything.

A final preliminary remark on method. Some memorable derogatory statements have been made in recent years about the practice of paraphrasing Mallarmé's poems. Most of those who issued such statements have produced unironic paraphrases of their own which tend to support their point. Clearly, Mallarmé's Gordian knots create an irresistible temptation, and, after rereading the later chapters of this book and noting the characteristic tone of conviction creeping in, I wonder if I have managed to resist it. Hopefully, any inappropriately dogmatic assertions will be blamed on the critic, not on his method. To read Mallarmé's poetry in accordance with the system of rules it observes and to which it refers is not to say that one correct interpretation is waiting to be woken like a Sleeping Beauty with the kiss of death. Simply, Mallarmé's poetry is organized according to the same sort of logic that forms the theoretical basis of most literary criticism. Much of its interest lies in the definable, abstract patterns it creates: metre, rhyme, syntax, and so on. One of these patterns consists of 'meanings': themes, motifs, ideas, groups of images, analogies (including abstractions), sequences of imaginary events. The ideological frame of the poem can be described in a cursory fashion just as one can describe its form or syntax. All the great (and little) themes are treated as the means to an end; the subject is sent back to its seat among the other instruments: the 'sujet apparent n'est qu'un prétexte'; in fact, the 'subject' is not the subject at all but a 'motif général'.[2] This explains why Mallarmé was able to sum up in a few 'barbaric' words the subject of some of his poems, on one occasion in English.[3] Effectively, he was making the same point as Oscar Wilde when he disembarked at Dieppe in 1897: 'Mallarmé is a poet, a true poet. But I prefer him when he writes in French, because in that language he is incomprehensible, while in English, unfortunately, he is not.'[4]

Either way, the difference in end-results is probably negligible. Brutal paraphrases depend for their usefulness on the sort of suspicious, antagonistic

reader they tend to produce anyway, while the paraphrase that gives prominence to what is after all the substance of the poem implies a manner of
reading which should relativize any particular interpretation – a pair of 3-D
spectacles rather than a picture-postcard.*

* I have tried to avoid applying words like 'ambiguity', 'equivocality' and even 'indeterminacy' to
Mallarmé's poetry *en bloc*. Not to channel his cascading images through a hermeneutical hose-pipe,
but because they can be highly misleading terms. They tend, for instance, to summon up a whole
aesthetics of multiplicity which may conceal or fail to account for particular features. Even if one
thinks only of the initial act of interpreting a Mallarmé poem, at least four types of ambiguity come
to mind. (The following pedantic distinctions are meant to serve as a reminder that readings
advertising themselves as multiplicitous are often univocal in most respects.)
1. **Provisional Ambiguity.** In 'A la nue accablante tu . . .', *tu* in line 1 may be taken at first to be
either a pronoun or the past participle of *taire*. However, when we realize that no verb corresponds to
the putative 'you'; when, moreover, we notice that the *tu* in line 5 is the pronoun and remember that
the prosodic rules prevent a simple repetition from counting as a rhyme; then, interpreting it
henceforth as 'silenced', we are unlikely ever to return to our original reading. (Which is not to say
that some aura of direct, intimate address might not still attach itself nostalgically to the opening line,
or that, in keeping with Mallarmé's idea, forgetting might not reactivate old potentialities.)
2. **Persistent Ambiguity.** This is the type of ambiguity which survives – but in a weakened form –
the organization of hierarchies wrought by successive readings. When we stumble for the first time
over the seemingly disconnected units of 'A la nue accablante tu . . .', we may clutch at the
recognizable adjectival phrase, 'A même' (flush with). Once 'A la nue' has been attached to the
participle 'tu', however, the reading 'tu à même les échos esclaves' (i.e. 'tu même aux échos esclaves')
will probably dominate. Nevertheless, the original reading, unlike the provisional 'tu', is still grammatically and semantically possible (and even desirable: see p. 203).
3. **Intrinsic Ambiguity.** The ambiguity of words like 'gisement' in 'Au seul souci . . .' or 'nues' in
'L'aile s'évanouit . . .' is so clearly embedded in the syntactic and semantic structure of the poems that
even the most clod-hopping paraphraser should acknowledge its existence. Not that this always
happens.
4. **Mysterious Ambiguity.** 'Basalte' may be construed as a contradictory composite of 'low' and 'high'
(H.J. Frey, in *Yale French Studies*, 1988, p. 254). 'Vertige' may be a verse assimilated to a stalk, etc. Are
we dealing here with the 'mysteries' of spelling, authorial intention, pure chance or private fantasy?
Open questions like these are among the hallmarks of Mallarmé's poetry. Closing them down rarely
leads to anything of interest.
5. **Universal Ambiguity.** There is perhaps a fifth type of ambiguity applicable to preliminary readings
of Mallarmé's poems: the ambiguity that results from a decision not to accept any prosodic, syntactic,
semantic or graphic barge-pole. This type of ambiguity, often advertised as one that treats the text as
text, may be attached quite firmly to an extraneous theory or even state of mind and allows the critic
to simulate free-style while running along the floor of the swimming pool. For practical and aesthetic
purposes, it is a poor substitute for 'la compréhension multiple' (however one interprets that expression).

6

Le mystère d'un nom

'Verlaine? Il est caché parmi l'herbe, Verlaine'

Names – rather than people – are, as we saw, the progenitors of the *Vers de circonstance*.[1] For Mallarmé, names are exceptional words which can nevertheless be rounded up into verse when treated with 'the magic of rhyme'. The verses are therefore constructed like cartouches designed to include the name, so that these seemingly arbitrary vocables are reproduced as necessary components of the poem. Foreign names present an even more satisfying challenge: they contain an extra trace of language's imperfection, reminding us that there are several languages, botched versions of the primal language. Finally, names offer a particularly vivid illustration of poetry's reality-eroding, idealizing effect, since they can designate a real person; and because of the illusion of 'meaning', some of that person's reality seems to be invested in their name. Even as adults, when someone plays with our name, we have a feeling of being insulted or trifled with. As adolescents, we obsessively write the name of the desired object to simulate or hasten possession. If we are an infant and someone gets our name wrong, we may even react violently in the defence of our public identity – and so we should. We will die but our signifiers have an indeterminate lifespan of their own, which means that when Mallarmé says that everything exists in order to end in a book, 'everything' should be taken to include human beings.[2]

The importance Mallarmé attached to these onomastic games can be gauged by the fact that he included some of them in the edition of his *Poésies*, assembled in the early 1890s and published after his death in 1899. They provide us with a relatively simple example of the drama with which to begin: the names themselves create a clear focus for the other elements in the poem.

Billet à Whistler

One such poem is the *Billet à Whistler*, which had already been published in two other places before it appeared in *Poésies*. *Billet* (its last intended title) is an octosyllabic sonnet written by Mallarmé at the request of his friend Whistler for a 'decadent', aestheticist London journal calling itself *The Whirl-wind*. Mallarmé took as his central image the heading of *The Whirlwind*, which depicted a dancer swathed in a whirlwind of muslin: an interesting example of a *transposition d'art* in which the mediocrity and simplicity of the parent form an almost ludicrous contrast with the brilliant complexity of its offspring. An example, too, of a poem that would surely be more difficult to interpret without extraneous data (i.e. the picture itself), though the absence of such data may well enrich our reading of it. (Mallarmé himself chose to reveal its origin in a note.)

The Whirlwind published Mallarmé's sonnet on November 15, 1890. The same issue contained an engraving by Whistler and an editorial written or dictated by Whistler in which Mallarmé was hailed as 'the most *vingtième siècle* poet in France' and as 'the *raffiné* Prince of "Decadents"'. Proof of the poet's decadence could be found in his sonnet's incomprehensibility – untainted by the official 'explication' which the editors appear to have wanted and from which Whistler happily 'saved' his friend.[3]

Billet

Pas les rafales à propos
De rien comme occuper la rue
Sujette au noir vol de chapeaux;
Mais une danseuse apparue

Tourbillon de mousseline ou
Fureur éparses en écumes
Que soulève par son genou
Celle même dont nous vécûmes

Pour tout, hormis lui, rebattu
Spirituelle, ivre, immobile
Foudroyer avec le tutu,
Sans se faire autrement de bile

Sinon rieur que puisse l'air
De sa jupe éventer Whistler.

Though the main reason for considering this sonnet is the showy rhyme at the end on Whistler's name, we shall have to prove our lack of aestheticist virtue by offering a thematic explication, mindful of the fact that the superficial meaning or meanings are so trivial (e.g. *The Whirlwind* is an exceptionally good newspaper) that blunders in this domain will be relatively inconsequential.

The gist of the first quatrain might be crudely defined thus. The artistic

Whirlwind is not the sort of newspaper to deal in the vulgar 'rafales' that (pre)occupy the man on the Clapham omnibus,[4] or rather, which produce the entertaining spectacle of a 'noir vol de chapeaux': a splendid image, as Whistler remarks – hats flying away in the wind like a cloud of starlings. (A recent issue of the paper, which Mallarmé had seen, carried a lithograph by Whistler entitled 'The Winged Hat'.)[5] The initial insinuation corresponds to Mallarmé's most revealing remark about the sonnet. He told Whistler that *Billet* combined his two suggestions, which were: a) to write 'un beau sonnet'; and b) to send 'deux mots de sympathie ou d'approbation – car vous devez bien approuver – en tout – un journal qui n'est pas de journalistes!' As Whistler knew, this was one of Mallarmé's pet topics: the moral and linguistic inferiority of newspapers which, he says with more direct sarcasm, 'dispense[nt], certes, l'avantage de n'interrompre le choeur de préoccupations'.[6]

   The Whirlwind, we hear, is not a mere gust of wind – a violent, unexpected, short-lived blast of air – but a 'tourbillon' (naturally): a more organized and aesthetically satisfying phenomenon.[7] Specifically, a whirlwind of 'mousseline ou / Fureur' which has incarnated itself as a dancer. The juxtaposition of concrete and abstract nouns is an example of one of Mallarmé's favourite rhetorical devices: the hendiadys (two nouns instead of a noun and a qualifier) – a furious whirlwind of muslin. The qualifying expression, 'éparses en écumes' shows the 'tourbillon' (by analogy with other poems) to be the poetic subject of the sonnet: frothy, impalpable reality, scattered into the various elements that verse will bring together. As in the heading of the newspaper (and as in a real ballet), the dancer raises this 'tourbillon' by raising her knee. 'Celle même dont nous vécûmes', applied to the dancer, perhaps refers to Art, which provides Mallarmé and Whistler with a living – spiritual if not financial. With the strong undercurrent of sexual motifs in the sonnet, the dancer could also be taken to represent Woman or a muse: in this case, Terpsichore, muse of dance and choral song. But the reading proposed by Chisholm is perhaps the most pleasing and modest: 'a superbly concise evocation of the ecstasy felt by the spectators ("nous") who had eyes for nothing else; this filmy, delicate spectacle was their very life.'[8] More generally, the dancer is presented as something essential, in both senses of the word – a symbol, as defined a few months later by another great aesthete: 'the mere shapes and patterns of things becoming, as it were, refined, and gaining a kind of symbolical value, as though they were themselves patterns of some other and more perfect form whose shadow they made real: how strange it all was! [Lord Henry] remembered something like it in history. Was it not Plato, that artist in thought, who had first analysed it?'[9]

   By the third quatrain, the whirlwind appears to have whirled itself into a tangle. The syntactical thread can be disentangled thus, on condition that we eventually leave it in a tangle: the whirlwind is raised 'Pour tout . . . Foudroyer'. (The 'pour' may indicate either intention or consequence.) The adjective or past participle 'rebattu', teasingly and confusingly placed before one feminine adjective and two of indeterminate gender, can be attached to 'tout' ('tout [ce qui est] rebattu'). *The Whirlwind* annihilates what is 'rebattu' – hackneyed or banal; in fact, to take 'rebattu' literally, it even contributes to the trivializing effect, flogging, as it were, a beaten horse. Alternatively – and simultaneously – it can refer to the raised tutu, especially if we mistake it for 'rabattu', by association with the hats.

Something apparently escapes this destruction; but the exception, 'hormis lui', is not immediately identifiable, partly because of the characteristic confusion of genders. Assuming that the antecedent of the masculine pronoun, unlike that of 'nous', actually appears in the poem, it could conceivably refer to 'tourbillon', 'tutu', 'genou', the 'vol de chapeaux' or (as Mauron and Favre[10] would have it) to Whistler. But for reasons that will become clear, we might tentatively attach it, with Chisholm, to the 'tourbillon' itself or to the tutu ('Tourbillon qu'elle soulève pour tout foudroyer, hormis lui-même'; or 'pour tout foudroyer avec le tutu, hormis lui – le tutu'). Everything is annihilated except the 'tourbillon' or the 'tutu' (masculine) raised by the *danseuse* (feminine).

The other adjectives – 'Spirituelle, ivre, immobile' – describe the dancer. The first may be both 'spiritual', alluding to her fairy-like, incorporeal appearance, and 'witty', as a compliment to the newspaper. 'Ivre' in Mallarmé's poetry usually signals an attempt at a creative act or, by a sort of pathetic fallacy, the unusual behaviour of reality when the observer is in a state of poetic excitement. 'Immobile', again, evokes the calm of the ballerina in the eye of her own storm, as does the phrase, 'Sans se faire autrement de bile'. The figure's immobility is attributed to a personal quality: she only gets worked up about almost nothing.* And that 'almost nothing' is the distich at the end:

> Sinon rieur que puisse l'air
> De sa jupe éventer Whistler.

This is the point (or *pointe*) of the sonnet. Evidence, too, of Mallarmé's almost imperceptible dandyism: his exquisitely polite, excessively appreciative homage to Whistler and *The Whirlwind* is actually a poem written in praise of itself, an appropriation by verse of all the *écumes* of its apparent subject. The 'air' (both the wind and, by musical analogy, the verse – 'l'air ou

---

* At the risk of turning this into a self-referential commentary, the last phrase could be cited as an example of something that often occurs when one tries to explicate a Mallarmé poem: unintentionally, as it happens, it describes the essential theme of the sonnet. The figurative language Mallarmé's poems persuade us to use occasionally acts as a key. What seems at first a rhetorical flourish suggested by the poem may reveal connections we have been invited to make. Consequently, old explications consisting primarily of rhetorical flourishes can be recycled with a view to extracting their accidental insights.

chant sous le texte') produces a 'laugh' because it gives rise to a punning
rhyme which, if not exactly hilarious, is at least technically amusing.
'Éventer' in this context can mean to waft or to fan ('agiter l'air autour de');
but it can also mean to reveal, as in 'éventer un secret'. 'Whistler' is the
biological entity whose lithographs appear in the pages that, literally, lie
under the dancer's tutu and who himself might therefore be said to have
issued from her skirt; but 'Whistler' is also the word itself, which the poet has
dismembered and reconstructed as a rich and unusual rhyme.

Without this technical perspective, the end of the sonnet is meaningless,
or, it must be said, superficially and profoundly *rebattu*. 'Le tutu d'une
danseuse, voilà – pensera-t-on – un sujet bien rebattu. Oui, pour tout autre
que Whistler', says Chassé, attaching 'rebattu' to 'tutu' and noting, as if to
make matters worse before they can get better, 'mais la construction de la
phrase est bien chaotique'.[11] Or, to follow Chisholm: the dancer is only
worked up about the thought that 'the *tutu* can reach Whistler across the
Channel'.

Just when Mallarmé seems to be at his most ornamental and flighty, he is
also at his most didactic. The topiarist's shears have cut the hedge into a
meaningful hieroglyphic. The actual, not merely decorative or descriptive,
significance of the rhyme is that poetry does not deal in material presences.
All traces of reality must be annihilated and even (as Chassé needlessly
worries) trivialized, for some (representation of an) ideal to be summoned up.
The motifs wound together in the poetic *tourbillon* – journalism, the hatless
masses, *The Whirlwind*, ballet, poetry, meteorology – have effectively disappeared in a blur or become unimportant. The focus is placed on the process
itself, with just a marker or a *témoin* (the rhyme) that the virtual victory has
been achieved on one level. This is what Mallarmé sees in a real ballerina in
Les Fonds dans le ballet:[12] the material of the tutu is a 'dégagement multiple'
which seems to 'dissolve' the 'central' figure that produced it. To the eye,
distracted by all the elements that surround it (one of which is defined as
'écume'), the central figure 'dies'; but as it does, it 'sums up' ('résume') or
'condenses' all the surrounding details.

In *Billet*, this is the ambiguous force of the crucial verb 'foudroyer'. 'Foudre'
is applied, as we saw, to rhyming verse – the bolt of lightning that appears to
'propagate' the sky around it, just as the rhyme on Whistler's name seems,
retrospectively, to have generated or to have been the aim of the poem. The
verb 'tourbillonner' is also applied to the action of rhyme in *Planches et
Feuillets*.[13] The ballerina annihilates like a whirlwind but also dynamically
brings together what she seems to scatter. Hence the rather camp or Wildean
paradox: the humorous association of 'foudroyer' and 'tutu' – not normally
thought of as a weapon of destruction. Or, as Whistler says of the rhyme:
'est-ce assez superbe et dandy en même temps!!' The only tangible product of
the whirlwind's fury is a Mallarmean pirouette: the virtuoso rhyme, produced
by a poem that is itself a *billet* – literally, a little ball.

Mallarmé's philosophy allowed him to pass himself off as an exemplary Decadent. For all its furious, drunken energy, *The Whirlwind*, unmoving or unmoved like the perfect dandy, refuses to funnel its energy into degrading satire and invective: 'bile' is traditionally applied to the indignation of the *genus irritabile vatum*. Mallarmé's scorn has a far wider sweep than that of the satirical poet or aestheticist in the street. Not only the real world but also the matter of the poem itself is abolished (or made difficult to reconstitute) and ends in a rhyme that is, of course, only a rhyme. We should not strain to find it more amusing than it is, but accord it the philosophical honours of its prosodic role.

This airy-fairy, circumstantial sonnet thus has the great interest of displaying quite vividly two characteristics of rhyme as it relates to the whole poem.

1. Mallarmé associates certain images with rhyme (for example, 'foudre' or 'tourbillon'). Many of these images are aural or oral – not surprising in a poet who wanted poetry to reconquer what it had lost to music. Smiles and laughs are often used to represent rhyme, and there is extra evidence of this association in Mallarmé's letter to Whistler announcing the arrival of the sonnet: 'Un petit sonnet de congratulation, avec votre nom à la rime, Ah! Ah! Ah!' To which Whistler's informed reply was: 'Oh! le sonnet! Si vous saviez comme je me fais d'avance une joie de le lire! Ah! Ah! Ah!'[14] Other images belonging to the same family will be introduced later on in this chapter: the two lips of a mouth or the two mouths that come together in a kiss (perhaps suggested by the term *rimes embrassées*). The value of these images seems to have been missed in the interpretation of Mallarmé's poems. They frequently create paradoxes, apparent nonsenses or synaesthetic images that demand some sort of explanation other than mere labelling or use of the word 'synaesthesia'. Any attempt at explanation in such cases is likely to prove rewarding since these images invariably reveal some common ground shared by the poem's 'apparent subject' and the construction of the verse.

2. *Billet* also provides a memorable reminder of the fact that rich, unusual rhymes like *puisse l'air-Whistler* tend to monopolize our attention to the detriment of the rest of the poem. Or, as Banville says with his usual bounding hyperbole: '*on n'entend dans un vers que le mot qui est à la rime*'.[15] Just as the furnishings of the *sonnet en yx* disappear to leave the final 'septuor', so the remainder of these little octosyllabic sonnets disappears, so to speak, behind the dazzling pinnacle of the poem. The predominance of rhyme corresponds to the 'instinct' that according to Mallarmé, 'dégage, du monde, un chant, pour en illuminer le rythme fondamental et rejette, vain, le résidu'.[16] In humdrum terms: when we read, we attach more importance to some elements than to others, even in Mallarmé's poetry, where each word seems potentially to be as important as any other. In fact, far from merely representing it, rhyme activates the instinct that the poems seem to want to short-circuit. Rhymes encourage us to read these poems as we intuitively interpret reality. Of

course, an 'instinctive' grasp would fail to work with most of Mallarmé's poems – at least it seems to fail with the sort of reader who feels the urge to write about them . . . But if we concentrate first on the 'meanings' or functions that prosody lends to the words, the amorphous, sponge-like text acquires asperities and ridges which give the probing mind some purchase. The visible, prior organization of the poem – the basically orthodox rhymes and rhythms that digest the raw material (including Whistler) – is the organism to which we should appeal for enlightenment, if only to walk away with what turns out to be a more profitable confusion.

Méry Laurent

As admitted at the end of Chapter 5, Mallarmé does not always give end-rhymes the lion's share of the poetic process, though they are usually the implicit goal or origin of the other forms of repetition.

His friend, Méry Laurent, provides a convenient way of describing some more complex variations based on a name which are then incorporated into the drama of verse. The poems addressed to Méry or which she can be said to have inspired are crystallized around recurring motifs which form a sort of distinctive paraph, like the signature of a close friend.

The reason for treating the 'Méry Laurent' poems as a continuation of the name game will become apparent in a moment: their principal motif is derived from Méry's name. And since the game is meaningless if no one knows how to play it, it would be as well to observe that Méry herself was perfectly capable of recognizing both the motif and its meaning. According to a distich inscribed in her album, she had a talent or shortcoming that set her apart from most of Mallarmé's contemporaries:[17]

> Elle a ce mignon travers
> De comprendre un peu mes vers

(If we were to worry even here about ambiguities, we might take this as a double warning: an impression of 'understanding' Mallarmé's verse is not necessarily a good thing, any more than partial understanding is a virtue. And the 'travers' in our case may not be quite so 'mignon'.)

The following poems – 'Toujours plus souriant . . .' ('Victorieusement fui . . .'), *Sonnet pour elle*, 'Méry / Sans trop d'aurore . . .', *Chanson*, *Éventail de Méry Laurent* and 'Surgi de la croupe . . .' – all have something in common: they all refer to a rose. Significantly, roses also appear in several *Vers de circonstance* addressed to Méry. In all the other poems written by Mallarmé from *Le Tombeau d'Edgar Poe* (1876) until his death in 1898, the word 'rose' (the noun, not the adjective) is used only twice: in a triolet of the *Théâtre de Valvins* and in *Huitain*, though the 'mignonne' to whom the poem is addressed may once again be Méry.[18]

The recurrence of the rose might be attributed to chance, were it not for the fact that, in each of these poems, it occupies a similar, vital position – thematic, prosodic or both. Twice, it appears in the last line of the poem: 'Une rose dans les ténèbres'; 'un casque guerrier . . . Dont pour te figurer, il tomberait des roses.' In three of the poems, the rose is associated with the idea of 'interruption'. In 'Surgi de la croupe . . .', the neck of the vase that would have contained the rose 's'interrompt'; in *Éventail*, the roses, 'Toutes la même', 'interrompront' Méry's 'souffle'; and in *Chanson*, Méry herself 'interrupts' the rose. As usual, a pattern emerges before a specific sense, the medium before the message, the effect before the cause, just as, in Corbière's do-it-yourself sonnet (but for a very different reason), the telegraph wires are more important than any hypothetical telegram.

The key to the game is that Méry Laurent's Christian name was Marie-Rose. Mallarmé often teases her about her vanity; apparently he also teased her about her original name – a name, Marie-Rose, that only her intimate friends would have known. The rose is a mystery, in the etymological sense: a secret rite performed by initiates in worship of a deity.

Once identified, this onomastic game makes it possible to interpret more fully even some of the seemingly transparent *Vers de circonstance*. When Mallarmé gave his friend a water-glass for Christmas in 1895, it came with the following quatrain (the technically 'incorrect' double hiatus in the second verse is surely a nice example of imitative disharmony):

> Ta lèvre contre le cristal
> Gorgée à gorgée y compose
> Le souvenir pourpre et vital
> De la moins éphémère rose.[19]

The trace of Méry's lipstick on the glass is compared to a rose. But is it supposed to be a *real* rose? Assuming regular dish-washing, the 'rose' on the glass probably would be more 'ephemeral' than a real flower; yet it does seem strange to call the flower 'moins éphémère' and to emphasize its relative durability, especially since roses are normally emblems of transience.[20] And why would the purple lipstick be the 'souvenir' of a rose? In fact, the fourth verse refers to Marie-Rose/Méry herself: the emblematic rose Mallarmé associates with her is a very special sort of flower which survives the changing seasons. In *Sonnet pour elle*, 'La même rose avec son bel été qui plonge / Dans autrefois et puis dans le futur aussi'; and in *Fêtes et Anniversaires* in the *Vers de circonstance*, Méry is said explicitly to be 'une vivace rose / De jardin royal'.

Marie-Rose/Méry can therefore be identified with the 'less ephemeral rose'; which would explain why the lipstick is a 'souvenir', a mark of the person who drank from the glass. Knowing this, we can see that the quatrain is constructed around a tripartite image of which the second element (the flower) is absent: the lipstick, a rose and Marie-Rose herself.

The rose is just one example of several *mots-motifs* connected with Méry Laurent. 'Bouches' and 'baisers' appear in three of the poems and, indirectly, in the 'lèvre' of the water-glass quatrain. Perhaps this is a predictable allusion to their politely romantic relationship. Less predictable and more intriguing is the recurrence of the past participle, *émané*. It occurs in three poems: in the 1889 version of *Chanson*, in *Sonnet pour elle*, where it refers to the odour of the absent rose, and in *Éventail*, where 'L'arôme émané de Méry' is announced by the rhyme supplied by one of her Christian names – 'émeri' (the stopper of the phial that would have contained the perfume). This, too, can be attached to the onomastic game. With her personal and partial understanding of Mallarmé's verse, Méry might have detected in the recurrent *émané* – which appears in no other poem – an allusion to their mutual friend, the artist who painted her on a background of flowers and introduced her to Mallarmé: É. Manet.

Sonnet pour elle

The Méry Laurent poems allude to or are organized around a game which remains quite private, though the distinction between 'public' and 'private' is probably more a hindrance than a help in reading Mallarmé's poetry. No doubt the usefulness of a biographical fact demonstrates a degree of poetic 'impurity' in the circumstantial and even, to some extent, the 'serious' verse; but that is hardly a reason to ignore it. Besides which, the potential significance of these motifs can be deduced from the poems themselves. Even poems of a personal nature, like the *Billet à Whistler*, show quite candidly the influence that the name game exerts on the poem as a whole. However mysterious, intimate or trivial the original cause, the effects on the phonetic, prosodic and semantic structures of the poem are visible enough to allow the spectator to join in.

To begin with one of Mallarmé's most undeceptively accessible later poems:

SONNET
pour elle

O si chère de loin et proche et blanche, si
Délicieusement toi, Méry, que je songe
A quelque baume rare émané par mensonge
Sur aucun bouquetier de cristal obscurci.

Le sais-tu, oui! pour moi voici des ans, voici
Toujours que ton sourire éblouissant prolonge

> La même rose avec son bel été qui plonge
> Dans autrefois et puis dans le futur aussi.
>
> Mon coeur qui dans les nuits parfois cherche à s'entendre
> Ou de quel dernier mot t'appeler le plus tendre,
> S'exalte en celui rien que chuchoté de Soeur –
>
> N'était, très grand trésor et tête si petite,
> Que tu m'enseignes bien toute une autre douceur
> Tout bas par le baiser seul dans tes cheveux dite.

As in the *gorze-quatorze* sonnet, the woman sabotages – in a very agreeable and rewarding manner – the poet's attempt to establish a satisfactory synthesis within the limits traced by the rules of versification. The 'last word' his heart seeks is replaced by a quite different 'douceur', supplied by the woman.

The two quatrains of this regular sonnet form what Mallarmé (in 1862) said the stanzas of a sonnet should form: 'des chants entiers' on which rhyme confers a noticeable unity.[21] The standard unity of end-rhymes is reinforced in a manner reminiscent of Banville's *Le Forgeron*. In the first verse of each quatrain and in the last verse of the first quatrain, the end-rhyme either echoes the beginning of the verse or 'pre-echoes' the beginning of the next verse:

> O si chère de loin et proche et blanche, si
>   si   si
> Délicieusement toi, Méry, que je songe
>   isi
>
> Sur aucun bouquetier de cristal obscurci.
> sᴙ   is   sᴙsi
>
> Le sais-tu, oui! pour moi voici des ans, voici
>   i   si   si
> Toujours que ton sourire éblouissant prolonge
>   s i   is

These phonetic circles are formed within a longer echo, which joins the beginning of the sonnet to the end of the octave by means of a so-called *rime équivoque* or *fraternisée*: 'O si' (v. 1) – 'aussi' (v. 8). Mallarmé's image of the poetic text as a piece of lace seems particularly appropriate here. Phonetic strands criss-cross the sonnet and, by foregrounding the 'material' components of the poem, tend to evacuate the intervening spaces of direct significance: connections rather than the things they connect.[22] This is the 'theme' or abstract pattern which is announced in the contrasting 'loin' and 'proche' of the first line.

There also appears to be a more personal, fetishistic reinforcement of the unity in the use of *si* as bonding agent. Several other poems suggest that when Mallarmé chose these phonemes to highlight the omnivorous rhymes of *Le Forgeron*, he was acting according to an established preference, one which may be susceptible only to psychoanalytic or semiotic analyses. This syllable and its mirror-image, *is*, are among his favourite motifs:

> S'*i*dyllisait le Cazal*is*

> Mon très vieux coeur ne d*is*simule
> *Ici* l'espoir

> Chaque fleur pense que Madame Al*i*ce
> Cazal*is* va respirer son cal*i*ce.

> Taciturne et vacille en le *si*gne que non[23]

The quatrain inscribed in Debussy's copy of *L'Après-midi d'un faune* forms the same sort of phonetic circle as *Sonnet pour elle* (with even a matching y):

> Sylvain d'haleine première
> *Si* ta flûte a réus*si*
> Ouïs toute la lumière
> Qu'y soufflera Debussy.

Other spectacular instances include: 'La Gloire, comme nulle tempe . . .' ('mi-sel / Ne s'y . . . / De si . . . missel, / Ce l'est'); the hundredth *Loisir de la Poste* (malice, fois-ci, Alice, Poissy); *Prose pour des Esseintes* ('sol des cent iris, son site', etc.); *Hérodiade* ('hérisse / Un révulsif ébat', in which the mirroring of *is* reflects the sense); the *Prélude* of *Les Noces d'Hérodiade*, beginning with an isolated 'Si' which is picked up not only in the remainder of the verse ('Génuflexion comme à l'éblouissant') but also in about half of the twenty-nine verses that follow:

> Alors, d*is* ô futur taciturne, pourquoi
> *Ici* demeure-t-il et s'éterni*se* coi
> Selon peu de rai*son* que le rich*is*sime orbe [etc.]

The effect is also amplified visually if not phonetically (as in the 'Ouïs' of the Debussy quatrain) by 'dis', 's'éternise' and 'raison'. Finally, in the dainty quatrain for Céline, the *si* provides three and almost four rhymes – not at the end of the verse, but at the penultimate syllable (technically, the last syllable in verse 3):

> Un beau nom est l'essen*ti*el
> Comme dans la glace on *s'y* mire
> Céline reflète du *ciel*
> Juste autant qu'il faut pour *sourire*.

It is also remarkable that such a high proportion of Mallarmé's poems begin and end with a word containing *si* or *is*. *Si* is a quality of the instrument as much as a note, and it serves as a reminder that, alongside the prosodic conceits which form the basis of this book, there are also patterns with purely abstract or subjective referents. Cohn cites Mallarmé's contention that *s* is the 'analytical' letter *par excellence* and deduces that *i* is the 'resuming' letter.[24] For Julia Kristeva, who also bases her remarks in part on *Les Mots anglais*, 'La dominance de /s/ indique une tension phallique urétrale'[25] – a view that has some authorial support in the lavatorial *Chanson bas* whose phonetic and semantic motif is supplied by the fourth item in the following sequence: *Ta paille, cil, s'il, tapisse, envahissante, ici, y sente, prémices.* Or perhaps *si* is simply *the* emblematic word of the imagination – affirmation (*si*) in the face of negation (*is*).

To return to *Sonnet pour elle.* The rhymes and echoes which weave such a visible web can and should be compared to the rose which plunges into both past and future – 'Dans autrefois et puis dans le futur aussi'. Just as some of Mallarmé's poems refer to their own topography, others allude to their existence in time – 'real' time (i.e. the past of memory and the future of posterity), but also the past and future of the sonnet in the reading mind. The prosodic sense of verse 8 is clear. Rhyme performs the function Mallarmé assigns to it in *Solennité*: a 'seal' to prevent the 'floating' elements of the poem from wandering off. The rose itself (that is, the three phonemes) also contributes to the synthesis:

> La même rose avec son bel été qui plonge
> **ROZ**
> Dans autrefois et puis dans le futur aussi.
> O R   Z   RO S

Lines like these are reminiscent of the conundrums of the *Vers de circonstance*; and so, having activated (or, as it may seem, over-activated) our cryptic sense by dwelling on the visiting-cards and rhymed addresses, we can tentatively introduce among our multiple readings the fact that the rose is present not just in the 'future' of the verse (ROS) but also in the 'past', anagrammatically in 'autrefois'. Another point, which will seem even further-fetched until we notice a similar feature in 'Surgi de la croupe . . .' (p. 91), is that the z in both verses falls on the fifth syllable: ro*se a*vec / autrefoi*s et*.

Next, in the first tercet, these unifying echoes actually become part of the explicit theme. The poet's 'coeur', at the beginning of the stanza, does indeed 'hear itself' ('s'entend') in the 'dernier mot': 'Soeur'. As in *Prose pour des Esseintes*, 'exaltation' accompanies the production of a rhyme, albeit a subtle rhyme that is only 'whispered'.

Unfortunately or not, the poet's quest for a rhyme does not in the end provide him with the conclusive punning synthesis of *Billet à Whistler*. Once again, the woman interrupts the game to produce a rhyme that the poet would not have found or used himself. This 'douceur' is enunciated 'tout bas', without trumpeting its triumphant consonance. It is expressed 'par le baiser seul': 'by the kiss alone', but also 'by the lone kiss'; not on another mouth but peripherally, in the hair. The poet's peacock-like display of impressive symmetrical rhymes ends almost disappointingly with hardly the most passionate sort of kiss. Yet the 'baiser', though 'seul', does still stand for a harmony established between two realities or in this case between two people. The final rhyme itself – significantly unannounced in the sonnet except by assonance with the *si* – is both simple (technically, *suffisante*) and unexpected, though it is 'enriched' by the phonetic proximity of *t* and *d*, and by the matching penultimate syllables: pe*tite*-che*veux di*te.

The apparent subject and the rhymes of *Sonnet pour elle* correspond in what we should allow ourselves to see as an obvious, even gimmicky fashion. A socio-prosodic reading might make something of the fact that the adjective *petit* is applied to Méry both here and in 'L'aile s'évanouit . . .'. On both occasions, she disrupts or redirects the poetic process. Her 'small head' may simply reflect a physical reality, or then again it may reflect the fact that the 'head' of the verse resulting from her 'instruction' is also rather small – like the 'cher cadeau qui varie' (from *caput*) in one of the *Rondels*, the unfortunately lovable 'petits bonnets' – imperfect rhymes – of 'L'aile s'évanouit . . .', or the 'chef fulgurante' of Poetry in 'La chevelure vol . . .'.[26]

It may be useful to reinforce the points just made by leaving Méry very briefly for Thérèse Roumanille, daughter of the Provençal poet and recipient of *Feuillet d'album*. In 1892, *Feuillet d'album* was presented typographically in *La Wallonie* as a traditional sonnet, with two quatrains and two tercets instead of the three quatrains and distich which Mallarmé claimed to have borrowed from English poetry.

> Tout à coup, et comme par jeu,
> Mademoiselle qui voulûtes
> Ouïr se révéler un peu
> Le bois de mes diverses flûtes,

Je m'aperçus que cet essai
Tenté devant un paysage
Eut du bon quand je le cessai,
Pour vous regarder au visage.

Oui, ce vain souffle que j'exclus
Jusqu'à la dernière limite
Selon mes quelques doigts perclus

Manque de moyens s'il imite
Votre si naturel et clair
Rire d'enfant qui charme l'air.

As we know, a contemporary reader would expect to see or hear the rhymes on *eu* and *ûtes* recur in the second quatrain (see pp. 5–7). The rhymes 'predicted' by the poem's form fail to materialize, as if the effort of pushing out the 'souffle' as far as the 'final limit' of each verse had been too much. Like Houssaye with his libertine muse, Mallarmé offers graphic evidence that his art or his 'flûtes' are incapable of rendering the natural beauty of the young girl. His 'air' or song falls under her spell. Unlike Houssaye, however, he perhaps also concludes that his art should not strive to be mimetic[27] – at least not in the normal sense.[28] True beauty is inimitable and inevitably undoes the game, as he says in 'Rien ici-bas que vous n'ayez . . .': 'Nos vains souhaits émerveillés / De la beauté qui les déjoue.' Or, in *La Musique et les Lettres*:[29] 'Les monuments, la mer, la face humaine, dans leur plénitude, natifs, conservant une vertu autrement attrayante que ne les voilera une description.'*

In one respect, this 'failure' is the condition of success. The distracting woman is the physical, trivial pretext that prevents the poems from wrapping themselves in a net of sonorous repetitions. More arresting and even discordant variations are introduced in the same way that rhymes are broken down into fragmentary but complementary echoes: 'encore peut-être faudra-t-il avoir précédemment posé les rimes fermes.' The chaos of reality can heighten by contrast the order of verse, just as the constrictions of verse bring out the charming incontinence of natural phenomena.

---

* More subtle treatments of the theme can be found elsewhere: in 'De l'orient passé des Temps . . .' (the first version of 'Quelle soie aux baumes de temps . . .' and probably the first poem written after the *Sonnet allégorique de lui-même*), the distractingly physical 'chevelure' (or 'la torse et native nue') reaches 'far beyond the jewels' of poetry (or beyond the mirror-frame of the sonnet). In 'M'introduire dans ton histoire . . .', the antagonism of sexuality and the 'glaciers' of pure poetry ends with a prosodic victory: the 'thunder' and 'rubies' of rhyme on the 'hubs' of the poet's chariot wheels or verses, and the assimilation of a rhymeless word (see p. 150). The same association of rubies, thunder and Poetry is made in 'La chevelure vol . . .' (see p. 231, n. 26 and, in the sonnet, 'astre', 'feux', 'son doigt', 'gloire', 'chef', 'doute' and 'torche'). All three poems deserve prosodic readings.

The designs that Mallarmé traces through the poem with rhyme add to the development of the theme a sort of prosodic commentary which may be more accessible at first than the 'meaning' of the poem. This commentary is not simply superimposed on the theme, contributing an extra, discrete layer to the poetic gâteau. It merges with the theme to such an extent that it becomes indispensable: the apparent subject may not be complete or even decipherable without it. This merging of form and theme is signalled most directly or concretely in the use of key words – the 'rire' of the *Billet à Whistler* or, in *Sonnet pour elle*, the 'sourire' which 'prolongs' the rose. More abstractly, it can be seen in the various permutations of rhyme which act out the poet's attempt to 'capture' – prosodically or romantically – the addressee of the poem.

However, Mallarmé's prosodic tricks are more complex and above all more ideologically interesting than Banville's. The prosodic commentary does not necessarily confirm the explicit message. It may work against the thematic grain of the poem, evoking, for example, a failure to emulate or even simply describe the beauty or disturbing exception. The attempt may consist in incorporating a person's name into the poem or, conversely, in imposing on the person a poetic 'name' or signature, as in *Sonnet pour elle*: 'de quel dernier mot [or end-rhyme] t'appeler'. 'Name' in this sense means, not the conventional label, but the ideal, synthetic word, the hypothetical signifier that is also the signified – 'name' in the sense it has in the paradoxical lines from *Toast funèbre*: 'le frisson final, dans sa voix seule, éveille, / Pour la Rose et le Lys le mystère d'un nom.'

These affectionate poems which seem to celebrate the more pleasant aspects of life also express a desire to transmute contingencies into something essential – something that, necessarily, cannot exist. A metaphysical variation on Baudelaire's 'Hymne à la Beauté': 'L'éphémère ébloui vole vers toi, chandelle, / Crépite, flambe et dit: Bénissons ce flambeau!'

Mallarmé's creative nihilism is only implied in these poems, and we have yet to wander very far from the *divertissements* of the *Vers de circonstance*, though some deeper perspectives have begun to open up. Some actors have flitted across the stage, half-costumed; some of the musical themes have drifted up from the orchestra-pit. It is time to raise the curtain on a more coordinated performance.

'Surgi de la croupe et du bond . . .'

In *Sonnet pour elle* and in *Feuillet d'album*, the non-appearance of the victorious rhyme – or, in 'L'aile s'évanouit . . .', the emergence of an inadmissible rhyme – constitutes a flattering acknowledgment of the woman's charms and a polite recognition of the inadequacies of that 'compteur factice', regular French verse. But the lesson, as we saw, can be construed as an encouraging reminder that verse is independent of the realities it pretends to capture: 'ce vain souffle . . . Manque de moyens s'il imite / Votre si naturel et clair / Rire d'enfant' – etymologically a *silent* laugh.

In 'Surgi de la croupe . . .', the absence of the rhyme (and, this time, of the rose as well) has more sombre connotations.

> Surgi de la croupe et du bond
> D'une verrerie éphémère
> Sans fleurir la veillée amère
> Le col ignoré s'interrompt.
>
> Je crois bien que deux bouches n'ont
> Bu, ni son amant ni ma mère,
> Jamais à la même Chimère,
> Moi, sylphe de ce froid plafond!
>
> Le pur vase d'aucun breuvage
> Que l'inexhaustible veuvage
> Agonise mais ne consent,
>
> Naïf baiser des plus funèbres!
> A rien expirer annonçant
> Une rose dans les ténèbres.

After such a vigorous attack, with its amazing combination of still-life and sexual energy, we might expect to see rising out of the 'verrerie éphémère' the 'less ephemeral' rose of Méry Laurent. But the neck of the vase is 'interrupted' or ends without even a stalk emerging. The virtual painting lacks its principal ornament and the upward surge is frustrated. True, the rose is mentioned at the end, but in a negative construction. The negation can be (and has been) interpreted as a contradictory proclamation of the poet's ability to conjure an imaginary something out of nothing: 'je dis: une fleur! et, hors de l'oubli où ma voix relègue aucun contour, en tant que quelque chose d'autre que les calices sus, musicalement se lève, idée même et suave, l'absente de tous bouquets'.[30] But the rose is named directly and can hardly be described as 'musical' or as a pure 'idea'. It exists only on a thematic level. Anyone can name a rose, but not everyone can evoke the 'absente de tous bouquets' and endow it with 'le mystère d'un nom'. The real achievement, in other words, would be to conjure up an imaginary nothing out of something.

Even thematically, the source of disappointment is not the absence of a rose, but the fact that nothing 'announcing' a rose is 'expired' (literally, breathed out). As a result, the final image, however delectable, is an example of what happens when a poet simply iterates: '*nommer* un objet, c'est supprimer les trois quarts de la jouissance du poème qui est faite de deviner peu à peu: le *suggérer*, voilà le rêve.'[31] Perhaps, then, it would be more appropriate to read it as an ironic reminder that the 'rose' is no less absent for being named. Pretending that poems contain things is an aesthetic 'error'.[32] The rose, absent or present, is largely unimportant; the process that produces it is not.

Superficially, the development of the sonnet can be compared to the first scenario from *Le Mystère dans les lettres*: 'commencer d'un éclat triomphal trop brusque pour durer; invitant que se groupe, en retards, libérés par l'écho, la surprise.' The 'delays' correspond to the verses leading up to the final image of a rose in darkness: like the parenthetical clauses of Mallarmé's prose, they postpone the end of the poem or the 'surprise'. They are 'liberated by the echo' just as rhyme liberates them from prosodic isolation. Except that, in 'Surgi de la croupe . . .', only incompletion and incapacity result. The vase (or, from the second quatrain, the philtre) is empty and unused. The 'agony', which sometimes signifies the moment at which all realities vanish to leave something pure, is wasted. And the poet himself remains attached to the 'plafond', unconnected to the empty poem on the page below – an illegitimate being; in fact, even less legitimate than a bastard because his mother and her lover ('ni son amant ni ma mère') never drank the same love-potion. A bastard uncreated.

To return to the prosodic facts: the poet is designated by the noun, *sylphe*, which, notes Gardner Davies, often refers to something uncreated;[33] likewise, Cohn interprets it as 'an event that does *not* occur'.[34] The most important clue is that *sylphe* is one of the hundred or so words that have no rhyme.* The sylph remains attached to the ceiling, and can therefore be contrasted with the rhyming, ambiguous 'nues' of 'L'aile s'évanouit . . .' which relate the 'plafond' to the rest of the room.

The second useful piece of prosodic information is that the rose, too, is isolated. It rhymes with nothing in the poem – which is what the poem itself tells us quite directly: nothing 'announces' it. In the *Chanson* discussed below, the 'baiser' announces or symbolizes a rhyme. Here, the kiss is described as 'naïf' (that is, natural, not *arti*ficial) and 'funèbre'. All it produces is that most banal of rhymes: *funèbres-ténèbres*, a rhyme which signally lacks the surprising, playful quality of *petite-dite*, *émeri-Méry* or even *gorze-quatorze*.

The only faint murmur of hope surviving the initial over-optimistic surge and thrust is a discreet little theme that struggles to make itself heard and to bring forth the rose in another 'éclat triomphal':

---

* Albert Glatigny applied the image of a 'sylphe ailé fait d'une haleine' to the half-formed verse that has yet to find a rhyme: the 'vers . . . informe, vagissant, / Qui demande sa rime et qui n'a pas encore / Su trouver son chemin dans le rythme sonore' ('A Ernest d'Hervilly', in *Les Flèches d'or* [1864]; *Poésies* [Lemerre, 1870], 99). As a professional improviser, Glatigny must have been particularly sensitive to rhymeless words – first, one imagines, as an embarrassing nuisance; then, from a more Mallarmean point of view, as a source of interest.

4th syllable
Le pur vase | d'aucun breuvage
z
Que l'inexhau | stible veuvage
z
Agonise | mais ne consent,
z
Naïf baiser | des plus funèbres!
z
A rien expi | rer annonçant
s
Une rose | dans les ténèbres.
z

The z of *rose* establishes itself from the beginning of the tercets at the position it will occupy in the final line (at the fourth syllable). But it hovers inside the verse as if inside the empty vase, not at the crucial rhyming position but buried in the body of the poem.

The object contemplated by the poet does not 'consent' to furnish the triumphant rhyme. As Mallarmé puts it in one of his prose poems (which also lend themselves to prosodic readings): 'reality' does not 'consent' to bring together in a single, privileged point 'tout ce rapprochement fortuit' that constitutes it. The 'rire strident ordinaire des choses' offers only a 'cacophonie à l'ouïe' and the poet 'reste à vif devant la hantise de l'existence'.[35]

The dynamic still life painted by the sonnet is an allegorical representation of the poetic machine. In *Crayonné au théâtre*, Mallarmé talks of 'rimes dardées sur de brèves tiges'[36] – an image that might be applied, thematically and technically, to *Prose pour des Esseintes*, with its flowery rhymes bursting out on their little eight-syllable stalks. Here, even the stalk is missing. Regressing almost to a point at which the poem cannot exist, the neck of the flower-vase itself is interrupted. With its linear, forward movement contradicted by the theme and prosodic conceits, the text can be compared to a telescope that sees back almost to the moment before creation. The stems of verse disappear and only a peculiar 'verrerie' is visible. 'Verrerie' is normally interpreted as 'vase'; Cohn's 'an ephemeral glassware' more accurately conveys its strangeness. None of the three meanings given by Littré corresponds to Mallarmé's use of the noun: 1. 'Usine où l'on fait le verre'; 2. 'Art de faire le verre'; 3. 'Collectivement. Toute sorte d'ouvrages de verre'. Mallarmé's 'verrerie' is a factory in which *vers* are produced, the mould of the sonnet or the poet's mind. (For other puns on *vers*, in *Salut, Autre éventail, Averses ou Critique* and *Prose*, see pp. 147, 155 and 190.)[37] But the factory is on strike. Accordingly, the masculine rhymes are among the poorest ever used by Mallarmé in the quatrains of a regular sonnet: b*ond*, s'interr*ompt*, n'*ont*, f*ond*.

Quite exceptionally, they have just one phoneme in common and fail even
to form a satisfying visual rhyme. The two mouths forming the kiss of rhyme
– so it seems to the sylph-poet – have never met. If they did, it would still, of
course, be the product of a 'Chimère', but the artificial unity would at least
have been established.

    'Surgi de la croupe . . .' is a delightfully and confusingly ironic little poem;
a successful evocation of failure, in which the art of absence is practised in the
'objects' of verse itself. Verse becomes an actor, capable of producing its own
interpretations and even of ignoring the fictional poet's intentions. There is
an especially pleasing example of this in a contrary phonetic image of the
theme, comparable to the often-cited *mort(e)* in the sonnet which celebrates
victorious flight from suicide ('sang par écu*me, or, t*empête', replacing the
earlier 'meurtrier'):[38]

> Je crois bien que deux bouches n'ont
> Bu, ni son amant ni ma mère
> y ni sɔ̃

– the 'unison' that should, but does not actualize itself in rhymes, 'Toutes
dans un frisson / A l'unisson'.

Chanson sur un vers composé par Méry

From cloud to silver lining . . . The *Chanson* (or *rondel*) *sur un vers composé
par Méry*, for all its formal and semantic differences, can be read as a counter-
part of 'Surgi de la croupe . . .'. Many of the same figures return in the same
roles and costumes: the sylph, the kiss, the rose and the interruption which
leads only to silence or absence. But the *Chanson* starts at a different point on
the dramatic continuum; it begins, roughly speaking, where the sonnet ends.
This is the second version (1896):

> Si tu veux nous nous aimerons
> Avec tes lèvres sans le dire
> Cette rose ne l'interromps
> Qu'à verser un silence pire
>
> Jamais de chants ne lancent prompts
> Le scintillement du sourire
> Si tu veux nous nous aimerons
> Avec tes lèvres sans le dire
>
> Muet muet entre les ronds
> Sylphe dans la pourpre d'empire
> Un baiser flambant se déchire

> Jusqu'aux pointes des ailerons
> Si tu veux nous nous aimerons

The *Chanson sur un vers composé par Méry* follows the second of the two scenarios in *Le Mystère dans les lettres*. As Mallarmé says, this is the opposite of the other: 'sont, en un reploiement noir soucieux d'attester l'état d'esprit sur un point, foulés et épaissis des doutes pour que sorte une splendeur définitive simple'.

The 'doubts' are built up or 'foulés' – 'trampled' like grapes by the metrical feet – in the following fashion. First, as the title indicates, the poem is extrapolated from a poetic problem posed by Méry: an isolated octosyllabic line – 'Si tu veux nous nous aimerons' – which is a fairly conventional opening for a song. She may for example have been remembering Glatigny's 'Partie de campagne':

> Pendant que le soleil luira sur nos deux fronts,
> Demain, si tu le veux, nous nous embrasserons.[39]

Or the song that came to Mallarmé's lips when he was thinking of another woman, Marie, in 1862:

> Je serai grand, et toi riche,
> Puisque nous nous aimerons.[40]

Her lover, always trying to make ends meet, takes the line both as a literal and as a poetic proposition: an invitation followed by no action; a verse with no matching rhyme. The line, 'Si tu veux nous nous aimerons', is a kiss – literally and figuratively – offered and then immediately withdrawn. Like Méry's song which stops short after its first verse, the 'rose' (a rosy kiss or poetic flower) is 'interrupted' as in 'Surgi de la croupe . . .' and gives rise only to a 'silence pire'; worse, perhaps, than the silence of a kiss, or the silence that Mallarmé considers an essential aspect of verse (see p. 117).

The similarity with 'Surgi de la croupe . . .' extends to the rhymes: a clear indication that thematic and prosodic elements circulate in the same complicated orbits. As in 'Surgi de la croupe . . .', Mallarmé represents the interruption at the end of the orphan verse with those visually disparate rhymes (though reinforced now by the preceding consonant, *r*): aime*rons*, inter*romps*, *prompts*, *ronds*. For, as the second quatrain tells us in a sort of commentary on the first, songs ('chants') never spring up promptly or spontaneously to produce a sparkling smile or rhyme. In the first version of the poem, the smile is silent – 'ton tacite sourire' – like the 'rire d'enfant' of *Feuillet d'album* (see p. 89). So far, the isolated line has not found its partner, and the problem is merely repeated, as Mallarmé's variation on the *rondel* form demands, in verses 7 and 8.

In the third stanza, the *Chanson* reaches that critical point that one can usually identify in Mallarmé's poems, even without the advantage of a plausible interpretation – just as ignorance of the plot does not necessarily prevent us from following the dramatic turns of an opera. This is the 'agonie' or the 'reploiement noir' which announces either victory or – as in 'Surgi de la croupe . . .' where the vase itself enters into agony – defeat, expressed in the repetition of 'muet'.

In these little poems of just over a hundred syllables, in which every word has what sometimes seems a value disproportionate to its surface meaning, any repetition is certainly significant. 'Muet muet' is a rhyme turned in on itself: a 'reploiement noir' or folding together of the poem's wings. A rhyme 'à soi pareille', which remains, as the poem says, 'entre les ronds', the 'magic rings' of rhyme which can be either fairy-rings or smoke-rings – 'plusieurs ronds de fumée / Abolis en autres ronds', like the rhymes themselves:

fumée
ronds
résumée
expirons

Not surprisingly, the entity described as silent is the sylph. As concrete evidence that the poet has yet to overcome the isolation of Méry's verse, line 10 contains two rhymeless, echoless words: 'sylphe' and 'pourpre'. How can the synthesis now be forged from such isolated elements to produce the 'scintillement du sourire'?

Just when all seems lost, the kiss solicited by the poet suddenly comes into existence in the antepenultimate verse; or rather, it is consummated and performed in the penultimate and final verses. In the Mallarmean *rondel*, the penultimate verse is the most important: it rhymes with the first verse, which returns at the end of the poem. It also contains the 'surprise', being the 'extra' verse which elongates the third stanza and pulls it apart like a Christmas cracker. The solitary verse composed by Méry finally finds its partner in the splendiferous rhyme, *ailerons-aimerons* – a gratifying contrast to the noticeably 'poor' masculine rhymes.

The kiss 'tears apart' as the lips separate in forming it: an almost simultaneous conjunction and separation, just as rhymes combine elements of identity and difference. In this particular case, the rhyme is split, so to speak, to the extremities of the rhyming words – 'Jusqu'aux pointes des ailerons': s *ai*(l)*erons* – s *ai*(m)*erons*. The objective characteristics of the rhyme are mirrored in the image of a wing. Just when it seemed to be disappearing into silence or incompletion, the poem attains that momentary balance of the hovering bird, the 'équilibre momentané et double à la façon du vol'.[41] The first, problematic verse returns, but this time at the end of the poem, no longer isolated or gratuitous but called for by the rhyme supplied by the poet.

It completes the circle and becomes an excuse for a kiss, or, as the 'baiser flambant' would suggest to anyone sensitized to Mallarmé's eroticism, a more intimate copulation. The 'déchirement' allows the insertion of the extra line.[42]

This is one of the most satisfying products of unrequited love imaginable. And perhaps the most satisfying reading of it is one that acknowledges the extent to which Mallarmé 'gives the initiative back' to verse. Reading the poem as a self-referential allegory helps the subject matter to erase itself into the abstract, where it recovers its proper triviality, and a new urgency. Even without a prosodic reading or awareness of the mysterious functions of verse, this self-involvement of the poem may be what makes these spare and tenuous images so resonant and memorable. Any work of art that refers to itself becomes more interesting. Whether knowledge of this technique lessens the impact of the images or not is ultimately a matter of taste and curiosity. Either way, it seems, ironically, to liberate them from the suspicion – by confirming it – that poems are only made of words.

The Méry Laurent poems can, of course, be appreciated for whatever merits one decides to find in them. The present appreciations contribute illustrations of certain precepts, demonstrate the inextricability of verse and theme, and show that Mallarmé's meditations on verse are not confined to his prose works. They also indicate the conscious completeness of his poems and the rewards of reflecting on the actual, practical task originally undertaken by the poet. *Chanson* in particular seems to benefit from a prosodic reading.

The full potential of the drama of verse has yet to be felt, however – partly because these poems retain some of the personal allusiveness of the *Vers de circonstance*. This chapter ends, therefore, with two poems in which the name game becomes a metaphysical drama and, at the same time, a concrete demonstration of what French verse actually does. The claim will now be made, at least provisionally, that only a prosodic reading is capable of producing a wholly satisfactory interpretation.

Hommage [*à Puvis de Chavannes*]

This curiously arrogant and unpretentious sonnet appeared in 1895 in a special issue of *La Plume* devoted to the painter, Puvis de Chavannes:

> Toute Aurore même gourde
> A crisper un poing obscur
> Contre des clairons d'azur
> Embouchés par cette sourde

The first quatrain is a grammarian's feast of adjectival constructions. First, 'gourde', applied to 'Aurore', makes the effect an attribute of the cause: the numbing is transferred, by a sort of hypallage, from the unnamed early bird to the cold dawn itself. Similarly and conversely, the chilliness (or the word that might have designated it) is transferred from the dawn to the owner of the 'poing obscur': the verb 'crisper' recalls the adjective 'crispé', as in Verlaine's 'vent crispé du matin'. These are illustrations of Mallarmé's precept: depictions of things by means of their effects. Finally, 'sourde' in line 4 is a substantival adjective referring back to 'Aurore'.

The dawn inspires whoever experiences its numbing effect with what appears to be impotent rage – surely a more comfortable reading than those which attach the fist to the dawn and conclude that its fist is numb 'à force de crisper': the dawn clutches the bugles of day. But 'contre' has then to mean 'on' or 'around', and 'cette sourde' is an awkward, superfluous repetition: 'Every Dawn, even numb from gripping the bugles blown by this [Dawn].'[43] 'Poing obscur' can be taken instead a) as a synecdoche, the obscurity being that of the puny human who shakes a futile fist at the dawn or the natural world at large; or b) as another hypallage, the hand that tries to blot out the cacophonous light or rubs a sleepy eye. We know this deeply troubled person from Mallarmé's early poems: the poet who longs for a 'trépas obscur' but who suffers under the azure sky which seems hostile or simply 'deaf' to the misfortunes of the human race. The bugles which rouse the poet and announce the dawn – discordant because the bugler is deaf – are a distant echo of the bells in L'Azur (1864 version):

> En vain! l'Azur triomphe, et je l'entends qui chante
> Dans les cloches. Orage, il se fait voix pour plus
> Cruellement goûter sa victoire méchante,
> Et du métal vivant sort en bleus angelus!

Three decades later, Mallarmé's theme is not the subjective miseries of human existence but the objective felicities of verse. From here on, things improve. Despite the fact that the feminine rhymes are identical ('gourde', 'sourde') and the masculine rhymes merely suffisantes, the drama takes a promising turn:

> [Toute Aurore . . .]
> A le pâtre avec la gourde
> Jointe au bâton frappant dur
> Le long de son pas futur
> Tant que la source ample sourde

Even with such an inauspicious dawn appears a shepherd equipped with a gourd and a stick. Already, prosody intervenes in the argument in an unmistakable fashion. As in the Vers de circonstance, rhyming puns announce a poetic victory. The identical feminine rhymes acquire entirely different connotations: negative in the first quatrain, positive in the second.

'Sourde' at first implied cacophony. Now, at the end of the quatrain, the noun becomes a verb implying fertility and, no doubt, the welling up of poetic inspiration: 'Tant qu'*ici* la source sourde', according to an earlier, more specific version. The addition of 'ample' suggests the 'fullness' of harmony flooding into the preestablished form of the sonnet (see p. 172 and n. 49).

'Gourde' at first signified a lack of sensitivity. Now, the adjective becomes a noun which designates a source of sustenance and is connected semantically, phonetically and prosodically with 'source' and 'sourde' in line 8. Despite what Gardner Davies claims,[44] Mallarmé does use the word 'gourde' in the sense of 'courge' in another text – admittedly in his translation of Whistler's lecture, *Le 'Ten O'Clock' de M. Whistler*.[45] There, the gourd represents both a vessel and a primitive form of art, the ancestor of the first vase. The adjective has been taken from the dawn and given to the shepherd. Brute reality has become an aesthetic breakfast.

The gourd might also represent music. 'Joined' to the 'bâton frappant dur', it sounds like a percussion instrument. The series of alliterations extends the technically *suffisantes* masculine rhymes into the verse: 'bâ*ton f*ra*pp*ant *dur*', 'de *son pas futur*'. The irritation and crispation of the sleepy poet for whom dawn is a jangling alarm-clock has given way to a vigorous, optimistic activity.

The tercets, as the conjunction 'ainsi' suggests, supply an example or relate the consequence of what is stated in the quatrains:

> Par avance ainsi tu vis
> O solitaire Puvis
> De Chavannes
> > jamais seul

> De conduire le temps boire
> A la nymphe sans linceul
> Que lui découvre ta gloire

The adjectives applied to Puvis de Chavannes bring together in an oxymoron the positive and negative connotations of the quatrains: 'O *solitaire* Puvis / De Chavannes / *jamais seul*'. The painter is identified with the shepherd and 'time' with his flock: his glorious *oeuvre* reveals to future generations the fertile well-springs of Art.[46] The well is symbolized, as it might have been in one of Puvis's mural paintings, by a nymph (a water-spirit) without a shroud – thus, immortal.

Setting aside the drama of verse, we should have to conclude, as some have, that this is a rather trite and simple homage: posterity will be able to send down its buckets into Puvis's fertile art. Redeeming features might be found in Mallarmé's exploitation of the *transposition d'art*, in which the poet claims to imitate certain characteristics of the painter's work: the use of allegorical figures (unclad nymphs are common in Puvis's paintings); the simplicity and sharpness of the lines which became increasingly noticeable in his work; intellectuality dominating the pictorial aspects of the painting;[47] and so on, until we run out of plausible analogies.

Why, then, should Mallarmé cloak such banality in so much obscurity? Does the art of suggestion really succeed in revitalizing the cliché? And, more importantly, why would anyone want to reread the sonnet having once savoured its rhythms and decoded its 'message'?

Because difficulties remain, notably the articulation of the quatrains and tercets. The very banality of the *Hommage* herds us towards more fertile pastures. Mallarmé tells us virtually nothing about Puvis de Chavannes; perhaps a few allusions to some of his typical motifs. But if the painter's name had not been used as a rhyme, the sonnet could easily have served for several other artists. After all, Mallarmé did not choose the subject himself; he simply accepted the proposal of the Puvis de Chavannes committee.[48] If he wanted to commemorate an artist in *Poésies*, Puvis would surely have stood far back in the queue behind Manet, Degas or Berthe Morisot.

The answer, with more than just a risk of repeating ourselves, is that the principal, initiating subject of the poem is verse. The shepherd ('le pâtre') represents not only the artist but also rhyme. Rhyme, which 'se révèle avec la fonction de gardienne et d'empêcher qu'entre tous, un [vers] usurpe, ou ne demeure péremptoirement'.[49] By assigning the role of *gardienne* or *pâtre* not to the poet but to a prosodic element, Mallarmé gives the old idea of the poet as Good Shepherd or *pasteur* a nice empirical twist. The *pâtre* in Mallarmé's sonnet is less sectarian or tendentious than he is in the employ of other poets, perhaps retaining from his Romantic past the association with music: the shepherd's pipes are one of the standard components of the Romantic landscape,[50] though the gourd and walking-stick are typical Mallarmean touches – down-to-earth and evocative, concrete and pregnant with abstract speculation.

In developing the image of the walking shepherd, Mallarmé also makes a memorable contribution to the repertoire of images that liken poems to roads and rhymes to lanterns or milestones. The first word of the rhyme, preceding the poet on the path of the idea, is the walking-stick, placed 'alongside his future step'. The foot which then falls beside the stick (with a metrical connotation) represents the second word; and the process continues, as long as the well does not dry up.

Hommage may be even more optimistic than that. The adverbial expression 'tant que' has been taken so far to mean 'as long as';[51] but are we necessarily asked to believe that the whole enterprise is dependent on a constant flow of inspiration? This reading would have to count as a 'provisional ambiguity' or, in simple terms, a mistake, since *tant que* in this sense normally takes the indicative. *Tant que* with the subjunctive means *jusqu'à ce que*, at least it did until the seventeenth century: 'Versez, versez toujours, tant qu'on vous dise assez.'[52] Taken in the sense of *jusqu'à ce que* or *si bien que*, it would mean that by beating out the regulated rhythms of verse, the poet, like Moses, actually makes the spring well up: 'vous frapperez la pierre, et il en sortira de l'eau, afin que le peuple ait à boire' (Exodus 17: 6). The paradox or inversion is too Mallarmean not to be taken seriously: inspiration is not the precondition but the product of the poem.

The drama of verse reveals the sonnet in its basic integrity and it can be seen now to form a single logical unit. The process described in the quatrains explains how it is that Puvis de Chavannes 'lives in advance' in the verse (specifically, in the rhyme of line 9). French has no other word ending in *uvis*; but by using a *rime complexe*, Mallarmé incorporates this mongrel word into the flock. Puvis's name – far more than Puvis himself, worthy though he is – provided Mallarmé with a challenge which, in spite of the occasion, he points out to us quite ostentatiously. He was hardly the most self-effacing giver of presents. As all Baudelaire readers know from 'Sed non satiata', it would have been easy to find some equally rich rhymes for *Chavannes*. Banville, for instance, says rather limply that to find the like of Puvis de Chavannes's murals, one would have to go much further than Vannes.[53] But that would have been too easy; it would have 'proved' nothing. So, with the insouciance of a virtuoso, Mallarmé dismisses the undemanding rich rhyme to the beginning of the next verse, leaving just a ghost of the 'obvious' rich rhyme *caravane* at the beginning of the tercet: 'Par avance'.

By following in the poet's footsteps, we can see immediately why the exceptional, provocative word, *Puvis*, is said to be 'solitaire'; and also why, after the production of the rich rhyme, *tu vis-Puvis*, he tells us reassuringly, with an apparent contradiction, that Puvis is 'jamais seul'. This can of course mean that Puvis is a trailblazer now but that, later, he will have plenty of followers; or that Puvis may stand alone but, as the homages testify, he is not lonely. The more interesting point, and the verifiable event that has actually occurred on the page, is that one more 'peremptory' sheep has been persuaded into the fold.

The opening (or 'dawn') of the poem evinces the doubts created by language which seems arbitrary and as if deaf to the needs it supposedly supplies. The bugles of daylight against which the fist is raised recall the 'Hilare or de cymbale à des poings irrité' of *Le Pitre châtié* or the 'rire strident ordinaire des choses et . . . leur cuivrerie triomphale' of *La Déclaration foraine*: this is reality in its untreated, cacophonous state, subjectively hostile until constructively annihilated by Art. To the deafness of things, the poet opposes the rhythm and tempo of poetry: the gourd, the step and the stick. However primitive these devices may be (in fact, because they are primitive and primal), they are effective. As an example and proof of the mystical power of verse, Mallarmé offers the cunning rhyme on Puvis's name. Verse in this way repudiates 'le Hasard' by exploiting the 'hasards' of language.

Two things, finally, can be said in defence of this little sonnet. First, it should be counted among Mallarmé's more direct and deliberate *arts poétiques*. The image of the walking-stick is comparable to the smoke-rings of 'Toute l'âme résumée . . .', which is often cited as Mallarmé's *art poétique* as if there were only one. In view of the generally unnoticed ironies of the latter poem, *Hommage* might even be considered a more 'official' (though less complex) statement of Mallarmé's poetic procedures.

Second, once the poem is grasped as a whole and the pretext put firmly in its historical place, it can be enjoyed for its aesthetic and philosophical properties. Gardner Davies says of the sonnet that its development and poetic content 'semblent relever davantage des *Vers de circonstance* que des autres *Hommages et Tombeaux*'.[54] Yet – even ignoring the fact that the sonnet is, as it turns out, ideologically significant – it has a certain beauty which it owes to its circumstantial origin. Its relative simplicity, which seems at first to be that of a commissioned compliment, inspired by little more than courtesy, accentuates the victory of rhyme and the poet's own precise pleasure. The numbing triviality of life, and the obstreperous nature of language which confines most of us to a linguistic wheelchair, are the adversaries that mobilize verse.

'Au seul souci de voyager . . .'

The *Hommage* to Puvis de Chavannes makes a good travelling companion for the octosyllabic sonnet on Vasco da Gama, 'Au seul souci de voyager . . .', and the two poems do actually appear together in this order in *Poésies*. They share the subject of posterity and a cheerful enactment of the drama of verse. Partly for this reason, the Vasco sonnet provides a fitting conclusion for this chapter: it forms another *art poétique* in which the rhyme on a name signals another happy ending to the drama. It also seemed sensible to leave it until the end because some of the things said about it would be implausible without the evidence presented in the preceding pages.

'Au seul souci de voyager . . .' is Mallarmé's last sonnet. It was written, appropriately enough, not under the impulse of an emotional emergency, but because an *Album commémoratif* was being prepared under the patronage of the Queen of Portugal to celebrate the fourth centenary of Vasco da Gama's discovery of a route to India (1498).

> Au seul souci de voyager
> Outre une Inde splendide et trouble
> – Ce salut soit le messager
> Du temps, cap que ta poupe double*

*   Mallarmé's reputation for cacophony deserves a little study of its own. Such a study would include comments on his frequent use of the proscribed hiatus, which, being covered by the rules that

Comme sur quelque vergue bas
Plongeante avec la caravelle
Écumait toujours en ébats
Un oiseau d'annonce nouvelle

Qui criait monotonement
Sans que la barre ne varie
Un inutile gisement
Nuit, désespoir et pierrerie

Par son chant reflété jusqu'au
Sourire du pâle Vasco

Mallarmé's 'salut' brings the anniversary message that Vasco da Gama has rounded the Cape of Time. Not only did the great adventurer sail to India via the Cape of Good Hope (formerly, in French, the *Cap des Tempêtes* and, here, perhaps punningly, the *Cap du Temps*), but he also reached the happy shores of Posterity, far beyond his original destination: '*outre* une Inde splendide et trouble'. The epithets might evoke the remoteness ('trouble' in the sense of cloudy, indistinct) and legendary wealth of India; perhaps also, since Mallarmé's *Hommages* often dwell on negative aspects of the subject's life, the political problems Vasco da Gama experienced and caused in his role as Viceroy.

Mallarmé observes, offers some objective measurement of cacophony.
    Chisholm calls this 'unfortunate line' a 'serious lapse': 'Mallarmé had an extraordinarily sensitive ear for the music of words', so why did he let slip such an 'unpoetic' 'cock-a-doodle-doo' and a verse whose every word begins with a plosive consonant? Tentative answer: because 'the sonnet was written to order' (*Mallarmé's 'Grand Oeuvre'* [Manchester University Press, 1962], 31–2). This kind of dismal comment still crops up from time to time, though usually in less dogmatic forms: the 'round consonants (*p, b*) and vowels (*o*) [also the Cape-shaped *u*'s?] may have something to do with the "rounding" idea. The cacophony of the line is harder to explain' (Cohn, *Toward the Poems of Mallarmé*, 193).
    A scientific answer to Chisholm's point might be this: *Poésies* contains 11,870 syllables. The composition of *Poésies* took about thirty-six years, which means that, on average, Mallarmé spent over one day on each syllable. The 'serious lapse' might therefore have occupied his attention for a whole week, which surely gave him enough time to spot and eradicate the 'fault' (especially since, with his knowledge of English, the offending syllables should have reminded him of the interjection 'Oops!').
    A second answer, to both points, is that Mallarmé's poetry – with obvious exceptions – was written to be read silently, and five plosive consonants sound quite different in the inner ear. (On Mallarmé's special concept of 'musicality', see p. 111)
    A third answer, peculiar to this line, is provided by the drama of verse. 'Poupe double' is an assonantal *rime couronnée*, a type of rhyme in which the last word of a line rhymes with the penultimate word. (Most *traités de versification* give examples of *rimes couronnées*.) The rounding of the Cape was Vasco's crowning achievement; 'couronne' and 'cap' are also semantically connected; and, to cap it all, the juxtaposition of identical vowels and similar consonants refers to the idea of 'doubler' . . .
    In short, Mallarmé's 'cacophony' can either be treated as proof of incompetence or carelessness, or as a clue that might lead to evidence of the contrary – unless, like Chisholm, we consider our ear more sensitive than Mallarmé's.

According to this reading, Mallarmé simply resurrected the conventional image of posterity suggested to him by Vasco da Gama's claim to fame – the image used by Baudelaire in the thirty-ninth *Fleur du Mal*:

> Je te donne ces vers afin que si mon nom
> Aborde heureusement aux époques lointaines,
> Et fait rêver un soir les cervelles humaines,
> Vaisseau favorisé par un grand aquilon,

The remainder of the sonnet appears to refer to the dangers of a long sea voyage. A bird cries as if to announce the approaching continent; the navigator steers a straight course through real or metaphorical darkness. He despairs; but his smile, somehow connected with the bird's cheering cry, presumably reminds us that he eventually reached the harbour of Calicut.

Once again, Mallarmé sails very close to the shallows of banality and gratuitous obfuscation. Indeed, it was not known until 1947 why he decided to assign Vasco da Gama a place in his pantheon of heroes. Austin Gill suggested as a remedy to Mallarmé's idiosyncrasy that the real subject of the poem was Chateaubriand – surely a more appropriate choice of hero.[55] When it was known that the sonnet had been composed for the *Album commémoratif*, Léon Cellier published an article in which he gloated over the fruitless ingenuity of his unwitting colleagues before marching with a side-long smile into the same bog of Vasco-centred complexity (though he does emerge on the other side holding a more balanced reading).[56] The present author could confess to having followed in Cellier's wake and waded through Camoens's epic poem in search of a significant 'oiseau d'annonce nouvelle' – in vain. The fact that the sonnet was commissioned from Mallarmé is a sharp, time-saving reminder that Vasco and his voyage belong to the froth and spume of the apparent subject: Magellan or Columbus would have done just as well; except, of course (and this is the lesson), they wouldn't. But not for any historical, biographical reason; only for what become, *post facto*, reasons of prosodic convenience. Vasco has to be there for the rhyme, and the poem itself establishes, in what we shall see as a surprising and pleasing fashion, the mock-inevitability of the name.

Mallarmé does in any case warn his 'scoliastes futurs' of the sonnet's allegorical function. The initial toast bestows the definite article on a general 'souci de voyager' and the indefinite article on the particular example, '*une* Inde': to the spirit of adventure, 'above and beyond' the present subject. The idea that Vasco da Gama is used as a mere instance is given further support by the conjunction 'Comme'. The insistence is on the poetic *salut* (greeting and salvation): '[Que] ce salut soit le messager du temps . . . comme . . . un oiseau d'annonce nouvelle'. The skimpy evocation of Vasco's voyage is a detailed image of the poetic 'message'; and the message, as our Mallarmean experience might lead us to expect, is embodied in a bird.

But what exactly is this bird about? Why does it perch, not on the crow's-nest or on top of a mast, but 'sur quelque vergue bas' – on one of the lower yards – where it 'plunges' into the waves with the tossing ship? Not the best position from which to sight land. In our perplexity, we can seize upon the biblical echo in the 'annonce nouvelle': the dove of the Ark which, unlike its predecessor the raven, returns to announce the end of the Flood. In this connection, Léon Cellier quotes Victor Hugo's 'Les Mages' in which Vasco da Gama, like Noah, is cheered up by a bird:[57]

> Un jour une barque perdue
> Vit à la fois dans l'étendue
> Un oiseau dans l'air spacieux,
> Un rameau dans l'eau solitaire;
> Alors, Gama cria: La terre!
> Et Camoëns cria: Les cieux!

We might even go so far as to note that Mallarmé could have learnt from his Littré that *colombe* came from a Greek word meaning *plongeur* . . .*

Whatever literary and linguistic echoes surround it, the bird is presented as a figure of the poet or the poem itself. Its 'ébats' connect it in Mallarmé's universe with the frivolous 'game' of poetry; 'écumait', referring to its fluttering feathers or the spindrift of the ocean, alludes to the surface realities that the poem will whisk together; its cries and its 'chant' are poetic expressions; 'monotonement' is applied elsewhere to the repetitions required by prosody and especially by rhyme; 'gisement' is a reminder of the hidden, scattered elements that the poem is supposed to 'forge' 'selon quelque richesse';[58] 'pierrerie' describes the words set in verse which 's'allument de reflets réciproques';[59] the tiller ('barre') suggests the control exerted by the master poet, as it does in *Un coup de Dés*; finally, the 'sourire' which announces the happy, rhyming conclusion of the poem. Even the 'little' words are important: 'avec', suggesting a coupling, and 'bas', which Mallarmé seems to associate with the writing down of the poem (see p. 173).

Before asking these words to help us retrace the drama of verse as performed in the poem, we should first take account of another organizing principle which, incidentally, provides us with the 'answer' before it can be

---

* Mallarmé's allusions to etymological connotations, particularly those given in Littré, were first pointed out in detail by Charles Chassé, whose valuable baby should not be allowed to drown in its over-ebullient bath-water – for example, 'linceul' has no macabre connotation because it originally just meant a piece of cloth (*Les Clés de Mallarmé*, 121).

recognized. Mallarmé often rhymes the beginning and end of a verse, and the beginning and end of a stanza, as in *Sonnet pour elle*. In 'Au seul souci . . .', the first syllable *Au* is also the last syllable: it recurs at the very end in the name Vasco and, of course, in its rhyming-partner, jusqu'*au*. The phoneme *o* is heard only four times in the poem: *Au*, jusqu'*au-*Vasco, and, in line 8 (just over half-way through), *ois*eau.

By forming a phonetic circle, 'Au seul souci . . .' succeeds where *Sonnet pour elle* and 'Surgi de la croupe . . .' both deliberately fail: the beginning of the poem announces the end; or rather, it is the *oiseau* (the word, not the bird) which relays or 'reflects' (literally, 'bends' into *verse*: from *vertere*, to turn) the monotone cry to *Vasco*. This cry is rhyme itself – 'une réciprocité de feux distante':[60]

> Susceptibilité en raison que le cri possède un écho – des motifs de même jeu s'équilibreront, balancés, à distance.[61]

The bird balances between the two yard-arms (the tapering ends of the 'vergue') on which the poem is stretched like a sail. Its crucial 'chant' is echoed by both extremities of the sonnet.

This 'distant' coordination of phonetic motifs is not quite as *recherché* as it seems – not for a poet who sometimes starts out with nothing but the alpha and omega of a poem, even a longish poem like *Toast funèbre*: 'Commençant par: O toi qui . . . et finissant par un vers masculin, je veux chanter, en rimes plates probablement, une des qualités glorieuses de Gautier'.[62] There are also intertextual precedents for such devices: in this case, a form that might be cited for its family resemblance is the *rondeau*, in which the first word recurs at the end of the second stanza and then again at the end of the poem. Mallarmé himself wrote a *Rondeau* for his mother in 1859, with 'L'art ose' at the beginning, 'la rose!' in the middle, and 'l'arrose!' at the end. A more conspicuous example is the sonnet 'Le bachot privé d'avirons . . .', where the phonetic wire is stretched over a shorter distance, but with the same object of connecting up a name with another part of the poem:

> Ce brusque mouvement pareil
> A secouer de quelque épaule
> ep ol
> La charge obscure du sommeil
> a   ar
> Que tout seul essaierait un saule
>
> Est Paul Nadar debout et vert
> e   p ol a ar
> Jetant l'épervier grand ouvert

To sum up: 'A*u*', by the song of the '*oiseau*', is reflected 'jusqu'*au* sourire du pâle Vasco'. The rhyme, like the bird (and like Banville's rhymes in *Le Forgeron*), 'triumphs right back to the initial syllable'. Like the '*baiser*', Vasco's '*sourire*' signals the happy rhyme devised for the isolated word – here, a foreign name which finds its home in French verse. In the same way, the '*sourire*' of *Sonnet pour elle* attaches the present to the past and future of the poem: 'ton sourire éblouissant prolonge / La même rose avec son bel été qui plonge / Dans autrefois et puis dans le futur aussi.' This would account for what has been deemed the enigmatic or inappropriate smile of Vasco: being lost at sea is no smiling matter.

The 'despair' of the third quatrain is also that of the poet, condemned to suffer a sea of troubles, the monotony and apparent futility of verse, which, as the poet frequently worries, may prove ineffective. The 'gisement' seems at first to mean the bearing of the ship, unvarying and 'useless' because no land appears. But then the word 'pierrerie' invites us to reinterpret 'gisement', without discarding our first interpretation, as a mineral deposit and to give it the geological and prosodic sense it has in *Solennité*:

> quelque suprême moule [un vers] n'ayant pas lieu en tant que d'aucun objet qui existe: mais il emprunte, pour y aviver un sceau tous gisements épars, ignorés et flottants selon quelque richesse, et les forger.[63]

'Pierrerie' comes as the final, last-minute saving grace, the secular *salut*. Those with a taste for or experience of Banvillesque rich rhymes may well detect a *rime-fantôme* and 'expect' to have heard the rhyme *varie-avarie*: i.e. damage, especially to a ship. (Cf., in *Autour d'un mirliton*, 'Comme un yacht princier Marie / Magnier va sans avarie'.) Apart from the fact that this entirely guessable rhyme has four identical phonemes, it also seems to be the next logical item in the sequence:

Darkness (*nuit*) → Despair (*désespoir*) → Shipwreck (*avarie*)

and not

Darkness (*nuit*) → Despair (*désespoir*) → Precious stone (*pierrerie*)

These mysterious stones – light sparkling on the waves, Vasco's dreams of Asiatic wealth, a reef or a guiding star[64] – are 'forged' and fused *in extremis* by rhyme, which, once again, pops up just when the poem was entering its agony and when Vasco was heading straight into the night and the void. The rhyme itself is set apart from the other rhymes both typographically and by its punning, 'complex' character. It even recalls the rhyme invented by Verlaine in his *Art poétique* to show how tinny 'ce bijou d'un sou' can sound: *cou-jusqu'où*.

The direction or *sens* of both poem and ship remain 'inutile': we are not asked to imagine Vasco da Gama cruising happily into Calicut harbour to the greater glory of the Portuguese nation. This is Vasco, sited without hindsight in the middle of his voyage, uncertain of his final destination. A sign in search of its referent, finding instead its place in a coherent, self-contained system. Or, in less mercantile terms: the 'obstiné chercheur d'un mystère qu'il sait ne pas exister',[65] smiling with desperate lucidity at his pseudo-victory. In the midst of darkness and the unnamed ocean, the hero impelled by that inhuman consistency that made Mallarmé such a miserable teacher and such an endlessly readable poet, the monotonous cry of the bird establishes a line of communication or sends a message – something shining and precious which can be seen and enjoyed as the sonnet itself. (Since it is only a poem.)

7

Le doute du Jeu suprême

'*Vers brûlants et sages proses*'[1]

It would seem so far that, for Mallarmé, every thing and person can potentially be assimilated by verse, transmuted into phonemes and slotted into the musical mould. The poems discussed in Chapter 6 might even lead us to assume that the drama consists in the relative success or absolute failure of this assimilation. Here, Mallarmé describes and exemplifies the triumph of rhyme; there, he shows how verse is humiliated and taught a lesson by natural beauty or a household object. To state this bluntly would be to fall into the trap of 'meaning'. 'L'enfantillage de la littérature a été de croire, par exemple, que de choisir un certain nombre de pierres précieuses et en mettre les noms sur le papier, même très bien, c'était *faire* des pierres précieuses' – in which case books would never close properly.[2] Similarly, the 'childishness' of the present approach is to take the theme as the last word on the poem's subject, to detail the fictional activities of personified rhyme and consider the connotations exhausted – which is what we shall have to pretend to do before the conclusion, invited in any case by Mallarmé's poetry to reach a practical compromise.

Yet we have also seen that Mallarmé's auto-allegorical poems are not just celebrations of poetic language or grumblings about its inadequacy. The apparent dysfunctioning of rhyme, as in 'Surgi de la croupe . . .', serves, not as direct evidence of failure (since these poems are technically correct) but, indirectly, as a warning of epistemological Thin Ice. On the one hand, those poems in which verse 'fails' to reestablish a hypothetical synthesis are comparable to some of Baudelaire's poems in which what Mallarmé might have called 'de savantes dissonances' enact the deficiency of poetic language and even language in general before exiting through the stage-door still in costume and make-up, still convinced that the fiction is a purer form of the reality it pretends to represent. On the other hand, this occasional imperfection is not only a topic of the poem; it also infects the text itself – inevitably (we can now say 'of course'), but in a manner that is strangely memorable, precise and analytical. The free play of the postmodern signifier is acted out inside a controlled environment, where reading, that 'pratique désespérée',[3] seems simultaneously possible and impossible, necessary and futile. No doubt Mallarmé sensitizes us to multiple interpretations, but by forcing on us the difficult task of coordinating the various levels of meaning and the elements that make up each level, he also activates our capacity for forgetting and in fact makes it an indispensable life-belt.* Every interpretation is an impoverishment (though it may convey an impression of what was lost), which is why so many commentaries end with a 'So now we can see . . .', meaning, in effect, 'Now that we can no longer see the rest of the poem . . .'. Along with a pleasant sense of authorial control and integrity, there should also be a feeling of urgency, impending catastrophe and forgetfulness – as indeed there often is in books written about his poetry.

For practical reasons, we shall return for the first part of this chapter to the frozen surface of the text and allow Mallarmé's comments on verse to give us the false sense of security without which no commentary would ever end.

The poet, unlike the author of the critical texts, constantly harbours doubts about the power of verse. Without these doubts, there would be no drama; or only a Banvillesque drama, endlessly rehearsing its happy endings. Mallarmé appears in most of his later poems as his own sceptical reader: the reader in the back row who wonders if *le vers* really does correspond to a primordial 'instinct' or whether it acts simply as a linguistic fig-leaf thrown over something incomprehensible, inhuman and scandalous.

In its simplest thematic terms, Mallarmé's poetry asks us to consider a dilemma often formulated by mediocre poets with a true sense of their worth, or by poets like Baudelaire: isn't versified poetry in some respects the opposite of what it pretends to express? Can something exceptional or ideal be conveyed by such a conventional vehicle? Specifically, in Mallarmé's poetry: are names simply pretexts – emblems of a 'materialistic' cult of verse, or can they also be made to act as proofs of a linguistic and metaphysical victory? However complex, ambiguous or partial the answer, the problem itself is formulated in a crisp, empirical fashion. Mallarmé's 'obscurity' coexists with a blindingly practical view of his art. His starting point is common sense – facts or phenomena which are thought or insincerely assumed to be generally acknowledged. Even in the least literal of his critical texts, the arguments are based on commonplaces. His prose is descriptive before it becomes polemical. Exaggeration, concision and even obfuscation are used as rhetorical devices,

---

* Mallarmé himself was quite capable of forgetting, not just the horrors of teaching, but also his own poetry, even if recently written: 'les premiers mots du Sonnet sont "toujours plus *abîmée*" (mais je ne suis pas sûr d'*abîmée*)' (letter to Édouard Dujardin, December 20, 1886; *Corr*, III, 76). Writing to Henri-Albert Haug, he refers to 'A la vie [sic] accablante . . .' and, appropriately, his 'vaine mémoire' (*Corr*, VII, 163).

but never the sort of impressionistic fantasy that confines the figurative text to a private universe.

Just as his poems create an illusion of necessity, Mallarmé's philosophy of language is based on a heroic, unbelieving act of faith and is inseparable from the doubts it creates. Worries about the efficacy of verse are the inevitable antithesis of the triumph proclaimed by the sonnets on Puvis de Chavannes and Vasco da Gama. The drama of verse can be envisaged as a curve which rises and falls. Each poem begins at a certain point on the curve and travels along it for a certain length. Poems like 'Surgi de la croupe . . .' come to an end before the curve begins to rise again. The presumed nature of language and verse never changes, but the poet's 'local' perception of it does, and this perception determines the 'behaviour' of verse in each poem.

Each poem develops its paradoxes and contradictions within a coherent dialectic. This dialectic is like an atheistic, linguistic equivalent of the Christian drama: Good and Evil do battle in human time, but in eternity Good is victorious. Verse itself, says Mallarmé, is a dialectic[4] – a 'discussion' – and since the subject here is rhyme, we might assume that alternating rhymes represent thesis and antithesis:*

> Nous promenions notre visage
> (Nous fûmes deux, je le maintiens)
> Sur maints charmes de paysage,
> O soeur, y comparant les tiens.

Though it does exist on an ideal level, the synthesis can only be implied by the dialectic: 'Oh! sache . . ./Que de lis multiples la tige / Grandissait trop pour nos raisons . . ./Et non . . ./Que ce pays n'exista pas.' The enormous rhymes bear witness to an ideal synthesis, inaccessible to rational thought (see p. 163).

This chapter is a tour around the periphery of the drama and an exploration of its limits. It deals primarily with three poems in which the doubts seem to gain the upper hand and where the dialectic fails to produce or even presuppose a synthesis. The first, the *Hommage* to Wagner, represents the lowest point on the curve, where no momentum is available. In order to proceed, the poet is forced to project a line towards another art. In *Petit Air II* and in 'Une dentelle s'abolit . . .', the drama is more strictly contained within the poem itself, but more diffusely than in the poems of the previous chapter.

---

* Is this why, with the exception of a few *triolets* and *rondels*, rhymes in Mallarmé's later poetry always come in twos or fours – a peculiarity emphasized by his use of the discrete, final distich in his shorter sonnets? With those exceptions, the last poem in which rhymes come in threes is the first version of the *sonnet en yx*, back in 1868.

Hommage à Wagner

This regular sonnet is generally agreed to be one of Mallarmé's most accessible in its general theme, one of the most difficult in its details. The following
remarks refer mainly to the quatrains, which express quite directly the pessimistic view of verse which other poems merely imply and which Mallarmé's
critical texts contradict.

> Le silence déjà funèbre d'une moire
> Dispose plus qu'un pli seul sur le mobilier
> Que doit un tassement du principal pilier
> Précipiter avec le manque de mémoire.
>
> Notre si vieil ébat triomphal du grimoire,
> Hiéroglyphes dont s'exalte le millier
> A propager de l'aile un frisson familier!
> Enfouissez-le-moi plutôt dans une armoire.
>
> Du souriant fracas originel haï
> Entre elles de clartés maîtresses a jailli
> Jusque vers un parvis né pour leur simulacre,
>
> Trompettes tout haut d'or pâmé sur les vélins,
> Le dieu Richard Wagner irradiant un sacre
> Mal tu par l'encre même en sanglots sibyllins.

As Cohn observes, 'Mallarmé uses the title *Hommage* for a dead fellow artist
who is not a poet, but a kissin' cousin, as it were; *Tombeau* was reserved for
Poe, Baudelaire, Verlaine.'[5] *Hommage* – originally, the act of respect and
allegiance made by a vassal to his lord – is also slightly ironic. The 'kissin'
cousin' may be little more than a pretext or the object of flattering remarks
with unflattering innuendos.

At the first attempt, *Hommage à Wagner* (its original title) can be read –
and usually is – as a poetic version of *Richard Wagner, rêverie d'un poëte
français*. Both essay and sonnet appeared in *La Revue wagnérienne* on August
8, 1885 and January 8, 1886 respectively. The central idea of the essay is
formulated in a convoluted exclamation which stands in a paragraph of its
own:

> Singulier défi qu'aux poètes dont il usurpe le devoir avec la plus candide et
> splendide bravoure, inflige Richard Wagner![6]

Wagner's 'challenge' was accepted by Mallarmé: poetry, as he famously said,
must 'reprendre son bien à la musique' – that is to say, its *musicality*, meaning,

not its 'sonorités élémentaires', its nice, recitable sounds, but its primordial, semiotic rhythms,[7] 'la musicalité de tout',[8] 'la Musique Intellectuelle',[9] 'les reprises et les jeux d'un chant intérieur méconnu jusqu'ici'.[10] Something like Baudelaire's musical and poetic 'prosodie mystérieuse et méconnue', 'dont les racines plongent plus avant dans l'âme humaine que ne l'indique aucune théorie classique'.[11] In *Rêverie* and *Hommage*, the tone is less triumphant: Mallarmé accentuates the fact that Wagner has 'inflicted' this challenge on poets as if, by so doing, he had already consummated their defeat.

The gloomy view of poetry's new historical status is confirmed by Mallarmé's own interpretation of *Hommage*. In an explanatory mood, he sent it to his uncle, Colonel Mathieu, with a copy of the sonnet:

> L'hommage est un peu boudeur; c'est, comme tu le verras, la mélancolie plutôt d'un poëte qui voit s'effondrer le vieil affrontement poétique, et le luxe des mots pâlir, devant le lever de soleil de la Musique contemporaine dont Wagner est le dernier dieu.[12]

'Sulking' even more than in *Rêverie d'un poëte français*, Mallarmé provisionally adopts the following point of view: Wagner's artistic (if not popular) success demonstrates the superiority of 'sibylline' music over words. Worse than that, it highlights the deficiencies inherent in that clattering old machine, French verse. Not only has poetry failed to redeem its birthright from music, music has muscled in on the territory of poets. Music, too, is inscribed on vellum, as the sonnet points out, but its notes, unlike letters, rise up triumphantly from the page.

The pallor and decrepitude of verse mentioned in the letter to Colonel Mathieu are conveyed in the morbid hues of the first quatrain. The news is that poetry is mortal. The 'effondrement' of the letter alludes to the 'tassement' of verse 3. Like a rotting piece of furniture, poetic constructions are unreliable, imminently useless and, when struck by 'the sunrise of contemporary Music', crumble into dust. The horizontal or downward motion of the quatrains contrasts with the upward 'jaillissement' of the tercets. The competition between the different arts is mere antagonism, an 'affrontement', which may refer to the dialectical nature of verse or to its unsuccessful assault on music. If Mallarmé's own reading turns out to be acceptable, the sonnet to Wagner would be the most generous and miserable of the *Hommages* – though it is a poem, not an aesthetic tract, and does not necessarily represent his final view on the subject.[13] It should even serve as a reminder that 'the poet' of these poems is not Stéphane Mallarmé: 'c'est . . . la mélancolie plutôt d'*un* poëte'.

Most critics have proposed interpretations which are far more limited than Mallarmé's. Albert Thibaudet set the tone by identifying the decor of the first quatrain with that of the stage: the sonnet, according to him, is constructed around the two intertwined motifs of theatre (first quatrain and first tercet) and book (second quatrain and second tercet).[14] Lloyd Austin plucked a more specific reading from an article in *La Revue wagnérienne* in which Mallarmé's friend, Dujardin, noted the symbolic fact that Hugo died on Wagner's birthday (May 22, 1885): the 'vieil ébat' might therefore be Romantic drama of which Hugo was the 'principal pilier'.[15] These theatrical readings can claim support from the various texts in which Mallarmé talks about Wagner: the 'ancien théâtre', lacking the 'vivifiant effluve qu'épand la Musique', now lies mouldering 'aux feuillets pieux du livre'; 'Son jeu reste inhérent au passé'.[16]

These and other interpretations have influenced successive readings as much as anything in the sonnet itself, and it seems that the more unusual or 'individual' the poem, the stronger the exegetical traditions it fosters in the community. Peter Hambly goes so far as to say that the pillar must be the audience without which no performance would take place: 'La mort de Wagner fait qu'on ne parle plus de créations d'opéras à son sujet. Les spectateurs risquent donc d'être moins nombreux à des représentations de son oeuvre (leurs effectifs vont "se tasser").'[17]

None of these readings should be ignored, but it should be noted, first, that they tend to particularize the sonnet and send it back to its circumstantial roots; second, that the problems they tackle may be muddles created by previous readers, not by the poem. If we try to chart the motifs identified by Thibaudet, they turn into dead ends, which is why Cohn, who more or less adopts the Thibaudet reading, uncharacteristically calls the sonnet 'excessively complex and not one of his best'.[18] The precise dynamics of the collapse – to mention just one apparent gaucherie – are hard to visualize. What, for example, is the main pillar of a stage, bearing in mind the fact that Mallarmé normally invites us to look for figurative meanings only after a recognizable concrete picture has emerged (even though the concrete picture may be the last thing to emerge)?

Other decodings have generalized the quatrains to include other forms of artistic expression. Gardner Davies, whose reading Lloyd Austin later preferred to his own,[19] sees the pillar as Wagner, dead and about to be forgotten. The 'folds' are those of a musical partition or a book of poetry, flatteringly and flutteringly described in the second quatrain. 'Notre' refers both to the poet and the musician: you and I, Wagner, play the same game. These items, surprisingly, should be stuffed away in a wardrobe. Why? In order to 'écarter les importuns' – true Art must be exclusive. Guy Michaud also sees the wardrobe as a means of preserving the 'dépôt sacré'.[20] Such readings are exactly in line with Mallarmé's exclusiveness, but they create more serious, unsatisfying difficulties. Even if one imagines the select few secretly consulting the sacred texts by torchlight, there remains the embarrassing problem of the vulgar verse 8: 'Enfouissez-le-moi plutôt dans une armoire.' 'Armoire', says Gardner Davies, was probably forced on Mallarmé by the rhyme; in any case, he claims, giving up, 'ce vers . . . ne saurait être considéré que comme une faute de goût, détonnant dans le sonnet de manière peu agréable'. Guy Michaud more politely finds it unbeautiful and 'un peu inattendu'.

Insults, like rhetorical flourishes, can be very revealing. Once we return, as we always must, to Verse and to everyday or universal realities, the poetic centre of gravity reasserts itself and pulls in most of these peripheral 'précisions'. The poem itself then enables us to accept rather than exclude, appreciate rather than niggle. Verse – the form which is 'simplement elle-même la littérature'[21] – constitutes a group of which theatre is a subset. And even Victor Hugo can be reinstated on one level of meaning, since Hugo 'était le vers personnellement'![22]

The recent history of French verse (to sum up in advance) is reenacted in the *Hommage* from more or less the same point of view Mallarmé was later to adopt in *Crise de vers*. The 'mécanisme rigide' of the 'vieux moule', heroically and despotically maintained by Hugo, but weakened by all the weight of tradition and overuse, finally snapped. The broken piece of furniture represents the *vers brisé* or, more generally, the collapse of the classical system, 'une brisure des grands rythmes littéraires'. The future 'manque de mémoire' may designate the increasingly noticeable absence of 'rimes fermes'[23] in French poetry. Another revealing disparagement offered at this juncture by Gardner Davies is that 'manque de mémoire' is 'une périphrase assez plate du mot *oubli*'.[24] So, presumably, it does not just mean that. Certainly, *oubli* of 'le vieux dogme du vers';[25] but this 'lack of memory' is not the result of the collapse, but part of it ('*avec* le manque de mémoire'). The 'manque de mémoire' is that of the *vers libre* with its 'infractions' and, more precisely, its lack of a balanced synthesis, the 'identité de deux fragments constitutifs *remémorée* extérieurement par une parité dans la consonance'.[26]

Next, in *Crise de vers*, 'les fragments de l'ancien vers' reconstitute another, instrumental 'intégrité': 'la Musique rejoint le Vers pour former, depuis Wagner, la Poésie.'[27] In the melancholy *Hommage* of 1886, this development is seen as the privilege of music.

Even ignoring the fact that this concurs with Mallarmé's own interpretation, the prosodic point of view is the only one that makes it possible to hold together in the mind all the recalcitrant details and contrasting tones of the quatrains. We can see now what the sulking poet thinks might be the premature final act of the drama of verse.

The 'moire', for Charles Chadwick, represents a dust cover draped over the furniture of a deserted salon. The salon is the poet's mind, once 'bien meublé', and the pillar the rest of Mallarmé, who, according to various letters written at the time, feels himself sinking into a deathly silence.[28] Without straying quite so far from the sonnet itself, we might retain the image of a shroud arranged over something which is 'already' dead or funereal and which will die a second death when it collapses. But is Mallarmé (rather, the poet) to be pictured as a composite creature, part 'mobilier', part 'pilier'? It would be unusual for both rhyme-nouns to designate exactly the same thing. 'Moire' in any case is a strangely precious material to use as a dust cover. Here, we may temporarily revert to Thibaudet's theatrical decor as a more logical reading.*

Both interpretations have the disadvantage of underrating and depreciating the other words, which then become simple dependants of whichever elements are elevated to the rank of key-words. Yet the astounding virtue of Mallarmé's poetry is that, the more one becomes aware of each word's figurative density, the more its capacity for contributing to coherent patterns becomes apparent. Eventually, we may be forced to suspect that the obvious irreducibility of his poems is not after all an infinity, but a very big number.

The 'plis', for instance, are often associated with the pages of a book – 'une longueur de plis convenable'; 'ses plis brodés d'arabesques significatives'[29] – and also with verses, by etymological allusion.[30] 'Moire' can therefore be seen as one of those synecdoches which conjure up the object in its partial absence. The 'moire' is the binding, the pattern on the binding or the 'papier moiré' of the book, as in these *vers de circonstance*:

> Tant de luxe où l'or se moire
> N'égale pas, croyez-m'en,
> Vers! dormir en la mémoire
> De Monsieur Louis Metman.[31]

With its 'silence déjà funèbre', the 'moire' is also a shroud. This couple of images can then be paired with one of Mallarmé's favourite analogies: the book and the tomb. Theatre, '*gisant* aux feuillets pieux du livre'; the splendid 'dalle funèbre du dictionnaire';[32] or, in the *Sonnet à Valère Gille*:

> Le beau papier de mon fantôme
> Ensemble sépulcre et linceul
> Vibre d'immortalité, tome,[33]

And so, back to the folds, often found in the vicinity of the Mallarmean tomb-tome: 'le pliage … offrant le minuscule tombeau, certes, de l'âme'. In the *Ouverture* of *Hérodiade*, the book, the tomb and the bed form an image-

---

* Heath Lees has discovered that 'moire' was also applied to the wave-patterns of music as they appear, for example, on a brass plate on which fine sand has been sprinkled (*French Studies Bulletin*, 51 (Summer 1994), 14–16) – a delightful and valuable interpretation which has been rejected in accordance with the only-one-reading-can-be-correct approach by Eileen Souffrin-Le Breton (*French Studies Bulletin*, 53 (Winter 1994), 16–18), though apparently still not the right one: see Charles Chadwick, 'More on *Moire*', *French Studies Bulletin*, 55 (Summer 1995), 17–19.

group whose principal members ('plis', 'grimoire', 'moire', 'dais sépulcral') appear in several places, notably in the surprising 'lit aux pages de vélin' (on which, presumably, the text is 'couched' or, in *Hommage*, 'pâmé') and the 'plis jaunes de la pensée'. These cohesive, recurrent analogies exist at a deeper, less turbulent level than the 'tone' or 'mood' of the poem. In *Le Livre, instrument spirituel*, for example, some of the same images (flight, folds, closure, silence and magic) appear with the same functions – except that, here, the poet wears his happy mask:

> cette extraordinaire, comme un vol recueilli mais prêt à s'élargir, intervention du pliage ou le rythme, initiale cause qu'une feuille fermée, contienne un secret, le silence y demeure, précieux et des signes évocatoires succèdent.[34]

The image of a 'vol recueilli', evoking the pages that can be folded out or closed, will reappear in the 'aile' of the second quatrain of *Hommage*. It occupies a similarly funereal context in the quatrain 'Pour la bibliothèque d'Alidor Delzant':

> Ci-gît le noble vol humain
> Cendre ployée avec ces livres
> Pour que toute tu la délivres
> Il faut en prendre un dans ta main.[35]

These images of death, sleep and flight are the new, improved product of clichéd comparisons. The improvement is obtained, partly by developing secondary details, partly by establishing complex relations between the different images. The book as corpse or tomb is especially common in Romantic poetry: 'ces quais poudreux / Où maint livre cadavéreux / Dort comme une antique momie'.[36] Mallarmé's achievement is to combine the images in such a way that almost all the levels can remain undetected without our enjoyment being impaired. In 'Le vierge, le vivace . . .', the same bookish analogies can be detected in the 'vols qui n'ont pas fui'; the 'déchirement' to be effected by a 'coup d'aile ivre'; the hard, smooth, frozen white surface like the 'transparent' page; the 'blanche agonie' and 'l'espace'; the 'fantôme' imprisoned in its icy tomb.[37] But it would be ridiculous to say that anyone who failed to see this could not appreciate the sonnet.

In *Hommage*, the 'moire' – book or, by implication, tomb – is 'déjà funèbre', but even more moribund than first appeared. For the time being, the furniture – 'mobilier' and not 'immeuble' – supports it (Mallarmé often imagines books standing on a piece of furniture[38]); but the structure is destined to collapse and precipitate the whole caboodle into oblivion. The word 'tassement' is one of those verbal repeater stations that relay the message in different directions. Far from being a mere synonym of 'affaissement' or 'effondrement', it contributes to the evocation of the book, as it does in the passage quoted above:

> le pliage est, vis-à-vis de la feuille imprimée grande, un indice, quasi religieux; qui ne frappe pas autant que son *tassement*, en épaisseur, offrant le minuscule tombeau, certes, de l'âme.[39]

When the pages of a heavy book are closed they continue to press together slowly under their own weight. In *Hommage*, this compression becomes a wholesale collapse. One sense of 'tassement' ('compression') leads to the other ('affaissement'). The dual significance of 'tassement' articulates the comparison of verse, page and book to a construction. Similarly, 'dispose' suggests the arrangement of letters as well as the placing of the folds on the 'mobilier'. 'Écrits', like the folds of the volume, are 'disposés' according to a principle; 'le sens enseveli se meut et dispose, en choeur, des feuillets'.[40] If the literary erection is faulty, it will of course be unstable. Another decayed analogy is renovated: literature and architecture. The column or pillar refers to the verticality or instability of the text or book.[41]

In this case, the literary referents in their physical order might be: a) the book; b) the page down which the poem progressively descends (*Un coup de Dés* contains some spectacular references – semantic and typographical – to the downward movement of text); c) the sonnet with its top-heavy form on which the folds of verse are piled up;[42] d) the verses themselves with their noticeably unbalanced structure and displaced caesuras – 'déjà | funèbre', 'pli | seul', 'tassement | du', 'avec | le', etc.

The 'principal pilier' does not have to be reduced to a static symbol representing Hugo, Mallarmé or Wagner. Neither should it be automatically attached to whatever meaning it seems to have in any other context: the reason for quoting other occurrences in Mallarmé's work is to point out its relations with other figures of the same group, not to assemble a dictionary of Mallarmean symbols. The 'pilier' of *Hommage* is associated first of all with the epithet, 'principal'. By this, we should understand not only 'the most important', but also 'which is the principle'. (Noun and adjective come, by different routes, from *princeps*.) What literary 'principle' can be said to act as a pillar? Perhaps syntax, that 'pivot' demanded by 'l'intelligibilité'.[43] Or, to adopt the more general point of view suggested by Mallarmé's letter to his uncle: 'le Vers', which is the 'principle' not only of poetry but of all literary expression. Apparently, however, Wagner's music is able to do without it (this is the paragraph immediately following Mallarmé's allusion to the 'challenge' presented by Wagner):

> Le sentiment se complique envers cet étranger ... d'un malaise que tout soit fait, autrement qu'en irradiant, par un jeu direct, du principe littéraire même.[44]

The poetic game – which, for Mallarmé, fully realizes its potential only in silent reading[45] – has become as habitual as a piece of furniture or a 'pli' (as in the expression 'prendre un pli'). Now, it threatens to disintegrate, not because of an external force but, as the word 'tassement' indicates, under the weight of its own tradition. The folds (verses or pages), though numerous, are 'seuls', forming no synthesis and without 'réciprocité'.[46] Just a multiplicity of singularities, a load of *ptychs* failing to make up a *diptych*. The overused alexandrine, like the 'insupportable colonne' of the newspaper, is literally and figuratively 'unbearable': the 'nombre fixe' of regular verse, 'lequel frappé uniformément et réel devient insupportable autrement que dans les grandes occasions';[47] or, more mundanely, 'si habile qu'en soit la facture, il est insupportable d'entendre toujours le même vers pendant cinq actes'.[48]

Hommage à Wagner is a rumbling echo of the 'malaise' Mallarmé claims to have felt at the emergence of free verse, his unease 'devant une brisure des grands rythmes littéraires'.[49] In 1894, in *La Musique et les Lettres*, he returned to the subject, but with fresh optimism, because, after all the cunning inventions of modern poets, verse was 'musical' once again and could 's'élever', 'fluide, restauré'.[50]

The tercets, then, contain ironies which may be visible only to readers of Mallarmé's critical texts. 'Mal tu', for example, hints at the deficiencies he normally associates with music – its unintellectual, tumultuous noise. Perhaps the first and, for some, last implication of this is that Wagner's music is so powerful that it makes itself heard even on paper. But this can also be seen as an unusual criticism of music in general: impressive it may be, but, unfortunately, 'poorly silenced'. The 'supreme art', on the other hand, consists 'à ne jamais en les chantant, dépouiller des objets, subtils et regardés, du voile justement de Silence sous quoi ils nous séduisirent'.[51] A related deficiency is its popularity, alluded to in the 'dubious deification'[52] of Wagner, 'the latest god' of contemporary Music: 'god' in the sense of deity, or 'god' in the sense of fad? Unlike poetry, music is 'pour la foule qui assiste, sans conscience, à l'audition de sa grandeur' (an opinion nicely exemplified by the appropriation of Wagner's music by the Nazis), whereas 'l'individu requiert la lucidité, du livre explicatif et familier'.[53] In the wider context of Mallarmé's thought (but only in that context), the poem can indeed be construed as an admission of defeat masking a private celebration of Mallarmean poetry. A picky Saussurean or, for that matter, Mallarmean approach may even detect the rival remnants of Mallarmé's name in the second tercet surrounding the name of Wagner.

Even without these ironies, the second quatrain of *Hommage* is quite firmly rooted in the first, and there is really no need to separate the two quatrains into two groups of distinct images. The 'plutôt' of verse 8 indicates the connection. The furniture which supports the book and the verse is destined to collapse; far better then to cast this old game into the pit of oblivion before it falls in itself.

> Notre si vieil ébat triomphal du grimoire,
> Hiéroglyphes dont s'exalte le millier
> A propager de l'aile un frisson familier!
> Enfouissez-le-moi plutôt dans une armoire.

'Notre', according to this interpretation, refers to 'we poets', not to Mallarmé and Wagner: the community of versifiers which Mallarmé habitually invokes in the first person plural as if assuming general agreement. Given the nationalistic slant of *Rêverie d'un poëte français* and several other texts, it also refers to 'we French and our prosodic tradition' – contrasted with 'cet étranger' – perhaps with the additional nuance of the magisterial 'we'.

Two sources of needless confusion have now been identified and should be mentioned before we go on to see exactly how depressed the poet is about his art. One is the tendency to locate a particular referent for the images in the 'real', historical world, as if it mattered to Mallarmé the poet. The remedy for this is the prosodic reading, which places the poem at the centre of the Mallarmean universe – a particular, real point, but a point from which other readings can be spun off so that they fall into orbits instead of careering off into intertextual space. The second source of confusion is the desire to know what the poet 'really thinks' about the facts he describes. Some strong opinion is implied, but is it positive or negative? Is this supposed to be a good or a bad thing? The remedy for this is acceptance of the poem's consistent ambivalence.

The adjective 'triomphal', for instance, associated with the poetic game, seems to be positive, but it also has a sarcastic nuance: triumphing, not triumphant. The 'jeu' or 'ébat'[54] is old; but 'vieil', in the cold light of the first quatrain, might suggest decrepitude rather than ripeness, senility rather than seniority. The same ambivalence – fertile tradition or sterile habit – is present in the two juxtaposed nouns: 'grimoire' and 'hiéroglyphes'.

Here, it would seem, is the hopeful idea that poetry is a Baudelairean 'sorcellerie évocatoire'. Words are magic symbols or hieroglyphics in a *grimoire*, signs with mysterious, latent properties like the recipes of an alchemist. As usual, however, the poem begins to struggle against the stream of meaning just when it seemed to be flowing smoothly. Words contradict their ostensible meanings. The hieroglyphics of poetry (literally, sacred carvings) are contrasted with the 'sanglots sibyllins' of Wagner's 'sacred' music, and this structural and thematic antithesis brings other connotations to the surface. Here are the relevant definitions from Littré:

Grimoire: Fig. et familièrement. Discours obscur, écriture difficile à lire.

Hiéroglyphes: Fig. Ce sont des hiéroglyphes pour moi, c'est-à-dire c'est une chose à laquelle je ne comprends rien.

Both nouns can be applied to a text whose obscurity is not the veil of a mystery but the public face of the author's ineptitude:

> Chaque vers qu'il complique a pour plus légers torts
> D'être grimoire, énigme et jeu de patience
> Où les forts en rebus briseraient leur science.[55]

The peeved poet of *Hommage* takes a view of his own verse that poets are supposed to consider typical of bourgeois philistines. His cynicism even affects the linguistic register of the poem, to the obvious distress of future critics: 'Enfouissez-le-moi plutôt dans une armoire.'

Unless we decide to agonize over possible defects or to assume that Mallarmé was having an off-day (actually – considering how long it took him to write his poems – an off-season), we can surely interpret this throwaway verse as an expression of the poet's exasperation at his own factitious, old-fashioned art. Intertextual and intratextual values are brought into play. The 'armoire' reintroduces the comparison of the book to the tomb; the cupboard is also a sarcophagus; and even outside Mallarmé's poetry and prose, it belongs to a group of images referring to the work of art that will (or should) never be read or which is inherently forgettable. 'Et toi, mon Alexandre, hélas! quelles armoires / Dérobent tes chefs-d'oeuvre à l'admiration?', Glatigny asks the putative father of the alexandrine.[56] Baudelaire also imagines himself languishing in an 'armoire' associated with a 'manque de mémoire', but with the possibility of an ironic resurrection:

> Ainsi, quand je serai perdu dans la mémoire
> Des hommes, dans le coin d'une sinistre armoire
> Quand on m'aura jeté, vieux flacon désolé,
> Décrépit, poudreux, sale, abject, visqueux, fêlé,
>
> Je serai ton cercueil, aimable pestilence! ('Le Flacon')

Mallarmé's 'armoire' acquires another dismal nuance from its immediate context. 'Armoire', as we know, was the only suitable remaining partner for 'grimoire'. It therefore has a dual figurative function. On the one hand, it connotes obscurity, closure, secrecy or neglect; on the other hand, the rhyme-word appears *qua* rhyme, and a pretty dreadful rhyme at that. The poetically 'tasteless' and mechanical 'armoire' is preceded by an implied ellipsis. The walking-stick posits the 'grimoire', then a weary boot plants a thudding 'armoire' next to it with a dull inevitability and the poem begins to look rather rickety. Unlike the rarer rhymes of the tercets, the rhymes of the quatrains are all 'rich', even *léonines*; but none of them have that engaging, synthesizing complexity so remarkable in other poems. Each rhyme is contained within a single word. As critics of Hugo and Banville pointed out, rich rhymes can reduce poetry to a tedious game. The rhyme that sticks out too obviously at the end of the verse is 'un bruit de trompette qui couvre le sens', a 'répétition toute matérielle [qui] ne peut ajouter à la phrase aucune beauté réelle, ni d'expression ni de pensée'.[57] Intellectual wealth is supplanted by a material luxury, riches picked up wherever language happens to have deposited them and ostentatiously displayed as a 'luxe essentiel à la versification'. This is Mallarmé's poetry pretending to be what his critics said it was.

The rhyme itself can be seen to illustrate the definition of the poetic act that precedes it:

> Hiéroglyphes dont s'exalte le millier
> A propager de l'aile un frisson familier!

Thibaudet familiarizes these lines by referring to the 'chant ailé' of 'la vieille poésie'.[58] Without discarding such a general interpretation, we can allow ourselves to be quite precise: the wing is (among other things) the end of the line which gives a 'heurt d'aile brusque' to the body of the verse.[59] Like wings, Mallarmé's verses come in pairs. Their duality or 'affrontement' is said to propagate a 'frisson'. The 'frisson' in turn can refer to a vital harmony: the production of significance and its communication to the reader, who is then able to 'recognize' a 'familiar' meaning or 'family' resemblance. 'Frisson' also seems to be applied specifically to rhyme or, generally, to poetic harmonies: the 'frisson final' of *Toast funèbre*; the 'frisson / A l'unisson' of *Le Cantique de saint Jean*; in *Symphonie littéraire*, a variation on the flower-stalk image – 'une plainte déchirante ... qui, parvenue à l'extrémité des branches, frissonne en feuilles musicales';[60] and, aptly, the 'frissons articulés proches de l'instrumentation' produced by the 'brisure des grands rythmes littéraires'.

The happy pictures painted in Mallarmé's critical texts often turn up as negatives or 'clichés' in the poetry. 'Familier' may have the sense it has in 'le trésor familier des Rythmes',[61] the known repertoire of French prosody. Applied to 'frisson', it can refer to the fact that rhyme-words are 'familiar' because they have been announced by their rhyming-partner. To Symbolist poets, it would also summon up the mystical *correspondances* of Baudelaire's sonnet, where symbols observe the passing human 'avec des regards familiers' (rhyming with 'piliers'). But the adjective also has a less esoteric sense. Without eclipsing the other nuances, it helps to create that characteristic atmosphere of semantic antagonism: 'ordinaire', 'habituel' or, in light of the verse that follows, 'vulgaire'. Rhymes that are both hackneyed and too colloquial.

If we credit Mallarmé with the knowledge that future readers would find the end of the octave jarring and bathetic, it is hard to see this simply as an expression of the need for mystery and exclusivity. The tone itself is as

'familier' as the would-be stimulating 'frisson' that so excites the hieroglyphics. In any case, the change of tense from present to perfect suggests that
the tercets are an explanation of why the old 'ébat' should be stored
away: 'Enfouissez-le-moi . . . [parce que] le dieu Richard Wagner . . . a
jailli.'

'Millier', which provides a leonine rhyme for 'familier', may indicate that,
however many hieroglyphics or rhymes there are, their number is not infinite.[62] It may also reach back to its Sanskrit root (given in Littré): *mil-*, to
combine or associate. The art of literature, unlike Wagner's divine art, is
finite, and the blatant harmony of rhymes only highlights the absurdity of its
pretensions. The 'smiling', rhyming 'fracas' (an etymological cross-reference
to 'tassement')[63] is 'originel' because it drinks directly at the fount of
language; but its ancient, divine function has been usurped by Wagner's
music. This is why it 'hates' him: an emotion that can be construed as a
compliment, coming from a poet who often applauds the works of fellow
artists by saying how heart-broken or stung he is by their excellence.

Poetry remains an intellectual game – and how can we tell from the
Hommage itself that, for Mallarmé, this is a mark of its superiority? Without
having asked us to leave the circles of verse, the sonnet brings us back to the
Rêverie d'un poëte français, where Mallarmé describes himself with either
arrogance or politeness as a 'humble qu'une logique éternelle asservit',
a victim of 'l'esprit français, strictement imaginatif et abstrait, donc
poétique'.[64]

The relative 'impurity' of the sonnet might excuse the disproportionate
length of this commentary. *Hommage à Wagner* is in most respects a 'reflexive'
poem in the simple sense – a poem that has poetry as its subject. It
alludes directly to the poetic game, offering only a few intrinsic examples,
and makes it impossible to follow one unbroken line of prosodic meaning.
The subject of the tercets is a different art altogether. The apparent contradictions with Mallarmé's critical texts are a further incitement to digression
and elaboration. But the sonnet is reflexive, too, in the Mallarmean sense,
though less completely than other poems: it exemplifies the dilemma it
describes.

The clod-hopping rhymes can be compared, because of their function, to
the rhymes of 'Le vierge, le vivace . . .', which all have the same vowel: *i*. One
could conceivably describe this as 'imitative harmony', and there are those
who hear in it the pathetic peeping of the trapped bird – though rhymes on
onques or *oi* would have been more realistic. It may be more profitable to see
it as a phonetic figure or the onomatopoeia of an abstraction. Even for critics
who find this sort of joky device unworthy of a great poet and mention it only
with reluctance, the repetition represents the immobility of the swan. In the
quatrains of *Hommage*, the obvious, 'text-book' character of the rhymes –
corns and calluses instead of onyx fingernails – indicates the futility of the

poetic game, which is neither lightened nor excused by the charming insouciance of the subject. Words which the rhyming phonemes leave intact are insufficiently dissolved phonetically to be anything other than themselves. The whole poem becomes a futile 'résidu'. The 'silence' of the beginning (that significant syllable again!) is answered by the 'sanglots sibyllins' of the end; but the 'sanglots' burst out of someone else's work.

And so, perhaps, they should – physical spasms, like the orchestra's 'éruptif multiple sursautement de la clarté, comme les proches irradiations d'un lever de jour: vain, si le langage . . . n'y confère un sens.'[65] Mallarmé refers to the disgraceful etymon of 'sanglot' in a letter which underlines the subtle criticism contained in *Hommage à Wagner*: 'Un hoquet ou deux sanglotent, interrompant le rythme à tort, seulement; on les pourrait effacer, parce qu'en poésie, il s'agit, avant tout, de faire de la musique avec sa douleur, laquelle directement n'importe pas.'[66] For the critical Mallarmé – hypothetically, the 'real' one – it is, in fact, the orchestra that is the 'industrial' machine, with its pipes and strings and pistons, pumping out its material noise for the pleasure of the infatuated masses.[67]

Petit Air II

According to the Goncourt brothers, Mallarmé was asked by Alphonse Daudet in 1893 if he was not perhaps trying to be even more hermetic and abstruse than ever.[68] The same year, Mallarmé adorned Daudet's album with one of his most difficult poems. *Petit Air II* sets us back in the midst of the drama which then enacts its mysteries without being obscured by another art. Despite this, the ending is no happier.

> Indomptablement a dû
> Comme mon espoir s'y lance
> Éclater là-haut perdu
> Avec furie et silence,
>
> Voix étrangère au bosquet
> Ou par nul écho suivie,
> L'oiseau qu'on n'ouït jamais
> Une autre fois en la vie.
>
> Le hagard musicien,
> Cela dans le doute expire
> Si de mon sein pas du sien
> A jailli le sanglot pire
>
> Déchiré va-t-il entier
> Rester sur quelque sentier!

Neglected by critics,[69] simplified by translators and criticized for its defects, *Petit Air II* is something of a *poème maudit*. The contradictions of what appears to be the argument are instantly and lastingly disconcerting. Provisionally, it can be reduced to a few elements: 'l'oiseau qu'on n'ouït jamais une autre fois en la vie a dû éclater là-haut; il restera, déchiré, sur quelque sentier.' But then the verbal forest covers up the path. Why, for instance, is 'Indomptablement' applied to a bird that plummets from the sky (the manuscript version has 'Tomber' instead of 'Rester')? The catastrophe may be a result of its wildness; but it still seems misleading to allow a five-syllable adverb stressing the bird's indomitability to take up over one-twentieth of a poem in which it suffers the final taming.[70] More confusingly, 'voix', 'ouït', 'musicien' and 'sanglot' all suggest that the bird emits a sound; yet when it exploded, it did so 'Avec ... silence'. Finally, if the bird is 'déchiré', how can it remain 'entier'?

These contradictions (and there are others lurking in the poem) do not perhaps create the state of mind most likely to produce a balanced reading. Innocent confusion may suggest that the seven-syllable lines are truncated alexandrines and the reader expected to supply exactly five-twelfths of the poem. Or perhaps it was written in accordance with the formula Mallarmé claimed to have invented and practised: always delete the beginning and end of what you write – 'Pas d'introduction, pas de finale'.[71] The reactions of Baudelaire's contemporaries to *Les Fleurs du Mal* are not always easy to understand without imagining that almost everyone alive in 1857 was a prude, but anyone can recapture the exasperation of Mallarmé's first readers. Those with the stimulus of a publisher's contract or an examination have a strong incentive to hang on to whatever reading first seems to offer a thread of logic. Intellectual self-preservation recommends a more cautious and distant approach. We may wish to treat it simply as a *petit air*, with its halting rhythms, tragic and inconsequential; its formation, in the absence of distracting meanings, of interesting phonetic combinations like non existent words, and enjoy the purely aesthetic qualities of this little bird that incubates no egg. We can scratch about for mental food in the crumbs of sense: the exploding bird, the 'bosquet' or the path. Alternatively, we can chicken out and generalize about poems that destroy themselves from the inside, signifying only unreadability.

The following approach is a compromise. If the relations between elements in the poem fail to offer even the shortest logical sequence, perhaps the poem's relations with other texts will show a path through the thicket. Then, we can reenter the poem by the gate of prosody, on a level where 'le regard intuitif [or even informed] se plaît à discerner la justice, dans une contradiction enjoignant parmi l'ébat, à maîtriser, des gloires en leur recul'.[72] (In reality, the following reading was reached by a mixture of the two.)

The comparison of the poet's hope to a soaring bird is a common image in poetry of any period. Mallarmé himself uses it in some of his juvenile poems:

'Sur les ailes de l'Espérance, / Que tes voeux, pleins de confiance, / Enfant, s'envolent vers le ciel!'[73] But since the bird of *Petit Air II* sings for the last time before falling out of the sky, the end of the poem may reflect the other side of the cliché. In Baudelaire's 'L'Albatros', the bird shot down by the sailors is compared to the poet. This, too, is a standard theme of Renaissance poetry. Following a Horatian model, the bird can be an Icarus, symbol of dashed hopes and crushed Promethean ambitions:

> Dois-je voler emplumé d'esperance,
> Ou si je dois, forcé du desespoir,
> Du haut du Ciel en terre laisser choir
> Mon jeune amour avorté de naissance?[74]

Mallarmé's sonnet could indeed be read as a pastiche of a Renaissance poem, not just because it contains the bones of a fable. The seven-syllable lines may be those of a *chanson* or, come to that, a *petit air*. The form of the poem also situates it historically: 'un mode primitif du sonnet ... usité à la Renaissance anglaise'.[75] Its archaic character is heightened by the scarcity of descriptive words (only 'bosquet' and 'sentier') and by the noun 'musicien', which was often used as a synonym of 'bird' in the sixteenth century, both in English and French poetry.

After anchoring the sonnet in various poetic traditions, we may feel confident enough to compare it to another Mallarmé poem in which the poet identifies himself with a bird: 'Le vierge, le vivace et le bel aujourd'hui ...'. Gardner Davies finds that the bird of *Petit Air II* has two features in common with the swan: a bird that is 'étranger au bosquet' and which, according to tradition, sings only at the moment of its death. From here on, confidence evaporates. Even before we leave the thematic surface of the poem – and even ignoring the fact that Mallarmé's swan never takes off – a significant difference emerges. The first person plays an important role in *Petit Air II*, whereas in the 1885 sonnet it appears only in one verse: 'Va-t-il *nous* déchirer avec un coup d'aile ivre'. Far from providing the moral or 'real meaning' of the fable, the *je* makes it impossible to identify the poet with the bird; the two parts of the conventional image – whether positive, negative or both – fail to stick together, and the bird flies off on its own like a free-floating signifier. The third quatrain, in which the poet wonders whether 'le sanglot pire' has burst from him or from the bird, establishes a difference rather than an identity. The detachment of the two protagonists is confirmed by 'là-haut' in line 3. The poet remains on the ground and, even when the bird joins him there, its location is uncertain: 'sur *quelque* sentier'.

Though we may resort to them in the hope of making things easier, intertextual comparisons have the power to tease out unsuspected difficulties. Here, the echoes of a bird-poet analogy draw attention to those pesky elements that prevent the metaphor from consolidating itself. Typically,

Mallarmé places the full weight of uncertainty on a mere grammatical word: '*Comme* mon espoir s'y lance' may allude to the traditional idea that the poet's hopes rise up 'in the same way as' the bird; or, given Mallarmé's peculiar combinations of tenses, it may mean that the bird exploded 'just when' his hope was rising; or even that the bird's demise was somehow the result of the poet getting his hopes up. Whatever the case, contrast seems more likely than identification.

Here again, the thematic repertoire of Renaissance poetry offers an intertextual straw. The poet sometimes appears as a bird-catcher or breeder, his aim being either to tame the bird or to kill it, perhaps even to eat or sell it. The bird itself may represent Love, Poetry or the poet's romantic or literary ambitions. The image of the 'oiseleur' or 'oiselier',[76] revived by Mallarmé's contemporaries, usually refers to the poet in his humble role as versifier – which brings us back to the image of winged verses. For Glatigny, the poet snatches swallow-winged rhymes from the air. Verlaine calls his 'Paysages tristes' 'l'oeuf de toute une volée de vers chanteurs . . . dont je suis peut-être le premier en date oiselier'.[77] The poet is a 'oiseleur', 'Qui cherche à prendre des pensées', in poem xxvi of Hugo's *Les Rayons et les Ombres*. The 'oiseleur' also makes a brief appearance in the *Odelette* by Banville to which Gautier's 'L'Art' in *Emaux et Camées* was a reply:

> Quand sa chasse est finie,
> Le poète oiseleur
>   Manie
> L'outil du ciseleur.[78]

Rhyme itself can be an indiscriminate bird-catcher who nets whichever winged signifiers happen to fly past.[79]

As we should have guessed before trying to shoehorn it into a poetic tradition, *Petit Air II* is an entanglement of recognizable but strangely modified or underdetermined motifs. In this case, there seems to be some sympathy with – or, neurotically, sarcastic allusion to – the reader's dilemma, since the poet also claims to be suffering from confusion. Is he in some way responsible for the fall, or is the bird a symbol of the poet?

> Cela dans le doute expire
> Si de mon sein pas du sien
> A jailli le sanglot pire

Is this genuine ignorance about an emotional event or simply a rhetorical doubt? The voice of a teacher: 'This may have hurt me more than it hurt you'? Or the poet emphasizing his affinity with the bird: 'It would be hard to say which was worse'?

The further we go along purely semantic paths, the more our doubts increase. The poem itself is largely 'foreign' to the 'groves' of French poetry and belongs only to the broadest category: bird, but of no known feather. The definition of the bird itself brings us to another clearing marked by another set of blank signposts:

> L'oiseau qu'on n'ouït jamais
> Une autre fois en la vie.

Is it, as Gardner Davies suggests, the swan that sings as it dies? But 'vie' seems to refer to the person who hears the bird, not to the bird itself; and why should it not be possible to hear the swan-song more than once? The implication is that this is a unique opportunity. Perhaps the mysterious 'oiseau' is a bird of ill omen whose song portends the death of whoever hears it. The poet and bird might then be engaged in an ironic musical contest: perhaps the poet's song is just as pernicious as the bird's. Fatal is the song of the night raven, says an epigram in the Greek Anthology, but when Demophilos sings, even the night-raven dies.[80]

We have now assembled a mess of possible interpretations and acquired one certainty: no single meaning imposes itself. The poem attracts literary comparisons like an electromagnet and then switches off the current. In fact, we are not even told whether or not the principal action of the sonnet has taken place. The bird 'must have' exploded, but has it? And is the final, inverted sentence really an affirmation or a question – 'va-t-il . . . Rester'? 'Cela dans le doute expire' (a 'singulière périphrase', notes Bénichou)[81] might be applied to the poem as a whole – flippantly because the drama expires in the suspicions and hesitations it arouses; speculatively because Mallarmé uses the verb 'expirer' (as in 'Surgi de la croupe . . .' and 'Quelle soie aux baumes de temps . . .') in a paradoxically positive sense – the expiration or expression of the poem which requires the 'death' or disappearance of its raw material, the transformation of each designated thing into a mere 'fait rythmique et transitoire où aboutira et dont repartira la période'.[82]

Now that futile erudition has battered us into the position we should have adopted in the first place, we can start again. We have in effect been treating the poem as a piece of 'commercial' literature and, as Mallarmé warned us, finding it 'obscure' instead of reading it as 'la manifestation d'un art qui se sert . . . du langage'.[83] The 'doubt' itself offers a new starting point by placing the poem in the drama of verse. It may even provide us retrospectively with a context for all the interpretative material we dug up in vain.

Doubts, as we saw, form part of the drama: like 'foi', the word 'doute' can be seen as another example of Mallarmé's secular use of Christian terminology.[84] On its simplest level, it refers to the doubts of the poet of *Hommage à Wagner* who wonders whether his own art has any virtue. In *Petit Air II*, it may be a question about the universal value of individual expression. For the reader, the doubts may concern the poetic treatment of reality. Language can make 'un fait de nature' disappear into a certain number of phonemes, but is this 'disparition vibratoire selon le jeu de la parole' only a game or can it suggest some 'notion pure'? Will ordinary language, 'comme le traite d'abord la foule', recover its 'virtualité'?[85] And, if it does, will our doubts not be exacerbated when we realize that the 'au-delà magiquement produit par certaines dispositions de la parole' is no more than a 'moyen de communication matérielle avec le lecteur comme les touches du piano'?[86]

To consider the material realities of the poem: rhymes are often the actors which have the job of proclaiming the poet's victory or defeat. In *Petit Air II*, the first feminine rhyme introduces a note of optimism. As in *Prose pour des Esseintes*, the *rime complexe* enacts the creation of a synthesis. The three vocables – *s[e] y lance* – come together to form a whole word, *silence*. Rhymes like these are a formal equivalent of the 'vers qui de plusieurs vocables refait un mot total'.[87]

The giant rhyme turns out to have been a false hope, another 'éclat triomphal trop brusque pour durer'. The last rhyme – *entier-sentier* – though almost as rich, fails to form one of those happy surprises with which Mallarmé often ends his poems: *ce l'est-bracelet, puisse l'air-Whistler, jusqu'au-Vasco*, etc. It falls into the inferior category of rhymes like *funèbres-ténèbres* in 'Surgi de la croupe . . .': technically perfect but trite or unexciting.

From discreet inadequacies to blatant 'mistakes' . . . Some of the rhymes are, to say the least, not very good. *Bosquet-jamais*, as Gardner Davies remarks, is plain 'unacceptable' according to the rules Mallarmé observes.[88] Paul Bénichou (along with all the unnamed Mallarmistes he asked for an explanation) is also 'perplexed' by this 'anomaly': 'les vers 5 et 7 riment fort mal, ou, pour mieux dire, pas du tout'.[89] Banville would have said the same thing, and one assumes that Mallarmé's disciples were too polite to ask the obvious question.

The answer lies in the poem itself. Contrary to what Bénichou claims, there are other examples of this type of rhyme in Mallarmé's work. Very illuminating examples: *jouait-fouet* and *reconnais-bonnets* – both unacceptable rhymes in the unacceptable *gorze-quatorze* sonnet to Méry Laurent which treats the theme of flouting rules. In *Petit Air II*, as befits a poem intended for public consumption, the deliberate mistake is pointed out far more plainly.*
In one of those key expressions that allow the poem to comment on its own progress or *impasses*, Mallarmé justifies and explains his inadequate rhyme: 'Voix . . . par nul écho suivie'. There is even a subtle counterpoint which, as it were, seeks to re-establish the full harmony and supply the voice with an echo, like the phonetic 'unisson' or the *ʒ*s which try to 'announce' the rose in 'Surgi de la croupe . . .':

---

* There is another significant *e-ɛ* rhyme in the first version of the *Chanson bas, La Marchande d'herbes aromatiques*, where it represents a more visceral form of incompletion: the WC, 'Où chacun jamais complet / Tapi dans sa défaillance / Au bleu sentiment se plaît'.

> Voix étrangère au bosquet
>   **waz**
> Ou par nul écho suivie,
>   **a**
> L'oiseau qu'on n'ouït jamais
>   **waz**
> Une autre fois en la vie.
>   **waz**

The bird's voice is echoed, but in the 'wrong' place – and an acrostic 'VOL'
in the second quatrain may be a similar, intentional irony. The bird of *Petit
Air II* can therefore be contrasted with the *oiseau* of the Vasco da Gama
sonnet which contains the whole poem within the span of its phonetic wing-
tips. The poet's 'sob' can certainly be considered relatively deficient, as can
the bird's. What has occurred (or 'must have' occurred) is a fault in the order
of things, an anomaly, a 'peremptory' exception, something that stands outside the rule-system.

These dysfunctionings and irregularities are important not just as subtle
clues to hidden meanings or illustrations of the theme, but because they
are what happens in the sonnet – perhaps they are even its only verifiable
truths.

Another, less obvious device owes its negative connotations to Mallarmé's
own particular prosody. Verse 11 contains an example of something that
often occurs at the critical moment or 'agony' of the poem: 'Si de mon sein
pas du sien'. 'Sein' and 'sien' form a sort of 'inverse'[90] or anagrammatical
rhyme which expresses – quite literally – the possible confusion of bird
and poet. In a boisterous poem written when he was seventeen, Mallarmé
did actually rhyme 'sien' with 'sein';[91] but here the rhymes are prevented
from 'exteriorizing' their consonance. To use Mallarmé's image, this is one of
those *reploiements* of the poem, which folds in on itself and threatens to
paralyse the dialectic. A prosodic ingrowing toenail, like the 'Muet muet' of
Chanson.

These internal rhymes are discreet but highly influential actors in the
drama of verse. The most famous and arresting example occurs in 'Une
dentelle s'abolit . . .':

> Mais chez qui du rêve se dore
> Tristement dort une mandore[92]
>   **temã doʀt e mã doʀ**
>
> Au creux néant musicien

The internal rhyme swallows up almost the whole verse. The linear development of the poem is bogged down in repetition and it seems to be on the
point of disappearing into itself.

Whenever these distracting internal rhymes appear, they come with some kind of commentary or allusion to prosodic features, like the 'par nul écho suivie' of *Petit Air II* or, in the example just quoted, the 'creux néant musicien'. In the *sonnet en yx*, the internal, self-reflecting rhyme, 'Aboli bibelot', is followed by the qualifying phrase, 'd'inanité sonore'. In the original version of the *Finale* of *Hérodiade*, the 'eyes' of rhyme are turned inward like the 'regard révulsé' of John the Baptist's severed head; as in *Petit Air II*, the inversion of *i* and *e* indicates a central 'néant':

> Ce que d'elle *détient* en son *éteint* génie
> Le regard révulsé par quelqu'un au néant.[93]

In 'Quand l'ombre menaça de la fatale loi . . .', the futility of versification, which merely rearranges what already exists, is suggested even more explicitly in another 'stagnant' rhyme: 'L'espace à soi pareil qu'il s'accroisse ou se nie.' It may be that this device had negative connotations for Mallarmé because he associated it with 'un vieux vice charmant' of 'poètes nos prédécesseurs': 'trop de facilité à dégager la rythmique élégance d'une synthèse'.[94] Above all, however, these pseudo-errors and deficiencies bring us back to one of his main preoccupations – and also to the Wagner sonnet. The bird-*musicien* is also a musician, and poetic expression is once again a 'sanglot'. At the time of writing the poem, Mallarmé was often complaining of the misunderstanding that led poets to remove their words from the 'mould' of traditional verse in order to achieve a superficial 'musicality' that had little connection with the structures and 'rhythms' of existence – 'Musique au sens grec, au fond signifiant Idée ou rythme entre des rapports; là [in poetry], plus divine que dans l'expression publique ou symphonique.'[95] The bird, 'là-haut perdu', is like the modern verse which 's'en va (pour devenir traits d'orchestre, chant éperdu . . .)'.[96]

This already provides us with a more promising and sustainable approach – a reading which is available only through the prosodic peculiarities of the sonnet and which makes it possible to deduce an objective guiding principle from the very minutiae and inconsistencies that seemed to sabotage the act of reading and invite carping criticism. The dysfunctioning of rhyme is a motif which complements that other motif 'incorrectly called the subject'. Just as the formal unities are 'disappointing', so 'entier', applied to the bird, indicates, not a satisfying synthesis, but a futile totality. The bird has been 'déchiré' like the 'baiser' of *Chanson*, but remains 'entier', untied but ununited with the rest of the poem – lost, inaccessible and still 'indomptable'.

The prosodic reading can then be compared to conclusions reached by purely thematic routes. According to Paul Bénichou, 'entier' would refer to the fact that the soul does not rise from the body but dies with it, as in *Toast funèbre*: 'Que ce beau monument l'enferme [Gautier] tout entier'. 'L'oiseau déchiré reste tout entier dans sa dépouille et . . . rien de lui ne survit ailleurs:

"entier" nie la survie.'[97] This is surely preferable to the hazy parallel established by Gardner Davies with Le *Cantique de saint Jean*. Basing his remarks
on a commentary by Jean-Pierre Richard, he compares the bird to the head
of John the Baptist and sees in *Petit Air II* an 'optimistic' poem expressing
Mallarmé's 'faith' 'in the completion of his *Oeuvre*'. In the *Cantique*, the
decapitation symbolizes (obviously not without irony) a 'refoulement' of the
'anciens désaccords' of body and spirit. But the idea of a 'baptême' or a 'salut'
(the last word of the *Cantique*) is absent from *Petit Air II* – as J.-P. Richard
points out.[98] The anonymous bird lacks the positive connotations associated
with John the Baptist, even in Mallarmé's work. It would be absurd in any
case to adduce Mallarmé's faith in the completion of the *Grand Oeuvre*.[99] The
principal characteristic of the *Livre* is that it never existed, just as Mallarmé
never wrote his thesis and never made a successful or enjoyable career of
teaching. The *Livre* – unless we decide to revel in Rimbaldian hero-worship
– can be seen as another non existent ideal which acted as the invisible,
coordinating point of reference, somewhere 'là-haut'.

Similarly, a comparison with 'Le vierge, le vivace . . .' hardly points to the
'hypothèse opposée'. The swan remains uselessly stuck in the ice, but the bird
of *Petit Air II* is no more triumphant. It may have 'chanté la région où vivre',
but its song is unheard, its flight or emigration interrupted. At least the swan
retained the movement of its neck. Perhaps there is a hint that this is just the
other horn of the same dilemma in the repetitive rhymes on *i*: every rhyme of
'Le vierge, le vivace . . .' and all but two of the seven rhymes of *Petit Air II*
contain an *i*. A more roomy comparison might bring in the other inhabitants
of the Mallarmean aviary: Vasco's balanced 'oiseau d'annonce nouvelle'
which is 'bas' but can still flutter its wings and is followed by an echo or at
least by a ko; or the 'fugace oiseau' of *Petit Air I*, which is 'à côté' and
associated with 'jubilation', the poet having sensibly lowered (*ab-dicated*)
his gaze from the inaccessible 'gloriole' of the sky, 'Haute à ne la pas
toucher'.[100]

A second test of the data obtained by prosodic means might take account
of Mallarmé's metaphorical statements about poetic language. Adapting the
old cliché, he often compares the poet's aspirations to a 'chant' which
's'élance';[101] 'voici le miracle de chanter, on se projette, haut comme va le
cri'.[102] The vital difference is that Mallarmé's definitions pertain, not to the
ideal itself, which necessarily remains ideal, inaccessible and unnamed, but to
the *expression* of his aspirations: 'on projette, à quelque élévation défendue et
de foudre! le conscient manque chez nous de ce qui là-haut éclate.'[103] 'Ce qui
là-haut éclate', like the bird, is not defined. The ambiguous verb, 'éclater',
suggests that whatever it is appears and disappears like a firework. However,
by using this hypothetical ideal as a focus, the poet creates a harmonious
'symétrie [qui] vole, outre le volume, . . . sur l'espace spirituel'.[104]

This still leaves us swimming in the vague and Romantic: 'espace spirituel'
and 'là-haut' are not precise concepts and it would be untypical of Mallarmé
to use them and consider something said. These blurry terms may reflect a

Platonic philosophy, but the more immediate interest of Mallarmé's criticism lies in his attempt to tie down the dithering generalizations of Romanticism and turn them into equations worthy of deliberation. Some of the appeal of his *Mardis* was surely his repeated demonstration that areas previously thought to be inaccessible to fruitful analysis had at least a useful metaphorical potential. The residual mystique of vast emotional or religious *topoi* gives his didactic observations an unusual thrill: the realization that, after all, he was talking about something real. A passage from *La Musique et les Lettres*, written shortly after *Petit Air II*, establishes the link between the high-flown rhetoric and ground-level language:

> Nous savons, captifs d'une formule absolue que, certes, n'est que ce qui est. Incontinent écarter cependant, sous un prétexte, le leurre, accuserait notre inconséquence, niant le plaisir que nous voulons prendre: car cet *au delà* en est l'agent, et le moteur dirais-je si je ne répugnais à opérer, en public, le démontage impie de la fiction et conséquemment du mécanisme littéraire, pour étaler la pièce principale ou rien.[105]

'Si je ne répugnais' is a rather mischievous formula since this 'démontage impie de la fiction' is precisely what Mallarmé's poems do in public.

As the sonnet suggests, the poet is like a bird but also like a bird-handler. By using a lure, he tames his aspirations which otherwise would fly off to the *au-delà*. The 'leurre' – 'morceau de cuir rouge, en forme d'oiseau, qui sert pour rappeler l'oiseau de proie lorsqu'il ne revient pas droit sur le poing'[106] – is also the artifice of prosody and, generally, all the tangible bits and pieces of organized expression.

The image of a lure takes up from a passage on the previous page where Mallarmé talks of 'Le tour de telle phrase ou le lac [*sic*] d'un distique'. The original edition of *La Musique et les Lettres* does indeed have 'le *lac* d'un distique',[107] which is hard to explain other than by saying it was a printer's error (Mallarmé's proofreading was not impeccable).[108] In view of the neighbouring 'leurre', 'lacs' (snare) is a more logical reading: Bertrand Marchal has kindly confirmed that the manuscript shows 'le lacs', replacing 'l'enlacement', and points out that 'lac' may be one of Mallarmé's 'licences orthographiques'. Thus, 'lacs' in the normal sense of 'Noeud coulant qui sert à prendre des oiseaux' and 'tour', not only in the sense of *tournure*, but also in the sense of *dévidoir* or reel ('cordage qu'on ne veut filer que peu à peu, malgré sa tendance à s'échapper'), in other words as a near-synonym of 'lacs'. Both words appear together in *Planches et Feuillets*: 'ces lacs et tours un peu abstraits'.[109] The image of a 'lacs' is particularly well suited to the final distich of *Petit Air II*, especially considering the semantic proximity of 'lacérer' and 'déchirer'.

The falconry image is a key to the rest of the passage from *La Musique et les Lettres*.[110] The poet imposes the constraints of verse on his 'untameable' passion. These constraints allow him to 'sing' or to postulate the *au-delà* which he knows does not exist – and must not exist, because if it comes true the dream is no longer a dream. The *au-delà* is simply the invisible 'moteur' of the poetic 'mécanisme'. If the 'incontinent' poet fails to 'contain' himself and casts aside the lure 'sous un prétexte' (that is, following some non-linguistic, 'pretextual' impulse), the bird flies off and is never heard again. The pleasure of the game – falconry or poetry – is lost, and the player's action, since it takes place outside the rules, bears witness only to chance or to 'notre inconséquence'.

This is what happens in *Petit Air II*. The hopeful poet-*oiseleur* launches the bird into endless space like a *vers-libriste* ignoring the margins; but in so doing, he relinquishes his authority over it. The bird is torn apart by something which remains invisible: atmospheric pressure, bird of prey, heart attack or lightning? It emits a 'sanglot', but not a Wagnerian 'sanglot sibyllin' – a silent, incommunicable cry of fury. 'Furie' and 'silence' are words Mallarmé often applies in his letters to successful poetic expression; but here, the cry has no echo and is not sustained or repeated. 'Genius', on the other hand, is an 'écho de soi, sans commencement ni chute'.[111] Verhaeren's verses are 'la forme verbale, intime, spontanée et de vous jaillie; à quoi s'en tient votre abondante furie' – but a 'furie *contenue*'.[112] As the sonnet's defective rhymes suggest, the bird fails to achieve that 'équilibre momentané et double à la façon du vol', that material ideal which consists in maintaining the various elements of the volume in a 'vol recueilli mais prêt à s'élargir',[113] a purely virtual flight like that of the falcon in the glove of the falconer, the embryo in the egg, the fan in a woman's hand or the sails on a mast. The bird, like the kiss in *Chanson*, is 'déchiré' but remains 'entier' because it finds no partner.

A possible objection is that the hypothetical swan has turned itself into a falcon. Both readings can be justified, and both readings should be seen as strictly partial. First, as others have pointed out, the word 'hagard' was originally applied to old falcons that could no longer be tamed: it is therefore connected with 'Indomptablement', perhaps even with the phonetic phrase, 'L'*oiseau* qu'*on* n'ouït jamais' (a decapitated '*faucon*'). Second, as Bénichou remarks, Mallarmé certainly used the general term 'oiseau' for a reason,[114] and there is little to be gained from materializing it and tying a steely footnote to its leg: 'Cet oiseau est le cygne . . .'[115]*

---

* In view of its 'vol', the adjective 'hagard' and a traditional symbolic value of birds, it might just as well be a 'pubis' (cf. *Le Tombeau de Charles Baudelaire*) and the sonnet an evocation of sexual intercourse – with an absent partner. Derrida gives a similar reading of 'A la nue . . .' in *Dissemination*, trans. Barbara Johnson (London: The Athlone Press, 1981), 266, as does G. Montbertrand (see p. 231, n. 37), and Rosemary Lloyd points out the erotic motifs of 'M'introduire dans ton histoire' in *Mallarmé, 'Poésies'* (Grant & Cutler, 1984), 18. The same binary oppositions are present in theme and prosody: rise and fall, rigidity and flaccidity, 'delay' and premature completion. Rhymes have either masculine or feminine connotations depending on whether they come at the end or in the middle of a verse. See also comments above on *Chanson*. The sexual/prosodic reading might be taken to several logical conclusions.

Thematically, *Petit Air II* is probably closest to *Le Pitre châtié*. In the hope of achieving some unmediated enjoyment of the ideal his art suggests, the poet sheds his artistic trappings and deceits – in this case, his make-up – which, as he discovers too late, was 'tout [son] sacre'. The clown regrets the loss of his artistic equipment, however 'ignoble', and the bird-handler the loss of his unique bird whose song will never again be heard.

The poet's 'hope' turns out to have been his weakness: thinking that an ideal could be attained without the machinery of verse. *Petit Air II* can be read as a more down-to-earth version of Banville's 'Saut du tremplin' at the end of the *Odes funambulesques*, where the clown, in trying to escape from the petty realities of daily life, jumps so high that he bursts through the cloth ceiling and reaches the stars (though the phrase 'sans règles' hints at a similar moral):

> Par quelque prodige pompeux
> Fais-moi monter, si tu le peux,
> Jusqu'à ces sommets où, sans règles,
> Embrouillant les cheveux vermeils
> Des planètes et des soleils,
> Se croisent la foudre et les aigles.

In Mallarmé's cosmos, the usual order of Poetry and Ideal is reversed. The humble origin – the trampoline or lure of verse – is actually the end from which the upper air, constellations and spiritual space are extrapolated. There is, then, no need to take a tragic view of events, because the poem exists and would not otherwise have been written. 'L'oiseau qu'on n'ouït jamais' may have produced the final, perfect expression, the 'frappe unique' of the prelapsarian word that would be 'matériellement la vérité'.[116] Something like the linguistic equivalent of 'voir Naples et mourir'. This ideal state of language could hardly be considered a professional advantage, hence the poet's question: was my (imperfect) version really worse than the perfect, echoless cry? Because, without the imperfections of language, '*Seulement, sachons n'existerait pas le vers*' . . .[117] Like the Wagner sonnet, *Petit Air II*, seen in the predominantly negative light of Mallarmé's poetics, can be shown to be less depressing than it seems. Whatever the ultimate destination of the poem, it comes close to achieving in the reader's brain that 'furious silence'[118] of the perfect poem, an 'admirable musique . . . inconnue à haute voix':[119] 'Tout le vol vital de traits composant ces chants brefs équivaut, sitôt leur évanouissement, au plus transparent silence, muet comme l'émotion de vivre.'[120] In Régnier's excellent phrase, 'l'hyperbole conceptrice n'entraîne pas avec elle la matière de sa fusée.'[121]

By sustaining the ambiguities and contradictions of the sonnet, 'recuperating' its supposed mistakes and presenting the words of the poem as words and functions, the drama of verse provides, not a definitive paraphrase, but a broad and coherent perspective. The sonnet emerges from the drama as another *art poétique* based on an extraordinary interweaving of the poetic connotations of birds: the folly of Icarus, praying, language tamed or trained by the poet, and the winged verses which are launched (in Mallarmé's case, reluctantly) into the public domain. The poet of *Petit Air II* launches his poetic bird, not towards the arrows of literary fortune but towards Chance itself, realizing, of course, that a bird in the hand is worth two in any other place.

The test of the prosodic reading is its failure to supply a single, unanswerable, global conclusion. *Petit Air II* can still be enjoyed as a nice example of a deconstructive allegory that establishes connections only to reveal the arbitrary, untameable nature of language. Unclenching his fist to throw the die, the poet 'yields the initiative to words' and the poem escapes from any paraphrase. Unlike the traditional poem which calls for a suspension of disbelief and a pretence that something physically or emotionally real is being described, this one actively encourages disbelief and imprints itself on the memory like a blind-spot. Perhaps even more unsettling is the suspicion that the enormous lacunae left to the reader's imagination have already been filled by the master and that all his questions have answers. This impression may have something to do with the characteristics attributed to the poet in the poems – a handler who usually maintains his 'authority' over language even while voicing the reader's doubts. In this sense, we can share his contemporaries' fears that all Mallarmé's poems were confidence-tricks – because they are, and the reader is either the dishonest lawyer upholding his client's improbable integrity against all the odds, or the willing victim.

'Une dentelle s'abolit . . .'

Petit Air II begins with 'hope' and ends with 'doubt'. In 'Une dentelle s'abolit . . .', 'doubt' makes an early appearance in the second line, which leaves enough time for a glimmer of hope to shine through before the end. The curve climbs back towards poetic success. Futility and sterility become the necessary conditions of a virtual birth.

> Une dentelle s'abolit
> Dans le doute du Jeu suprême
> A n'entr'ouvrir comme un blasphème
> Qu'absence éternelle de lit.
>
> Cet unanime blanc conflit
> D'une guirlande avec la même,
> Enfui contre la vitre blême
> Flotte plus qu'il n'ensevelit.

> Mais chez qui du rêve se dore
> Tristement dort une mandore
> Au creux néant musicien
>
> Telle que vers quelque fenêtre
> Selon nul ventre que le sien,
> Filial on aurait pu naître.

Nearly everyone with an opinion on the subject agrees that the quatrains depict – though only just – a lace curtain which disappears or is eclipsed in the sunrise (the 'doute . . . suprême').[122] As it disappears, it reveals no bed. Twisted into a 'garland', the curtain faces itself in the window ('conflicting' with itself) or is blown up against the pane by a gust of wind. Like the absent bed, it symbolizes sterility or death.

To pick holes in the curtain reading, one could say that it treats the poem as a series of circumlocutions. Compared to the glittering *tableaux* of Mallarmé's prose texts, the sonnet seems thin and wispy, with only an abstract or aural interest once the brute meaning has been jotted down: 'Strophe I. Description des rideaux d'une fenêtre.'[123]

This is not to say that the reading is somehow invalid. Even the skimpiest 'translation' of the poem may make some useful and interesting generalizations possible. For example: most of Mallarmé's poems can be read as negative images of a 'normal' depiction. The absent norm here would be a window, a curtain and a scene within a room. Instead, the window and the curtain cancel each other out and the room is either empty or not there. The poem remains on the surface of its frame, as if the glass protecting the potential painting was a mirror. Following the conventional structure of the sonnet form, 'Mais' introduces an antithesis in the tercets. But the opposite of the absent scene is not its presence. Instead, the focus is on a hollowness or concavity. The frame itself effectively disappears: 'la vitre', with the definite article, becomes 'quelque fenêtre', and the present tense a past conditional, 'aurait pu'. Flatness in the quatrains gives way to emptiness in the tercets.

The impenetrable surface, however, is far richer than supposed. On closer inspection, the 'dentelle' only *seems* to coagulate into a curtain. Several problems nag us back into the text even if the first reading seems to fit. Where, for instance, is the poet? Standing in the room, or outside, peering through the window, or inside and outside at the same time? The curtain disappears but then returns in the form of a garland and performs three distinct functions in the second quatrain. Also, is 'le doute du Jeu suprême' just the sunrise? In fact, is it necessarily the sunrise at all? 'Doubt' might just as well suggest the darker dusk, the 'supreme' moment of the day; and the 'Jeu', of course, could also be verse, with emphasis on its 'supreme' component, rhyme. The most confusing and influential difficulty occurs in line 8.

'Flotter' is contrasted with 'ensevelir', apparently hinting at something more hopeful than death. But then how should one explain the 'Mais', which apparently heralds a positive antithesis? The 'mandore', as J.-P. Richard notes, indicates a sleeper and a possible awakening,[124] though 'tristement', 'creux' and 'néant' hardly point to a traditional happy ending.

These difficulties can be shown to arise, not just from the concise complexity, but also from critical over-simplification. If the other 'couches d'intelligibilité' are restored (especially the *mille-feuille* of prosodic significance), the sonnet begins to perform more coherently – as Cohn has shown with a wider thematic sweep than the present analysis.

Lace looms large in the scenery of the drama of verse. As a visual image, it portrays the empty page of a book on which letters are the knots and strands of the material: 'ce pli de sombre dentelle ... assemble des entrelacs distants.'[125] As an abstract image, it refers to the interrelated parts of the poetic work, most of which is made up of blank space: 'je tisserai *aux points de rencontre* de merveilleuses dentelles, que je devine, et qui existent déjà dans le sein de la Beauté.'[126] Lace represents an 'extrême complication' of motifs which nonetheless appear 'nettement'.[127] Typically, these figurative functions have a humble ancestry: the image of a 'trame', an 'écheveau', a 'fil enchevêtré'[128] or a 'tissu' – a word Mallarmé associates with its close etymological relation, 'texte', and also with verse ('ce tissu transformable et ondoyant') and music ('une infinité de mélodies brisées qui enrichissent le tissu',[129] or the 'entrelacs de la mélodie' which is materialized in the 'guipure' on the shoulders of women in the audience).[130]

'Dentelle' is also used in its normal sense in *Pour un baptême* and in the *Ouverture* of *Hérodiade*: the 'dentelles pures' and the 'belles guipures' of a shroud. There, too, the image is implicated in the circles of a relentlessly literary universe – the 'plis jaunes de la pensée', the 'plis roidis' of the book, 'Percés selon le rythme' and the 'lit aux pages de vélin'.

A long journey can be undertaken into Mallarmé's universe before the bookish connotations of 'dentelle' are exhausted. It also has a technical sense: 'Dessin poussé sur le bord des livres ou sur le plat de leur couverture' (Littré). A more distant alliance with books emerges in some prose texts which also shed light on the verb 'flotter'. The lace ('dentelle', 'effilé' or 'gaze') is the rain that flows down the window of the poet's library and, by reflection, down the panes of glass of the bookcase: '*l'effilé* de multicolores perles qui plaque la pluie, encore, au chatoiement des brochures dans la bibliothèque. ... j'aime ... , *contre la vitre*, à suivre des lueurs d'orage';[131] 'L'interminable pluie, aux carreaux, met une *gaze* à un paysage admirable de verdure'.[132] The 'blanc conflit' of the sonnet might then also be the 'échevèlement d'ondée [aux] carreaux',[133] 'enfui contre la vitre', down which it flows like hair or a garland. These images hover eccentrically around ordinarily solid figures of speech. The conventional word may be jettisoned but its connotations are retained and tied to other images: the absent progenitors here may be 'moire' and 'nappe', applied to rain, and 'ondé' (via 'ondée'), applied to hair or material.[134]

Thus, 'Une dentelle s'abolit . . .' begins with one of those prismatic images that radiate paths of meaning towards letters, words, lines, poems, pages, leaves, sheets (folded to make the leaves),[135] books, bookcases, libraries and the non-existent *Grand Oeuvre* itself, and, from there, towards the rest of the universe: folds, curtains, shrouds, sheets, beds, rooms, tombs, wombs, and so on. Without folding away the relatively boring curtain (which is certainly there among the other coincident objects), 'dentelle' can be seen as a figure of poetic creation in all its aspects. The sonnet joins the long list of Mallarmean poems that open with an image of writing, either explicitly ('vierge vers', 'langage', 'grimoire', 'Mes bouquins', 'plume', 'Ce salut') or figuratively ('le Phénix', 'la Chimère', 'Le temple enseveli',[136] the 'lac dur oublié', 'Le silence . . . d'une moire', 'Cette rose', 'mes diverses flûtes', 'Basse de basalte',[137] 'ronds de fumée'). Another *Sonnet allégorique de lui-même*.

Now that we can send interpretative probes into the poem in several different directions at the same time, it should seem less unyielding or periphrastic. In the 'Jeu suprême' of poetry, the poet weaves verses which, like the threads of a piece of lace, form a 'gouffre central'.[138] Words and their meanings disappear, 'concourant au rythme total, lequel serait le poème tu, aux blancs'.[139] Hence the doubt: will anything be left after the operation? Will poetic language, as in *Hommage* and *Petit Air II*, lose even its virtuality? The 'bed' in which the ideal synthesis or 'troisième terme' might be conceived is eternally absent. The rain on the window, the bindings in the bookcase and the words on the white page indicate only absence – 'comme un blasphème'. More than the Promethean 'creations' of Romantic poets, Mallarmé's actual production of absences (the single, verifiable achievement of any user of language) is a 'blasphemy'. Just as the opening of a book is a violation of its 'reploiement vierge',[140] the self-referential exposure of the poetic process is a 'démontage impie de la fiction et conséquemment du mécanisme littéraire, pour étaler la pièce principale ou rien'.[141] All that results is an 'unanime blanc conflit' – the white pages which face one another like the 'unanime pli' of the fan, the two transparencies of rain and window or the repeated rhymes of the regular sonnet which, in an analogous moment in 'De l'orient passé des temps . . .', literally cancel each other out:

> Mais les rideaux en leurs plis *vagues*
> Cachent des ténèbres les *vagues*
> Mortes, hélas![142]

The image of the garland draws attention to particular semantic strands of the 'dentelle'. It suggests the coordinated spirals of the poetic thyrsus, its complex regularity. Again, it designates the book itself. A 'guirlande', in Littré, is a 'Choix de petites pièces de poésie. Une guirlande poétique'; and also in Mallarmé: 'Mises à part les *Premières Poésies* pour ne les suspendre ici que comme la guirlande d'un pubère hommage à . . . la Muse.'[143] In the ebony room of a library (for example), 'Se tordent dans leur mort des guirlandes célèbres' – poems vaingloriously published 'pour séduire un roi', the traditional patron and addressee of poets ('Quand l'ombre menaça . . .'). The book, in the book, confronts itself, or the poem in the poem. Its conflict is not that of the Romantic text, opposed to a hostile world; everything that happens happens within the text itself.

The 'vitre blême' against which this conflict occurs is the window of the bookcase or, as in the *sonnet en yx*, the frame of the sonnet itself, which may or may not become a window opening onto another dimension. The 'vitre blême' is also the page – the 'papier blême de tant d'audace'[144] – more easily imagined nowadays as a computer screen.

Seen in this literary light, 'flotte', opposed to 'ensevelit', has a negative value, which explains the positive antithesis of the tercets. The disparate elements that form the poem 'float' or vacillate[145] until the poet affixes a seal to them – the seal on a tomb or the rhymes at the end of each verse. The meaning of the poem must be 'buried' in the tomb-tome where its mystery will remain intact. The fact that this has yet to happen is underlined by the rhymes which, so far, have been only *suffisantes* whereas the rhymes of the tercets are rich and even *léonines*.

The quatrains can now be reread as an abstract and concrete description of the poetic game. The scene, on one level, is a library or a bookcase within a library – a 'docte sépulture' containing 'l'or des titres, confrontés à eux-mêmes'.[146] One emptiness contains another. The bookcase is empty, and the absent book contains no bed on which the text can be couched, laid to rest and authenticated.

We now find ourselves back at the critical point of the drama, signposted by the self-absorbing internal rhyme (see pp. 128–9). The phonetic and semantic similarities with the *sonnet en yx* are striking. The 'Mais' of the first tercet, the internal rhymes on *or* and the '(T)elle' that opens the second tercet. But this time, something hopeful is about to happen.

The *Sonnet à Valère Gille* offers a clearly bookish example of this hope extracted from despair, or a more lucid form of despair. The 'Gloire' is simultaneously the glory of the poet, the halo with which the lamp surrounds the reading face and the gilded edges of the page. The key point here is the identification of the poet or reader with the book itself:[147]

> Le beau papier de mon fantôme
> Ensemble sépulcre et linceul
> Vibre d'immortalité, tome,

This is another of Mallarmé's recurrent analogies, which might be traced back to figurative uses of 'lire' or the comparison of human skin to parchment – Hérodiade's nurse with her 'esprit pâli comme un vieux livre ou noir';[148] the flower of 'Las de l'amer repos . . .', grafting itself onto the 'filigrane bleu de l'âme'; Victor Margueritte, urged to sit down at his writing-desk and to 'fixer le fameux papier blanc de notre âme, sous une lampe'.[149]

The point of this brief excursus is to show that the prolongation of the literary images in 'Une dentelle s'abolit . . .' is entirely probable. Gardner Davies thinks that the 'periphrasis', 'chez qui du rêve se dore', denoting the poet's room, 'n'est pas particulièrement heureuse',[150] thereby inviting a reinterpretation. First, is this not the poet (or any poet who gilds himself with dream) rather than his room: 'chez [celui] qui du rêve se dore'? Second, resettled in its multiple contexts, the image looks perfectly happy and even illuminates the obscure analogies of the quatrains. If the gold of bindings and illuminations is that of 'dream' – for example, the dream of the perfect poem as in the *sonnet en yx* – then the cancelling out of opposing elements (rain and window, word and object, both parts of the huge internal rhyme in line 10) is confirmed, buried rather than left to float like linguistic jetsam. The book (or poet) then 'vibrates' like Valère Gille's 'tome' or like the sound-box of a musical instrument – or like a womb. No real birth or creation takes place; the poem has only internal relations and cannot procreate itself. Similarly, in the first sonnet of the *Triptyque* of which this is the third panel, the 'sépulcre' 'Ne s'allume pas d'autre feu / Que la fulgurante console' (i.e. the visible sonnet itself). The book or poem is then 'Ensemble sépulcre et linceul' – like language, emptiness and the veil that conceals its vacuity. However, the *potential* of birth is established: 'le dire, avant tout, rêve et chant, retrouve chez le Poète . . . sa virtualité.'[151] In the 'creux néant musicien' of the text, something sleeps which the act of reading can reveal or rudely awaken: 'Ce pli de sombre dentelle . . . assemble des entrelacs distants où dort un luxe à inventorier.'[152]

The three sonnets examined in this chapter are notably bad examples of the drama of verse, and, for that reason, highly informative. The central thesis of this book might have been more persuasively developed in other ways: for example, by analysing the poems mentioned briefly in the Conclusion as possible subjects of further prosodic readings, or some of the poems that were ransacked for illustrations in this chapter. But this would have meant ignoring an important aspect of the drama.

The reciprocity of the poetic game and the verses that make up the poem is established only intermittently in these sonnets, either because the principle itself is called into question or because the drama is frozen at a particular moment: it begins at the point where it breaks down or fails to begin at all. Perhaps this is what makes these sonnets unusually difficult. In most of Mallarmé's poems, existential despair is the implicit condition of a provisional linguistic optimism, not a helplessness that expresses itself directly in the verse.

Mallarmé's poetry is a counter-image of nineteenth-century fantasies about poetic activity (creation is abolition, the subject is not the subject, the *au-delà* is the pretext). *Hommage à Wagner*, *Petit Air II* and 'Une dentelle s'abolit . . .' are, in turn, counter-images of the poetic process as Mallarmé normally decides to see it, which is why they seem to contradict his critical texts. In prose, he almost never describes the failure of verse, just as his intensely courteous comments on other poets nearly always refer – obliquely if need be – to their Mallarmean virtues.

These poems are reminders that doubt and despair are the black backcloth of the drama, even in the triumphant *Prose pour des Esseintes*. For not only is there a lurking conviction that verse has no transcendent value, but also a more general and nastily infectious malaise:

> ce jeu insensé d'écrire, s'arroger, en vertu d'un doute . . . quelque devoir de tout recréer, avec des réminiscences, pour avérer qu'on est bien là où l'on doit être (parce que, permettez-moi d'exprimer cette appréhension, demeure une incertitude).[153]

8

Un subtil mensonge

'*le poème tu*'[1]

Éventails

Reading Mallarmé, one grows accustomed to seeing tangible truths emerge from the most imaginative operations; it therefore seems almost reasonable to ask whether the poetry he talks about so cheerfully in his critical texts and letters actually exists on the printed page. Are there any verses in his work which lead the drama to something other than the possibility of creation or the production of happy rhymes and pleasant patterns, or are we doomed to disappointment?

The first answer is 'no, it does not exist', for the simple reason that Mallarmé places the limits of poetry at the very beginning of the whole enterprise. All he can then do is represent the starting point in different ways or describe the consequences of any attempt to move beyond it. And this, too, however indirectly or incomprehensibly expressed, is still representation – discourse about discourse which cannot exist. The drama of verse provides a literal and allegorical structure by which these attempts can be suggested without being directly described, but it also engages every element of the poem in the same rehearsal of its initial conditions. The show must not go on.

The second answer is a qualified 'no'. Since, according to Mallarmé, verse is itself the mystery it fails to express, the perfect poem may exist but cannot be directly apprehended. The real question is: if it did exist, would we recognize it? This chapter is devoted to a group of poems which give us the clearest view of our failure to perceive the ideal poem. With patience, they create an enjoyable kind of exasperation by demanding an intellectual reading and then proving its inadequacy; imposing conditions which make it hard to read the poem; seducing, refusing and offering a consolation (or, in extreme critical cases, forcing the victim to agonize over relativity, indeterminacy and what might have been). Just when the prosodic approach seems inapplicable or superfluous, it highlights the extra-linguistic ambitions of the poem, enhances our ability to read it from different angles, and paradoxically prevents us from becoming 'les spectateurs . . . d'un drame sans le pouvoir de gêner même par de la sympathie rien à l'attitude absolue que quelqu'un se fit en face du sort'.[2] In the end, the drama of verse might be seen to come into its own precisely at the moment when every other sort of drama disappears.

Mallarmé wrote twenty-two poems on fans (literally): eighteen quatrains and a distich in the *Vers de circonstance*, a sonnet each for Méry Laurent and Mme Mallarmé (1890 and January 1, 1891), and a poem for Mlle Mallarmé (1884 or earlier) in *Poésies*. As the longest of the fan poems, *Autre éventail de Mademoiselle Mallarmé* provides a focus for the others, though it is in some ways unique in Mallarmé's work.[3]

> O rêveuse, pour que je plonge
> Au pur délice sans chemin,
> Sache, par un subtil mensonge,
> Garder mon aile dans ta main.
>
> Une fraîcheur de crépuscule
> Te vient à chaque battement
> Dont le coup prisonnier recule
> L'horizon délicatement.
>
> Vertige! voici que frissonne
> L'espace comme un grand baiser
> Qui, fou de naître pour personne
> Ne peut jaillir ni s'apaiser.
>
> Sens-tu le paradis farouche
> Ainsi qu'un rire enseveli
> Se couler du coin de ta bouche
> Au fond de l'unanime pli!
>
> Le sceptre des rivages roses
> Stagnants sur les soirs d'or, ce l'est,
> Ce blanc vol fermé que tu poses
> Contre le feu d'un bracelet.

Each quatrain, except perhaps the third (which is the only one with significant variants), could have appeared on its own in the *Vers de circonstance*. Each one consists of a single sentence, as if designed to be written on a separate panel of the fan. The result of this compartmentalized structure is that the poem seems at first to lack the dramatic, dialectical development of Mallarmé's other poems. The impression is reinforced by the slender subject and possibly by prejudices about what constitutes an important theme. *Autre éventail* has the same form as *Prose pour des Esseintes* – octosyllabic quatrains in *rimes croisées* beginning with a feminine rhyme – but the urgent, human interest of the other poem is not much in evidence. The two protagonists are not the poet and a mysterious sister but Mlle Mallarmé and her fan. The speaking voice, at least in the first quatrain, is the fan itself (in the same way that clocks and park benches bear inscriptions in the first person), apparently pursuing a selfish, hedonistic ideal. Can we be expected to join it in its 'pur délice sans chemin' while following the 'chemins' of verse? Instead of tracing a path from hope to despair or *vice versa*, *Autre éventail* merely describes the motion and the physical or visual effects of the fan. Wafted by a hand, placed against the corner of a mouth, then closed and rested on a braceleted arm. In line with Mallarmé's contention that the poetic voicing of an emotion should be treated as a 'simple note dans le chant de la parole',[4] all the elements of a potential human drama – ecstasy, imprisonment, exploration, madness, frustration, laughter, sex, birth and death – are subsumed in the evocation of the fan. *Autre éventail* is like a *metafora di decettione* in which the more trivial or material of the images has taken over. Whatever drama there is is so rarefied and abstract as to be inaccessible by normal means. The mouth itself is silent, its only expression a suspiciously liquid communication, quite possibly undetected by the person herself, just as the reader half-consciously drools over a pleasing sound or image. No doubt the poem is the linguistic residue of vitally important ideas and perceptions, but all that remains of the poet's thought is a self-sufficient image. Moreover, this is obviously what he meant to do: 'Tout mon rêve! une raréfaction des images [the images by means of which we think] en quelques signes comptés un peu comme . . . l'esquissa le divinatoire dessin japonais.'[5] The poem then becomes a mnemonic for something unremembered, unknown or unlearnable.

Yet, as Jean-Pierre Richard suggests in his commentaries on the *Éventails*, each one illustrates an *art poétique*.[6] This can mean two things: a) the poem may not be about very much, but, like any work of art, it implies a certain technique and a set of opinions – which then allows us to salvage some academic data from it; b) it can mean that prosody is the principal, organizing wheel of the machine. Not only can the poem be read as an exercise in the art of symbolic description, it can also be treated as the expression and exemplification of a 'game' – poetic creation symbolized as the art of manipulating a fan. A close thematic reading should in any case produce some sort of prosodic interpretation; there are plenty of clues to lead us back to versification, and, with such a trivial subject, most critics have felt free to read the *Éventails* as poems about poetry or at least as poems which use prosodic images. That may even be the full extent of the poem's reflexivity: the

Éventails as busman's holiday. But if the drama of verse is frozen into a *tableau vivant*, pillaged for images and typical events, that too indicates another dimension to the drama. Not because the whole operation is sent packing as in the *Hommage* to Wagner, but because the drama itself is shown to imply its own dissolution; the poem is its own *raison de ne pas être*. If these poems can be read as active *arts poétiques*, rather than just illustrations of precepts and techniques, they would have to be seen as negative versions of Boileau's style of treatise: demonstrations that the conditions of true poetry are to be found in whatever makes it impossible to write it.

The analogy between fan-waving and the writing of poetry is established so directly in the opening of the *Éventail de Madame Mallarmé* that there is really no reason to be tactful and pretend not to have seen the producer rushing off the stage as the curtain went up:[7]

> Avec comme pour langage
> Rien qu'un battement aux cieux
> Le futur vers se dégage
> Du logis très précieux
>
> Aile tout bas la courrière
> Cet éventail si c'est lui
> Le même par qui derrière
> Toi quelque miroir a lui

The pivotal word, which joins 'verse' and 'language' to the fan, is 'battement'. It appears in all three *Éventails* of *Poésies* – in the second quatrain of Mlle Mallarmé's and in the second quatrain of Méry Laurent's:

> Mais que mon battement délivre
> La touffe par un choc profond
> Cette frigidité se fond
> En du rire de fleurir ivre

'Battement' has three functions. It refers to the waving of the fan which spills out its painted roses as Méry Laurent shakes it in the air. As a metrical term, it refers to the rhythm of a verse: 'la mesure suivant laquelle on bat un vers'.[8] In the two family *Éventails*, it has a third referent – the wing (perhaps implicitly in Méry Laurent's: 'A jeter le ciel en détail').

Like those plastic 3-D pictures found in cereal packets, the central image performs its transformations and remains consistent with its background. Each peripheral item in the image-group (not just the pivotal 'battement') shares elements with all the others. The wing corresponds to the paper panel of a fan or to the whole fan. Seen from another angle, it represents the page of the book on which the poem is printed or the whole book which opens in the hand like a fan – an analogy made explicit in *Étalages*: the book is an 'éventail à la différence près que cette autre aile de papier plus vive'.[9] Tilted differently, the wing is a rhyme that enables the verse to fly. In Mme Mallarmé's *Éventail*, the 'future verse' (announced by its anterior rhyme) is the wing-fan reflected in a mirror: the 'same' fan, just as the rhymes – 'lui' and 'lui' – are spelt the same. (Mallarmé uses exactly the same conceit in at least two other poems: see p. 171). The 'logis très précieux' may refer to the person holding the fan or to the hand that holds it, or it may be used in its figurative sense, 'imagination'. Then again, it may suggest the 'corps de logis': the main part of a building to which the wings ('ailes') are attached – in other words, the body of the verse.[10]

These interconnected images which fan out through the poem also set up connections with other poems. In *Autre éventail*, Mlle Mallarmé is invited by her fan to keep its wing in her hand: 'Sache, par un subtil mensonge, / Garder mon aile dans ta main.' The 'subtle lie' is the sleight of hand that makes the captive fan appear to fly independently. A lesson for the over-exuberant poet of *Petit Air II*. Thanks to the 'subtil mensonge' of prosody – the illusions it creates and deflates at the same time 'under the tissue' of the text[11] – the bird bearing its silent, poetic message appears to take flight but remains under the control of its handler. Hence the paradox that the wing's 'coup prisonnier' is able to push back the horizon, like a fan lowered in front of a face. The association of fan- and bird-handling is reinforced (though this is perhaps not visible to the mind's naked eye) by 'délice' and 'délicatement', both of which have the same etymon: *de-lacire* ('faire tomber dans un lacs'). The wing, like the 'aile-courrière' of Mme Mallarmé, remains 'tout bas', silent, under human control, 'down' on the page.

If read for its apparent subject, *Autre éventail* offers a happy resolution of the drama, or rather a happy state which escapes the ups and downs of the drama: a 'pur délice sans chemin' – a repetitive, rhythmic ecstasy produced by the 'subtil mensonge' of prosody, but which transcends the paths or 'sentiers' of verse. 'Language' that is nothing but a 'battement'. The *art poétique* of the *Éventails* could be said to consist in an attempt to eradicate the subject matter of representational art. Just as the ash of reality in 'Toute l'âme résumée . . .' is to be knocked from the 'skilfully burning' cigar, so the poem is to be kept spotlessly clean: 'Un peu d'invisible cendre / Seule à me rendre chagrin' (*Éventail de Madame Mallarmé*). The invisible remnant of reality (or what seems to be the trivial subject) is the only impurity in the mirror or in the 'reflets réciproques' of the words,[12] which indicate the absence of the things they designate, form their own phonetic, visual or prosodic patterns and, hopefully, conjure up a 'tiers aspect fusible et clair présenté à la divination'[13] which lies far beyond the scope of the present analysis.

More than that, the *Éventails* propose a form of poetry which implies, not just the abolition of reality, but its own disappearance. Like the 'unanime pli' of the closed white pages, the fan is literature purified of its literariness, the ideal poem, written without dirtying the paper or throwing the die: 'Aussi je crois, poète, à mon dommage, qu'y inscrire un distique [on the fan] est de trop'.[14] Poetry, in the *Éventails*, is written 'to its own detriment', which may account for the variety of critical approaches which try to save these poems from themselves. The first verse of Mme Mallarmé's *Éventail*, where the poem seems to dust off any representational language – 'Avec comme pour langage' – would have to be regretted by subject-seeking criticism as a uniquely clumsy opening line, with its prepositions, adverb and abstract noun referring to itself. Instead of admiring the poet for finding the perfect match of message and medium, we should have to pity him for finding the exact opposite. Poetic language tends in the *Éventails* towards poetry without language; lyricism which compacts all experience into 'a few signs'; intellectual poetry with an unintellectual ideal; verses whose referents are their own words, inscribed on a form which Mallarmé associates with 'délicieux illettrés'; literature for the illiterate (again, a point could be made about the gender of the addressees); a highly conscious use of language whose symbolic equivalent has 'pour vertu, mobile, de renouveler l'inconscience du délice sans cause'.[15]

Traditionally, in poems where things are held to be themselves, fans perform a function that should disqualify them from acting as symbols of poetry:

> Lorsqu'une dame, vers sa joue,
> Du mobile éventail secoue
> Les bouts soyeux,
> C'est pour dérober une larme,
> Un sourire, un aveu qui charme,
> A tous les yeux.[16]

Like the tomb-tome, the fan-poem is a paradoxical image. Fans are used to conceal expression. 'Ensemble sépulcre et linceul', the poetic *éventail* is a container for the realities it abolishes and the veil which prevents us from seeing their absence. For all its *approfondissement* of the rules of prosody and grammar, Mallarmé's poetry can be deemed as 'detrimental' to literature as Rimbaud's non-linguistic *dérèglements*. It can especially be considered detrimental to organized reading. Abstractive criticism is forced to work against the grain and to do the dusting in reverse, restoring the ash of reality to the surface of the page.

As the last, abstract refuge of the subject, the drama of verse marks out an area in which poem and abstractive critic can work together. From a different point of view, the *Éventails* provide a good test of the prosodic approach. They contain none of the blatant conceits of the onomastic games, nor the deliberate 'mistakes' of the poems of doubt, nor the attention-grabbing internal rhymes and echoes which convey a strong impression of the poet's intention. Only 'En du rire de fleurir ivre' in *Éventail de Méry Laurent* suggests the sudden blooming of multiple rhymes as the metrical 'battement' 'releases' the elements that form them.

Even when its disappearance or stasis is implied, elements of the drama – as we have been unable not to see – are still present, creating tensions and resolving them, if only to 'renouveler l'inconscience' . . . At the very least, there are several details which, without the drama, could only be interpreted in isolation, smeared with Mallarmean analogies and stuck back on the *éventail*.

The image of poetic flight held in the snare of verse is developed in the second quatrain of *Autre éventail*. The 'battement' gives a 'coup prisonnier', just as the metrical 'battement' or rhythm has its 'coup final': rhyme.[17] But why 'prisonnier'? Like the 'échos esclaves' of 'A la nue accablante tu . . .', rhymes are imprisoned by the constraints of prosody, as Boileau said they should be: 'La rime est une esclave et ne doit qu'obéir.' Mallarmé's rhymes, though enslaved, have the power to push back the horizon, as the enjambment shows: 'Dont le coup prisonnier recule / L'horizon'. Each rhyme, like the shepherd's walking-stick, postulates or introduces a new perspective.

The process is illustrated in the third quatrain. The pocket of air which is alternately pushed away and tugged back by the fan is also the 'frisson' or 'baiser' of rhyme, looking for its 'futur vers' like the isolated verse composed by Méry Laurent. The frustrated 'espace' will eventually find its distant echo in the last word of the poem – 'bracelet' – but for the moment its existence is unjustified. This is the intermediate, worrying stage, between the proposition and the kiss, the initial advance and final consummation.

In earlier versions of the poem, the quatrain began with the words 'Chaste jeu', then 'Vaste jeu'. This is interesting for two reasons. First, 'jeu' emphasizes the connection with the play of verse. Second, since 'chaste' and 'vaste' are semantically disparate, not to say unconnected, we can assume that Mallarmé was looking for a phonetic effect: in this case, an anticipatory half-rhyme (but in the 'wrong' place) for the frustrated 'espace'. In the final version, the phonetic effect is sacrificed for a meaningful pun.[18] 'Vertige', with its echoes of Baudelaire's 'Harmonie du soir' ('Voici venir les temps où, vibrant sur sa tige' rhyming with 'langoureux vertige'), is also a *vers-tige*[19] – which might seem like a Saussurean free-gift were it not for the authoritative confirmation of a variant. In the same quatrain, 'fier de n'être pour personne' was changed to the final 'fou de naître pour personne'. As in *Prose pour des Esseintes* and *Crayonné au théâtre*, the verse is a stalk on which the rhyme, it is hoped, will blossom. The hidden meaning of the word 'Vertige', announcing the flower image at the end of the poem, is a sign of hope; but so is the device itself. Puns and homonyms are implicit rhymes, unrealized but virtual, like the stem awaiting its flower or the air which oscillates in limbo.

This subtle moment of crisis leads at first to the 'unanime pli' of the closed fan, like the 'unanime blanc conflit' of the pages, leaves or sheets in which the mirror-images and repetitions seem to cancel each other out, creating only a stagnant singularity: the flowerless *vers-tige* or, in the final quatrain, the closed fan which is also a flower-stalk or a 'sceptre' – that is, a rhymeless word.

Despite the premature foreclosure of the 'unanime pli', the fourth quatrain establishes the vital connection between human expression and the enclosed poetic system with its inexpressible ideal, or between the hermetic poem and the reader seated in front of the 'écran de feuillets imprimés'.[20] The isolated kiss of the previous quatrain is brought against a mouth by the closed fan, used to conceal or to 'bury' a laugh. The untamed, 'farouche' elements of the poem, the 'paradis' scattered in the air, the skies it hopes to reach,[21] come back under the handler's control – the fan, like the verse, is now an 'aile tendue; mais avec des serres enracinées à vous'.[22]

At the last moment, the crisis of the closed, 'stagnant', ideal work of art reaches a climax. The last quatrain contains two crucial elements of the drama: the only *rime complexe* in the whole poem – *ce l'est-bracelet* – and its only rhymeless word, 'sceptre':

> Le sceptre des rivages roses
> Stagnants sur les soirs d'or, ce l'est,
> Ce blanc vol fermé que tu poses
> Contre le feu d'un bracelet.

The 'sceptre', as several critics have said, stands for a moral quality: the poet's sovereignty. Visually, it represents the closed fan. So much is clear and even conventional. The same dual analogy occurred to the writer of the 'Éventail' entry in William Duckett's *Dictionnaire de conversation à l'usage des dames et des jeunes personnes* (1841) – in the seventeenth century, the fan became 'le sceptre indispensable des femmes élégantes' – and Eileen Souffrin-Le Breton has pointed out several other examples in fan poems quoted by Octave Uzanne in a study of *L'Éventail* published in 1882.[23] In *Autre éventail*, the fan-sceptre is also a flower and its natural setting. The three colours, we happen to know, are those of the fan on which the poem was written – white paper, red ink, gilt edges – but also the colours of a landscape, summed up in the closed fan or flower.[24] The flower in turn is a bird with its wings closed. The panorama is condensed into a thin line. As in Mallarmé's poems, minimalism increases in proportion to the complexity it implies.

The prosodic-metaphysical implications of the fact that 'sceptre' is a rhymeless word can best be described and confirmed by analogy with the prose poem, *Le Nénuphar blanc*, written shortly after *Autre éventail* in 1885. In his mind, the poet plucks a lily from the 'végétations dormantes' of the riverbank (cf. the 'rivages . . . stagnants') as an imaginary memento of the 'site' where he heard a woman's step. The flower, being 'closed', envelops in its hollow whiteness 'un rien, fait de songes intacts',[25] like the 'mot intact et nul de la songerie' which the 'battements' of the fan bring to the lips.[26] The lily is then an imaginary 'trophy' of the imagined ideal, inexplicit enough not to destroy 'le délice empreint de généralité'. Like the sceptre of *Autre éventail* – the 'blanc vol fermé' held in the hand – the lily is 'un noble oeuf de cygne, tel que n'en jaillira le vol'. Flight so purely potential as to be an egg. In the same way, the whole poem is the 'témoin' of an 'intact' ideal which would vanish if expressed, hatched or launched into the air. The fan represents a delicate, hypothetical point of balance between the bird of *Petit Air II* and the swan of 'Le vierge, le vivace . . .'. Neither trapped nor freed but held in an unsustainable equilibrium.

As a purely prosodic reading would suggest without reference to any thematic meaning, 'sceptre' indicates the futility of verse which, like the 'grand baiser' of the air, can neither reach the ideal sky nor find its transcendental 'délice sans chemin' in silence.

The sceptre plays a similar role in two other *Éventails*, both in the *Vers de circonstance*. There, however, its threat is defused. In both the circumstantial *Éventails*, phonetic repetitions incorporate the 'peremptory' word into the body of the verse, performing the function Mallarmé attributes to alliteration: 'effort magistral de l'Imagination désireuse . . . d'établir un lien entre [les spectacles du monde] et la parole chargée de les exprimer'.[27] The contrasting *Vers de circonstance* emphasize the 'rhymelessness' of the sceptre in *Autre éventail*:

> Fermé, je suis le sceptre aux doigts
> ɛʀ   ə s ɛptʀ
> Et, contente de cet empire,
>   ə ə sɛt   pʀ
> Ne m'ouvrez, aile, si je dois
> Dissimuler votre sourire.[28]

> Toujours ce sceptre où vous êtes
>   sə s ɛptʀ   et
> Bal, théâtre, hier, demain
> t   tʀ   ɛʀ
> Donne le signal de fêtes
>   et
> Sur un voeu de votre main.[29]
>   tʀ

This is a typical effect of rhymeless words in Mallarmé's poetry. The rhymeless virus enters the poem, and immediately half-rhymes and echoes flock around it like antibodies:

D'enfoncer le cristal par le *monstre* insulté.
    ɔ̃ s   ʀst   ɔ̃ stʀ

Comme mourir *pourpre* la roue.
    u ʀʀ u ʀ ʀ   ʀu

Ce fruit à quelque arbre confit
s   f i   f i
Cueilli par un *sylphe* ou tout comme.[30]
    i   si f

In a quatrain for the Eugène Manets, a rhymeless word is made to 'rhyme' with two 'difficult' rhymes:

Vous me prêtâtes une ouïe
Fameuse et le *temple*; si du
Soir la *pompe* est évanouie
En voici l'*humble* résidu.[31]

In 'Tout Orgueil . . .', an alternative strategy is used. The *u* and *l* of the rhymeless 'sépulcre' recur in the same position (at the third syllable) as if trying to make it rhyme (see also, on the 'sépulcre' of *Prose pour des Esseintes*, p. 162):

3
11   Le *sépulcre* de désaveu,
      ə s yl
13   Ne s'allume pas d'autre feu
      ə s ly
14   Que la fulgurante console.
      ə   yl

In *Autre éventail*, as the theme demands, 'sceptre' remains 'intact', enclosed in itself like the fan, the flower or the egg. Yet the poem does end with a synthesizing *rime complexe*, which brings us back to an image of the poet's control: the bracelet which decorates and 'imprisons' the arm. 'Feu' is a word Mallarmé sometimes applies to rhyme or to words in a verse;[32] here, it is applied to the bracelet which is itself the rhyme.

Like the 'sceptre', the poem remains intact, self-sufficient, closed, stagnant and crepuscular; but, juxtaposed with something outside itself, by being manipulated or read, it conveys its silent message – or so, ironically, the poem tells us.

Mallarmé's *Éventails* can be seen as a return to the 'extase pure' of 'Las de l'amer repos . . .'. The drama of verse is used to create a reflexivity and self-sufficiency in keeping with the aesthetic ideal of the 'illiterate' fan: 'un chant pur presque de tout écrit, où fulgure le mot'.[33] At the same time, it provides a dramatic, abstract framework for the description of the fan, like a template that will be discarded before the finished work is displayed. This is what distinguishes *Autre éventail* from the 'Chinese' depiction in the second part of 'Las de l'amer repos . . .'. The painted landscape is an explicit example of the poet's solution to a directly stated emotional and philosophical problem. In *Autre éventail*, the original cause is implicit. It contributes only an impression of purposefulness (with no obvious purpose) and didacticism (without axioms or precepts).

Autre éventail is the finest and first example of how Mallarmé's later poems invite us to read them against the grain and then emerge triumphantly intact, unless we try to rip the adult flower from the bud. The reflexivity of these poems, which is often alluded to quite directly, inevitably introduces an unusual degree of abstraction and self-consciousness into the process of reading. But, barring obsessional convictions, the subjective effect of this is to disengage the poem (or most of it) from the abstract, philosophical *armature* it implies. The 'logic' of the poem, in the final despairing or relaxed analysis, may be simply its musicality – a 'chiffration mélodique tue, de ces motifs qui composent une logique, avec nos fibres';[34] or its pictorial motifs, like the 'fraîcheur de crépuscule' suggesting both the physical sensation and the shadow cast by the fan on the young woman's face.[35] These things are best left to individual sensibilities. Any systematic approach is sooner or later inappropriate or obtrusive. After all the intellectual probing it seems to demand, the poem sends us back to our own reading: 'le va-et-vient successif incessant du regard, une ligne finie, à la suivante, pour recommencer'.[36] Though by this time it may be far too late: 'je me figure que les vers n'ont aucun sens s'ils ne frappent pas tout de suite et n'éveillent une divination chez qui les lit; alors il ne faut pas les chercher, s'évanouissant de plus en plus.'[37]

Those elements referred to as the drama of verse which, on one level, 'explain' the poem, are shown, by the optical illusion of reflexivity, to be themselves a part of the illusion – a 'mensonge *subtil*': etymologically, 'under the tissue' or weave of the text, like the ribs of the fan, the body of the dancer[38] or the 'subtil secret des pieds [sous] les dentelles d'une jupe'.[39] But the drama of verse, as much as any extraneous theory, helps to account for that consistent incomprehensibility and possibility of understanding which allowed Mallarmé to be famous without suffering the effects of familiarity and informed expectations, to exercise his greatest influence through misunderstandings, and, in effect, to write the same poem over and over again for thirty years.

9

Un jeu qui confirme la fiction

'un coup d'état . . . spirituel'[1]

Prose pour des Esseintes

Prose pour des Esseintes, Mallarmé's famously obscure celebration of lucidity, contains elements of all the poems studied in the previous chapters. These fifty-six octosyllabic lines give the drama of verse its longest, most complete performance, despite the fact that the poem probably dates from 1884[2] – or perhaps for that very reason. *Prose* confirms the fundamental consistency of Mallarmé's poetics, but it also shows that the few principles which form its early foundations became the basis of more complex developments which refine or contradict their substructure. The drama is seen here in its Golden Age – and so are Mallarmé's astounding ambitions for it. In retrospect, the other poems can now be seen as fragments, variations or, in view of the criteria established in *Prose*, failures.

    The following pages are not an all-out attempt to explain everything in the poem – for several reasons. *Prose* has attracted not only the dogmatic and the divinely inspired but also some excellent textual critics, and it would be silly to reformulate insights that can be found elsewhere in their pristine form (though, naturally, I have made full use of them).[3] Second, even after so many commentaries, the poem gives every sign of being inexhaustible. The title in its liturgical sense may allude to des Esseintes's predilection for the *laudi spirituali* of the Renaissance and the plain chant of the Middle Ages – 'hymne permanente élancée depuis des siècles vers le Très-Haut' (like the 'hymne des coeurs spirituels'); but it may also refer to itself as an example of des Esseintes's ideal prose poem, an ideal suggested to him by his reading of Mallarmé's prose poems: 'un roman concentré en quelques phrases [où] les mots choisis seraient tellement impermutables qu'ils suppléeraient à tous les autres; l'adjectif posé d'une si ingénieuse et d'une si définitive façon qu'il ne pourrait être légalement dépossédé de sa place, ouvrirait de telles perspectives que le lecteur pourrait rêver, pendant des semaines entières, sur son sens, tout à la fois précis et multiple.'[4] Third, the idea is to display the drama of verse as enacted in the poem without charting every secondary path. The conclusions obtained by this partial method can be compared to those reached by other routes, and their broad agreement can be taken as a test, either of this reading or of others. The affirmative present is used for the sake of convenience and concision; the argument should be sprinkled with 'for example's and 'might be's, but not too many: the prosodic thread pulls in all the others far more efficiently than any thematic motif, and there are several parts of the poem, perhaps even the poem as a whole, which would retain their surface obscurity without a prosodic reading.

Neither is this supposed to be the one and only set of conclusions that can be reached by prosodic paths. Whatever the particular conclusions, I hope it gives some idea of the method's virtues. The drama of verse should make it possible to rescue the poem, not from its own difficulties, but from the sort of erudition that presupposes an omniscient poet, ignores Mallarmé's refusal to indulge in arcane historical allusion, forgets that these poems are 'manifestations of an art that uses language', and probably has a dispiriting effect on readers who fail to realize that, in the face of such infinities, there is not as much difference between 'experts' and 'beginners' as one would like.[5] Anything in the following pages that looks like erudition is an attempt to establish usage, not to 'fourbir jusqu'à une transparence l'allusion'.[6] Mallarmé was one of the great communicators of his time, and *Prose* itself is partly the story of a heroic compromise between the ecstatic perception of an ideal and its imperfect expression, the discovery of a mystery and the establishment of a ritual by means of which it can be communicated to a congregation. *Prose*, as Cohn has pointed out, may be a typically self-deprecating title, in contrast with the later unversified 'Poème', *Un coup de Dés:*[7] a straightforward discourse or *prosa oratio*, a poem which, after all, was published in a well-known magazine and several of whose uninterpretable verses have made their way into quotation dictionaries. It may also be a typically messianic title, proclaiming the poet's function as the author of new religious texts.

Equipped with an authoritative guiding principle, we should be able, not to concoct the ultimate crib, but to derive from *Prose* a more lasting pleasure than Mallarmé's maid who, entering the salon during the recital of a piano piece by Schumann, 'trouve cela beau parce qu'elle n'est pas rebelle à l'harmonie des accords'.[8] Like *Igitur*, *Prose* is clearly not 'dénuée absolument de signification pour tout le monde', though the pleasure we experience may not be quite the same as the joy of total understanding: when the passing reader extracts a satisfactory interpretation and gets his money's worth, 'Il croit comprendre, et, selon le mot du Maître, *cela n'en est que plus sinistre*'.[9]

> Hyperbole! de ma mémoire
> Triomphalement ne sais-tu

Te lever, aujourd'hui grimoire
Dans un livre de fer vêtu:

5   Car j'installe, par la science,
       L'hymne des coeurs spirituels
       En l'oeuvre de ma patience,
       Atlas, herbiers et rituels.

In the first published version, these two stanzas were separated from the others by a small dash. They form an introduction or invocation. The subject of the poem is to be the composition of the poem. Will it be successful or not? 'Grimoire', 'mémoire' and 'triomphal(ement)' bring to mind the inauspicious *Hommage* to Wagner, where the spell-book ended up in the wardrobe. Here, it is bound in a 'livre de fer', iron being the usual emblem of an unpoetic age but also, in this context, the clasps of an ancient book. The victory will apparently not be easy. Something of the familiar tone of Baudelaire's 'La Muse malade' might be detected.

'Hyperbole' may be slow in rising, but the poet has optimistically gone ahead with the preparations. The 'hymn of spiritual hearts' is to be 'installed' in his work by means of 'science', which appears to be represented here by codified texts: 'Atlas, herbiers et rituels'. These texts are to the realities of the poem – sky, paths, flowers, 'exaltation' – what prosody is to the poetry itself. The opposition of conscious, even crudely mechanical craft and natural inspiration is familiar from other poems, especially the *Éventails* and *Le Pitre châtié*. 'Hyperbole', springing from the poet's memory, is to be the catalyst that will make the operation possible.

Hope, it seems – once we start to read the poem as a poem – is justified. The gigantic rhymes which so vividly typify the whole work have already begun to sprout. *Mémoire-grimoire* is perhaps not very remarkable, and *sais-tu-vêtu* is one of only four *rimes suffisantes* (depending on pronunciation) in a poem in which the average number of matching phonemes per rhyme is four;* but then, in the second stanza, the rhymes begin to perform as energetically as in the *Vers de circonstance*: la *science-patience* and *spirituels-rituels* have five and six identical phonemes respectively. The grimoire is already taking over, and, to take a worm's eye view of the words, it appears to have infiltrated other parts of the verse as well. 'Hymne' is practically a rhymeless word (it rhymes only with 'médimne');[10] but it picks up the first two letters of the poem and introduces one of those promising, suggestive homonyms which act as self-contained rhymes. 'Hymne' would normally be associated with 'choeurs' rather than 'coeurs'. A hypothetical listener would almost certainly hear 'choeurs', just as 'vers' in *Salut* would have been interpreted by

---

* The others are *loin-soin*, *pas-pas* and *rie-Pulchérie*, though the last is a special case (see p. 176).

its original audience as 'verre'. In the early poem, *Pan*, Mallarmé used the same pun: the 'coeurs' of the flowers mingle with the 'choeurs' of the church with their 'hymnes moroses', 'coeurs' and 'choeurs' being placed at the rhyme. These rhymes and echoes are in themselves evidence of a 'rituel' (a book which gives the prescribed order in which rites are to be performed) – a 'rituel' that is 'spirituel' in both senses of the word.

There are also other signs that the *grimoire* is active and that the poem, while describing 'real' events and intentions, is also performing its own self-referential mysteries. Just as atlases and herbaria apparently have some poetic virtue, so dictionaries, for Mallarmé, are also 'grimoires'. What we generally think of as the purely artificial convenience of alphabetical order can reveal the mysterious, primal interrelations of words. Spelling is part of the poet's 'fonds'. So, in this case, the poet 'scientifically' introduces subtle allusions to the essential components of the work: verse and rhyme. Several examples of allusions to *vers* are given in this book (see p. 91). The main point to remember is that these allusions do not necessarily require any semantic or etymological authority. The title of the article, *Averses ou Critique*, for instance, contained a word that would probably have passed unnoticed had the title not been changed to *Crise de vers*. *Averses* and *vers*, for the traditional scholarly mind, have only the most tenuous connection: one comes from *versare*, the other from *vertere*. Mallarmé is not the only nineteenth-century poet to make a meal of such coincidences (Baudelaire's *verre/vers* in 'Le Flacon' or 'vers' as verses and worms in 'Le Soleil' are well-known examples), but he is unusual in attaching precise philosophical connotations to them. In *Prose*, the last three letters of 'lever', coming before a vowel, can be pronounced VƐR.* (The earlier version had the same letters, reversed, in 'ne rêves-tu'.) 'Ver(s)' then forms two anagrammatical rhymes and one *rime suffisante* with the verse that follows:

> Te le*ver*, aujourd'hui grimoire
> Dans un li*vre* de *fer* vêtu:

These graphic correspondences, for Mallarmé, come, precisely, from the 'grimoire' – the collective, ancient legacy of language: 'l'ingénuité de notre fonds, ce legs, l'orthographe, des antiques grimoires'.[11] There, in the material, impractical areas of language, the legacy of ancient *grimoires*, lie its mysteries and its real effectiveness: 'une secrète diction confusément indiquée par l'orthographe et qui concourt mystérieusement au signe pur général qui doit marquer le vers.'[12] Significantly, the 'grimoire' itself contains another

---

* The first rhyme of Baudelaire's 'La Cloche fêlée', so often cited as an aesthetic sin, actually rhymes both aurally and visually: 'Il est amer et doux, pendant les nuits *d'hiver*, / D'écouter, près du feu qui palpite et qui fume, / Les souvenirs lointains lentement *s'élever* / Au bruit des carillons qui chantent dans la brume.' See also, above, p. 24.

prosodic motif: *rime* (or *rythme*), whose letters and sounds are also present in 'Hyperbole', 'mémoire', 'Triomphalement', 'hymne', 'spirituels' and 'rituels'. The last two words also refer semantically to the idea that the twenty-four letters of the alphabet, arranged in verse, imply notions that are 'au-delà de l'ordinaire atteinte': 'telle rénovation de *rites* et de *rimes*';[13] 'le vers, système agencé comme un *spirituel* zodiaque'.[14] The allusions to magic and religion are therefore ironic and potentially misleading: once the philosophical premise is accepted, these games are signs of a deliberately pragmatic approach to language, not a frantic grasping after mystical evidence. The mysteries of language, for the time being, can only be guessed at, glimpsed in the writings of great poets; but one day, 'la Science, possédant le vaste répertoire des idiomes jamais parlés sur la terre, écrira l'histoire des lettres de l'alphabet à travers tous les âges et quelle était presque leur absolue signification'.[15] A glimpse of the ideal future (now a little closer) from which Mallarmé's poetics is retrospectively extrapolated.

Verse makes it possible to analyse, manipulate and communicate these mysteries. 'Hyperbole' itself, as the necessary main-spring, associated with the *grimoire*, can be identified (among other things) with rhyme. First in its rhetorical sense: rhyme amplifies similarities and 'exaggerates' by postulating connections between semantically dissimilar words like 'spirituels' and 'rituels'. Rhymes like the eight-phoneme *désir, Idées-des iridées*, which holds enough phonetic material for two *rimes riches* and one *rime suffisante*, are 'hyperbolic' because of their size and because, as the poet's 'sister' will suggest, they represent a distortion of normal realities. Second, etymologically, 'hyperbole' points to the fact that verses are thrown or projected beyond themselves by rhyme. The image is related to the smoke-rings of 'Toute l'âme résumée . . .' and the walking-stick and 'pas futur' of *Hommage*. Two similar elements, placed in relation to one another, project a third element which contains them both but transcends them by the operation it performs. 'Parole' comes from *parabola*. Rhyme, on the other hand, is a super-word, a *hyper(par)ole*, not a parallel but a transcendence. The mathematical sense of 'hyperbole' might then provide an abstract model for the functioning of rhyme:

> Courbe telle qu'en menant d'un quelconque de ses points des rayons à deux points fixes nommés foyers, la différence de ces rayons est toujours la même. [L'hyperbole] est formée de deux branches indéfiniment ouvertes et se tournant mutuellement leur convexité.   (Littré)

The key elements are the two lines that form a single figure and the two fixed points that define it – the 'foyers'. The idea of a mathematical operation which 'magically' establishes a pattern or unity is present in most of Mallarmé's definitions of rhyme (the connection is metaphorical or, optimistically, archetypal, and calls for no great mathematical knowledge): 'équilibre momentané et double à la façon du vol, identité de deux fragments constitutifs remémorée extérieurement par une parité dans la consonance';[16] or the magic circle which is constantly opened and closed by rhyme.[17] The hyperbola, with its looping *jaillissement* and reversion, might be taken as the blueprint of a successful poem. In 'La chevelure vol . . .', the 'vol' of verse is joined to the image of a 'foyer', which, in view of the hyperbola, can be given, along with its usual meaning, its geometrical sense. 'Le foyer d'une ellipse, d'une hyperbole, d'une parabole, le point ou les points où se réunissent et d'où partent les rayons vecteurs':

> La chevelure vol d'une flamme à l'extrême
> Occident de désirs pour la tout éployer
> Se pose (je dirais mourir un diadème)
> Vers le front couronné son ancien foyer

The paradox of rhyme is that, in order to be fully deployed, it must return to its starting point. This is one of the ways in which the drama of verse and the ritual of rhyme reenact the trajectory of the sun: 'Le soleil que sa halte / Surnaturelle exalte / Aussitôt redescend / Incandescent'.

Precisely what role is Hyperbole called on to play in *Prose*? Like rhyme, it will be asked to provide a poetic 'name', to define something undefined – as the earlier version suggested:

> Indéfinissable, ô Mémoire,
> Par ce midi, ne rêves-tu
> L'Hyperbole, aujourd'hui grimoire
> Dans un livre de fer vêtu?

'Trouble' enters the poem in stanza 4 when the 'site' is said to bear no name that is cited by the gold of Summer's trumpet. The problem is one of naming, and a solution of sorts is supplied at the end, as we shall see, by rhyme in its most hyperbolic form: 'ce nom: Pulchérie!' This name, noun or rhyme may represent the final triumph of 'Hyperbole', projecting itself from the initial *i*. But then there seems to be another, pre-emptive triumph in the word 'Anastase!' – perhaps the other 'foyer' of Hyperbole, to which it is connected semantically but not phonetically. Could it be that the poem has more than one conclusion? Is this supposed to be tragedy or comedy, a destination or a crossroads?

>   Nous promenions notre visage
> 10   (Nous fûmes deux, je le maintiens)
>   Sur maints charmes de paysage,
>   O soeur, y comparant les tiens.

The poetic adventure proper now begins. The pointless question which the prosodic reading will allow us not to ask is: who is the 'sister' or, as she is later called, the 'child'?[18] Candidates have included Méry Laurent, Memory, Hyperbole, Patience, Life, Mallarmé's reader, members of his family, including his sister Maria, who died in 1857 and who presumably announces her own resurrection at the end. A sister in the religious sense has not been proposed, which is surprising considering the spiritual rituals; nor has it been pointed out that 'Soeur' is the title by which kings address their queens when writing to them (Littré). This might account for the royal 'we' in line 9 – Man as king of creation? – except that one would have to assume that the king had mistaken a linguistic convention for a psychological fact: 'Nous fûmes deux, je le maintiens'.

Anyone who has agonized over this question owes a debt of gratitude to Malcolm Bowie, who first observed that the 'soeur' is 'a complex presence', that she should be viewed in the light of her several contexts, and that 'such shifts and fusions of identity are an important source of tension in the poem'.[19] If something more precise is wanted, Cohn's interpretation has the merit of sticking closely to what is actually said: the sister is 'the woman principle in the poet's self and cosmos', representing, ironically enough, sympathetic common sense and sanity – 'sensée et tendre'.[20]

In the context of the third stanza, the 'soeur' can be described in the abstract terms the poem implies. The sister is one element of a pair that forms a new unity. Singular and plural are fused in the phrase 'notre visage', and the following line stresses that 'notre' is indeed a plural: 'Nous fûmes deux'. The poet and his sister, whose 'charms' (from *carmen*: song) are compared to those of the landscape, are therefore analogous to rhyme, which is also a dual entity – and which also consists of masculine and feminine.

This is not to say that the sister *is* rhyme. She and her relations with the poet, and then the relations of the couple with the outside world, are representative of an archetypal process. In the same way, the rising and setting of the sun is not a symbol of rhyme any more than the functioning of rhyme is a symbol of the 'drame solaire'. Remembering that the ultimate referent is missing or implied should prevent us from seeing one of its images as the 'true subject' of the poem.

The tangible, definable reality here is verse itself, and its analogies with what we know of the sister can be usefully established.

First, the synthesis of poet and sister is reflected in the enormous rhymes, many of which, as Bowie notes, enact the fusion of two separate elements: 'de visions' becomes 'devisions', 'de voir' 'devoir', 'par chemins' 'parchemins'. The reaction of poet and sister to the blooming of the huge flowers and the rhymes that represent them (or which are represented by the flowers) is revealing: 'Sans que nous en devisions' – with etymological connotations of 'division'. Analysis is unnecessary; the synthesis is there, ready-made. The same notion of completeness is conveyed by another striking peculiarity of the rhymes in *Prose pour des Esseintes*. The rhyme-endings, without exception, are graphically identical. The phonetic identity of each rhyme is stressed by its visual identity. *Prose* can be contrasted in this respect with *Toast funèbre* in which many of the rhymes have disparate, Banvillesque endings: *suffire-porphyre*, *muet-transmuait*, *dits-jadis*, *Terre-s'altère*, *nom-non*, etc. In *Prose*, the rhymes not only sound the same, they look the same. This visual uniformity is quite unusual in Mallarmé's poetry and was certainly a deliberate effect. In the whole of *Poésies* (fifty-seven poems counting the *Chansons bas* as one), only eight poems contain no visually disparate rhymes; and the longest of these poems have only seven rhyme pairs. (*Prose* has twenty-eight.)*

The second prosodic feature that bears analogy with the poet-sister relationship is the comparison of the sister's 'charms' to those of the landscape. Two things combined are placed in relation to a third reality. The two things may be rhymes or they may be the poet and something else – for example, his art. Typically, Mallarmé describes the act of writing poetry as the collaboration of a couple: the clown and his muse, the fan and the hand, the bird and the handler, the shepherd and his stick, the cigar and the smoker, the kiss. The closest equivalent to the poet and sister of *Prose* is probably the Faun and his pipes, an instrument which is also a double unity, a 'jonc vaste et jumeau'. The player and his instrument then become a plural being in turn: 'notre chant crédule', like 'notre visage'. This song then institutes relations between itself and the outside world: 'confusions' are to be established between 'la beauté d'alentour' and 'notre chant crédule'. In *Prose*, the action is defined by the verb 'comparer', which can be taken in its older sense of 'equate': 'mettre de pair avec', 'égaler à'. The theme is that of a traditional *galanterie* – 'Shall I compare thee to a summer's day? . . .' But the process is also that of verse, projecting lines from its dual 'foyers' to form a hyperbolic version of itself in a different dimension: 'Quelque symétrie, parallèlement, qui, de la situation des vers en la pièce . . . vole, outre le volume, à plusieurs inscrivant, eux, sur l'espace spirituel, le paraphe amplifié du génie, anonyme et parfait comme une existence d'art.'[21]

> L'ère d'autorité se trouble
> Lorsque, sans nul motif, on dit
> De ce midi que notre double
> Inconscience approfondit
>
> Que, sol des cent iris, son site,
> Ils savent s'il a bien été,

15

---

* The same holds true for the earlier version, the only different rhyme being *tendre-rendre* (instead of *entendre*).

> Ne porte pas de nom que cite
> 20   L'or de la trompette d'Été.

This is where the trouble begins. From now on, the nameless 'site' will be the object of the operation. In this Garden of Eden, something has not been named. The poet's god-like task will be to create for it 'le mystère d'un nom': this is the duty (the word 'devoir' will appear in the eighth stanza) that Mallarmé associates with Gautier in *Toast funèbre*, 'le devoir / Idéal que nous font les jardins de cet astre', and the theme of so many of his poems, including most of the *Vers de circonstance*. The name is produced, of course, not by simply consulting a dictionary, but by practising the art of verse, an activity which is a form of 'inconscience'[22] or partly subconscious activity, drawing not on conventional, pragmatic wisdom, but on the archetypes inherent in verse: 'Le vers qui de plusieurs vocables refait un mot total, neuf, étranger à la langue et comme incantatoire.' Will verse be equal to the challenge implied by the first word of the earlier version: 'Indéfinissable'? For that matter, will the problem itself be clearly defined?

Exactly whose 'site' or, in the last stanza, 'sépulcre' this is, is another red herring, at least for the moment. The emphasis at first is on the author – or his quality: 'autorité' – and his ability (or rather, the ability of author and art combined) to produce an adequate, poetic expression of reality and thus transpose it onto a spiritual plane. The problem can be reduced for the sake of argument to the most basic problem of expression. Baudelaire's essay on Gautier mentions a very similar situation:

> Ce fut justement à propos des dictionnaires qu'il ajouta *'que l'écrivain qui ne savait pas tout dire*, celui qu'une idée si étrange, si subtile qu'on la supposât, si imprévue, tombant comme une pierre de la lune, *prenait au dépourvu et sans matériel pour lui donner corps, n'était pas un écrivain'*.[23]

For Mallarmé, the problem of finding a name casts doubt not just on the writer's skill, but – something potentially far more catastrophic – on the art he practises. 'Ere' may refer to his poetic sovereignty, the writer's 'reign'; but in its etymon, *aera* (number), it also refers to the mechanical, arithmetical nature of his art, the poetic 'air'. In effect, this is a practical problem with a calculable solution: the site is marked by a hundred irises; the place or time is 'midi'; 'multiple' lilies grow on the stems; 'atlas', 'herbiers' and 'rituels' are finite works of reference; 'hyperbole' is a geometrical figure; and the poem is written in octosyllabic lines. Verse itself is a 'numérateur'.[24] The problem of namelessness is exacerbated by the fact that the very statement that reveals it is somehow detached from these arithmetical operations: 'sans nul motif'. The very gratuitousness of the act is troubling – and not only that: there is no 'motif' to suggest a pattern. The essential component of versification is missing: 'l'acte poétique consiste à voir soudain qu'une idée se fractionne en un nombre de *motifs* égaux par valeur et à les grouper: ils riment.'[25] Rhyme is a 'proof' that one reality corresponds to another, that 'le cri possède un écho – des *motifs* de même jeu s'équilibreront, balancés, à distance'.[26] These prosodic motifs which can be heard and seen on the page are also the 'purs motifs rythmiques de l'être',[27] so that the technical, professional dilemma is also an existential and metaphysical one: 'Toute âme est une mélodie, qu'il s'agit de renouer.'[28] In this case, the process of 'comparison' or equating has failed to turn up a poetic equivalent. The integrity of verse is called into question by an exceptional reality – or perhaps just by reality itself, described in *La Déclaration foraine* as 'une vociération . . . dans tous sens à la fois et sans motif'.

It now seems appropriate to ask after the nature of this troubling reality. A clue is provided by the end of the poem, where line 19 – 'Ne *porte* pas de *nom*' – is echoed by line 55: 'De *porter* ce *nom*: Pulchérie!' The subject of line 55 is the 'sépulcre' – presumably, therefore, the 'site' or resting-place of the unnamed 'il' who did indeed exist ('Ils savent s'il a bien été'). We might at this point send down a diver from the mother-ship of prosody into the seas of intertextuality. The disturbing 'sépulcre' whose name is not cited by the gold of Summer's trumpet brings to mind the old theme of Death in the midst of Life and Beauty: *Et in Arcadia ego*. The 'island' of *Prose* is like the Island of Cythaera in Baudelaire's poem. The island paradise that contains a rotting corpse: 'Dans ton île, ô Vénus! je n'ai trouvé debout / Qu'un gibet symbolique où pendait mon image . . .'. We can then go on to note that the same *topos* is associated with the absence of a name, without inferring any erudite allusion. At the time, this is simply general literary knowledge:

> La mort ne nous laisse pas assez de corps pour occuper quelque place, et on ne voit là que les tombeaux qui fassent quelque figure. Notre chair change bientôt de nature: notre corps prend un autre nom; même celui de cadavre, dit Tertullien, parce qu'il nous montre encore quelque forme humaine, ne lui demeure pas longtemps: il devient un je ne sais quoi, *qui n'a plus de nom dans aucune langue, tant il est vrai que tout meurt en lui, jusqu'à ces termes funèbres par lesquels on exprimait ses malheureux restes.*[29]

Bossuet took his text from Ecclesiastes, via Tertullian, where the nameless corpse and the sun recall the nameless grave and the 'trompette d'Été' of *Prose*:*

> Car c'est en vain qu'il est venu au monde, il s'en retournera dans les ténèbres, et son nom sera enseveli dans l'oubli.
>
> Il n'a point vu le soleil, et n'a point connu la différence du bien et du mal.[30]

---

* Cf. similar solar images in *Le Pitre châtié* ('Hilare or de cymbale') and *Symphonie littéraire* ('de rayons purs contournés en trompettes').

Pursuing the biblical connotations, the trumpet and the namelessness (or rather, the fact that its name, if it has one, is not cited by the trumpet) may be an allusion to the Apocalypse: those whose names are inscribed in the Book of Life will not be saved when the Last Trump sounds, the trumpet that announces Resurrection ('Anastase').[31] The biblical reading also fits the earlier version: 'Ne porte pas de nom que cite / Entre tous ses fastes, l'Été.' 'Fastes' are the 'registres publics contenant le récit des faits mémorables'; 'monuments écrits qui conservent le souvenir et la suite des événements' (Littré). The trumpet is that of poetry. The 'fastes' are the 'éternels parchemins' on which, in the end, the word 'Anastase!' – and not the name 'Pulchérie!' – will be engraved. (The 'fastes', incidentally, also point forward to the final, earthly destiny of the drama of verse; but that will have to wait until the end of the chapter.)

These thematic motifs which are active on the surface of the poem are entirely consistent with its underlying material and metaphorical structure; in fact, it is only the prosodic structure that shows up their complete coherence. The fact that Christian symbolism is devalued – or revalued – by its inscription in an atheist philosophy[32] is already a sign of its purely relative importance. Its 'meanings' are not the poem's 'last word' but one of its functions. If we cling to these meanings or mistake their importance, the poem will probably seem like a series of distractions from something which has yet to be identified or which may be unidentifiable.

Without returning immediately to the physical, prosodic realities, the metaphorical threads of the poem can also be attached to verse. The trumpet, as an audible sign of triumph, is often used – not just by Mallarmé – as an image of rhyme. Rich rhymes are 'un bruit de trompette qui couvre le sens'; rhyme is an 'écho qui prend . . . l'éclat de la trompette'; for Banville, rhyme 'résonne comme un clairon'.[33] Typically, Mallarmé teases every last strand of comparability from the image. Describing his vision of *Les Fleurs du Mal*, he places it alongside three other images of rhyme – wings, cymbals and thunder: 'des anges . . . chantent leur extase en s'accompagnant de harpes imitant leurs ailes, de cymbales d'or natif, de rayons purs contournés en trompettes, et de tambourins où résonne la virginité des jeunes tonnerres.'[34] Each verse is a trumpet in sound and, with a little synaesthetic imagination, shape. 'Contournés' refers to the etymon of *verse*; and the 'rayons' which are literally twisted together are also the 'rayons' that form the hyperbola.

The prosodic realities confirm the metaphor. The trumpet of rhyme has no name for the site, for a perfectly verifiable and unmetaphorical reason: 'sépulcre' has no rhyme. This site, both prosodically and thematically, is the exceptional element that threatens to remain 'péremptoirement' and to nullify the poet's 'science'. Which then explains the extraordinary, almost ludicrous accumulation of sibilants: 'Inconscience . . . sol des cent iris, son site, / Ils savent s'il a bien été.' These are the emblematic *si*'s and *is*'s signifying an attempt by verse to assimilate every reality, to reestablish unity and to heal the rift between language and the world, or to prove that, from a superior point of view, the rift does not exist. Again, the rhymeless 'sépulcre' has invaded the body of verse and the sibilants come flocking around in what seems at this point to be a vain attempt to find a name for it and thus to annihilate it or, in straightforward reality, to bring about its 'disparition vibratoire selon le jeu de la parole'.[35] For all its superficial obscurity, the poem quite patently performs the actions it describes, like a beehive seen through a glass panel: 'Voici les rimes dardées sur de brèves tiges, accourir, se répondre, tourbillonner, coup sur coup, en commandant . . . l'attention à tel motif de sentiment';[36] 'le principe qui n'est – que le Vers! attire non moins que dégage pour son épanouissement (l'instant qu'ils y brillent et meurent dans une fleur rapide . . .) les mille éléments de beauté pressés d'accourir et de s'ordonner dans leur valeur essentielle' – a passage which is followed by the image of the 'gardienne': 'les vers ne vont que par deux ou à plusieurs, en raison de leur accord final, soit la loi mystérieuse de la Rime, qui se révèle avec la fonction de gardienne et d'empêcher qu'entre tous, un usurpe, ou ne demeure péremptoirement.'[37]

The iris is the perfect flower-rhyme for the job: it contains the emblematic *i* and *s*; its family, the 'iridées', brings with it other rhymes and motifs – 'glaïeul' and 'lis'; it also means 'rainbow', announcing a new covenant between heaven and earth; and a rainbow is a natural hyperbola.

> Oui, dans une île que l'air charge
> De vue et non de visions
> Toute fleur s'étalait plus large
> Sans que nous en devisions.

> 25   Telles, immenses, que chacune
> Ordinairement se para
> D'un lucide contour, lacune
> Qui des jardins la sépara.

The 'Oui' at the beginning of the sixth stanza seems to reaffirm the trouble or perhaps explain it. The troublesome, problematic site was indeed an exception. Otherwise, the flowers were blooming with their enormous, hallucinatory lucidity in an entirely satisfactory fashion. There was no need for discussion or analysis – until the problem with the site was pointed out. Similarly, in *La Déclaration foraine*, the 'tacite félicité' of the poet and his female companion was disrupted by the motiveless 'rire strident' of reality which induced him to seek an 'explication figurative plausible pour mes esprits'. In *Prose*, the silence (of the Mallarmean verse) was broken by the first oral expression, 'on dit'. Direct, conscious analysis was introduced into the synthesizing 'double inconscience' of verse. The contrast is underlined by the distinction between 'vue' and 'visions'. Just as poetry contains no material presences but is a process or a series of interrelations, so the admirable quality of the island was that the (poetic) 'air' imbued it, not with particular, analysable visions, but with the pure capacity of seeing.

The connection between the peremptory site and this delightful ideal state in which the flowers, like the rhymes, are so big and vivid as to appear to detach themselves from their surroundings, is not immediately apparent. Except that the site was covered by flowers – the 'cent iris' . . . The flowers, it now seems, prevented the exception from being noticed. They form their own discrete realities, realities which the 'Esprit de litige' (perhaps the same 'on' that pointed out the failure of rhyme to provide a name) will denounce as unreal. Not only is there a reality that your art is incapable of 'naming', the compensatory realities it conjures up in reaction to the exception are not realities at all.

Whatever the validity of this objection (the question will be answered later on), it is the function of rhyme to try to integrate the exception into its scheme. Accordingly, the flower-rhymes continue to grow: in these two stanzas and the following one, they have an average of five matching phonemes – eight and six respectively in stanza 8. They are, contradictorily, 'immenses' (literally, immeasurable):

> Gloire du long désir, Idées
> 30   Tout en moi s'exaltait de voir
> La famille des iridées
> Surgir à ce nouveau devoir,

The 'devoir' of the flowers was referred to before in the adverb 'Ordinairement', suggesting not just the astounding matter-of-factness of their extraordinary growth, but also that they were acting in a manner appropriate to their function. The 'duty' they rise to perform is the 'function' attributed to rhyme in the passage quoted above – 'la fonction de gardienne' – and, generally, to the poet: 'l'explication orphique de la Terre, qui est le seul devoir du poëte et le jeu littéraire par excellence'.[38]

Were it not for the missing name, this would probably have been the perfect happy ending: hyperboles, of some kind, are leaping up all over. The eighth stanza has the longest rhyme in the poem – probably the longest rhyme in a 'serious' poem for several centuries. Its beginning rhymes with its end, enclosing two symmetrical vowels: de zi ʀi de. Similarly, the beginning of the stanza, 'Gloire', rhymes aurally with its end, 'devoir', and also with 'moi' and 'voir'. 'Surgir' rhymes with 'désir'. Several motifs of the poem are echoed phonetically and graphically – 'grimoire', 'midi', 'iris' – as well as semantically: 'surgir' and 's'exaltait' are both hyperbolic actions, presumably satisfying the poet's 'long désir'.

But has a name for the site been found, or will the 'trouble' persist? The poet's 'exaltation' is surely a good sign, but we might remember that, in *Sonnet pour elle*, the poet 's'exalte' at finding the rhyme that binds the first tercet together, *coeur-Soeur*, only to be taught a different lesson by his 'sister'. The irony is that, even as the poem describes in perfect rhymes a final victory, this victory is seen to be not entirely adequate. The poem will go on to insist that this synthesis is not just the trivial, artificial product of poetic (over-)enthusiasm, but a reality, a 'mystery' beyond the grasp of normal logic but existing nonetheless. Even so, the site still exists as part of that reality.

The implication is not that poetry is just a beautiful fantasy and that unpleasantness remains but *qu'importe?* We can see for ourselves that it is real: the letters of the *grimoire* perform their 'multiples fusions' before our very eyes and imply their 'doctrine propre, abstraite, ésotérique comme quelque théologie';[39] their rarefied 'Idées'. But the nameless grave – Death, Absurdity, Chance – is still there. The reality of both grave and ideal realm is affirmed (vv. 18 and 48); yet the 'glory' of the flowers depends on their very distinct-ness and detachment from the world in which they grow: 'lacune / Qui des jardins la sépara'. The problem, then, is one of far greater import: not the old *mensonge/réalité* dilemma (this is dealt with in the eleventh stanza), but a fact which, like the rhymeless word, calls the whole verse enterprise into question:

> Mais cette soeur sensée et tendre
> Ne porta son regard plus loin
> 35   Que sourire et, comme à l'entendre
> J'occupe mon antique soin.

The sister's unexpected reaction – introduced by the crucial 'Mais' – is the turning point and the beginning of a solution to what seemed an impossible predicament.

However well the rhymes appear to perform their poetic duty, the poet's more sensible half merely smiles. Not quite the characteristic 'rire' which, as in Mallarmé's personal prosody and as at the end of the poem (though only hypothetically), signals a victorious rhyme. Accordingly, the rhymes shrink. The last three stanzas all contained *rimes complexes* (if *se para-sépara* is counted); this stanza does not. *Loin-soin* is one of only four *rimes suffisantes* in the poem, and in some respects the poorest of the four.[40] The enjambment, 'Ne porta son regard plus loin / Que sourire', is a further detraction from the rhyme: the stress falls on the verb 'sourire' as if to emphasize that a more discreet synthesis is to be formed, contrasting with the laugh at the end. Finally, an additional interruption to the huge flower harmonies is created by the only hiatus in the poem (except the less noticeable 'vue et' in line 22): 'sensée et tendre'.* The suggestion is that a more conventional, rational,

---

* A phonetic motif, it seems, expressing the crucial moment of doubt. Cf., above, p. 71: 'foulés et épaissis des doutes'.

prosaic discourse has broken in. Instead of the organic activity of realities independent of the poet – like the functioning of verse and rhyme – the poem now describes the actions of the poet and his sister. Connections are now to be established between him and her, to the apparent exclusion of the outside world. Another function of rhyme has been introduced and an alternative approach which seems at first to entail a rejection or diffusion of the bigger harmonies.

The process is still the 'reciprocity' typified by rhyme. The poet's 'antique soin' ('vieil', 'ancien' and 'antique' typically refer to the traditions of verse) consists in 'listening' to the 'sourire' or 'regard' of his sister. These synaesthetic figures, like the later 'ouïr tout le ciel et la carte', are important references to the visual and aural nature of verse: the rhymes are both seen and heard. But now, for what is apparently a 'sensible' reason, the focus is shifted. In the earlier version, the inception of a self-contained circle of rhyme was more clearly indicated. The poet returns his sister's gaze, literally in the same form ('tels'), just as the rhymes respond to each other with identical phonemes. The signifying process becomes a more exclusive affair:

> Mais cette soeur, sensée et tendre,
> Ne porta ses regards plus loin
> Que moi-même: et, tels, les lui rendre
> Devenait mon unique soin.

The hyperbole of rhyme has come bounding up to provide a poetic 'name' for the 'site'; but the other half of the dual 'visage' – perhaps the rational and productive half – makes a separate demand on the poet's attention; and he decides, according to his 'antique soin', to listen to her:

> Oh! sache l'Esprit de litige,
> A cette heure où nous nous taisons,
> Que de lis multiples la tige
> 40   Grandissait trop pour nos raisons

> Et non comme pleure la rive,
> Quand son jeu monotone ment
> A vouloir que l'ampleur arrive
> Parmi mon jeune étonnement

> 45   D'ouïr tout le ciel et la carte
> Sans fin attestés sur mes pas,
> Par le flot même qui s'écarte,
> Que ce pays n'exista pas.

The sister is now left smiling and the poet listening to her. The next three stanzas form a long, parenthetical sentence: a comment from the present poet on the past events. ('Taisons' in line 38 can be read as a historic present: it was 'corrected' in the copy made by the poet, Luigi Gualdo, to 'taisions', which weakens the rhyme with 'raisons': the structure of rhyme naturally takes precedence over superficial temporal divisions.) The skeleton of the sentence is usually, and plausibly, constructed thus: 'Sache que la tige grandissait trop pour nos raisons et non que ce pays n'exista pas.'

The 'litigious' spirit of (for example) the sceptical reader may quite reasonably, it seems, object that this hyperbolic poetic hymn with its plainly mechanical harmonies, rhythms and convenient coincidences is just a pretty prosodic face. The extraordinary realm the poem describes is an effect of language and prosodic rules. The 'iridées' and 'Idées' have no real connection, and the whole scene has no claim to existence whatsoever. This is what the silence and smile of the sister might be thought to indicate; and so the poet hastens to explain . . .

As the final stanza will show, the 'Esprit de litige' is raising a serious objection. The poet may simply be trying to exorcize his authorial disquiet or 'trouble' at finding some exception in the world – an exception which threatens to disprove his rule-system and to show that his science is, at least in some cases, incapable of establishing a link between reality and itself. His epistemology, which is after all a suspiciously alchemical, old-fangled sort of system, is fundamentally flawed. The poet is just a versifier, a player of games, and he tries to cover up the inadequacy of his art by producing huge, flowery distractions. Plenty of rhyme but not much reason.

The objection is worth considering at some length, because the entire poem is an answer to it and, in fact, the objection remains intact at the end, still a part of the argument like the antithesis of a dialectic. The 'Esprit de litige', as shown by the phrase beginning 'comme pleure la rive' and ending 'le flot même qui s'écarte', cannot be dismissed out of hand, because there are conditions in which it would be right, as the poet himself accepts. – For enlightenment we shall look to the flowers.

Flowers are emblems of the poet's art in several contradictory and complementary ways which make them the perfect image of the dialectical poem. First, the flowers are rhymes bursting out on the 'tige' of each verse (see pp. 91 and 237, n. 19). The complex, 'multiple' rhymes – end-rhymes, internal rhymes, anagrammatical rhymes – spring up to provide a 'name' for the troublesome 'site'. The whole stem of the verse is covered with flower-rhymes: 'de lis multiples la tige / Grandissait trop pour nos raisons'. They may seem to be only coincidental harmonies, but they bear witness to and incarnate those 'mysterious' relations which, for Mallarmé, exist even in the alphabetical order of words in the dictionary. The ideal 'pays' they conjure up actually does exist – they are in themselves 'proof' of it – but it cannot be apprehended by reason. This is where verse comes into its own: it alone can suggest and illustrate the existence of the ideal realm. The reality it evokes is not a particular island the poet may happen to remember. It is the archetypal reality that can only be implied or evoked by verse and the connections it establishes: a pattern not a picture, 'vue' and not 'visions'. The usual Romantic dichotomy of Real and Ideal is misleading, though this is the trap the 'Esprit de litige' falls into. It has understandably failed to realize that this poet is a Structuralist anthropologist *avant la lettre* using the vocabulary of Romanticism. The reality in question is a hyperreality, inaccessible by normal means, just as the par(ab)ole used to describe it is a (hyper)parole.

In his letter to Huysmans, Mallarmé made exactly the same point as in the poem: however mystical and unreal the visions may appear, the connections and interrelations themselves undoubtedly and demonstrably exist:

> L'admirable en tout ceci, et la force de votre oeuvre (qu'on criera d'imagination démente, etc.) [the 'on' here would correspond to the 'Esprit de litige'] c'est qu'il n'y a pas un atome de fantaisie: vous êtes arrivé, dans cette dégustation affinée de toute essence, à vous montrer plus strictement documentaire qu'aucun, et à n'user que de faits, ou de rapports, réels, existant au même point que les grossiers; subtils et voulant l'oeil d'un prince, voilà tout.[41]

Words arranged according to the rules of prosody are like the visible particles whose motions and interreactions reveal the presence of invisible neutrinos. In a heightened state of awareness and with patient mastery of his art, the poet discovers these magical 'flowers' almost effortlessly; the hyperbolic garden blooms as he walks through it. Seen without its philosophical ramifications, this is simply a splendid evocation of artistic ecstasy, when all the right words come to mind, when the message exactly fills the mould and when the means of understanding the world enhances it. The experience was described with the same image, by, of all people, Boileau in his section on epic poetry:

> Ainsi, dans cet amas de nobles fictions,
> Le poète s'égaye en mille inventions,
> Orne, élève, embellit, agrandit toutes choses,
> Et trouve sous sa main des fleurs toujours écloses.[42]

Unfortunately, the flower is also a fitting image from the sceptical, 'litigious' point of view. 'Flowers of rhetoric' are literary conceits which take the place of positive expression; they refer to themselves rather than to realities. The expression 'fleurs de rhétorique', 'se dit d'un discours où les fleurs de rhétorique, prodiguées sans mesure et sans goût, tiennent lieu de ce qui aurait dû être dit' (Littré). Which is exactly what people did say (and sometimes still do) about *Prose*.

A more sinister connotation will be developed in the final stanza but is already present here: 'cacher sous des fleurs' means to conceal something dangerous 'sous des apparences séduisantes'. Flowers in poetry are often found growing on the edge of precipices. Is the poetic 'hymn' with its implication of a spiritual dimension or after-life merely masking the final reality, which is Death?

Mallarmé's use of the flower image – which is itself so detailed and sustained as to be a parody of what is after all one of the most banal of poetic clichés – also fuels the argument of the 'Esprit de litige'. From the idea of flowers, the poet elicits an absurd assortment of vocables: 'iris', 'iridées', 'lis', 'glaïeul', which are all incorporated quite visibly or audibly into the phonetic patterns. These words can be construed as ostentatious, clumsily erudite examples of the poet's flowery 'science', which might then be thought to consist, not in some mystical wisdom, but simply in knowing the terms that are listed in the 'herbier'. 'Iridées' (the *Iridaceae* family) is so learned that one critic assumed that Mallarmé made the word up himself.[43]

There is indeed a sense, deliberately created, that this 'science' is little more than the accumulation of terms which will enable the poet to find rhymes for almost every circumstance (every circumstance except, of course, the rhymeless 'sépulcre'). The impression of pedantic virtuosity, noted by some commentators, should not necessarily be ignored in the interest of proper admiration. Attention is drawn to it anyway when the commonsensical sister seems to be relatively unimpressed by it: 'ne porta son regard plus loin que sourire' – an entirely appropriate reaction to the sort of botanical erudition that produces grandisonant, exotic words like 'iridées' to make an eight-phoneme rhyme. Flowers, here, are the typical objects of spurious learning: nomenclature and classification masquerading as wisdom; science that is little more than labelling. In one of Balzac's early novels, Barnabé Granivel plans out his nephew's education along similar lines:

> Pour complément de ces sciences, tu ajouteras l'histoire naturelle et la botanique, avec un examen scrupuleux des systèmes; et tu sauras les noms de tes bouquets à Chloris dans les terminaisons as, us, ex et is. Si l'on prononce le nom gracieux de Narcisse, dis que c'est un *liliacée*.[44]

Or, if presented with an iris, call it an *iridée* . . .

Surely – we might go on to complain – this is just a refinement of the vulgar, 'commercial' use of language; vocabulary gone to seed. In fact, to stand outside the poem for a moment with its author, this cheapening of words, which seems almost a mockery of poetic language, is the necessary prelude to a poetic and existential victory. The display of would-be impressive nouns, which reaches its notorious 'Byzantine' climax with Anastase and Pulchérie, refers to two fundamental aspects of Mallarmé's philosophy. Words must lose their conventional values in order to regain their poetic potential. This is simply common experience: the same thing happens when we hear not just a poem (especially in a foreign language) but also, as *Prose* suggests, a talk full of technical terms: 'ce à quoi nous devons viser surtout est que, dans le poème, les mots – qui déjà sont assez eux pour ne plus recevoir d'impression du dehors – *se reflètent les uns sur les autres jusqu'à paraître ne plus avoir leur couleur propre, mais n'être que les transitions d'une gamme.*'[45] It turns out that what was needed was something like the opposite of erudition. The poeticization of these words, whatever their face value, also introduces the notion of 'scientific' reflection: language is to be the object (and vehicle) of study. As usual, when something previously taken for granted is submitted to analysis, the effect is humorous or even slightly scandalous. Reactions to the two proper nouns in the last stanza of *Prose* are characteristic. The real subject, which transcends all the others, is fiction: the only possible object of exact analysis, because fiction is 'le procédé même de l'esprit humain'.[46] The question then is: how can final human truths be examined when these truths are linguistic in nature and the means of examining them also linguistic? (The old dilemmas of Deconstruction looming.) The answer is verse, in which language is made to reflect on its own procedures; but this presents its own set of problems.

There are, then, conditions in which one might accept the objection that correspondences between poetic language and reality or the occult realities which poetic language is said to evoke are entirely spurious. The poet himself goes on to describe just such a case (to requote stanzas 11 and 12):

> Et non comme pleure la rive,
> Quand son jeu monotone ment
> A vouloir que l'ampleur arrive
> Parmi mon jeune étonnement
>
> D'ouïr tout le ciel et la carte
> Sans fin attestés sur mes pas,
> Par le flot même qui s'écarte,
> Que ce pays n'exista pas.

The ideal land could be said to exist when the 'monotonous' or rhyming 'game' of poetry is just an aesthetic lie. The banks or shores of the island 'cry' with the melodious, emotional 'sanglots' of rhyme, as in one of Banville's apostrophes to Rhyme:

> Ou tu gémis, comme les flots
> De la mer qui songe et qui veille.
> O Rime, exhale tes sanglots
> O bas, tout bas, à mon oreille.[47]

The waves which ebb and flow at regular, rhythmic intervals are like the rhymes which break at the end of each verse, each one giving way to the next. 'Pleure' and 'ouïr' stress the fact that this is an audible phenomenon. The 'rive' is also another image with a literary facet: 'rive' is the printer's term for the edge of a sheet of paper, in this case the edge of the poem where the rhymes appear. 'Même', in 'le flot même', draws attention – as does 'monotone' – to the sameness of rhymes. And so do the rhymes themselves: *pas-pas*, another example of Mallarmé attaching semantic values to *rimes homonymes*. Evidence of his intention can be found in the fact that on two other occasions the word 'même' appears between the identical rhymes: lui / Le même . . . lui (*Éventail de Madame Mallarmé*); tu . . . A même . . . tu ('A la nue . . .').[48]

As in the *Hommage* to Puvis de Chavannes, the poet walks along, pacing out the metrical feet and, as the rhymes part like the waves of the Red Sea, he hears in them the proof or 'attestation' of a higher sphere: 'tout le ciel et la carte' – perhaps a hendiadys for 'la carte du ciel' – evoking once again the analogy of letters and the celestial alphabet, the stars mapped out on paper. The correspondence or 'reciprocity' of verse and universe, 'exchanging proofs', is confirmed by these seemingly material harmonies. Hence the poet's delighted 'étonnement' – a word which, by its etymon, *attonare*, is tied to the idea of verse as 'foudre'. This cosmic unity which is reproduced in the dynamic structures of verse is real enough. The 'lie' consists in the poet's straining to make his verse reflect the fullness and completeness he perceives: 'A vouloir que l'ampleur arrive . . .'. The effort, here, produces what are *almost* the biggest rhymes in the poem; but, significantly, unlike 'Gloire du long *désir*, *Idées* / La famille *des iridées*' and other rhymes in the same section, the phonetic groups that 'try' to match perfectly are interrupted by dissimilar phonemes:

> Et non *comme pleure la rive*,
>
> A vouloir *que* l'am*pleur arrive*
>
> Quand *son jeu* mono*tone ment*
>
> Parmi m*on jeune étonnement*

These two stanzas also contain the only examples (except for *se para-sépara*) of what are, strictly speaking, derivative rhymes: *rive-arrive* (both from *ripa*) and *pas-pas*. The other rhymes, as Bowie points out, are all quite distinct etymologically and, despite their glaring similarities (*spirituels-rituels*, *par chemins-parchemins*, etc.), are related only phonetically. Here, the synthesis is too facile, too dependent on 'les mots de la tribu'. The harmony is riddled with subtle imperfections.

In such conditions, says the poet, your objection could be sustained: my youthful exhilaration leads me to try and introduce all sorts of phonetic correspondences *à la* Banville, which might express and illustrate what I know to be true but which are themselves factitious, the product of conscious effort rather than the unconscious attuning of linguistic structures. (This explains the much interpreted phrase, 'ment / A vouloir'.) The desired 'ampleur' has been construed as either negative or positive, usually the former; but since the context explains that two different instances of the same process are being considered, 'ampleur' is both negative and positive depending on which side one takes – poet or 'Esprit de litige'. For the latter (as for Cohn), 'ampleur' would suggest facile production, perhaps the 'source ample' of Puvis de Chavannes; for the former, it would suggest the fullness of harmony that fills up the mould of verse, or the fullness of verse itself.[49]

So, like the Faun, the poet sometimes 'amuses' 'La beauté d'alentour par des confusions / Fausses entre elle-même et notre chant crédule'. The false confusions of rhyme would not in this case have found a credulous audience ready to believe that these coincidences were revealing an essential link between verse and universe.

These parenthetical stanzas come at a point when the poet and his sister have fallen silent ('A cette heure où nous nous taisons'). The poet listens to her and waits for her to speak. The intervening description of the lying poetic game is an example of the rhetorical device that consists in explaining in detail what the text is *not* about. It also highlights what seems to be an *impasse*. The nameless 'site' which prevents this from being a perfect linguistic paradise can be covered up or disguised by the enormous rhyme-flowers. But it still exists, disturbingly; and the 'sensible' sister accompanying the poet only smiles and remains silent, apparently offering no solution to the problem. Even the poet, with his 'jeune' (or juvenile?) 'étonnement', realizes that poetry may simply mask or patch up any 'motiveless' reality with its 'motifs'. Its 'ampleur' would be that of the artificially emotional incantation with which the poet of *Le Démon de l'analogie* hopes to 'ensevelir' his anxiety 'en l'amplification de la psalmodie'.

A solution, as usual, comes just when all seemed lost (though exactly what the solution might be is not immediately apparent):

> L'enfant abdique son extase
> 50   Et docte déjà par chemins

> Elle dit le mot: Anastase!
> Né pour d'éternels parchemins,
>
> Avant qu'un sépulcre ne rie
> Sous aucun climat, son aïeul,
> 55 De porter ce nom: Pulchérie!
> Caché par le trop grand glaïeul.

Here we are then, finally, at the most famous piece of incomprehensibility in French literature. Having come so far, we arrive, it seems, just in time to see the boat pulling out and can either plunge into the abyss of error and falsehood or date the poem from the early 1870s and treat it as a youthful prank, instead of treating it as the mature prank it really is. The stickiest problems are the apparently unprepared tomb image, which, for Marshall Olds and others, 'has somewhat of a disturbing effect on the composition as a whole',[50] and the two names, Anastase and Pulchérie, which were much ridiculed at the time and are now puzzled over instead. Paul Bénichou notes that 'Anastase' and 'Pulchérie' 'certainly conceal a joke' but that, contrary to his usual practice, Mallarmé failed to provide us with the means to understand it.[51] For Jacques Gengoux, the two names are examples of words which, for the common herd, are uninterpretable, which is why Mallarmé made them meaningless.[52] The following reading explains everything – on one level.

The sister, now 'learned', ends her silence by 'abdicating' her 'ecstasy' and uttering the word 'Anastase'. The verb 'abdiquer', as we saw, is used etymologically: she 'says' or writes 'down' her 'ecstasy'. The normal connotation of 'abdicate' is that something is lost: she renounces her silence and the delightful, unexpressed vision is translated into a word that can be published on 'eternal parchments'. The spatial dimensions in which the action takes place are those of nearly all the other poems. The rising up of the ideal flowers, like the soaring of the bird, must be transposed into the flat dimension of the real page. The hyperbola must be completed. But verse, which is 'bas' – both 'low' and 'silent' – implicitly contains the original upsurge: 'chanter, au gré d'un bondissement allègre intérieur, quoique bas, en vers'.[53] Its rhymes are like dual coordinates which project an arc into a third dimension. 'Anastase', in the earlier version, was a 'terme' – a rhyme at the end of the verse and a conclusion:

> Ce fut de la finale extase
> Le sens, quand, grave & par chemin,
> Elle dit ce terme: Anasthase! –
> Gravé sur quelque parchemin,

The loss or abdication consists in renouncing the incommunicable ecstasy. 'Par chemins', as Bertrand Marchal points out, contrasts with the 'pur délice sans chemin' of *Autre éventail*.[54] The paths of verse,[55] the organized channels of prosody, are to receive the linguistic expression of the vision which would otherwise exist only in its transitory, sensual state. 'Anastase!', referring to resurrection and, more familiarly, to 'ne sais-tu te lever' in the first stanza, suggests that a hyperbola will after all have risen from the poet's memory; or rather, the ideal hyperbole of the miraculous island are mapped onto a different plane. The 'extase', as the earlier version says, is given a 'sens': both direction and meaning. A natural phenomenon, expressed in language, acquires a sense. The 'multiple sursautement de la clarté', like that of the flowers, will be 'vain, si le langage, par la retrempe et l'essor purifiants du chant, n'y confère un sens':[56] a 'sens' which, from the conventional point of view, may sound very much like a nonsense.

Not everything is resolved by this. In fact, the penultimate stanza is not entirely comprehensible on its own. The last two stanzas both form part of the same sentence, and though each one presents a different conclusion, neither is complete without the other.

'Anastase' has the prosodic merit of completing another rhyming circle: it forms a rich rhyme with 'extase'. It also prematurely completes the poem by sending us back to the beginning: the poetic act must end with another poetic act. But, semantically and prosodically, this closure or circularity leaves problems unsolved. The rhyme itself cannot compete with the enormous, synthesizing rhymes which began to form themselves so spectacularly in reaction to the namelessness of the 'site'. 'Anastase' in any case is described as a 'word', not as a 'name'. The connection between 'Anastase!' and the initial 'Hyperbole!' is etymological, semantic and intellectual, not purely poetic or 'mysterious'. No obvious phonetic motif, no anagrams or inverted rhymes are echoed in the word. There is, in the poem's terms, a distinct lack of 'ampleur', and we may feel, before we find out what the alternative was, that 'proper nouns are almost always too limited or determinate – or else "unearned" – for good poetry', especially when, as in this case, 'no convincing historical reason' has been found for it.[57]

The last stanza supplies what might be seen as the false conclusion of the poem. The word 'Anastase' was uttered *before* a tomb laughed at bearing the name 'Pulchérie', and the subjunctive – 'Avant qu'un sépulcre ne rie' – hints that there was some urgency to the final utterance, as if, by uttering the word, the sister prevented the tomb from having the last laugh.

In one respect, this stanza is also the final test of the reader. If we try to imagine some putative scene, mental or otherwise, that the poem is supposed to be describing, all is lost. 'Pulchérie' then becomes another Gordian knot. A guessing game with a practically infinite number of answers.

One can hardly overemphasize the fact, which the poem itself underlines, that 'Pulchérie' is not primarily 'pure Beauty', 'instinctive poetry' or whatever,[58] but a 'name' and a 'noun': 'ce nom: Pulchérie!', just as 'Anastase' is a 'word'. The 'principle', as always, is Verse, and the words that make up these verses are not just labels or approximate lexical equivalents of something else like gladioli, tombstones or the concept of Beauty, but groups of phonemes which are being made to perform a prosodic function – which is not to say that their conventional use should be ignored. But the 'meaning' of these words lies principally in their interrelations. This is what Mallarmé meant when he said that a poem should be composed not of 'words' but of 'intentions'.[59] 'Dans le Langage poétique – ne montrer que la visée du Langage à devenir beau, et non à exprimer mieux que tout, le Beau.'[60] As far as I know, the only critic to have approached the poem consistently from this Mallarmean point of view is Malcolm Bowie; and this is what enables him to make the following useful comment about 'Pulchérie': ' "Pulchérie" and "Hyperbole" have four phonemes in common (plʀi) and of these the consonants have appeared, in sequence or with one other consonant intervening, on fourteen further occasions.' 'Pulchérie', then, is one of the 'summative words' of *Prose* – a word which brings together several phonetic motifs. 'Trompette', for instance, is the focal point or universal set of other words in its vicinity:

> Ne *porte* pas de n*om* que cite
> L'*or* de la *trompette* d'Été.[61]

What then is the function of 'Pulchérie'? Is it simply the rather loose knot of several phonetic strands? If so, this would hardly justify it, even in the *Vers de circonstance*.

The keystone of the whole stanza, which will probably seem provocative and flippant if approached from the conventional angle, is a pun. Not a very original pun either. Long before Mallarmé, the same witticism adorned the 'unbeautiful tomb of a beautiful woman' (whether or not Mallarmé knew the inscription is of no importance): 'Heic est sepulcrum hau pulcrum pulcrai feminae'.[62] Mallarmé's version of the pun was slightly more obvious in the earlier version, where 'sépulchre' was spelt with an *h*, as it sometimes still is in the surname. (The *h* may have been inserted by Luigi Gualdo, who made the copy – and at least one mistake – but even so it demonstrates that the mind is naturally led to make the link between the two words.) Though no etymological connection exists ('sépulcre' comes from *sepelio* and 'Pulchérie' from *pulcher*), the graphic, anagrammatical and phonetic resemblance – especially if the *ch* of 'Pulchérie' is given its etymological pronunciation, k[63] – creates a 'poetic' link between Beauty and Death. *Sépulcre-Pulchérie* is one of those linguistic free gifts which Mallarmé treats with such respect and much less distrustfully than Saussure. It appears to offer an example of language preempting the poet's attempt to remedy its defects, claiming after all a certain mysterious, logical integrity. Yet at the same time, a suspicion is introduced that this is just a fluke.

Even if it is only a trivial coincidence, there is another secret in the ritual which makes this ancient pun worthy of its place at the end of the poem. 'Sépulcre' is one those 'peremptory' words that cannot be rhymed. Like Death itself, it stands alone, making a nonsense of everything; the great nuisance and exception. Here, it manages to insinuate itself into the rhyme-scheme. Technically, the rhyme is only *suffisante* – *rie* and Pulché*rie* have two matching phonemes – but the rhymeless word comes very close indeed to forming another enormous flower-rhyme:

> sépulcre ne rie
> s pylk   ʀi
> ce nom: Pulchérie.
> s   pylk ʀi

Sépulcre-Pulchérie is like a luxury version of that ordinary old rhyme, *beau-tombeau* – a rhyme, interestingly enough, which Mallarmé was soon to use, with a similar philosophical-prosodic conceit, in 'Victorieusement fui . . .'. Again the association of the tomb and a rhymeless word – 'pourpre' – suggesting beauty and unwanted consecration is greeted with a 'laugh'; and, again, the victory is attributed to a woman:

> Victorieusement fui le suicide beau
> Tison de gloire, sang par écume, or, tempête!
> O rire si là-bas une pourpre s'apprête
> A ne tendre royal que mon absent tombeau.

In *Prose*, on finding that it bears within itself the noun 'Pulchérie' ('De porter ce nom: Pulchérie!'), the 'sépulcre' laughs or would have laughed the laugh that signals a successful rhyme – a laugh which is now more reminiscent of a grinning skull than of the laughing ballerina of *Billet*. Death, the 'ancestor' of all things, has threatened to make a mockery of the poet's art. In a punning combination of prosodic and semantic elements, the poem not only says but actually demonstrates that the material harmonies of verse are (or can be) just a reaffirmation of mortality. They can do nothing to alter the conditions of their production. 'Un coup de dés jamais n'abolira le hasard.'

The end of the stanza – 'Caché par le trop grand glaïeul' – stresses the fact that this is not an enigmatic pirouette at the end of the poem but its formal and semantic conclusion, in which everything that precedes is summed up, interpreted, explained and exemplified. The flower-rhymes which flocked around the nameless 'site', rising up, to the poet's delight, to perform their 'duty', were behaving like those words which, as we saw in the last chapter, try to incorporate rhymeless words like 'monstre', 'pourpre', 'quatorze', 'sceptre' and 'sylphe' into the rhyme-scheme. Faced with the final, deathly example, we can now understand why the poet's sister sensibly drew him away from the flowers into communication with her. Because the 'sépulcre' is able – almost – to bend the rules of rhyme and get away with its trick by hiding behind the 'trop grand glaïeul'. 'Trop' indicates a qualitative judgment. These huge flower-rhymes were beautiful, dangerous distractions which only the alert, 'scientific' mind would perceive as evidence that language, even in verse, is governed by chance and that the poet's word-games are just another throw of the dice. *Sépulcre-Pulchérie* turns out to have been another example of straining to reproduce the 'ampleur' of those ideal correspondences that *do* exist in his poetry. The rhyme – interrupted by dissimilar phonemes – significantly recalls the *almost* very rich rhymes of the eleventh stanza. But this poetic 'exaltation' is seen to be a form of suicide: by giving the initiative back to words, the poet created a danger that his poem would be nothing more than 'an idle, tinkling pageant'[64] – as indeed it seemed to be. ('Victorieusement fui le suicide beau . . .' could be read as a treatment of the same theme.)

The 'glaïeul' might now be thought to be entirely justified in terms of the rest of the poem. Just in case it isn't, and just to emphasize the extraordinary conjugation of motifs and images at the end of the poem, a few more things might be said in its favour.

It has been pointed out that a 'glaïeul', etymologically, is a 'glaive', and therefore a possible allusion to the fiery sword that guards the path to the Tree of Life (Genesis 3:24). Perhaps so; but this mainly serves to show that as soon as the poem is treated as versified prose all kinds of fruitless difficulties arise. The Tree of Life is also the Tree of Death, so that it could conceivably be termed a 'sépulcre'; but why is the sword 'too' big? Too big not to hide the tomb? But swords are rarely broader than trees or tombs and the function of the fiery sword was not to hide the Tree but to guard the way to it; and so on, until the attempt is made to fit it all in with the first part of the sentence in the preceding stanza, which leads to an impossible, illogical mess which is really not worth going into.

If the 'glaïeul' is a symbol of anything, it is a symbol of what it is or belongs to – a verse, both sword and flower: 'à ne sortir, épée, fleur, que peu'.[65] It also harks back to figurative uses of the word 'fleur'. With its prosodic and linguistic context, it might be more plausibly attached to the idea of 'whited sepulchres': 'des sépulcres blanchis, qui au-dehors paraissent beaux aux yeux des hommes, mais au-dedans sont pleins d'ossements de morts, et de toute sorte de pourriture' (Matthew 23:27). In the end, of course, the 'glaïeul' is a rhyme that is said to mask the inanity of the poetic game, a hypocritical, hyperactive hyperbole. And, though we can count up its phonemes and call it 'rich', 'le *trop* grand glaïeul', for a nineteenth-century poet, is perhaps *too* rich and sweet, even independently of its context; a familiar favourite with 'materialistic' poets who prefer cute coincidences to common sense. Half a century before, Balzac placed it as an insult in the mouth of Baron du Châtelet (the Baron had been forced to sit through a recital of Lucien de Rubempré's poetry):

'Autrefois nous donnions dans les brumes ossianiques. . . . Aujourd'hui,
. . . c'est des lacs, des paroles de Dieu, une espèce de panthéisme christianisé,
enrichi de rimes rares, péniblement cherchées, comme émeraude et fraude,
aïeul et glaïeul, etc.'[66]

The end of the poem, in keeping with most performances of the prosodic
drama, is a trick; but this one, like *gorze-quatorze*, is also a 'lie' produced by the
poet's desire for hyperbolic expressions, whatever they might accidentally
say. And this particular, cheating rhyme contains its own deflation in the
absent rhymes it implies: for 'Pulchérie', the word that Mallarmé applies to
the poetic 'jeu' – 'supercherie'; and, for 'sépulcre ne rie' – 'duperie'. 'Duperie'
is the other face of authoritative expression, a form of literary suicide:
'Autrement, si ce n'était cela, une sommation au monde qu'il égale sa hantise
à de riches postulats chiffrés, en tant que sa loi, sur le papier blême de tant
d'audace – je crois, vraiment, qu'il y aurait duperie, à presque le suicide.'[67]
The 'riches postulats chiffrés' of *Prose* are its verses and rich rhymes. These
are not cabbalistic mutterings but scientific 'equations' for the universe,
'comparisons' of the 'charms' of Art with those of reality. Otherwise, the
poem would just be a deception, a trivial array of patterns whose endless
meanings were the result of chance.

Returning to the penultimate stanza, it seems that after all there must be
an intellectual limit or foundation to this linguistic trickery. There is a danger
(one which des Esseintes should have heeded) that by trying to make up for
the deficiency of language the poet only distracts himself and us from its
imperfection, thereby reaffirming it; a doctor turned beautician or a surgeon
embalmer. Sooner or later, the poetic 'ecstasy' must be 'abdicated', renounced
and written down, made public and, in its way, comprehensible: 'car, enfin, il
faut bien que le génie ait lieu en dépit de tout et que le connaisse chacun'.[68]
'Anastase!' can be read as a command: the work must be written, extracted
from the personal and collective memory – and we have indeed seen it
writing itself, not just discussing its plans for its own future.

The sister, in the penultimate stanza, proffers her own deceptive, witty
rhyme – *par chemins-parchemins* – devoid of any etymological authority.[69] Yet
she does nothing to incorporate her own rhymeless word – 'docte' – into the
rhyme-scheme. It is left with its conventional meaning entirely intact:
'learned'. This relative straightforwardness and even prosaicness is her prosodic mark, as we saw in the stanza in which, 'sensée et tendre', she only
smiles. Similarly, 'Anastase!', which is the equivalent of 'Pulchérie!' grammatically, syntactically and metrically (both in position and number of syllables),[70] is also its partner or antagonist in relation to the initial 'Hyperbole!'
It offers a choice: should the 'flowery', phonetic link or the etymological,
semantic and 'scientific' link be accepted? By accepting the latter, the poet
has some hope of inscribing his words on 'eternal parchments', of being an
intellectually interesting Mallarmé instead of a laughing Banville. With our

own little hundred-year measure of eternity we have to say that he made the right choice.

The end of *Prose* is a suitably ambiguous last act of the drama (though not the only last act, and the 'end' depends on whether we accept the order of the text or the order of the tenses). The sister, who can be thought of as a muse since that concept is equally open to interpretation, or, generally, as the art of verse, plays the role she plays in *Sonnet pour elle*. There, too, the poet 's'exalte' when he finds a seemingly definitive, synthesizing consonance for his 'coeur' in the word 'Soeur'; but then the learned sister 'teaches' him a different 'douceur' which consists in a real action – and a less technically spectacular rhyme. Death still exists, and so, too, does the coincidence that marries 'sépulcre' to 'Pulchérie': both are part of the poem, which inevitably reproduces the impersonal structures of language, ultimately governed by chance. The 'lie' which the rhyme is said to exemplify is also a textual truth. 'Le vers . . . *niant*, d'un trait souverain, *le hasard demeuré aux termes* malgré l'artifice de leur retrempe alternée en le sens et la sonorité'.[71] This contradictory achievement is the peculiar fascination of *Prose pour des Esseintes*: the poet, 'omitted' as a coordinating, active force by 'chance', still manages to produce an instructive, even didactic work, which will be published, hopefully, on eternal parchments, thus realizing the ambition of the famous writer in *A bout de souffle*: not to commit suicide but 'devenir immortel, puis mourir'. The game of verse is still a game – in fact, more a game than ever – but 'un jeu . . . qui confirme la fiction'.[72] A game which makes it impossible not to see that this is indeed fiction, but also which authenticates it, offers proof of its integrity, ensures that it carries the full authority and logic of verse and demonstrates that 'fiction' is the only possible basis for science, the only available 'sense' – 'le procédé même de l'esprit humain'.[73] In short, a happy version of *Igitur*, who, in his solitude, has 'oublié la parole humaine en le grimoire' and confronts the universe alone and in prose and, significantly, in an unpublished work.

The 'hymne' of the first stanza – which, in *Igitur*, refers to the 'chant personnel du Héros'[74] – has been 'installed' by the 'science' of prosody in the impersonal work, '[le] vers impersonnel ou pur'.[75] In *Prose*, the poet is not alone. His 'memory' is also the collective memory of the race, incarnated in verse, 'que personne n'a inventé et qui a jailli tout seul de l'instrument de la langue';[76] 'le vers n'étant autre qu'un mot parfait, vaste, natif, une adoration pour la vertu des mots'.[77]

'Adoration' . . . This was supposed to be the final destiny of the drama of verse, and it leads to an aspect of Mallarmé's work that can only be touched on here: the idea that Literature, 'reprise à sa source qui est l'Art et la Science, nous fournira un Théâtre, dont les représentations seront le vrai culte moderne'.[78] Poetry that will be the text of a new religion, with its rites, in which the poet officiates, its anthems and – naturally – its proses.[79] A new Bible which would be the creation of individuals and a collective spirit and offer a new explanation of the world. The exact opposite of what it seemed to be: 'inutile' and 'désagréable'.

'Terme', applied to 'Anastase' in the earlier version of *Prose*, is both the rhyme itself and the necessary end of the drama of verse – its realization and production: 'car il faut bien en revenir au terme quand il s'agit de vers'.[80] This is the simultaneously practical and megalomaniac conclusion reached in the passage on Banville's play, *Le Forgeron* (first published in 1887, like *Prose*, in *La Revue indépendante*). The intricacies of verse are no longer just the technical tricks they were in the Renaissance. They have become a part of the instrument itself. The mysteries of verse can now be projected from the stage and become active in the world they used to describe or ignore:

> Que l'acteur insinué dans l'évidence des attitudes prosodiques y adapte son verbe, . . . j'affirme que, sujet le plus fier et comme un aboutissement à l'ère moderne, esthétique et industrielle, de tout le jet forcément par la Renaissance limité à la trouvaille technique; et clair développement grandiose et persuasif! cette récitation, car il faut bien en revenir au terme quand il s'agit de vers, charmera, instruira, malgré l'origine classique mais envolée en leur type des dieux (en sommes-nous plus loin, maintenant, en fait d'invention mythique?) et par-dessus tout émerveillera le Peuple; en tout cas rien de ce que l'on sait ne présente autant le caractère de texte pour des réjouissances ou fastes officiels dans le vieux goût et contemporain: comme l'Ouverture d'un Jubilé, notamment de celui au sens figuratif qui, pour conclure un cycle de l'Histoire, me semble exiger le ministère du Poëte.[81]

What other justification could there be for a form of poetry that was denied by its own theoretical basis, and what other role for its writer but Poet Laureate of the Universe?

10

Conclusion:
Tangage

'On ne doit jamais s'expliquer.'[1]

The drama of verse, or the allegorical representation of the functions of verse, offers a new way of reading Mallarmé's poetry that is consistent and relatively easy to apply. It has the advantage of being based on a well-known set of rules and on Mallarmé's own poetic principles. It offers plausible and rewarding explanations of certain images and verses and, in many cases, exposes the logical structure of the whole poem. It acts as a key which proves its usefulness, not by supplying final answers, but by revealing, on the one hand, even more difficulties, unexpected events and deviations from what would otherwise be an invisible norm. Despite what parts of this book may have suggested, it obviates the need for that speculative erudition which tugs the poems all over Western civilization and brings them home in pieces. By describing what the poems actually do, the drama of verse supplies convincing answers for those who identify aesthetic defects instead of relishing the excuse to keep reading. Above all, it supports Mallarmé's claim – so often endorsed and invalidated in the same breath – that his poetry is not obscure if read as the product of an art that uses language. Its principal disadvantage is that of any explanatory approach: it creates strong preferences for certain readings where several are possible. But this is something that the reader will easily correct.

Historically, the prosodic reading underlines Mallarmé's methodological distance from his fellow Symbolists and his enormous lack of influence: how many of those who thought they were imitating his poems understood the principles of his verse? The vagueness of his admirers' comments is often a disappointing contrast with his own precise assertions. In so many eulogies, nothing concrete is said: religious awe and the impossibility of doing justice to the master's work – even to the nonexistent *Oeuvre* – are offered as reasons not to investigate further. Sometimes, violent admissions of perplexity turn out to be more useful. One cannot help being slightly worried about the fact that one of the earliest, most thoughtful appreciations of

Mallarmé's poetry was written by someone who claimed not to like it: 'Cet antipode absolu de mes préférences m'a permis d'émettre des idées vraiment malades et de célébrer la gloire de Mallarmé, ce qui m'a semblé être d'une assez affable blague', Huysmans bragged in a letter to Zola.[2] Many of those who admired Mallarmé seem to have ignored the obvious: that verse in all its mechanical complexity is the origin and end of his poems. At the time, it was difficult to say this without implying criticism. Perhaps if Mallarmé had been judged as morally reprehensible and mysteriously influential as Philip Larkin, he would have been read the way he wanted to be read. (Curiously, the same thing happened to one of Mallarmé's most sensible readers, Paul de Man.)

Mallarmé's insistence that the potential of Verse was still largely unrealized was not the self-vindication of a fuddy-duddy; it was a clue to the foundations of his work and the whereabouts of a *mode d'emploi* which he hoped might serve one day as an explanation of the universe. It was also a warning of possible misunderstandings, a reminder to Romantic relativists that his poetry was based on fixed laws and on a conviction that art is not the fallacious depiction of 'another world' but the 'transposition' of existing structures – reality in its purest perceptible state. His poems were read as children of their supposed literary parents, as he feared they would be: the personal sense of the 'poison tutélaire / Toujours à respirer si nous en périssons' in *Le Tombeau de Charles Baudelaire* seems to be that this fertile, protective, authorizing influence may retrospectively destroy the work it inspired: 'Je suis heureux que vous ayez goûté Poe, le poëte, qui est une mortelle eau de source: peu de poèmes tiennent après le chant de ceux-là, trop rares.'[3] Alternatively, though rarely nowadays, his verses were seen as belated examples of the professional pranks which, for several centuries – perhaps even since the end of the Western Empire or the reigns of Anastasius and Pulcheria – had been left to the satirical fringe.* The drama of verse helps to put these similarities into perspective and, though it places Mallarmé in a far wider sphere of influences, shows him to have been one of the most effective grape-vines of French poetry. As he said himself, his poems were visiting-cards to a period from which, in many ways, he was absent.[4] Stripping

---

* The present reading might open the way to a new and less impressionistic examination of Mallarmé's relation to other poetic traditions. For example, bearing in mind his friendship with the leading French Egyptologist of the time, Gaston Maspero, it might be said that he was persuading the French language to behave like the hieroglyphic script of Ancient Egyptian, in which the concurrence of ideograms and phonograms produces sequences of multiple puns and linguistic patterns which are often instantly visible to the otherwise ignorant eye. Some of Mallarmé's devices appear to have precedents only in Egyptian poetry of the 'classical' period (First Intermediate Period and Middle Kingdom). There are also some curious formal as well as linguistic similarities with Ancient Egyptian love poetry (well known to Maspero), where, for instance, the name of a flower supplies the basis of rhyming puns which form a litany of the loved one's virtues (conventionally addressed as 'sister' or 'brother'). The Egyptian motifs of Mallarmé's poetry and prose, like so many other seemingly decorative elements, may prove to be signposts – in this case, to a tradition which had lain dormant for three thousand years.

poetic language of its non-linguistic pretensions, leaving intact only the broadest abstract structures, treating the old icons as ornaments, rejecting traditions in favour of fundamentalism, legitimizing the latter by appealing to the former, Mallarmé's treatment of the poetry of his predecessors is perhaps best described by analogy with the vacuum-cleaner (an image unfortunately not available to him at the time of writing *Éventail de Madame Mallarmé*).

My most sweeping hope is that this book will help to rehabilitate the sort of prosodic-semantic reading that still has a bad name. Why this type of approach has remained in disrepute (despite Malcolm Bowie's book) is difficult to say: perhaps past excesses – statistical structuralism or a determination to discover intention behind every effect; or a fear that systematic aids of any kind are inimical to the reader's *jouissance* or a suspicion that applying simple, limited criteria means taking an old-fashioned, essentialist view of language. Without (or even with) a Mallarmean synthesis of theme and technique, such readings can be extremely tedious. Some readers may be willing to acquire the information but reluctant to believe that a great poet could harbour such a nihilistic view of trivial, universal concerns: not everyone likes to see the great subjects of poetry turned into the ash that is supposed to reveal the invisible ink of more abstract 'texts'. There is, as Sartre pointed out, a destructive spirit at work in this endless formation of structures: by making verse a reflection of itself, Mallarmé contributed to the relativization of the old forms of poetic discourse as efficiently as Rimbaud or Verlaine. Reading these texts for their emotional or philosophical insights can be a worrying business, and if this is how Mallarmé's contemporaries tried to read them, then, in his own terms, *Poésies* is not a masterpiece: 'Un livre que son esthétique spéciale met d'accord absolument avec le mode d'en user que peuvent apporter ses lecteurs, est un chef-d'oeuvre.'[5] The possibility that precise, prosodic conceits are most easily detected by small and nervous imaginations is no reason not to use them. They may sometimes provide the push that sends us back into a poem which, after years of probing, seemed to have retreated forever into its shell. Even the *Vers de circonstance* can be reinspected, not as isolated postage stamps, but as little four-paned windows into Mallarmé's workshop.

The implications of the idea have not been exhausted, nor, perhaps, its potential for disproving itself. The remainder of this book proposes four ways in which the drama of verse might be allowed to affect Mallarmean reading habits. It also provides the chronological end to the drama and the necessary disaster without which the game would never have existed.

Hérodiade

The prosodic reading could be extended, not just to those poems which clearly demand a prosodic reading, but also to other poems which are less completely and intrinsically reflexive. Some of these have been mentioned briefly in the course of this book. The following seem to be particularly rewarding examples: 'La chevelure vol . . .', 'Quand l'ombre menaça . . .', 'Victorieusement fui . . .', 'Tout Orgueil . . .', 'Quelle soie . . .', 'M'introduire dans ton histoire . . .'. Virtual commentaries might be pieced together by referring to the Index of Works by Mallarmé.

The biggest omission is *Hérodiade*, whose various versions span most of Mallarmé's literary career. I have quoted *Hérodiade* only in fragments largely because of another, corresponding omission. With patience, the drama of verse, once identified in detail, could be retraced chronologically. A short history might show the following. The drama first emerges episodically in the early 1860s in the form of isolated conceits or simply in poems about poetry (which, after Baudelaire, was hardly something new). This might be seen as a residue of his humorous *juvenilia*. There follows a period of consolidation, heralded by Mallarmé's reflections on language and marked by the first *sonnet en yx* which, for a time, remains exceptional. *L'Après-midi d'un faune* (first edition: 1876) conjugates thematic and prosodic elements, though the combination lacks the philosophical, dynamic structure of later poems. The drama reaches its Golden Age with *Prose pour des Esseintes* and *Autre éventail* (1884). Once the principles are established, along with all the attendant details – rhymes, significant images, narrative models – the drama becomes more complex, notably in the three poems of *Triptyque* (1887). Mallarmé's own prosody, like the 'national' prosody it grew out of, is settled enough to become the basis of new variations which sometimes undermine it. *Un coup de Dés*, interpreted below as the last act or epilogue of the drama (in biological and prosodic time), introduces other principles of unity which allow for a less integrated, more catastrophic performance. The drama itself survives, either in a highly condensed form or, more or less explicitly, in the theme: a reflection on the self-reflecting drama or a meta-meta-text.

Hérodiade belongs to the earliest period of the drama. Even in the last version (a revealing return to a prosodic square one), Mallarmé's initial experiments with auto-allegorical poetry conduct their conversations behind the scenes. The poem contains long passages in which Hérodiade's own self-reflection is mirrored in the verse; though, rather than a drama, these are chains of isolated references to verse, more in the manner of Banville's *Le Forgeron* than *Prose pour des Esseintes* or other poems which we can now describe as 'narrative'. The drama is still conveyed primarily by the theme: the prosodic conceits are voices which comment on the action like a Greek chorus. To analyse these passages in detail would take another chapter – and perhaps require a different approach: the absence of the clear, prosodic framework of the shorter poems would produce a running commentary rather than a structured argument. I mention it here in the hope that someone might care to pursue the point.[6] Perhaps the early *Ouverture* (c. 1866) would be the best place to begin such a study, since it contains what are probably the earliest signs of an attempt to propagate a poem from its prosodic base. Hérodiade's nurse is the first Mallarmean character to describe implicitly the problems of poetic expression – the isolated voice, 'sans acolyte':

> Qui jettera son or par dernières splendeurs,
> Elle, encore, une antienne aux versets demandeurs
> A l'heure d'agonie et de luttes funèbres!

The simultaneous production of harmony and complaints about its futility is already one of the 'fils conducteurs' of the text. The most noticeable expression of this is the 'failure' of rhymes to materialize at the end of the verse: 'plis / Inu*tiles* avec les yeux ensevelis / De siby*lles*'. In particular, the 'étoile' is denied its rightful place – 'un chant d'étoile, mais / Antérieure, qui ne scintille jamais'; or in the 'vieil éclat voilé' – '(ô quel lointain en ces appels celé!)'. At the end of the same passage, in a later version, the 'chosen' rhyme that should close the circle does not: 'pour voir les diamants élus / D'une étoile, mourante, et qui ne brille plus!' The finger of verse is raised with its translucent rhyme in the window of the poem, 'according to the memory of the trumpets'. It turns into a candle, which, like the verses, burns at both ends and melts into its 'ancien passé':

> Et bientôt sa rougeur de triste crépuscule
> Pénétrera du corps la cire qui recule!
> De crépuscule, non, mais de rouge lever,
> Lever du jour dernier qui vient tout achever,
> Si triste se débat, que l'on ne sait plus l'heure
> La rougeur de ce temps prophétique qui pleure
> Sur l'enfant, exilée en son coeur précieux
> Comme un cygne cachant en sa plume ses yeux,
> Comme les mit le vieux cygne en sa plume, allée,
> De la plume détresse, en l'éternelle allée
> De ses espoirs, pour voir les diamants élus
> D'une étoile, mourante, et qui ne brille plus!

'L'éternelle allée / De ses espoirs' . . . Verse – especially in *rimes plates* with huge internal echoes – goes on and on forever, backwards. The end-rhymes chase their own tails: yl, e, œʀ, œ, e, ly.

Read prosodically, successive versions of *Hérodiade* might be asked to reveal the various stages in Mallarmé's exploitation of his discovery: from a descriptive, 'imitative' use of prosodic features, to a metaphorical use – in which the events of the poem are reenacted in the verse itself or described in terms that can also be applied to verse. A static situation is provided with a dynamic framework.* Finally, to the full prosodic allegory, where verse is treated as the primary structure of everything. This development might be seen as the equivalent of the poetic process itself: the progressive absorption of reflected images by the mirror.

Even without a prosodic reading, *Hérodiade* is remarkable, as we saw at various points, for its episodic allusions to verse. These fragments of a generally unsuspected drama are perhaps its most conspicuous influence on later poets. I mention this influence thinking particularly of Valéry's *La Jeune Parque*, a philosophical monologue which is also an 'exercice' in 'l'art des vers'. In several parts of the poem, prosodic conceits are placed in the foreground, dressed in those recurrent symbols which attach the theme to the language of the poem and to French verse in general. Some of Valéry's symbols appear to have retained their Mallarmean connotations, as if the drama extrapolated from traditional French prosody had become a tradition in itself – the dawn, the diamonds at the extremities of the verse, the mirror, the lips, the smile, the Orient, the prison, the ring and the horizon. But all this would fill another book . . .

'Toute l'âme résumée . . .'

Hérodiade also suggests a valuable corollary of the prosodic reading: Mallarmé's views on the art of verse can be looked for not just in capsules of explicitness but in all his poetic expressions. By the same token, it may be worth reexamining those poems in which 'the poet' flaps his messages at us quite ostentatiously, as if, all of a sudden, the apparent subject were more important than verse – which is unlikely to be the case even if the apparent subject is verse.

The poem that might be thought the most obviously self-referential in Mallarmé's work has been deliberately ignored in accordance with what was said in the introduction on the subject of reflexivity. 'Toute l'âme résumée . . .' always used to be quoted and anthologized as Mallarmé's *art poétique*. The assumption was that, when *Le Figaro* asked for his opinion on free verse, he took the opportunity to make a final statement on the subject. Before he died, everyone would know exactly what he thought poetry should be: 'l'ultime conseil de celui qui entrevit peut-être la véritable nature de la poésie'.[7] If that was his aim, he failed completely.

---

* For example in the *Prélude*: the 'choc malencontreux' of 'divers *monstres* nuls'; the candelabra, the 'pièce héréditaire de dressoir' on which the 'équivoque' of rhyme arranges a 'gloire'; the 'vaisselle' with its 'avares feux' (like stingy rhymes offering few possibilities); the 'vains bras hasardeux' of verse. In the third part: the 'psaume' that is to be 'buried', the 'écho latent' which '[perpétue] du faîte / Divers rapprochements scintillés absolus'; the 'joyau géant' or 'noeuds' of rhyme. Finally, the 'plat nu' of the poem which 'dusts' and 'wipes' itself, with its silent, white edges beyond which multiple, contingent meanings do not exist: 'Toute ambiguïté par ce bord muet fuie'.

Toute l'âme résumée
Quand lente nous l'expirons
Dans plusieurs ronds de fumée
Abolis en autres ronds

Atteste quelque cigare
Brûlant savamment pour peu
Que la cendre se sépare
De son clair baiser de feu

Ainsi le choeur des romances
A la lèvre vole-t-il
Exclus-en si tu commences
Le réel parce que vil

Le sens trop précis rature
Ta vague littérature

Read with the subtler *arts poétiques* of the prosodic drama in mind, this tiny poem seems even more circumstantial than many of the *Vers de circonstance* (as recent commentators have suggested),[8] and perhaps this is why Mallarmé never wanted to include it in any edition of his poems. A serious, dogmatic exposition of a consistent theory it is not: 'Toute l'âme résumée . . .' is an exercise in ironic self-contradiction. In a positivistic fashion, it emits the precept that poets should exclude 'Le réel' from their work, and precisely formulates the idea that 'Le sens trop précis rature / Ta vague littérature'. Consequently, the attempt by *Le Figaro*'s interviewer to present it as an expression of 'le flou du flou' is entirely implausible, though in line with most later interpretations.[9]

The key to the anomaly is the fact that Mallarmé wrote the poem 'par jeu' as a postscript to his comments on the *vers libre*. Like Verlaine's judiciously clumsy defence of regular verse (see p. 48), it can be read as a deliberate failure. The 'vague littérature' is surely not supposed to be Mallarmé's, but the self-conscious meanderings ('vague' from *vagus*, wandering) of the *vers-libristes* who score their *états d'âme* through with clear meanings, allowing the ash of reality to pile up on the end of the verse which ought to burn with its bright rhyme like a 'clair baiser de feu' – *clair* not *vague*. Vagueness is sometimes associated by Mallarmé with vulgarity and commercial literature: 'Le vague ou le commun et le fruste, plutôt que les bannir, occupation!', he wrote sarcastically in *Étalages*; and, in *Or*, 'du vague, du médiocre, du gris'. Vagueness betrays the poet's failure to achieve the exact concentration that would reveal the pure, underlying 'rhythms'. Contrary to popular Symbolist belief, vagueness is a mask for untransmuted reality, not the mark of imaginative detachment from it. Both terms – the vague and the real – can refer to the same deficiency. In June 1894, Mallarmé defined the poetry of Léon Dierx as 'une entière forêt de maux' with 'le vague qui les rend vrais!'[10] The vagueness of the poem prevents emotions from becoming 'rhythms' and structures. Poetry that tries to be something other than language ends up being nothing but a representation and rehearsal of the real.* Ironically, the 'sens trop précis' (or, in a manuscript variant, 'trop marqué') is not an ink-blot on a desirable cloudiness, but the result of it: the problem with your 'vague littérature' is that its meanings are too precise.

The first part of the sonnet is another clear and complex metaphor for Mallarmé's verse, with its patterns as exact and 'chaotic' (in the scientific sense) as smoke-rings; its raw material (smoke) unimportant but not the processes it performs (smoke-rings); its supposed 'obscurity', as Claudel noted in a letter to Mallarmé, 'non le vague, mais la précision extrême'[11] – linguistic and prosodic precision. Some confusion has resulted from similarities with Verlaine's 'Art poétique'; but family resemblances do not inevitably indicate agreement. The comparison can also emphasize the unMallarmean connotations of 'vague': *flou, obscur, indécis*. The 'nous' of the first quatrain is the collective voice or 'soul' of French prosody, as Mallarmé's comments in the interview imply: 'le vers officiel dit demeurer, car il est né de l'âme populaire.' The singular 'ta' in the final line hints at the isolation of each *vers-libriste*, each ploughing his own little furrow: 'notez bien', he warned Gustave Kahn, 'que je ne vous considère pas comme ayant mis le doigt sur une forme nouvelle devant quoi s'effacera l'ancienne. . . . Vous ouvrez l'un des sentiers, le vôtre: et faites ceci de non moins important qu'il peut en être mille.'[12] It follows that the injunction, 'si tu commences', is not a piece of professional advice to beginners; it has the sense of, 'If you really must . . .'. If your lips are moved by romances, then try to filter out the base reality; let your smoking be at least a 'poison tutélaire'.

It is in the nature of extreme courtesy to leave its victim perpetually in doubt. Most translators have adopted the usual interpretation but some appear to have realized that 'vague literature' is not the most fitting description of Mallarmé's verse. Arthur Ellis has 'The airy shapes thy Muse enjoys',[13] and Antony Hartley 'your mysterious literature'.[14] Without thinking about the poem, the smoking analogy might be taken to mean that vagueness is a good thing: conventionally, the poet allows his meandering mind to drift with the wisps of smoke, as for instance in Mallarmé's *La Pipe*. But this

---

*   This is not to say that vagueness for Mallarmé is *always* either negative or positive. Vagueness and smoking are associated in two other, quite different contexts. 'Mais auparavant ne convint-il spacieusement de s'exprimer, ainsi que d'un cigare, par jeux circonvolutoires, dont le vague, à tout le moins, se traçât sur le jour électrique et cru?' (OC, 371). (Mallarmé promises however to 'éclairer' the subject in some later digressions.) And 'J'imagine [que] le nom soudainement d'Arthur Rimbaud se soit bercé à la fumée de plusieurs cigarettes; installant, pour votre curiosité, du vague' (OC, 512). Also, as a contrast to the remark on Dierx and a belated warning against the use of decontextualized images: 'ces parages / du vague / en quoi toute réalité se dissout' (*Un coup de Dés*).

particular development of the cliché shows something quite different: this is the highly structured activity of verse. Exhaling clouds of smoke is child's play; blowing smoke-rings through other smoke-rings takes years of practice.

Salut

If poems with an explicitly prosodic theme can be usefully devalued, other brief allusions can be taken as invitations to extend the prosodic reading to the rest of the poem – which, after all, is one of the advantages of reading Mallarmé from his own point of view: the poems can be grasped as complex, coherent texts rather than as precepts and conceits arranged in the display cabinets of traditional forms. References to verse are not just in-jokes or signs of professional obsession but prefatory remarks from the producer or conductor, programme notes designed to prevent us from reaching the mistaken conclusion that this poetry is 'obscure' by reminding us that every 'énoncé d'un objet poétique pris au sentiment ou dans notre mobilier' is a simple 'fait rythmique et transitoire où aboutira et dont repartira la période';[15] 'la manifestation d'un art qui se sert . . . du langage'.[16] Seemingly isolated allusions to the substance of poetry – the 'langage', 'vers' and 'battement' of the *Éventails* or the 'vers composé par Méry' – should be welcomed, not as an opportunity for a note on reflexivity, but as part of the general instructions or tips of the prosodic iceberg.

A good test of this is the slender *Toast* written for a banquet held by *La Plume* and then used by Mallarmé as the introductory poem of *Poésies*.

SALUT

Rien, cette écume, vierge vers
A ne désigner que la coupe;
Telle loin se noie une troupe
De sirènes mainte à l'envers.

Nous naviguons, ô mes divers
Amis, moi déjà sur la poupe
Vous l'avant fastueux qui coupe
Le flot de foudres et d'hivers;

Une ivresse belle m'engage
Sans craindre même son tangage
De porter debout ce salut

Solitude, récif, étoile
A n'importe ce qui valut
Le blanc souci de notre toile.

The splendid contradictory beginning is clearly self-referential. The first two lines, as we said before, refer both to the 'coupe' of the 'vers' that is recited and to the 'verre' of the 'coupe' that is raised for the toast, which makes the restriction, 'ne . . . que' slightly ironic: the verse designates 'only' the 'coupe', but *coupe* is more than one thing. The verse is 'vierge' in the sense in which Mallarmé uses the word in a letter to Albert Boissière:[17] 'inédit' – this previously unpublished verse, launched on its maiden voyage at this banquet. Virginal, too, because unmarred by any vulgar meaning, and also because, as the first verse of the sonnet, it has yet to be coupled with another. It remains for the moment intact, doing nothing but the bare prosodic minimum.

The difficulty arises in the next two lines. Here, the poem seems to stop referring to itself and starts on what is generally assumed to be its proper theme: what, for example, could be the prosodic significance of a troupe of drowning sirens? Despite the apparent change in subject a connection *is* indicated by 'Telle': the functioning of verse (or this verse) has something in common with the manner in which sirens drown, many of them upside-down. Interpretations have been varied and ingenious. Sirens, like nixies, represent fleeting, ungraspable beauty, 'symbols of the airy yet sensual art which the poet favored':[18] 'le vers, dans ses transformations si fugaces et presque de nixe'.[19] This, then, would be the drinker's equivalent of faces in the fire, as used in a recent television commercial in which the consumer sees the black-haired girl of his dreams in a glass of Guinness. The 'écume' of Mallarmé's sonnet is not the head on a pint of stout but bubbles of cham-pagne – a seascape made interesting by blurred vision and as if miniaturized by distance. But the details of the hallucination are hard to explain. Jacques Gengoux's stunningly precise diagnosis is that some of the sirens are upside-down because their busts are heavier than their tails,[20] though this would surely have had the opposite effect.

If verses 3 and 4 are reattached to the opening of the poem – as 'Telle' invites us to do – several more plausible interpretations present themselves. Sirens, like verses, sing (Littré traces the word back to the Phoenician *sir* meaning 'song'). Like Mallarmé's poetry, sirens are associated with death, luring reality into a 'gouffre central'. Horace's comparison of heterogeneous works of art to beautiful women with the tails of fish also springs to mind, or – an appropriate reading in this case – works of which one can make neither head nor tail. There may also be a less literal image of suggestive incom-pletion in the half-perceived sirens. An idea, says Mallarmé, may quite happily 'finir en queue de poisson; seulement refuse qu'on déroule celle-ci et l'étale jusqu'au bout comme un phénomène public.'[21] In view of this, the sirens could be a metaphor for the art of suggestion as exemplified by the almost content-less opening of the poem. Only half of each idea is presented 'en sa presque disparition vibratoire'.

Though in line with the explicitly poetic theme of the sonnet, these

readings are still quite general; they refer back to the poem, but only thematically not prosodically. The delightful, unexpected exactness of the analogy
depends, as so often in Mallarmé, on a seemingly peripheral, though perfectly
knowable feature of the image. A reminder is provided by *Un coup de
Dés*: '*une stature mignonne ténébreuse debout / en sa torsion de sirène / le temps /
de souffleter / par d'impatientes squames ultimes bifurquées / un roc*'. The siren
remains upright just long enough to flick her forked tail (her 'squames
ultimes bifurquées') against a rock. Sirens or mermaids, as everyone knows,
are divided at the end, just like the verses with their twin rhyme-words,
many of which are indeed 'à l'envers': *Salut* contains probably the highest
number of *rimes inverses* of any Mallarmé poem – *loin-noie*, *Rien-sirènes*,
désigner-de sirènes, *vierge-divers*, *Nous-naviguons-vous*, *naviguons-avant-
NAV*,[22] *naviguons-divers*, *d'hivers*; / *Une ivresse*,[23] *salut* / *Solitude*, etc. If we
remember, too, that Mallarmé envisions verses vertically as well as horizon-
tally,[24] the sirens' heads and tails are also the patterns made by the rhyme-
scheme –

A   AA   ACC E E
 BB   BB   D D

– and a representation of the lines of uneven length as they dive off into the
whiteness of the margin.

   Finally (and even more precisely), the reference to the *coupe* of the verse
(or *contre-rejet*, in which a short phrase is tied closely to the following verse)
draws attention to the mirror-image structure of the quatrain. The *coupe* is
matched by a *rejet* (in which a short phrase is closely tied to the preceding
verse):

vierge vers
A ne désigner que la coupe;

Telle loin se noie une troupe
De sirènes

Rejet and *contre-rejet*, *vers* and *envers*. The sirens are biological enjambments
or the sonnet's structure in half-human form. This could, just conceivably, be
a coincidence. Except that the verses continue to drown, right side up and
upside-down, in the second quatrain. The *coupe* and *rejet* are followed by a
rejet and a *coupe*:

Nous naviguons, ô mes divers
Amis,

qui coupe
Le flot de foudres et d'hivers;

Prosodically, verses 3 and 4 are a precise, descriptive image of the poem, not a bleary fantasy. Thematically, they develop the initial proposition and open up the argument from cup of champagne to ocean and the wider, though still literary, perspective of the second quatrain.

The siren image now assumes its full intertextual potential. Like Ulysses and his men, Mallarmé, the reluctant captain of a generation of poets, is engaged on an odyssey. But there is an important difference. The sirens are a paradoxical image, like Baudelaire's Midas-in-reverse who turns gold into base metal. Mallarmé's sirens, improbably enough, are drowning in the ocean; dying instead of luring sailors to their death.* What, then, is the point of the voyage? The poet stands erect, like Ulysses bound to the mast, drunk with beauty, but with no enchanting song to hear. As in 'A la nue accablante tu . . .', no 'perdition haute' justifies his heroism, which in any case consists simply in trying to remain upright.

Pointlessness is of course the point of the sonnet – a *salut* to 'n'importe ce qui valut / Le blanc souci de notre toile': paper canvas or sail – 'la page blanche da la *voile*' being the absent rhyme.[25] Similarly, the 'seul souci' of the Vasco da Gama sonnet was the transcendental voyage itself, not the discovery of India. Verse is its own object and the pretext absolutely unimportant. What did Mallarmé's audience think of the sonnet? Its original title was *Toast* – but a toast to what? Surely the person presiding over the banquet should have found something complimentary to say about *La Plume*. The audience may, however, have detected a polemical nuance which anchors the poem in its circumstantial setting and shows it to be a suitable preface for *Poésies* – in one respect, the ideological partner of 'Toute l'âme résumée . . .'.

As usual, Mallarmé distinguishes himself from his 'divers / Amis' (perhaps an echo of the English noun?)[26] – those diverse, divergent poets of the avant-garde, thrusting onward into new poetic domains, all fashioning their own personal variations on regular verse, pursuing individual paths and neglecting the collective *vers*; cutting through 'Le flot de foudres et d'hivers', just as free verse cuts through the 'foudre' of rhyme and the icy sterility of the ideal Mallarmean text. Mallarmé's young friends are part of the ship itself, driven by something they cannot control and, despite this, 'fastueux'. Sumptuous and festive, with a proper sense of the occasion but also, as Cohn suggests, 'showy'.[27] Full of pomp and pomposity. Mallarmé himself is at the stern, on the poop deck – a human being, behind the others, but in a position from which the ship can be steered. The image is Mallarmé all over: a polite concession – you are at the forefront of modern poetry while I am the old sea-

---

*   There may also be an allusion here at the opening of *Poésies* to Orpheus, who sailed with the Argonauts and drowned out the sirens with his music. As a result, the sirens dived into the sea and were turned into rocks. This might be related to the position of 'Mes bouquins refermés . . .' at the end of *Poésies* (apart from the reference to the closing of the books): Orpheus was torn apart by the maenads and his head floated to the island of Lesbos, there to found the poetic tradition represented by Sappho (see p. 18).

dog bringing up the rear – which is actually a reaffirmation of the rightness and necessity of his own position. And, as Bertrand Marchal points out, we must unfortunately consider ourselves a part of the audience. When the *Toast* becomes a *Salut* at the opening of *Poésies*, Stéphane Mallarmé on the title-page, the reader is 'appelé à son tour à l'incertaine navigation de la lecture'.[28] We, too, paper-knife in hand, are at the cutting-edge, slicing through the hermetic text with our own up-to-date pomposity.

Despite the pitching and tossing, Mallarmé, still under the influence of 'a beautiful drunkenness' or the 'ivresse' attendant on the pursuit of beauty, erects his regular verses on the ship of French versification with the wind of tradition or a 'vent de poupe' behind. 'Sans craindre même son tangage' – without worrying about the disruption of traditional rhythms, and surely not just (or even), 'so drunk he no longer fears that his poetry may be as uneven as the pitching of a boat'.[29] In fact, the inevitable result of steering such a fragile craft in a state of 'ivresse' is shipwreck – 'récif'. The letters themselves are not upright (Mallarmé specified italics); 'langage' is 'tangage', the 'récit' a 'récif', the 'salut' 'Solitude'; the sirens are drowning and the drunken poet hard to understand; but the implied disaster reveals (or is said to reveal) the primal, archetypal, absolute reality immanent in verse and universe – the significant rhyme for the blank page: *toile-étoile*.

The dénouement of the drama could only be another comment on its own nature: 'A travers un nouvel état, sublime, il y a recommencement des conditions ainsi que des matériaux de la pensée.'[30] If verse simply spells out its secrets it loses its mystery; yet, as we saw, that is precisely what it does. With its competing and complementary distractions, the self-consciousness of Mallarmé's verse perhaps prevented it from ever revealing those musical structures. Mallarmé very rarely quotes his own poems, and it may well be that his own poetry was not the best approximation of his ideal; or perhaps, in reading the poems, it would have been better to keep the critical texts entirely separate . . .

But there is also a more worrying question. As the century draws to a close and as verse in its decline asserts its eternal, absolute credentials, replacing its geographical Empire with a Holy one, have the original conditions remained the same, or was the drama of verse concealing a crisis of a more general and catastrophic nature?

Epilogue: Naufrage

'*sauf*'[1]

'A *la nue accablante tu* . . .', Un coup de Dés

It probably had to end like this anyway . . . The poem decomposed, deprived of its spatial, typographical, prosodic and even intellectual integrity, its syntax no longer a single 'pivot' but several conflicting centres of gravity, its rhymes either invisible or so weak as to seem coincidental, its resolutions loose ends. Stripped of the lanterns of rhyme and the masts of regular metre, severed from its ancestral roots, verse lies scattered over the page like wreck-age on the sea. *Salut* was a technically sound vessel under a captain's control; *Un coup de Dés* is the poem after it hits the reef. How can the drama of verse be applied to the great exception of French poetry, in which Mallarmé so spectacularly failed to follow his own commands? What happened to 'the old dogma of verse', its familiar, symmetrical 'mould', its definitive appearance? If 'le vers résume toute émanation flottant alentour',[2] then the truncated lines and isolated words of *Un coup de Dés* must be the opposite of verse, or, in view of a superficial resemblance with the printed *ébauches* of *Hérodiade*, the embryos of verses. Why such a sudden progression from regular verse to chaos without passing through the intermediate stage of free verse? Did Mallarmé start to worry about falling behind his fellow sailors? While the crew were fiddling with the classical knots, he decided to show them what a real disaster would be, swung the boat around, swept them overboard and headed north towards the 'plus purs glaciers de l'Esthétique'.[3]

Approached from the regular shores of Mallarmé's verse poetry, *Un coup de Dés* appears, in fact, as a logical consequence of the drama of verse, from which it can be shown to have developed prosodically, philosophically and historically. At least it can be shown to participate in the drama at the risk of replacing Mallarmé's shipwreck with our critic's swimming medal. A more accurate view of how *Un coup de Dés* excites, frustrates and manipulates the organizing mind, and an antidote to the epistemological medicine administered below, can be found in Malcolm Bowie's *Mallarmé and the Art of Being Difficult* and, naturally, in the poem itself.

Prosodically, one could say that in *Un coup de Dés* Mallarmé gave free rein to the elements of disintegration that were so cautiously and paradoxically alluded to in the regular poems and which, according to him, are inherent in modern rhyming verse where each line modifies, completes or undermines the other: 'Là est la suprématie des modernes vers sur ceux antiques formant un tout et ne rimant pas; qu'emplissait une bonne fois le métal employé à les faire, au lieu qu'ils le prennent, le rejettent, deviennent, procèdent musicalement: en tant que stance, ou le Distique.'[4] The lines or 'verses' of *Un coup de Dés* could be seen as the next stage: first, the 'mould' was the single verse, then the stanza or distich, and now the page or poem.

Philosophically, *Un coup de Dés* allows us to return to the starting point and to remind ourselves that 'Verse', for Mallarmé, is a structure or 'rhythm' – an archetypal form reflecting what might now be called the collective unconscious. The binary oppositions acted out thematically and prosodically in the verse poems are reflected in the daily human drama of hope and despair, and in every activity of the physical world: expansion and contraction, fragmentation and integration, rising and falling, darkness and light, absence and presence. Just as the 'apparent subject' is the froth on the surface of prosodic structures, so these prosodic structures are 'witnesses' of still deeper rhythms: over time, verse, like folk music, has absorbed the essential, abstract patterns of the human psyche. The methodological consequence of this is that the prosodic reading can also be applied to Mallarmé's critical texts and prose poems, just as he himself applied his own criteria to the work of any other writer and, theoretically, to anything else, even top hats.[5]

Historically, *Un coup de Dés* tells the story of its own origins and offers itself as an example of a cataclysmic moment in the historical unconscious. Of that, more in a moment.

Like most of Mallarmé's texts, *Un coup de Dés*, while suggesting several infinities – subjective interpretations, potential alternatives, the role of chance in artistic invention – does appear to present the reductive mind with a golden opportunity to prove its worth, and since we shall be accepting one of its structural supports as if it were solid (the thematic and formal vestiges of the drama of verse), some comment on the usefulness of invoking verse in an unversified poem may be in order.

Though the temptation to impose a neat semantic grid on the text is obviously there to be resisted, there is a contrary danger in sounding too tritely alarmist about *Un coup de Dés*, since it does exist on paper and was published and is still read, apparently with increasing profit. Mallarmé's most revolutionary poem contains some of the clearest examples in his work of what seems to be straightforward mimesis: typographical representations and visual references to the poem's structure, which are all the more noticeable for being unusual. The path of understanding provided by these hints and allusions lies parallel to the path we shall try to follow in a moment and suggests a state of mind in which the prosodic drama can be usefully applied. They can be related, for example, not just to external realities, but also to the traditions of Mallarmé's own work. We have seen how sensitive he was to the spatial dimensions of poems. Enjambments for instance are not just prosodic features but also typographical conceits. Some verses allude to both fields at the same time and, without scattering the poem over the page and across the central margin, point their syllabic fingers to all the unexplored space beyond the conventional frame. In *Hérodiade*, the gulf between sky and sea is displayed quite openly:[6]

> Et je déteste, moi, le bel azur!
>
>   Des ondes
>   Se bercent et, là-bas, . . .

The solitary 'jamais seul' of the *Hommage* to Puvis de Chavannes is another text-book example – and a nice illustration of Mallarmé's fondness for making one aspect of the poem contradict another.[7] 'Jamais seul' is a simple relative of the more sophisticated imitative devices of *Un coup de Dés*: its isolation on the page reinforces by contrast its obvious meaning; while the typographical oddities of *Un coup de Dés* go one step further, performing a representational function which may well be independent of the theme. The connection with the earlier verse poems can still be made on one level.

A similar logical development of his own procedures could be discerned in the use of blank space. The average length of Mallarmé's poems decreases towards the end of his life. This visible shrinking of the text is an allusion to a fact of poetic life. Short or lyrical poems, as he points out in his preface with what sounds like *fausse naïveté*, generally take up about one-third of a page. The same standard unit of space, we are told, was used for *Un coup de Dés*: 'je ne transgresse cette mesure, seulement la disperse'. The Page (or double page) instead of the Verse is the unit of measurement. A quick glance at the poem suggests that this may be true at least some of the time: it is possible to imagine that the hundred words beginning 'ancestralement à n'ouvrir pas la main' could be melted down and remoulded into the giant 'N'ABOLIRA' on the facing page. In other words, the obviously new and daring aspects of *Un coup de Dés* were there before but in a different form.

All these consoling comments about unities and traditions are of course practically useless, at first, in the face of such a fragmented text. Plain self-contradiction is simple enough, but not half-finished propositions, deconstructive allusions to negatives with no corresponding positives, modes of reading proposed then starved of text with which to try them out. Any sighting of a coherent principle is likely to be greeted with a 'Yes, but'. The unities are invoked – or so it seems when we try to read the poem – as a cruel mirage. Knowing that *Un coup de Dés* occupies approximately the normal amount of space per page is hardly an aid to interpretation in the way that the sonnet form may help us to organize our reading of the *sonnet en yx*. Comparisons with other poems which display their words in the shape of objects only highlight the refusal of the typographical conceits to set us on the right path, whatever that may be.[8] A shipwreck, a tilting deck, a fallen mast, perhaps; yet there is something provocative about the poet's decision to depict, not a vase or a candlestick or something as regular as rain, but an event that is characterized by randomness and dispersal. The one thing that might lend itself to typographical representation – Ursa Minor – is, according to the usual criteria, poorly drawn: where are the seven stars of the 'Septentrion', and is 'EXCEPTÉ' supposed to be the Pole Star?[9] Come to think of it, why is this valuable tool not made available to us when we really need some auxiliary explanation? Why does it tell us what we already know? 'UNE CONSTEL-LATION' is spelt out in capital letters; *'plume solitaire éperdue'* is perfectly understandable without its physical isolation; and we know from early on, without being shown the wreckage, that a 'NAUFRAGE' has taken place.

Playing with the idea of representation may disrupt our usual reading practices and suggest that even if we manage to resolve one set of ambiguities, we shall be no closer to a truth; but it also performs a philosophical function and gives some hope that the intellect may come in useful after all. The present author, as an undergraduate, copied out the poem rather sketchily onto large sheets of paper which he stuck on his wall, putting his faith in osmosis and the insights of visitors. This, as we shall see, was based on two crucial misconceptions, one of which will be dealt with immediately. (Actually, three, since I was using the unreliable Mondor edition.) Allusions to representation indicate the existence and presence in the poem of fundamental patterns and designs. *Something* is being represented, whether or not it shows itself directly. This is what Mallarmé stressed in the letters to Gide and Mauclair in which he explained some of the aesthetic and philosophical principles of *Un coup de Dés*: 'le rythme d'une phrase au sujet d'un acte ou même d'un objet n'a de sens que s'il les imite et, figuré sur le papier, repris par les Lettres à l'estampe originelle, en doit rendre, malgré tout quelque chose.'[10] The poet should try to imitate an action or even an object, not because of any individual, personal significance it may have – like the Colonne Vendôme – or because it provides a memorable image or a focus for interesting thoughts – like a Grecian urn – but because the process of representation can extract from it the impersonal archetypes it contains, the 'primitives foudres de la logique'.[11] Poems can be judged, theoretically, by the extent to which they reveal these underlying, immanent structures. Poetry should be mimetic, even if the object of imitation is invisible.

Mallarmé's mimesis is that of a ritual, the imitation of 'rhythms' rather than clumps of details.

The usefulness of the drama of verse in reading *Un coup de Dés* is that it allows us to follow one recognizable strand through the poem: a strand which is still subject to the contradictions and interruptions of the text but which runs more closely than any other alongside the concealed, 'latent' 'armature intellectuelle du poëme'.[12] It refers to the most visible and analysable manifestation of those primal rhythms – verse – and makes it possible to point to one of the vines of the thyrsus *as if* it were the immanent structure itself. It also has the interest of situating this meteoric work in the development of Mallarmé's poetry by confirming its close relations with such later poems as *Salut* or the Vasco sonnet, in which the 'Maître' keeps his hand on the tiller. The differences between these texts may seem so great that the point of comparison will appear too general and abstract to account for particular details. The remarks that follow do inevitably represent a crude, beachcombing approach to the shipwrecked text. Mallarmé himself points out in his preface that verse, in the restricted, technical sense, is absent from *Un coup de Dés*: 'il ne s'agit pas, ainsi que toujours, de traits sonores réguliers ou vers – plutôt, de subdivisions prismatiques de l'Idée.' A case could also be made for deliberate 'de-versification'. Read line by line, *Un coup de Dés* contains only four groups of twelve syllables (three of them regular alexandrines), but five of thirteen and eight of eleven, despite what some structuralist *coups d'état* have tried to suggest.[13] The principal proposition – 'Un coup de dés jamais n'abolira le hasard' – by which, says Claude Roulet, 'le Poème célèbre encore le triomphe du grand vers classique, rajeuni et qui gagne d'être isolé' is 'loin de ressembler à un alexandrin ordinaire'[14] (it contains thirteen syllables). However, the absence or dislocation of verse are still prosodically significant. They can be related to poems like 'Surgi de la croupe . . .' or *Hommage à Wagner* which accommodate elements of disintegration in their regular schemes. Moreover, if we return to the idea of blank spaces and typographical representations without taking Mallarmé quite so literally, this, too, implicitly recommends a prosodic reading. Mallarmé himself refers to these new principles as a 'prosodie' as if their peculiarity was not that of individual invention but the strangeness of a myth or archetype – something that owed its existence more to 'the popular soul' than to Stéphane Mallarmé.

First, the organization of the poem is directly analogous to the structure of the verse poems: 'la Page: celle-ci prise pour unité comme l'est autre part le Vers ou ligne parfaite.' The structural basis of the poem has simply been shifted up one plane, from verse to page. Second, the huge white spaces – philosophically if not actually – are those of regular verse poems: 'la versification en exigea [des blancs], comme silence alentour, ordinairement'. In practice, there may be huge differences, but the principle is the same, and its usefulness will become apparent when we read the poem. Another piece of infrastructure which survives the wreck of the verse poems (though not mentioned in the preface or anywhere else) is the use of a special vocabulary with prosodic connotations. Or, more simply, themes which are also treated in the verse poems. One of the themes, as most commentators have noticed, is writing.[15]

Mallarmé's preface also ties *Un coup de Dés* to the drama of verse by placing its most obviously unsettling feature in a historical context – the lack of any but the skimpiest (and perhaps accidental) prosodic regularity: 'reconnaissons aisément que la tentative participe, avec imprévu, de poursuites particulières et chères à notre temps, le vers libre et le poème en prose.' The reference to a historical moment, 'notre temps', is highly significant. Alluding to these modern pursuits is not just a literary-historical comment on the poem. The 'exquise crise, fondamentale' of verse, for Mallarmé, is far more than a literary fashion whose currency might help to make his own poem more acceptable or familiar to the reading public. The *crise de vers*, as Bertrand Marchal has shown so thoroughly, is part of a much wider picture. Historically, it embodies the spirit of an age in search of new structures. Art and society are directly interrelated; the disintegration of one can only be understood in terms of the other:[16]

> dans une société sans stabilité, sans unité, il ne peut se créer d'art stable, d'art définitif. De cette organisation sociale inachevée, qui explique en même temps l'inquiétude des esprits, naît l'inexpliqué besoin d'individualité dont les manifestations littéraires présentes sont le reflet direct.[17]

An 'organisation sociale inachevée' produces an incomplete prosodic organization. One suspects Mallarmé of simplifying the relationship between the two for the benefit of Huret's audience: this is really just the old idea that Art mirrors Society – surely a 'Decadent' would have said the exact opposite. The crisis of verse (or an actual case like *Un coup de Dés*) is more than just a 'rénovation de rites et de rimes';[18] but the social crisis itself is more than just a change of régime or a spate of anarchist bombs. The relationship of art and society is not a simple one of mutual or one-sided influence. Both are manifestations of fundamental structures. The prime cause is not directly defined, just as the thing itself is not depicted in the poetry, 'mais l'effet qu'elle produit'. The French Revolution and the emergence of free verse are part of the same archetypal drama. Mallarmé's preface introduces *Un coup de Dés* as an example of that crisis, but also as an investigation of it and perhaps an indication of what a new order might consist of. The poem, in other words, can be read as a discussion of its own form, as an answer to the question it so obviously poses: why is it not in regular verse? The prosodic revolution that followed the setting of the Hugolian sun is one of its subjects and guiding principles. By referring to its own structures and destructions, it recounts and enacts an attempt to discover the underlying pattern of the crisis. The story it tells, both thematically and formally, is, once again, an allegory. An allegory which is also a dramatization of a historical phase of the collective unconscious. Precept and example.

The drama of verse is projected here onto the broader planes it always implied in the regular poems. The philosophical difference is one of degree rather than substance. As its self-referential title suggests, *Un coup de Dés* is a gamble: can the poem be prolonged beyond its 'agony'? Can the moment of disaster be depicted at length? Can the underlying pattern still be displayed without the 'compteur factice' of regular verse? Was this pattern universal or simply an effect of versification? And can fundamental linguistic structures be investigated by means of language?

The answers lie in the problem itself. This is not a rational disquisition on the erosion of traditional verse and the dissolution of an old society; the poem participates in the crisis. All around the strands of logic, the storm continues to rage; and it may well be that this kind of critical writing, which seems to work with the verse poems, takes us further from the poem's ultimate refer-ents than even the most confused and cursory of silent readings. It may, however, prevent the poem from being swamped by theoretical dithering without being another attempt to pack it all away into little numbered boxes and pretend not to have been disappointed. Verse is a theme which inevit-ably generates its share of implausible remarks, but its practical virtue is that it makes it harder to pluck off all the thematic feathers and reconstitute them as an impossible bird. Ideally, it would reveal the basic simplicity of *Un coup de Dés*. The general semantic structure of the poem, in fact, is almost too obvious to be visible. It was very silly of Geoffrey Brereton to say that 'a typewriter would have been fatal to [Mallarmé's] art':[19] *Un coup de Dés* is a brilliant example of a poet combining modern technology with his art and indescribable ideals with a process of meaning which is quite literally placed in our hands.

The best poetic route to *Un coup de Dés* is another of Mallarmé's maritime poems: the sonnet which Tolstoy famously declared to be meaningless[20] – 'A la nue accablante tu . . .'. I realize this entails a lengthy digression, not least because of the difficulties the sonnet presents; but it makes it possible to take bearings in the world of *Un coup de Dés*. Even if the world is entirely unfamiliar to us, we can still try to find out where we are in it.

> A la nue accablante tu
> Basse de basalte et de laves
> A même les échos esclaves
> Par une trompe sans vertu
>
> Quel sépulcral naufrage (tu
> Le sais, écume, mais y baves)

Suprême une entre les épaves
Abolit le mât dévêtu

Ou cela que furibond faute
De quelque perdition haute
Tout l'abîme vain éployé

Dans le si blanc cheveu qui traîne
Avarement aura noyé
Le flanc enfant d'une sirène

The first part of the sonnet can be read as follows (several other readings are possible). The subject of the quatrains is the 'sépulcral naufrage': the poem is not just the inevitable failure (like any throw of the dice, it cannot alter the conditions of its production), but merely the ghost or representation of a failure, the simulacrum of a disaster. The 'écume' of the waves knows it to be a phantom but still, figuratively, foams at the mouth as if destroying a real ship (taking 'le' in 'tu le sais' as the invariable direct object pronoun referring to the ghostliness of the 'naufrage'). 'Tu' in line 1 agrees with 'naufrage' in line 5: the 'trompe sans vertu' is incapable of sending up a distress signal, even to the lowering cloud above.

Typically, Mallarmé's agreements are a source of disagreement, as in *Billet* (see p. 77). 'Basse', perhaps more than any other word, has been the object of a sometimes quite acrimonious tug-of-war whose contestants appear not to have realized they were all pulling in roughly the same direction and hurtling towards the 'horizon unanime'. The initial temptation is usually to attach 'basse' to the feminine 'nue', either as noun ('bass' in the musical sense or 'shoal') or as adjective. But the picture is just as coherent if 'basse' in the sense of 'shoal' is attached to 'naufrage', meaning not just the event itself but the resulting wreck (the shoal is compared to a ship and *vice versa*). 'Basse' is – for instance – in apposition, so that 'tu' agrees not, of course, with 'basse' but with 'naufrage'. The feminine appositional phrase, 'Basse de basalte', precedes its masculine subject, 'naufrage'. The same arrangement can be seen in *Petit Air II*: 'Voix étrangère au bosquet . . . L'oiseau qu'on n'ouït jamais.' Similarly, in the second quatrain, the appositional 'Suprême une entre les épaves' precedes the 'mât dévêtu'. Thus: 'What sepulchral shipwreck – a wreck which is (comparable to) a shoal of basalt and lava – cut off from the overwhelming cloud by an ineffectual horn, abolishes (or abolished) the stripped mast, which is (or was) the only remaining bit of wreckage?' The sentence forming the quatrains is an unusually complicated though entirely characteristic Mallarmean phrase, built up around what Scherer calls 'enclaves' (this is only one possible construction):

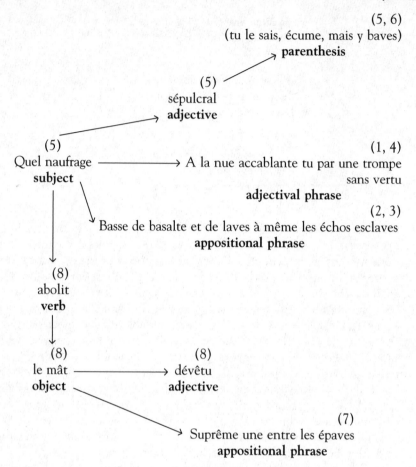

(5, 6)
(tu le sais, écume, mais y baves)
parenthesis

(5)
sépulcral
adjective

(5)   (1, 4)
Quel naufrage ⟶ A la nue accablante tu par une trompe
subject   sans vertu
                    adjectival phrase
                                        (2, 3)
          Basse de basalte et de laves à même les échos esclaves
                    appositional phrase

(8)
abolit
verb

(8)   (8)
le mât ⟶ dévêtu
object   **adjective**

                                                (7)
          Suprême une entre les épaves
                    appositional phrase

The subject, 'naufrage', is postponed until the start of the second quatrain, as in *Sainte*: 'A la fenêtre' (v. 1) . . . 'Est la Sainte pâle' (v. 5). In *Petit Air II*, the subject, 'oiseau', does not appear until line 7 and is preceded by a similar accumulation of syntax: adverbs, comparison, verb, appositional phrases. In 'A la nue . . .', the whole complex structure of the first seven lines is abruptly resolved (grammatically) and dissolved (thematically) in line 8, when the other principal members of the sentence come tumbling out as if a syntactic log-jam had suddenly been breached. Then those eight lines in turn are undermined by the tercets: 'Ou cela que . . .'. The quatrains are shown to have been a mere hypothesis of a disappearance of a ghost of a wreck of what might once have been a ship. Four removes from reality, five if one counts the fact that the poem itself is fiction.

'A la nue . . .' is a valuable example in regular verse of that arrested destructiveness which governs *Un coup de Dés*. However, the main point of this digression was to show the metaphorical space in which Mallarmé places his shipwreck poems: a space which has an exact equivalent in the real dimensions occupied by the printed text on the page. The topography of the sonnet is that of 'L'aile s'évanouit . . .' or 'Surgi de la croupe . . .': a connection is established (or not) between the ground-level reality (floor, mouth of vase or surface of the ocean) and the ceiling or sky. Verticality (whether the action goes up or down) signifies successful poetic communication – the falling feather, the rising flower or the standing poet of *Salut*. In 'A la nue . . .', the upright mast has sunk or was never there in the first place.

Now that the main axes of the picture can be envisaged, it should seem entirely plausible that 'basse de basalte et de laves à même les échos esclaves' can be an appositional phrase describing, not the cloud, but the shipwreck. A 'basse', defined by Littré, is a 'Banc de roches ou de corail, situé à faible profondeur, mais que l'eau ne découvre pas à marée basse'. We have seen that 'basalte' is used by Mallarmé to refer to the poem itself:[21] the solidified remnant of an original volcanic (or Vulcanic) upheaval. Just as the text remains flush with ('à même') the page, the rock never protrudes above the surface of the water. The 'echoes' are trapped in the self-referential text, postulating a third dimension, but incapable of projecting themselves into it. The surface of the ocean or the flat page is like the event-horizon of a black hole where images are frozen at their point of disappearance:

nue

---

basse

'A même' refers to the fact that the poem consists only of language and has meaning only in relation to itself. This is how Mallarmé uses the phrase when describing Verhaeren's verse: 'un élément . . . à même et soi, nu et dévorant ses propres mots.'[22] Nothing – not even a sound – escapes the epistemological shipwreck, and the alternative hypothesis – introduced by 'Ou cela que' – is no more hopeful: the siren has drowned; it is an 'enfant' (etymologically, silent); only one element of a pair is mentioned ('flanc' – and, in *The Odyssey*, there are only two sirens); and 'sirène' forms the only visually heterogeneous rhyme in the sonnet: *sirène-traîne*.

These metaphorical and physical dimensions of the poem, both the message and its medium, provide the basis for a prosodic reading of *Un coup de Dés*; or rather, since the longer poem is far more complex, a point of view from which the prosodic drama can be seen performing itself throughout the poem.

One possible reading might go something like this:

After setting the unusual prosodic scene with an eleven-syllable line and what, in our innocence, we might assume to be the vestige of a significant enjambment – ÉTERNELLES – lurching off into eternal empty space, the first double page opens with the closing of the book. Both sea and page are 'blanchi': strictly speaking, paper is whitened, not white. The verb 'blanchir' can also refer to the practice of aerating text with white space. The second adjective, 'étale', describes, again, both the theme and the medium: motionless, neither rising nor falling, flat. The flat page displays the first real and metaphorical descent of letters around the central gulf. (Bowie and others have pointed out that Mallarmé alludes typographically to the central margins, here only just bridged by the precarious 'par avance' as later by 'sauf que' and – expressively – 'aigrette de vertige'.)

Like all of Mallarmé's and almost everyone else's poems, the 'wing' of text has inevitably fallen 'in advance' down to the bottom of the page: 'retombée d'un mal à dresser le vol'. The initial impetus or 'heurt d'aile brusque' of verse gives it a temporary elevation or buoyancy like a feather or balloon; but, even in verse, what goes up must come down. In a similar phrase from a letter written a few months later, Mallarmé used the related analogy of a fountain to describe the verses of Maurice de Faramond: 'il semble que chaque jet d'eau s'alimente à son élan déjà retombé et qui scintille la minute nécessaire.'[23]

Each page – and the whole poem – can be read in terms of this conventional typographical descent. Here, the 'aile' descends like the writing pen which works its way down the page. Later, the 'plume solitaire' (feather or quill)[24] hovers momentarily at the top of the page. Later still, in words that recall the letter to Faramond, the 'aigrette de vertige' (*vers-tige*) 'scintille' and seems to evoke a standing figure ('une stature') which remains upright 'le temps / de souffleter . . . un roc' – or 'la minute nécessaire'. The brief moment during which verse appears to have a tiny impact on reality. This typical process, and its banal physical equivalent, is described in greater detail towards the end of the poem:

> Choit
>   *la plume*
>   *rythmique suspens du sinistre*
>   *s'ensevelir*
>   *aux écumes originelles*
>   *naguères d'où sursauta son délire jusqu'à une cime*
>   *flétrie*
>   *par la neutralité identique du gouffre*

'Rythmique suspens du sinistre' is a splendid description of Mallarmé's poetry. Rhymes and other rhythms are a postponement of the inevitable disaster – the inability of language to alter its conditions, to abolish chance. The 'suspens' is always followed by a descent into the void, the text by whiteness: 'indéfectiblement le blanc revient'.[25] The verse returns to the 'original froth' of reality from which it was extrapolated just a moment before ('naguères'), from which the lyrical 'délire' leapt up to a poetic peak. The poem, so far, can be read as one of Mallarmé's metaphorical evocations of writing. The advantage *Un coup de Dés* enjoys over the prose texts is that it acts out on the paper the processes it describes.

The end of the phrase – *'flétrie / par la neutralité identique du gouffre'* – refers to another of the simultaneously philosophical, prosodic and physical 'fils conducteurs' of the poem: the positive of poetic expression is effectively eradicated by the negative of silence. Meaning serves only to emphasize meaninglessness; text – contrary to the normal view – highlights the surrounding blankness. The motif is introduced on the first double page:

l'ombre enfouie dans la profondeur par cette voile alternative

jusqu'adapter
à l'envergure

sa béante profondeur en tant que la coque

d'un bâtiment

penché de l'un ou l'autre bord

The abyss of the sea matches the empty hull of the ship: trivially, the ship is filled by water. The emptiness of the vessel is neutralized by a corresponding fullness; and this is what actually happens as we read, whether or not with understanding. Philosophically, the idea is very Mallarmean, but in practice it is something which *Un coup de Dés* shares with every other poem and which is quite unmysteriously a part of the physical act of reading.

When the page is turned, appropriately after the word 'bord', the text is 'buried' in the book, between the sheets. This cancelling-out effect is accentuated by the fact that the words on the left-hand page are covered by blank space on the right, while blank space on the left falls over the words on the right-hand page. Whichever way the textual vessel leans, it disappears in the white abyss.

Most of the other double pages follow a similar pattern. There are two main types. Either the words fall on top of each other as if crossing themselves out; or, as here, the text is swamped by a corresponding blankness. The effect can best be appreciated by holding the pages up to the light, and perhaps this is what Mallarmé intended to suggest in the *Cosmopolis* version, where 'transparence' took the place of 'profondeur': 'l'ombre enfouie dans la transparence par cette voile alternative'. The 'voile alternative' is the facing page which covers the other – 'voile' and 'toile' being images of the white page or canvas. As with the downward movement of text, the same process is repeated, inevitably, throughout the poem. Some of the nautical metaphors refer to it quite directly: for example, the regular alexandrine that closes the central italicized section: 'par la neutralité identique du gouffre'. This process is the equivalent, on a larger scale, of rhymes like *vagues-vagues* or 'Tristement dort une mandore': words create a disappearance of the things they designate, and then the words themselves dissolve in their phonemes and graphemes.

A third humdrum, tangible reality referred to on the first double page (as in some of the verse poems) is the flatness of the poet's medium: 'couvrant les jaillissements / coupant au ras les bonds'. Like the basalt shoal of 'A la nue . . .', the text is flush with ('au ras', 'à même') the page. No actual presence, as Mallarmé reminds us in *Crise de vers* ('hors de toute pierre, sur quoi les pages se refermeraient mal'), prevents the closing and perfect correspondence of the matching 'voiles'. The 'jaillissements' and 'bonds' of so-called creation are cut off at the surface like the absent flower of 'Surgi de la croupe . . .'. The 'reploiement vierge' of the closing pages castrates, as it were, the poet's 'petite raison virile'.[26]

To sum up so far: the organizing principles of *Un coup de Dés* are directly related to the drama of verse. The archetypal actions are the same – the rise that implies a fall, the self-erasing of words, the imprisonment of text in its own dimensions – but transposed onto another plane: Page and Volume instead of Verse. Thematically, the drama is present as vividly as in the verse poems. Many of the same metaphors and key words are used, and even if the poem was and is exceptional in the world of French poetry, it can still be related intratextually to the rest of Mallarmé's work. The theme or 'apparent subject' is in some ways more prominent and accessible than in many of the verse poems. The formal elements of *Un coup de Dés* do not, of course, have a familiar, traditional set of prosodic codes as a point of reference; without a large amount of analysis and knowledge of how Mallarmé usually applies them, the rules of versification are practically useless. But the poem does refer to more universal realities: space, paper, page and book. Like the largest word on the map, these may be the last things to be noticed.

If the poem makes us feel that we are thinking too much for our intelligence, then perhaps we have simply not adapted our reading to the text. Trying to make everything fit as soon as possible is the shortest route to confusion and boredom. The repetition of characteristic actions and the partly circular arrangement of themes suggest that one or even several linear readings are unlikely to bear much fruit. The paradox is that *Un coup de Dés*, like the *Éventails*, seems to demand an unusual degree of mental agility if the lacunae of the text are to be crossed, when perhaps a little further down a bridge was already built. On the other hand, simply crossing the bridge would fail to provide much in the way of excitement.

Each part of the poem is structurally related to the dimensions indicated on the first double page. The horizontality and verticality of the text, including its white margins and central crevass; the flatness of the page; and – the only real possible projection into a third dimension – the turning of the page. Rather than introducing a new dimension, however (since *Un coup de Dés* is not a pop-up book), the turning of the page neutralizes the other dimensions. Nothing is created; in fact, the opposite occurs. In Mallarmé's commonsensical view of the matter, this annihilation or conjuring away of realities is the only thing a poet can claim to produce – 'la seule création humaine possible';[27] 'A l'égal de créer: la notion d'un objet, échappant, qui fait défaut.'[28]

All actions related to this topography are described in the smaller fonts, and the same actions, as we saw briefly, are repeated with variations throughout the poem. Each peak is 'sullied' by an abyss; a convexity is cancelled out by a concavity, one page by the following or preceding page, in the same way that, even with the best of memories, reading involves far more forgetting than remembering.[29] The dramatic tension is constantly recreated: which peak will be reached before the inevitable fall? – Looking ahead, the highest peak, thematically and physically, will be that of the constellation 'à l'altitude', like the wave that is higher than the others. This recurrent circular pattern is implicated in the larger structures, represented by the largest letters (that is, those which form discrete sense-groups rather than those which simply emphasize certain elements of the longer text, like 'SOIT', 'LE MAITRE', '*COMME SI*'): 'UN COUP DE DÉS JAMAIS N'ABOLIRA LE HASARD'; '*SI C'ÉTAIT LE NOMBRE CE SERAIT* LE HASARD'; 'RIEN N'AURA EU LIEU QUE LE LIEU EXCEPTÉ PEUT-ETRE UNE CON-STELLATION'.[30]

Typographically, the title of the poem provides a linear structure along which the circular patterns are arranged; but this too can be imagined as another all-encompassing circle: the argument itself is circular – an act performed under certain conditions will not affect those conditions – and a faint tautology has been detected in the fact that 'hasard' comes from a word for a game played with dice. Structurally, too, the poem is a giant chiasmus – 'UN COUP DE DÉS . . . COMME SI . . . COMME SI . . . un Coup de Dés' – with a miniature model of the structure on the third double page: 'la mer par l'aïeul tentant ou l'aïeul contre la mer'.[31] The circle of *Un coup de Dés* contains the life-spans of several Mallarmé poems. The bird of *Petit Air II* is repeatedly launched into the air and repeatedly falls to the ground, while each separate act is reflected or reenacted in the wider structure which contains and, thematically, negates them all.

The problem has now been posed, as in so many other poems – often in the quatrains of a sonnet, before the 'Mais' of the tercets. Cancelling out, futile correspondence, words erasing the realities they describe and then each other, alternatives but no solution. What we have seen so far is not so much the beginning of a drama as a description of some of its recurring components.

Similarly, allusions which first appear on the first double page will continue to tug our minds back to the unchanging realities of the text: its two directions, the flatness and whiteness of the page, the margins, the progressive closing of the book. Mallarmé complained of the pathetic contrast between the supposed variety of human feelings and the uniformity of verse. Here, this literary incongruity has a metaphysical application. For all the apparent chaos, there is an overriding immutability and uniformity. Seen from a certain height, even in such an irregular poem as this, elements of sameness dominate the local variations.

But this time, as we can hardly fail to realize from the form of the poem, something different has happened. Other solutions to the problem are being considered. They may have no effect whatsoever on the original dilemma; the conditions under which the dice are thrown or the poem composed will certainly be unaltered; but the exploration of alternatives, previously considered in separate enactments of the prosodic drama, is about to introduce a new complexity and a spectacular radiation of paths – even as the inevitable descent and closure continue. The impetus for change comes from the thematic, intellectual aspect of the drama: its investigation of its own history, its literary context and antecedents, and the historical archetypes it implies.[32]

Suddenly, 'LE MAITRE' appears, significantly, 'surgi'; and, with him, a partial explanation of what has happened to the old verse forms: 'hors d'anciens calculs / où la manoeuvre avec l'âge oubliée' and 'jadis il empoignait la barre'. The Master (the poet himself or his means of expression, Verse, 'dispensateur, ordonnateur du jeu des pages, maître du livre')[33] stands now 'beyond' or 'outside' the 'former calculations' of prosody (or, on the merely thematic level, of navigation), perhaps too old to remember or bother about the necessary operations. Once, as we know, and as the poem reminds us, he had a firm grip on the tiller like Vasco da Gama; but now he seems more like Captain Ahab in his self-destructive pursuit of the great white whale. We can see for ourselves that the verses have been allowed to drift apart and disintegrate. They form patterns which seem to be random or which, like constellations, may be only subjectively meaningful in the reader's interpreting eye.

Why has the Master rejected his nautical/prosodic science or[34] consigned it to the locker of oblivion as in the Wagner sonnet? The key prosodic reference here is 'horizon unanime': the flat horizon of the *Éventails* at which the coincident 'lights' or 'fires' of words (*con-flagration*) cancel each other out and imply the 'gouffre central' – here quite literally in the trough of the two pages, straddled by the text, as if figuring the hesitation of the Master, the suspension of the act, or the attempt to keep his balance: will he throw the dice or not? On this and the next page the problem is considered even as the Master drowns. If some inevitable, necessary 'unique Nombre' or final reality is forming itself, what is the point of writing the poem? For, as we learn later on, after the italicised performance of a typical Mallarmean poetic act, even if the expression exactly matched the final reality, it would still be pure chance.

In *Prose*, the poet rejected the formal, factitious synthesis of rhyming verse and proclaimed the necessity of expressing some communicable wisdom. Here, any expression at all is seen to be a futile rehearsal of its initial conditions. The phrase 'Esprit / pour le jeter / dans la tempête / en reployer la division et passer[35] fier' refers to the divisions and resolutions of the poetic work; the poet's pride at having thrown the poetic dice again. Significantly, 'fierté', not 'orgueil': any notion of Promethean damnation is noticeably absent from what would normally be a Promethean situation. Reality is indifferent. There is no 'perdition haute' to give a moral sense to the act. The rational, creative mind – '*sa petite raison virile / en foudre*' (organized in the 'foudre' of verse but, quite literally, belittled) – makes no difference to anything. Hence the Master's hesitation. The writing arm is lifeless ('cadavre par le bras') and sinks without throwing the dice, ironically and contradictorily, with the most obvious rhyme in the whole poem: 'le chef . . . sans nef'. The poet of *Salut* has lost his vessel. Metaphorically, this is the historical crisis or 'bouleversement' described by Mallarmé in *La Musique et les Lettres*: 'l'acte d'écrire se scruta jusqu'en l'origine. . . . A savoir s'il y a lieu d'écrire.'[36]*

These considerations are now appropriately faced with the vast, blank space of the page containing only the words 'N'ABOLIRA'. The text, written in the face of the void, is negated in advance. When the same roman typeface reappears, the human drama will be over and only an impersonal reality will

---

* The whole futile situation, tragic though it is, is strongly reminiscent of farce and might have been nicely performed, in a silent film of course, with Ben Turpin as the 'maniaque chenu' sinking beneath the waves with one arm aloft. Similarly, Charlie Chaplin can be imagined 'Oubliant [son] habit de pitre au tronc d'un hêtre' or tugging at the bell-rope in *Le Sonneur*. A typical first reaction to Mallarmé's poetry, before the anxious gloom of exegesis descends, is hilarity – which is also an important theme of the poems. The temptation to keep a straight face is definitely to be resisted. Reading Mallarmé's poetry for laughs is almost always illuminating, perhaps because it creates an incentive to consider all possibilities. The precious wit of the letters and the *Vers de circonstance* is just one constricted aspect of his sense of humour. Roger Fry points to some formal analogies with wit in his translation of Mallarmé's *Poems* (Chatto & Windus, 1936), 298; Paul Bénichou emphasizes the jokiness of *Prose pour des Esseintes* (see p. 238, n. 5); and I hope to have indicated the funny side of other 'serious' poems – quite apart from all the puns and conundrums: the flowerless vase of 'Surgi de la croupe . . .', the wardrobe of *Hommage à Wagner*, the topsy-turvy sirens of *Salut*, etc. The dead are prevented from leaving their tombs by the weight of mourners' wreaths ('Sur les bois oubliés . . .'). 'Calme bloc ici-bas chu d'un désastre obscur' is a description of a nasty piece of public sculpture (see OC, 226 on Poe's monument as drain-cover and note 'du moins' in the sonnet). A logical surrealism *à la* Monty Python might be detected in the incongruous exchanges of Hérodiade and her nurse, the missing *ptyx*, the flying pubis of *Le Tombeau de Charles Baudelaire* and, generally, in Mallarmé's use of Christian symbolism. See, for example, *Le Cantique de saint Jean* and cf. the crucifixion scene at the end of *Life of Brian*: 'Always Look on the Bright Side of Life.'

remain. Having said that the dice will not be thrown, the poem returns in time – the drowning Master's life passes before his eyes – in an effort to investigate the act of writing 'jusqu'en l'origine'. The past, at this point, is the only way forward.

The 'legs' (among other things) is the 'legs prosodique',[37] now in the process of disappearing. The alexandrine, 'l'instrument héréditaire',[38] has been softened up and liquefied like a body picked clean by the waves: 'caressée et polie et rendue et lavée' is, perhaps ironically, one of only three regular alexandrines in the poem. The image of polishing refers again, on one level, to the art of verse, to lines that are gradually honed and polished: 'Polissez-le sans cesse et le repolissez.'[39] As usual, the poetry implies a gloomy view of what sounds quite cheerful in the critical texts: 'Les fidèles à l'alexandrin, notre hexamètre, desserrent intérieurement ce mécanisme rigide et puéril de sa mesure.'[40] The skeleton of the old verse forms has fallen apart. The 'ultérieur démon immémorial' – the ancient 'demon of verse', 'né / d'un ébat' – has led the Master to his death. Its (or his) 'ombre puérile', the childish, half-conscious stuttering that Mallarmé associates with free or 'fluid' verse: the 'ingénuité' of Moréas and Dujardin, the 'mutinerie' of Laforgue, the 'primitives épellations' of Verlaine, the 'balbutiement' of the later Rimbaud[41] (or the semiotic rhythms of Julia Kristeva). Just as poetic prose, 'soustraite à ce laisser-aller en usage',[42] contains elements of versification, so the invertebrate shadow of verse, 'soustraite' from its unifying structure, produces only a futile gamble. The chiasmic phrase, 'la mer par l'aïeul tentant ou l'aïeul contre la mer', which is reminiscent of several palindromic verses in *Poésies*, expresses and exemplifies the engagement ('Fiançailles') of poet and reality, with a view to an ultimate marriage – a marriage to which the poet brings his prosodic legacy. But now that 'the veil of illusion' has gone, the structure of verse cast off, all sense is lost and the result is madness. 'Folie' is the last word on the double page – specifically, the poem itself, which Mallarmé described to Valéry as 'un acte de démence'.

In one respect, this is the end of the poem. After the next four double pages in which the text is mostly in italics, in lower and upper case, the roman font reappears, but this time without the Master. The secondary text which conveyed the details of the allegorical drama has become an 'inférieur clapotis quelconque comme pour disperser l'acte vide': not the harmonious, rhythmical 'flots' or 'ondes' of regular verse but an irregular lapping ('inferior' also on the page) which 'scatters' the 'empty' poetic act , 'qui sinon / par son mensonge / eût fondé / la perdition'. If the dice had been thrown, a heroic, Promethean gesture might have been accomplished: a Baudelairean 'lie' of artistic creation. (We shall see that this is indeed what has – hypothetically – happened in the italicized section.) All that remains, as in the *sonnet en yx* and 'Le vierge, le vivace . . .', is a constellation, independent of human expression: 'hors l'intérêt / quant à lui signalé / en général / selon telle obliquité par telle déclivité / de feux'. The Master no longer practises the 'anciens calculs' of sextant and compass, and so the constellation has no practical sense or purpose in human terms.

The irony is that this constellation in its 'impersonnelle magnificence'[43] is the symbol of the successful 'musicality' of the poem, its ability to recapture and display in its new prosodic structure the 'primitives foudres de la logique':[44] 'Quelque symétrie . . . vole, outre le volume, à plusieurs inscrivant, eux, sur l'espace spirituel, le paraphe amplifié du génie, anonyme et parfait comme une existence d'art.'[45] The philosophical conclusion, from a humanist point of view, is depressing. But the contradictory fact that the poem was produced, 'hors d'anciens calculs', is ironically alluded to in terms that make this the end, the new beginning and the nostalgic recollection of the drama of verse. The preposition 'vers' is given what may seem to be undeserved prominence by its isolation. The strong, typographical hint is that it can also be taken as a noun in apposition to the constellation (preposition and noun share the same etymon): 'le vers, système agencé comme un spirituel zodiaque';[46] 'le terme surnaturel, qu'est le vers'.[47] The proximity of the noun 'feux' suggests a typical pattern of Mallarmé's prose – for example: 'selon telle obliquité par telle déclivité de feux – Vers! ce doit être le Septentrion'. The stars, spilling over the sky like dice on a table with their 'heurt successif', are analogous to words in verse, 'par le heurt de leur inégalité mobilisés; ils s'allument de reflets réciproques comme une virtuelle traînée de feux sur des pierreries'.[48]

Ironic too is the unexpected regularity of the last half-page. Two five-syllable lines – 'le heurt successif / sidéralement' – add together to make a ten-syllable line: 'd'un compte total en formation' (aptly enough). Then four even-numbered lines, all rhyming with each other and internally, make up a regular alexandrine – 'veillant / doutant / roulant / brillant et méditant' – and two six-syllable groups rhyming on e, followed by the penultimate 'qui le sacre'. The final irony is that the 'point dernier' of the poem is a straightfor-wardly formulated maxim enshrined in a decasyllabic line which reaffirms the metaphysical futility of the organizing mind: 'Toute Pensée émet un Coup de Dés'.

This characteristic self-contradiction – a philosophical counterpoint which can be compared to the unimitative harmonies or conceits of the regular poems – allows us to adopt either a positive or a negative attitude to the fact that 'Un coup de dés jamais n'abolira le hasard'. There is in the end a necessary structure which the poem can reveal, thus proving its 'auth-enticity'. The nature of the universe and the archetypes of existence are immutable and inescapable; and from a philosophical point of view there is nothing more to be said: 'Nous savons, captifs d'une formule absolue, que, certes, n'est que ce qui est'; 'La Nature a lieu, on n'y ajoutera pas'.[49] But Mallarmé was first of all a poet and second a human being. The 'crisis of verse', which is one of the subjects of *Un coup de Dés*, is moved on a stage by the poem itself, and its principal, technical question is answered: 'en dehors

des préceptes consacrés, est-il possible de faire de la poésie?' The answer is
'yes', because, as Mallarmé told Jules Huret, 'Le vers est partout dans la langue
où il y a rythme'.[50]

The question of quality is harder to answer (which has not prevented some
critics from answering this, if no other question). The deversified poem may
simply be an attempt to salvage something from the wreck brought about by
the tinkering of the *vers-libristes*; or perhaps their experimentations have
made it possible to transpose onto the page 'quelqu'un des poëmes immanents
à l'humanité ou leur originel état'[51] or, as he suggests in his preface, the
abstract patterns of thought ('son dessin même'). Whether or not it actually
achieves this, *Un coup de Dés* is Mallarmé's most daring attempt (or most
daring description of the attempt) to take back from Music 'plusieurs moyens
m'ayant semblé appartenir aux Lettres', this being just the first stage in a
greater plan of conquest: 'nous en sommes là, précisément, à rechercher,
devant une brisure des grands rythmes littéraires . . . et leur éparpillement en
frissons articulés proches de l'instrumentation, un art d'achever la transposition, au Livre, de la symphonie ou uniment de reprendre notre bien'.[52] The
real defeat consists, not in the fiction of the drowned Master, but in the
discursive, intellectual presence of the poet who does not entirely yield
the initiative to words. *Un coup de Dés* was not after all 'l'oeuvre pure' but a
'tentative', an 'état' which still contained 'certaines directions très
hardies . . . à l'état élémentaire' – apparently out of politeness to his host, the
magazine: a poor substitute for 'eternal parchments'.

In an equally practical spirit, *Un coup de Dés* also offers an answer to the
question implicit in Mallarmé's self-reflecting, self-erasing drama: how can a
poem which starts with the premise of its own futility be sustained? Why do
Mallarmé's poems not all consist – as Richard Wollheim thought they might
– of blank paper?[53] Cynically, it could be said that the title phrase in big
letters, strung out over sixteen pages, is a way of making the pointlessness last
as long as possible. An extreme example of journalistic 'blanchissement' or
'remplissage'. But there is another answer which gives a curtain-call to all the
major themes of the drama and confirms that it owes its textual existence, not
to specific fictional events, but to a process.

It so happens that the dice *are* thrown, but hypothetically, in the italicized
text introduced by the words 'folie' and 'N'ABOLIRA'. 'Tout se passe, par
raccourci, en hypothèse', as Mallarmé says in his preface. 'SOIT / que', on the
first double page, presents the whole poem as a hypothesis, so that any further
hypothesis in the poem is twice removed from the base reality. The four
double pages of italics are the last, virtual enactment of the drama, the 'mad
scene' of *Un coup de Dés*, a poem within a longer poem that denies the smaller
one the reality of its existence – and even the reality of its absence – and
which allows it to perform itself only when all its actors have drowned and
disappeared, except the pen that would have written it.

The poem within a poem is, almost literally, a self-effacing text. For Mallarmé (and not just for him), italics have a special connotation. In letters to the publisher, Edmond Deman, he describes them as the printed equivalent of handwriting; they indicate, not a definitive text but a draft,[54] fiction and hypothesis rather than final reality. In *L'Après-midi d'un faune*, italics were used to represent the artistic recreation of reality or even pure fantasy. The nymphs may already be an illusion of the senses; in the italic passages, they are the fictional representation of an illusion in a work of fiction.

In *Un coup de Dés*, typography is related to meaning in a similar though slightly more complicated fashion. The straight, roman letters refer to straight, incontrovertible truths; the bigger the letters, the more general the truth. The title phrase is a universal constant. The smaller 'CONSTEL-LATION' is also a fact, but peculiar to this situation. The roman section in upper- and lower-case letters describes one infinitesimal human event but an event which, in terms of the poem, is supposed to have actually occurred: the disappearance of the Master. The capitalized italics '*SI C'ÉTAIT LE NOMBRE CE SERAIT*' refer to the universal truth of the title but are a conditional proposition, a true statement about a hypothetical situation (though the imperfect subjunctives in roman type appear to be an exception to the rule, if rule it be). The italicized section which occupies the three central double pages and part of the fourth therefore ranks lowest in the typographical hierarchy: the most fictional point on the scale that runs from imaginary to real, and the most circumstantial on the scale that runs from particular to universal. It is in this almost non-existent space that the verse drama is acted out for the last time. The hypothetical result of the hypothetical gamble.

The section is placed under the sign of '*COMME SI*' – the poet writes *as if* it made a difference – and, consequently, as it were, in the key of *si*. Here, again, are the characteristic *i*'s and *s*'s of harmonious, integrated poetic expression, signs of the 'desiring imagination''s effort to make language and reality correspond: '*COMME SI* / Une in*si*nuation simple / au *si*lence enroulée avec *i*ron*i*e / ou / le mystère / préc*i*p*i*té', etc. The italics (202 words) contain twenty *si*'s or *is*'s, compared to twenty-five in the rest of the poem (510 words) – without counting purely visual examples like 'simple', 'invisible', 'raison', or words where the two phonemes appear close together: 'solitaire', 'expiatoire', 'scintille', 'suite'. The italic section also contains eleven words with two contiguous *i*'s ('précipité', 'minuit', 'rigide', 'virile', etc.) compared to six in the rest of the poem. The phonetic integrity of the first double page is apparently confirmed by its clear circularity, and also by the circular theme which begins now to retrace the typical itineraries of Mallarmé's verse poems. (The following paraphrase is not supposed to be the only possible prosodic reading, but it is supposed to establish the coherence of the principle.)

An insinuation (for example an idea or anything 'insinuated' into the book)[55] is twirled around a central silence; or the mystery or secret rite of writing is cast down onto the page and into the poetic 'tourbillon' – like the laughing, annihilating whirlwind of *Billet* ('tourbillon d'hilarité'). The idea floats like a feather (the small *p* of 'plume' indicates an appositional phrase since upper-case letters are also used in this section) around the 'gouffre central', which it neither escapes nor bestrews.

This hypothetical equilibrium is disrupted in several ways. The visual circularity or centripetal force suggested by the symmetrical 'COMME SI . . . COMME SI' is diffused by the open-endedness of the proposition. In fact, it is far from clear that the sentence it seems to introduce is ever resolved. 'COMME SI / COMME SI / SI / C'ÉTAIT LE NOMBRE / CE SERAIT' could, with some mental exertion, be construed as a triple conditional clause, almost qualified out of existence; or, reading the double 'COMME SI' as a hesitant repetition, 'as if, were it to be the number, it would be' – and then, in roman, like a punch-line, adding a final, ironic confirmation of the purely conditional, perhaps impossible nature of the hypothesis: 'LE HASARD'. Even if this part of the poem within a poem has a certain perceptible, though slightly asymmetrical integrity, and even if these words 'se trouveraient, par une frappe unique, elle-même matériellement la vérité',[56] it would only be by chance. Besides which, the vertiginous descent of words down the page continues; the whiteness inevitably returns; and the letters appear, by contrast with the preceding pages, to be gravitating ever closer to the 'gouffre central' of the sheet – 'quelque proche   tourbillon'. Finally, for all the obvious phonetic repetitions, no obvious prosodic principles have asserted themselves. Perhaps there are echoes of the 'vers officiel' in 'voltige autour du gouffre' (six syllables), 'sans le joncher ni fuir' (six syllables); but one could just as well allege a deliberate avoidance of regular rhythms:

> *comme si une insinuation simple* (11)

> *au silence enroulée avec ironie* (11)

> *ou le mystère précipité hurlé* (11)

The point is not that there either are or are not elements of prosodic regularity, but that the very criteria by which such a decision might be made have been removed.

After this imperfect example of the 'équilibre double et momentané à la façon du vol' which verse is supposed to create, the imbalance becomes extreme. On the last double page there were ten words on the left, thirty-one on the right. Here there are four on the left and fifty-six on the right. The pen or the feather, alone in an ocean of white, establishes a link with the other side of the abyss by means of a rhymeless word: '*sauf   que*'. It now becomes apparent, or at least possible, by one of those characteristic retro-spective obfuscations, that this conjectural, italicized poem, cowering under the shadow of the larger, dogmatic text, has not yet been written, even hypothetically. The pen hovers over the white page, 'solitaire' and 'éperdue', 'sauf que la rencontre ou l'effleure une toque de minuit'.

The feather, in the usual reading, against the darkness, suggests a hat and a figure underneath it: imaginary realities extrapolated from the feather or pen. But this is also a brilliantly lunatic description of the act of writing, more or less directly displayed here in the printed equivalent of handwriting. The 'toque de minuit' is the black inkwell with which the 'plume' comes into contact: the hat that is implied by a quill as it quivers in the writing hand like a feather on a non existent cap. The 'velours chiffonné par un esclaffement sombre', suggesting the snickering sound of nib on paper, is like the 'pli de sombre dentelle' of the text on the 'blancheur rigide' of the page – 'derisory' in its 'opposition au ciel', because, for Mallarmé, the text projects a tiny, negative image of the night sky. The whole process is con-cisely described in *L'Action restreinte*: 'Ton acte toujours s'applique à du papier; car méditer, sans traces, devient évanescent. . . . L'encrier . . . avec sa goutte, au fond, de ténèbres. . . . Tu remarquas, on n'écrit pas, lumineusement, sur champ obscur, l'alphabet des astres . . . l'homme poursuit noir sur blanc. / Ce pli de sombre dentelle, qui retient l'infini', etc.[57] The act of writing – 'ce jeu insensé d'écrire' – is simultaneously heroic and derisory: 's'arroger, en vertu d'un doute – la goutte d'encre apparentée à la nuit sublime – quelque devoir de tout recréer'.[58] The same idea of absurd pretension is conveyed here by the verb 's'en coiffer', suggesting infatuation or the assump-tion of an important role. The quill and the inkwell, in an image reminiscent of an Odilon Redon and, according to Cohn, represented visibly on the page, are the writer's emblematic, cylindrical 'toque' – with connotations, here, of 'toqué' . . .*

The act of writing imbues the writer with a sense of Romantic heroism and shows him fleetingly as a Baudelairean 'prince amer de l'écueil'. But what does it actually produce? On the next double page, the narrative appears to split into two separate descents, and the turbulence increases.

The top line may describe the attributes and emotions of the writer, or one possible outcome of the act of writing: the poetic 'souci' (as in the Vasco sonnet), the heroic sense of expiating a crime or blasphemy (or, etymologically by *pius*, referring to the poet's 'duty'), and pubescence (i.e. the ability to reproduce). What follows is a vast contraction of the Mallarmean poetic process as described in *Chanson* and other poems: the ominous silence

---

* Curiously, the same punning association of inkwell and madness was made in *Igitur*, the key word being the '*fiole* de verre . . . qui renferme la substance du Néant': 'La fiole vide, folie' (*OC*, 439 and 443). Also in *Igitur*, the 'fiole [qui] contient le néant' is the only object salvaged from a shipwreck (*OC*, 450–51).

('muet') and the 'rire' that signals the production of a poetic harmony. In this case, the laugh is not of course the sign or product of a triumphant rhyme but more like the sardonic laugh of the 'sépulcre' in *Prose*. If the top line is followed over the page – as the syntax and the capital 'L' of the sentence beginning 'La lucide et seigneuriale aigrette' seem to demand[59] – the laugh must be the result of the heroic poem being *the* number: '*rire | que | SI | C'ÉTAIT | LE NOMBRE*'. Which, as we know, would be pure chance, just as 'sépulcre' rhyming with 'Pulchérie' was a seductive fluke. The poem is then seen objectively, from the outside, in roman type, as a 'hallucination éparse d'agonie', 'denied' as soon as it rises up and hermetically sealed in its self-referential frame when it does appear: 'sourdant que nié et clos quand apparu'. 'Tout se passe, par raccourci' is in this case something of an understatement. The whole of *Prose* can be relived in the eight words at the top of the page: '*soucieux | expiatoire et pubère | muet | rire | que | SI | C'ÉTAIT   LE NOMBRE*'

The lower line describes the transient effect of the poem when it is not 'the Number' or when a chance synthesis suggests a facile victory. An ambiguous figure – the siren – merely implied by the preceding operation which then in turn implies a structure: a 'roc', perhaps a symbol of the poem itself which, like Poe's tomb, 'imposa une borne à l'infini'. But the rock turns out to be a ghost, a 'faux manoir', nothing inhabitable, which immediately vanishes. It may have set a limit to the infinite but it did so only temporarily. Either way, it makes no difference.

As we saw before, the pen returns to the 'écumes originelles'. And so ends the poem within a poem, on a double page which contains six different typefaces, at least six different tenses, and which depicts the chaotic dispersal of the drama of verse when acted out in 'eternal circumstances'. And in circumstances like these we unfortunately have no way of knowing whether or not the right number would have been thrown. Though we do know from the 'numérateur divin de notre apothéose'[60] that it would probably have had to have been a double six.

> – Arcane étrange; et, d'intentions pas moindres, a jailli la métrique aux temps incubatoires.[61]

Un coup de Dés may plant its sophisticated feet in the primal, metrical mud, but there is, as Bertrand Marchal observes, no trace in Mallarmé of a Romantic 'nostalgie des origines'.[62] There is, however, a *nostalgie des fins*. A desire to see how it all must logically end and, generally, to escape the influence of the past. This, ironically, was a reason for making the traditional forms of French verse the substance of his poetry and treating them as manifestations of an archetype. Because then, the major influence on his work would not be Hugo or Baudelaire or any other poet, but the Universe; and his work would be extrapolated, not from the achievements of his predecessors, but from future possibilities. His ambition was not to found a new school but to be the end of a tradition.[63] This creates an interesting dilemma. Mallarmé, by his original aesthetic decision, and then by philosophy, experience, habit[64] and gambler's instinct, never stopped writing in verse – worshipped it, in fact, and wanted it to provide the *rituels* of a new religion. *Un coup de Dés*, he wistfully remarks in his preface, 'laisse intact l'antique vers, auquel je garde un culte'; and after *Un coup de Dés* he returned like a 'pitre châtié' to the starting point – *Hérodiade* and the 'vers officiel', in rhyming couplets no less. But since verse was supposed to be an instance of more fundamental structures, it had in theory to prove its own essential abstractness and, as far as its moral, emotional and descriptive components were concerned, destroy itself like a prosodic John the Baptist.

The drama of verse acts out in advance a century of increasingly self-referential, suicidal art. It may be another hundred years before we can form a clear opinion of Mallarmé's unversified finale to the drama of verse – which is itself an explanatory prelude: was it a more accurate equation for reality or a more convincing justification of poetry than any other 'élégance scripturale'? Wisely, he wrote it 'sans présumer de l'avenir qui sortira d'ici, rien ou presque un art'. That nothing, which so eloquently bears witness to the self-destruction implicit in the drama, may one day prove to have been Mallarmé's unique contribution to the history of verse.

The broader historical irony is that even as Mallarmé was making verse disappear into itself, the prosodic operation was irradiating other arts. Musicians and painters – unencumbered by the intellectual nostalgia and competitiveness of the literary tradition – have often proved more willing than writers and critics to accept Mallarmé on his own terms, to use the 'intellectual framework' as a stencil, or to respond intuitively to what appeared to other readers to be a parody of, or a challenge to, their own sentimental rationalism.

Seen from this point of view, Mallarmé's poetry provides the most startling example of the Romantic paradox: as each art asserts its independence and boils itself down to its essential ingredients, so the interpenetration of the different arts increases. Today, the same paradox is evident in Mallarmé's conflicting reputations: the fact of his enormous importance beyond Parisian culture and beyond literature, and the fact that some people who write on nineteenth-century poetry are still convinced that all his adult poems were a hoax.

Could it be that Mallarmé was not writing poetry at all, but practising an unknown art-form or inventing a new science? If so, it may not be unreasonable to hope that the unlocking of his laboratory will do nothing to stop the spread of the disease.

Appendix I
Rhyme Lists

'l'être humain n'approche pas impunément d'un mécanisme, et
ne s'y mêle sans perte'[1]

The following three lists of rhymeless words and of words offering only one or two rhymes are based on Jacques Heugel's *Dictionnaire des rimes françaises* (Editions de 'Psyché', 1941), with additions and corrections from various other sources. These lists can be used to verify assertions or simply to satisfy curiosity. They may also prove useful in studying the rhyming habits of other poets or as a parlour game.

Not all words described in this book as 'impossible rhymes' will be found here: rhymeless words which Heugel classifies as ungallicized foreign words have been omitted ('golf', 'khôl', 'punch', 'Rothschild', 'turf', etc.), though they are used by some poets (see p. 47). I have ignored the principle of visual rhymes which is presumably what makes Ferdinand de Gramont treat 'isthme', 'porc' and 'soif' as rhymeless words (unless, in the last case, he had simply forgotten about 'gnaf', 'Falstaff', 'paf' and 'pilaf'). A few words whose use dates from after Mallarmé's death have also been excluded.

'Derivative' rhymes – e.g. *microcosme-macrocosme* – count as one rhyme and are listed by the suffix (in this case, *cosme*), preceded by a hyphen. It should be noted that some words ('enfle', 'meuble', 'rompre', 'vaincre', etc.) form only derivative rhymes.

A glance at the second and third lists will show that many words with only one or two possible rhymes are effectively rhymeless: for example, 'perdre' rhymes with 'Erdre' (a tributary of the Loire) or 'luxe' (luxury) with 'luxe' (luxate). Similarly, a list of words forming only three rhymes would throw up several extra candidates for the first and second lists; but the line had to be drawn somewhere.

On the extra difficulties and impossibilities Mallarmé creates for himself, see pp. 58–9.

For the purposes of this book, words are listed in alphabetical rather than phonetic order. The lists are short enough for this to present only minor inconveniences.

1. Rhymeless words
(Total: 111)

abrupt	genre	radoub
abrupte	girofle	rafle
Agde	goinfre	relapse
algue	holocauste	répugne
Anvers	hourque	rompre
Auch	hum!	rostre
Aups	humble	Sainte-Menehould
Banyuls	hurle	sarde
belge	incurve	sauf
birbe	indemne	sceptre
Broglie	jeûne	sépulcre
Buch	jouxte	Sercq
bulbe	Just	Seudre
Cambodge	Langres	solde
camphre	lorsque	-solve
chanvre	lunche	soulte
Charybde	lynche	sourdre
chauffe	meuble	stupre
cirque	meurtre	syllepse
clephte	moeurs	sylphe
cophte	monstre	sylve
-cosme	-morphe	talc
-dextre	mound	tertre
docte	muscle	teugue
dogme	orle	-teuque
Dresde	ours	thyrse
Edme	oust!	triomphe
Elbe	pampre	tuf
enfle	peuple	turc
éructe	polke	-uple (quadr-, etc.)
Eusque	Polyeucte	usurpe
exècre	pourpre	vaincre
extirpe	propre	Vanves
fenouil	quatorze	Vertumne
fichtre!	quelque	volsque
fourche	quetsche	volt
gaufre	quinze	welche

2. *Words offering one rhyme*
(Total: 164, or 82 rhyme pairs)

absurde – kurde
Albe – galbe
Anselme – Saint-Elme
aphte – naphte
apophtegme – flegme
Apt – rapt
arbre – marbre
ardre – Ardres
Ars – m(M)ars
Auvergne – vergne
bigle – sigle
borgne – lorgne
boucle – escarboucle
bougre – lougre
Bourg – Ourcq
Bourges – courges
bugle – remugle
busc – musc
caroube – (r)adoube
Celse – Paracelse
cercle – couvercle
chambranle – (é)branle
Chanturgues – Lycurgue
cherche – perche
chiourme – gourme
Chypre – Ypres
cintre – peintre
comble – omble
concept – transept
coulpe – poulpe
couple – souple
crispe – Harispe
crypte – Égypte
-culpe – pulpe
défunte – emprunte
déjeune – jeune
diaphragme – syntagme
distincte – succincte
divulgue – promulgue
dogre – ogre
donc – onc

Émyrne – Smyrne
épargne – hargne
Erdre – perdre
Étaples – Naples
Eudes – leudes
Euterpe – serpe
faible – hièble
fiat lux – Pollux
filtre – philtre
-firme – firme
fisc – tamarisc
fougue – la Hougue
glauque – rauque
gonfle – ronfle
greffe – Josèphe
Hanovre – pauvre
heurte – Meurthe
hymne – médimne
joug – toug
lèpre(s) – vêpres
logarithme – rythme
luxe (n.) – luxe (vb)
masturbe – perturbe
médiocre – ocre
mont Aigoual – poil
morve – torve
moult – Soult
nèfle – trèfle
ourle – Vidourle
(re)laps – schnaps
salse – valse
salve – -valve
scalde – Smalkalde
-sexte – texte
siècle – Thècle
simple (adj.) – simple (n.)
sud – Talmud
Tartufe – truffe
tînmes – vînmes
tinrent – vinrent
ulve – vulve

3. Words offering two rhymes
(Total: 123, or 41 rhyme pairs)

Accurse – Quinte-Curse – Tiburce
Albuquerque – Aulerque – Dunkerque
Alpe – palpe – scalpe
ample – exemple – temple (see p. 237, n. 31)
andrinople – Constantinople – sinople
âpre – câpre – diapre
Aspe – hydaspe – jaspe
aveugle – beugle – meugle
bis/tris-ulque – inculque – pulque
bonze – bronze – onze
borborygme – énigme – paradigme
boude – coude – soude
boxe – -doxe – équinoxe
bronche – jonche – tronche
buffle – insuffle – mufle
cadre – escadre – ladre
Calixte – mixte – sixte
celte – svelte – velte
cerf – nerf – serf
chiffre – fifre – piffre
cingle – épingle – tringle

cinq – Mézenc – zinc
congre – hongre – Tongre
cotre – notre – votre
couleuvre – -oeuvre – pieuvre
Delphes – elfe – guelfe
double – rouble – trouble
écorche – porche – torche
Électre – plectre – spectre
exergue – Rouergue – vergue
flirte – myrte – syrte
furoncle – oncle – pétoncle
grimpe – guimpe – Olympe
Ingres – malingre – pingre
involucre – lucre – sucre
jongle – jungle – ongle
kiosque – Manosque – osque
legs (pron. lɛg) – thalweg –
   Touareg
lymphe – nymphe – paranymphe
merde – Monteverde – perde
morgue – orgue – Sorgue

Appendix II

The Date of *Prose pour des Esseintes*

The exact date of composition of *Prose pour des Esseintes* is not known. The published version, assuming it to be contemporaneous with its title, must date from some time between May 1884 (publication of *A Rebours*)[1] and January 1, 1885 (publication of *Prose* in *La Revue indépendante*).[2] Two earlier versions, one in Mallarmé's own hand, are usually said to date from the 1870s, even the early 1870s. There is no evidence for this, as Lloyd Austin points out.[3] For all his *clair*'s and *hors de doute*'s, Barbier says nothing that allows one to prefer a hypothetical earlier date.[4] Pending a computer analysis of the autograph, the known date (second half of 1884) should stand.

On the other hand, there are arguments in favour of the known date.

1. Possible allusions to *A Rebours* (see, for example, p. 152). These are not conclusive but they do demonstrate the plausibility of the 1884 dating.
2. Mallarmé's letter to Huysmans after reading *A Rebours*: some passages are quoted above (p. 168). Mallarmé's opinion of des Esseintes's 'tragic' end shows why *Prose* might have been thought to provide him with a lesson: 'Il n'y a rien pour lui, rien, au delà de cette phase étudiée de la jeunesse, pis que rien.' The 'studies' undertaken by the poet in the world of the senses will only reaffirm mortality unless they end in creation; 'science' must contribute to the 'oeuvre'. Des Esseintes never transcends his magic island: 'ces fleurs! vision absolue de tout ce que peut, à un individu placé devant la jouissance barbare ou moderne, ouvrir de paradis la sensation seule.'[5]
3. Like most of Mallarmé's later poems, *Prose* would therefore have been written in response to a particular circumstance – in this case, Huysmans's praise of his poetry and the resulting publicity: 'Vos *Poètes Maudits*, cher Verlaine, *A Rebours* d'Huysmans, ont intéressé à mes Mardis longtemps vacants les jeunes poètes.'[6]
4. A new argument is supplied by the prosodic reading. *Prose* enacts the drama of verse in a relatively simple form. Yet it does exist as a coherent, detailed narrative on several levels which contrasts with the more directly oratorical *Toast funèbre* (1873) and even with later poems like *Le Tombeau*

d'Edgar Poe (1876) or the first edition of *L'Après-midi d'un faune* (1876), in which the prosodic conceits are less integrated and bear less philosophical weight. In *Autre éventail*, the drama of verse is acted out fully on all levels, and in a manner highly reminiscent of *Prose*. *Autre éventail* was published a few months before *Prose* in 1884. Both poems have the same form.

Conclusion: not only is there no reason to believe that *Prose* was written in the 1870s, there are several reasons to think that it was indeed written 'pour des Esseintes' in the latter half of 1884.

Notes

Foreword

1 OC, 851. Pending the new Pléiade edition by Bertrand Marchal, page numbers refer to the following editions: *Oeuvres complètes*, ed. Henri Mondor and G. Jean-Aubry (Gallimard, 'Pléiade', 1945) and *Poésies*, ed. Carl-Paul Barbier and Charles Gordon Millan (Flammarion, 1983), respectively abbreviated OC and P. Where possible, I have corrected the text and said so in the notes. For reliable, short editions: Lloyd James Austin, ed., *Poésies* (Flammarion, GF, 1989) and Bertrand Marchal, ed., *Poésies* (Gallimard, NRF, 'Poésie', 1992).

2 'The Phoenix of Mallarmé's "Sonnet en -yx"', *French Studies Bulletin* 24 (Autumn 1987), 13–15.

3 OC, 646.

4 There are some pertinent remarks on the 'expressivist' approach in Malcolm Bowie's *Mallarmé and the Art of Being Difficult* (Cambridge University Press, 1978), 25.

5 Rev. W. Awdry, *The Eight Famous Engines* (Edmund Ward, 1957), 20–34: 'Gordon Goes Foreign'. For a real-life example, see the 'discussion' following Charles Chadwick's paper in *Colloque Mallarmé (Glasgow, November 1973) en l'honneur de Austin Gill*, ed. C.P. Barbier (Nizet, 1975), 83–102.

6 Peter Bowler, *The Superior Person's Book of Words* (Dell Publishing, 'The Intrepid Linguist Library', 1982). The *OED* gives one example from 1846.

7 See p. 63. Other spurious enigmas include: whose 'site' is described in *Prose*? which parts of the swan's body are trapped in the ice? and the Faun – did the nymphs exist, whether or not he saw them?

8 OC, 283.

9 This example of the *metafora di decettione* is given by Antoine Adam in his edition of *Les Fleurs du Mal* (Classiques Garnier, 1961), 307.

10 *Oeuvres*, ed. Jean Hytier (Gallimard, 'Pléiade', 1957), I, 670. On the same notion, see Georges Rodenbach, 'Notes sur M. Stéphane Mallarmé', *Revue franco-américaine* (July 1895), quoted in *L'Amitié de Stéphane Mallarmé et de Georges Rodenbach*, ed. François Ruchon (Geneva: Pierre Cailler, 1949), 131.

11 OC, 644. See also Jules Huret's *Enquête*: 'en vérité, il n'y a pas de prose: il y a l'alphabet, et puis des vers plus ou moins serrés, plus ou moins diffus' (OC, 867).

12 OC, 361.

13 OC, 334.

14 'Regards en arrière' (1912), in *Documents Stéphane Mallarmé* (hereafter: DSM), IV: see p. 311.

15 Letter to René Ghil, March 13, 1887; *Correspondance*, ed. Lloyd

James Austin (hereafter: *Corr*), III, 95.
16 *OC*, 382.

1 Poetry on the Production Line

1 *OC*, 867. Some examples in this chapter are taken from G. Robb, *La Poésie de Baudelaire et la poésie française, 1838–1852* (Aubier, 1993).
2 May 17, 1867; *Corr*, I, 249. See also a letter to Lefébure, February 1865: 'Enfant, je faisais des narrations de vingt pages' (*Corr*, I, 155).
3 *P*, 65–7, 76.
4 'Regards en arrière', *DSM* IV, 306–7.
5. W. Ténint, *Prosodie de l'école moderne* (1844), ed. P.J. Siegel (Champion-Slatkine, 1986), 229.
6 *Le Voleur littéraire et artistique*, March 20, 1848.
7 I include those sonnets which were never collected in *Les Fleurs du Mal*. Three of them can be found in the *Amoenitates Belgicae*: *Oeuvres complètes*, ed. Claude Pichois (Gallimard, 'Pléiade', 1975–6), II, 968–9, 977, 978.
8 'La Muse', *La Poésie dans les bois* (1845), in *Poésies complètes* (Charpentier, 1850).
9 Banville, *Petit traité de poésie française*, 198; Gautier, preface to the 1868 Lévy edition of *Les Fleurs du Mal*.
10 June 4, 1862; *Corr*, I, 31.
11 'Germe final' is the expression Mallarmé uses in a slightly different context in 1869 (*OC*, 1629).
12 Étienne Eggis, 'Plus loin!', *En causant avec la lune* (Parisse, 1851).
13 'M. Alfred de Musset', *Revue des Deux Mondes*, January 15, 1833, 171–85. Reprinted in *Portraits contemporains* and quoted in *Poésies complètes*, ed. Maurice Allem (Gallimard, 'Pléiade', 1939), 589.
14 Definitions of what constitutes *rimes suffisantes*, *pauvres* or *riches* vary. Nearly all nineteenth-century defi-

nitions, however, can be reduced to the following formula: one identical phoneme = *pauvre*; two = *suffisante*; three or more = *riche*.
15 See J.A. Hiddleston, 'Baudelaire et l'esthétique du choc', *L'Age nouveau* I (1987), 13–17.
16. 'Éveil' (November 1845), from the first part of *Évohé. Némésis intérimaire*. See *Odes funambulesques*.
17 Letter to Maspero, November 2, 1873; *Corr*, III, 394.
18 As Baudelaire seems to have noticed: 'Tout . . . est pour ainsi dire *apothéosé*. . . . le mot *apothéose* est un de ceux qui se présentent irrésistiblement sous la plume du poète quand il a à décrire . . . un mélange de gloire et de lumière' (*Oeuvres complètes*, II, 165).
19 'Évohé! fouaille la veine . . .', *Les Amours jaunes*.
20 *P*, 458, vv. 21–3 and 216, vv. 41–3.
21 P. Citron and R. Dragonetti, quoted by Bertrand Marchal, ed. *Poésies* (Gallimard, NRF, 'Poésie', 1992), 242.
22 Letter to Dierx, June 1894; *Corr*, VI, 275; my emphasis.
23 *OC*, 647.

2 The Rules of the Game

1 *OC*, 401.
2 *OC*, 362.
3 *OC*, 870, and in a letter to Camille Mauclair, October 9, 1897; *Corr*, IX, 289. See also *OC*, 491, 644, 866 and 867; and cf. Hugo, almost seventy years before, in the *Préface de Cromwell*: 'L'alexandrin les avait tant de fois ennuyés, qu'ils l'ont condamné, en quelque sorte, sans vouloir l'entendre. . . . Il fallait condamner, non la forme employée, mais ceux qui avaient employé cette forme; les ouvriers, et non l'outil.'
4 See Mallarmé's own remarks on *L'Après-midi d'un faune* in Huret's *Enquête*: 'J'y essayais, en effet, de mettre, à côté de l'alexandrin dans toute sa tenue, une sorte de

jeu courant pianoté autour' (OC, 870).

5   OC, 362.

6   OC, 363.

7   OC, 386.

8   Letter to Cazalis, July 1865; Corr, I, 168.

9   P, 495 and 674; 718; 492 and 621.

10   P, 617.

11   P, 567 and 684; see also Billet à Whistler, infra, pp. 77–9.

12   P, 481.

13   P, 674.

14   Au fil de l'heure (1898; Flammarion, 1929). The volume contains an unrecorded publication of the quatrain inscribed in Margueritte's copy of L'Après-midi d'un faune with minor variants in the punctuation.

15   Actually, eight, if one includes Truffaut and Fô.

16   Maurice Schaettel, 'Lecture d'un sonnet de Mallarmé', Revue des Sciences Humaines (January–March 1973), 139–49. See p. 141 and n. 3.

17   Toward the Poems of Mallarmé, expanded edition (University of California Press, 1980), 260.

18   P.S. Hambly and C. Roubaud, quoted by B. Marchal, ed., Poésies, 257.

19   L'Oeuvre poétique de Stéphane Mallarmé (Droz, 1940).

20   Dix poèmes (Droz, 1948), 114. Rachel Killick (art. cit., p. 230, n. 1), without mentioning Sappho, notes that 'c'est justement cette absence fixée par l'accident phonétique Paphos-faux qui constitue le thème' (242).

21   OC, 526.

22   OC, 532; see also, infra, p. 17.

23   Letter to Édouard Dujardin, May 5, 1891; Corr, IV, 230.

24   OC, 265 and 521.

25   OC, 510–11.

26   Letter to François Coppée, December 5, 1866; Corr, I, 234; Cohn, Toward the Poems of Mallarmé, 159 and 169, n. 2.

27   OC, 872.

28   P, 495.

29   OC, 529–30.

30   Judy Kravis, The Prose of Mallarmé (Cambridge University Press, 1976), 15–17.

31   Toward the Poems of Mallarmé, 196–9.

32   OC, 663.

33   Judith Ryan, '"Une chute antérieure de plume": Mallarmé's "Le Démon de l'analogie"', French Studies XLVII, 1 (January 1993), 33–42. See p. 35. If 'le Maître' in the sonnet en yx is Orpheus descending to the Styx, something might be said about the ten or's of the sonnet and the rhyme, lampadophore-amphore.

34   OC, 521.

35   'Alphée', 'Céphée', 'coryphée', 'Morphée' and 'nymphée'.

36   The text of P ('Tout orgueil') should be corrected.

37   OC, 1041.

38   P, 552.

39   Cf. v. 46: 'Resté là sur ces fleurs dont nulle ne se fane.'

40   P, 680, 491 and 566.

41   P, 498 and 482.

42   According to Aragon in 'La Rime en 1940' (reprinted in Le Crève-Coeur, nouvelle édition [Gallimard, NRF, 1946], 78), rimes complexes are rhymes in which the rhyming phonemes stretch over two or more words. The term rimes équivoques (or équivoquées) is also used, but this term can also refer to rimes homonymes (see p. 35).

43   P, 564 and 570; my emphasis.

44   Quoted by Abel Grenier as an instance of rimes batelées, in which the end of one verse rhymes with the caesura of the following verse: Marot, Oeuvres complètes (Garnier, n.d.).

45   P, 653.

46   P, 182–3.

47   P, 258.

48   Cf. the rime léonine, meaning, usually, an extra-rich rhyme with four or more identical phonemes.

49   Mallarmé and the Art of Being Difficult, 75.

50   P, 253.

51   P, 256.

52 Littré gives *treuver* as an archaism 'employé jusque dans le XVIIᵉ siècle'. La Fontaine uses it several times as a rhyme.

53 *OC*, 333.

54 *OC*, 663. Mallarmé often applies the word 'jeu' to poetry and writing in general: *OC*, 327 ('la multiple répétition de son jeu'), 330 ('la Poésie, ses jeux sublimités'), 368 ('le jeu de la parole'), 481 ('ce jeu insensé d'écrire'), 512 ('jeu ancien'), 647 (quoted at the end of Chapter 1). 'Jeu' also figures in several poems (see pp. 137, 147 and 178).

55 *Le Vers français*, 2nd edn (SEDES, 1973), 18–19.

56 *P*, 228, 336 and 418.

57 *P*, 180, v. 8 and 185, v. 8. The thirteen-syllable verse is: 'Mais confuse de soupirs si jeunes que je meurs', changed to 'Et jeune de soupirs si confus que je meurs'.

58 See also p. 138. For the other 'césures enjambantes': *Le Guignon*, v. 59 ('n'endo | sser'); *Le Tombeau de Charles Baudelaire*, v. 11 ('vai | nement'); and, in *Hérodiade*, *P*, 451, v. 2 ('glo | rieux') and v. 10 ('héré | ditaire'), 455, v. 15 ('pre | ssentiments') and v. 20 ('surna | turel'). Banville, Henri de Régnier and Verlaine also indulge in 'césures enjambantes'. Rimbaud was impressed by the latter's 'Et la tigresse épouvantable d'Hyrcanie': 'Dans la grotte', in *Fêtes galantes* (1869). On caesuras – *enjambantes* or otherwise – see Clive Scott, *French Verse-Art* (Cambridge University Press, 1980), 61–74.

59 *OC*, 366.

60 *P*, 85.

3 The Metaphysics of Rhyme

1 *OC*, 333.

2 *OC*, 300.

3 *OC*, 371.

4 *OC*, 332. See also, below, p. 66.

5 For a discussion of the same topic in the context of the whole of Mallarmé's work, see Bertrand Marchal's *La Religion de Mallarmé* (Corti, 1988), especially Part V: 'Une Théologie des Lettres'.

6 *OC*, 868.

7 *Le Figaro*, August 3, 1895; quoted in *P*, 433.

8 See G. Robb, *La Poésie de Baudelaire*, chapter 12. In orchestral music, for example, Mallarmé hears an 'ébauche de quelqu'un des poèmes immanents à l'humanité ou leur originel état' (*OC*, 367). A precise comparison of Mallarmé's verse to forms of *chanson* has yet to be made. See his own hints in letters to Grégoire Le Roy, May 21, 1889 ('tremper [notre vers] à une source de chansons, comme le font les Anglais') and Catulle Mendès, June 2, 1895 ('la ballade et . . . notre chanson, le rondel, ces formes désarchaïsées et déromanisées') (*Corr*, III, 316 and VII, 218). For further comments on Mallarmean music, see pp. 110–12, 117, 232, nn. 7 and 13, 233, n. 45.

9 *Oeuvres complètes*, I, 183.

10 *OC*, 375.

11 On the cabbalist's misconception, see *OC*, 850: 'détacher d'un Art des opérations qui lui sont intégrales et fondamentales pour les accomplir à tort, isolément, c'est encore une vénération, maladroite.'

12 *OC*, 867.

13 *OC*, 644. See also *OC*, 867: 'en vérité, il n'y a pas de prose: il y a l'alphabet et puis des vers plus ou moins serrés: plus ou moins diffus. Toutes les fois qu'il y a effort au style, il y a versification.'

14 *OC*, 386.

15 *OC*, 855.

16 *OC*, 855.

17 Albert Thibaudet, *La Poésie de Stéphane Mallarmé, étude littéraire* (Gallimard, NRF, 1912; 1926), 246.

18 *OC*, 856; my emphasis.

19 *Desire Seeking Expression: Mallarmé's 'Prose pour des Esseintes'* (Lexington, KY: French Forum, 1983), 99,

commenting on an article by
P.-O. Walzer, 'Prolégomènes à toute
exégèse future de la "Prose"', in
Festgabe H. von Greyerz (Lang,
1967), 809–15.
20 *L'Art poétique*, I, 28–37.
21 OC, 273. Barbara Johnson points to
an eventual 'rhyme' with 'même'
(*Défigurations du langage poétique*
[Flammarion, 1979], 207).
22 See 'Rat' in *Brewer's Dictionary of
Phrase and Fable*.
23 OC, 327.
24 P, 224 and 226.
25 *Oeuvres complètes*, II, 11. The review
in which Baudelaire uses this image
was not reprinted until 1908.
26 OC, 365.
27 Letter to Charles Bonnier, March
1893; *Corr*, VI, 65–6.
28 OC, 333.
29 OC, 327.
30 OC, 327.
31 OC, 363.
32 OC, 333.
33 OC, 364.
34 OC, 921.
35 OC, 368. The verb 'retremper' (to
'requench' metal in order to main-
tain the molecular structure it has
when hot) is related to the forging
image. See also pp. 41, 66–7 and 229,
n. 14.
36 OC, 855.
37 August 7, 1891; *Corr*, IV, 293.
38 OC, 333.
39 OC, 400.
40 OC, 644.

4 Un poëte en quête de rimes: Difficult Rhymes and Impossible Rhymes

1 OC, 374.
2 May 3, 1868; *Corr*, XI, 110.
3 *La Comédie humaine*, ed. P.-G.
Castex, Pléiade, X, 211.
4 'Satire II. La Rime et la Raison. A M.
de Molière', vv. 15–18.
5 *Scènes de la Vie de Bohème*, ed. L.
Chotard and G. Robb (Gallimard,
Folio, 1988), 50 and 83–4.

6 See for example OC, 332 and 653.
7 'Une folle entre dans ma vie . . .'.
8 For example, Glatigny, in 'Improvisation': 'Saisir au vol la rime aux ailes
d'hirondelle.' But there are dozens of
other examples.
9 'A Edmond et Jules de Goncourt'
(1856), in *Odelettes*.
10 'A feu Vert-Vert', in *Crâneries et
dettes de coeur* (Dolin, 1842).
11 *Oeuvres complètes*, I, 183.
12 Letter dated February 16, 1857.
Correspondance, ed. Cl. Pichois
and J. Ziegler (Gallimard, 'Pléiade',
1973), I, 377.
13 References are to the 'édition
définitive' of the *Odes funambulesques*, which includes *Occi-
dentales* and *Idylles prussiennes*
(Charpentier, 1878): 106; 106 and
166; 40 and 289; 273.
14 *Odes funambulesques*, 266; 145; 33.
15 Ibid., 20; 43.
16 OC, 523.
17 'Retchezken' (= Édouard Wacken),
'Phénomènes littéraires (La
Nouvelle école parisienne). II. M.
Théodore de Banville', *Revue de
Belgique*, November 1848, 285.
18 Used by Mallarmé in *Les Loisirs de la
Poste* (P, 489).
19 *Oeuvres complètes*, II, 499 and
510.
20 Wilhem Ténint, *Prosodie de l'école
moderne*, 166–7 and 181.
21 *Les Vers français et leur prosodie*
(Hetzel, n.d.), 43–4.
22 'La Rime en 1940', in *Le Crève-coeur*,
48–9.
23 *Odes funambulesques*, 153.
24 *Les Vers français et leur prosodie*, 45.
25 In 'Le Château du souvenir' (*Émaux
et Camées*), Gautier rhymes *Love's
labours lost* (sic) and *Faust*. According to Jacques Heugel, the only possible rhyme for *Faust* is *toast*. See also,
however, in *Le Carrefour des
Demoiselles*, privately printed by
Mallarmé and Emmanuel des Essarts
in 1862: *toast-Morning-Post* (P,
123–4).
26 *Oeuvres complètes*, II, 126.
27 Edmond Scherer, 'Baudelaire' (July

1869), in *Études sur la littérature contemporaine* IV (Calmann Lévy, 1886), 290.

28 Not included in Appendix I because 'gouge' and 'bouge' both have two meanings.

29 OC, 333.

30 Ibid.

31 Paul Claudel, 'Réflexions et propositions sur le vers français', *Nouvelle Revue française*, October 1 and November 1, 1925, republished in *Positions et Propositions I: Oeuvres en prose*, ed. J. Petit and Ch. Galpérine (Gallimard, 'Pléiade', 1965), 7.

32 Maybe the sort of ceiling Mallarmé dreamt up for Méry Laurent in 1891: 'un ciel, nuagé, léger, avec rares oiseaux peut-être' (April 26, 1891; *Corr*, V, 329).

33 OC, 374.

5   Composing the Poem

1 OC, 1050.

2 May 3, 1868; *DSM* VI, 369. See also René Ghil, *Les Dates et les Oeuvres* (G. Crès et Cie, 1923), 222: 'et, me dit-il à moi-même, comme il lui manquait un mot en la série yx, il en avait inventé un, le mot: ptyx.'

3 La Harpe, quoted by J. Dessiaux, *Traité complet de versification française, ou Grammaire poétique de la langue française* (Vve Maire-Nyon, 1845), 43.

4 Quoted by P.S. Hambly in the *Bulletin des études parnassiennes* V (December 1983). Banville's sonnet appeared in *La Revue française* (May–July 1858).

5 Ferdinand de Gramont, *Chant du passé, 1830–1848* (Giraud, 1854), Sonnet clvi. The quatrains are as follows:

Puisque, troublant toujours nos
  pieuses études,
Le monde à nos regards fait trembler
  le grand X,
Et dans les cieux voilés revoler
  Béatrix,

Cherchons plus loin encor d'austères
  solitudes.

Écartons-nous surtout des viles
  habitudes,
Aux syrtes de Lybie, aux cavernes
  d'Éryx
Des dipsades, des dards, des sepes,
  des natrix
Moins hideux sont les coups et les
  poisons moins rudes.

6 Ghil and Valéry quoted by J.-P. Richard, *L'Univers imaginaire de Mallarmé* (Seuil, 1961), 583.

7 See G. Robb, *La Poésie de Baudelaire*, chapter 13: 'Richesse de la rime, misère de la poésie'.

8 Letter to Henri Cazalis, July 18, 1868; *DSM* VI, 375.

9 *Ptyx* means 'fold', then 'writing tablet' and, in later Greek, 'document' and 'diploma': see Ross G. Arthur, 'When is a Word Not a Word?', *Romance Notes* XXVII, 2 (Winter 1986), 167–73. Hugo applies the word to a hill in *Le Satyre* (v. 19) and seems to have been particularly fond of the ending. Other *yx* words used by him include *Nyx*, *Othryx*, *pnyx*, *Spryx*, *Stryx* and *Thryx*.

10 Adolphe Racot, 'Les Parnassiens', *Le Gaulois*, March 26, 1875. Quoted by Michael Pakenham, then by C.P. Barbier and C.G. Millan: *P*, 222.

11 OC, 647.

12 OC, 332.

13 Théodore de Banville, *Poème inédit. Le Forgeron. Scènes héroïques* (Maurice Dreyfous, 1887). See respectively pp. 14, 21, 9 and 17. For another example of *rimes batelées*, see Marot's poem quoted on p. 24.

14 For a similar association of 'forging' and 'devouring', see Mallarmé's letter to Émile Verhaeren (April 14, 1891; *Corr*, IV, 223): 'le Vers, emprunté certes à la parole, *se retrempe* tellement, selon la furie de votre instinct, en autre chose, qu'il devient . . . un élément nouveau, à même et soi, nu et *dévorant ses propres mots.*'

15 See Banville's letter thanking Mallarmé for his article: 'Vous m'avez loué avec autant d'amitié et de délicatesse que d'intention impeccable' (quoted by E. Souffrin, then by Lloyd Austin in *Corr*, III, 116n).

16 OC, 332.

Programme

1 OC, 384–5.

2 Letters to Villiers de l'Isle-Adam, December 31, 1865 (*Corr*, I, 193) and René Ghil, March 13, 1887 (*Corr*, III, 95).

3 Mallarmé's 'traduction barbare' of *Le Tombeau d'Edgar Poe* is quoted in *P*, 275. See also *Corr*, II, 154 (letter to Sarah Helen Whitman, July 31, 1877).

4 Quoted in *Gil Blas*, November 22, 1897, and by Richard Ellmann in *Oscar Wilde* (Hamish Hamilton, 1987), 320.

6 Le Mystère d'un nom

1 Generally, see Rachel Killick, 'Les Noms propres ou "The Game of the Name" chez les Parnassiens et chez Mallarmé', in *Patterns of Evolution in Nineteenth-Century French Poetry*, ed. Lawrence Watson and Rosemary Lloyd (The Tallents Press, 1991).

2 OC, 872 and 378.

3 *Correspondance Mallarmé-Whistler*, ed. C.P. Barbier (Nizet, 1964), 75–7.

4 Mallarmé uses 'rafale' to mean a welter of preoccupations or distractions in a letter to Gustave Kahn, November 27, 1897: 'parmi la rafale qui souffle sur mon retour à Paris' (*Corr*, X, 42–3).

5 See Robin Spencer, ed., *Whistler: A Retrospective* (New York: Wings Books, 1991), 305. Whistler's hat is firmly attached to a head.

6 OC, 386.

7 See however OC, 369: 'les déversoirs à portée maintenant dans une prévoyance, journaux et leur tourbillon'.

8 A.R. Chisholm, in *L'Esprit créateur* IX, 1 (Spring 1969), 28–36. See also Émilie Noulet, *L'Oeuvre poétique de Stéphane Mallarmé* (Droz, 1940), 463: 'la danseuse à qui nous devons d'avoir intensifié par sa danse quelques moments de notre vie.'

9 Oscar Wilde, *The Picture of Dorian Gray* (1891; Oxford University Press, 1981), 36.

10 Charles Mauron, *Mallarmé l'obscur* (Denoël, 1941; Corti, 1968) 1968 edn, 143; *Oeuvres* (Garnier).

11 *Les Clés de Mallarmé* (Aubier-Montaigne, 1954), 150.

12 OC, 309; quoted by Y.-A. Favre, 511.

13 OC, 327.

14 Letters dated October 25 and 29, 1890; *Correspondance Mallarmé-Whistler*, 72 and 73.

15 *Petit traité de poésie française* (1872; Lemerre, 1891), 53. Banville's emphasis.

16 OC, 655.

17 *P*, 677. See also *La Déclaration foraine*: 'et j'en sais une [femme] qui voit clair ici' (*OC*, 279).

18 *P*, 286 and 434. 'Roses' also appear in the revised *Hérodiade* of 1887, but their initial appearance dates back to the 1860s (*P*, 208, 228 and 336). I have associated 'Surgi de la croupe . . .' with Méry Laurent on the basis of similarities with *Chanson* and the appearance of the emblematic rose.

19 *P*, 614.

20 Two famous examples: 'De mémoire de rose, il n'y a qu'un jardinier au monde' (Fontenelle); 'Et, rose, elle a vécu ce que vivent les roses, / L'espace d'un matin' (Malherbe).

21 Letter to Henri Cazalis, June 4, 1862; *Corr*, I, 32 and V, 189.

22 'Mais la littérature a quelque chose de plus intellectuel que cela [Zola's novels]: les choses existent, nous n'avons pas à les créer; nous n'avons qu'à en saisir les rapports; et ce sont les fils de ces rapports qui forment les

vers et les orchestres' (OC, 871).

23 P, 566, 123, 615, 621 and 453.

24 OC, 855; Mallarmé's 'Un Coup de Dés', 65.

25 Julia Kristeva, La Révolution du langage poétique (1974; Seuil, 'Points', 1985), 246.

26 Austin Gill points out that, in 'La chevelure vol . . .', Poetry can logically be taken as the antecedent of 'Celle', as it can in Le Tombeau de Charles Baudelaire: Mallarmé's Poem 'La chevelure vol d'une flamme . . .' (University of Glasgow, 1971), 14.

27 See Rachel Killick, 'Mallarmé's "Feuillet d'album"', Essays in French Literature XXIV (November 1987), 19.

28 Mallarmé does claim a mimetic function for poetry at the time of Un coup de Dés, in which typographical representations are a surface sign of a more abstract mimesis: 'le rythme d'une phrase au sujet d'un acte ou même d'un objet n'a de sens que s'il les imite' (letter to André Gide, May 14, 1897; Corr, IX, 172). See also his letter to Camille Mauclair, October 8, 1897 (Corr, IX, 288) and, infra, p. 197.

29 OC, 645.

30 OC, 857.

31 OC, 869.

32 OC, 365–6.

33 Gardner Davies, Mallarmé et la 'couche suffisante d'intelligibilité' (Corti, 1988), 279.

34 Toward the Poems of Mallarmé, 202.

35 OC, 279.

36 OC, 327.

37 Perhaps also in 'A la nue . . .': 'vertu'/'vers tu'. See Gérard Montbertrand, '"A la nue . . ." ou le déshabillage d'un poème de Mallarmé', Nineteenth-Century French Studies XV, 3 (Spring 1987), 294.

38 'Soupirs de sang, or meurtrier, pâmoison, fête!'

39 From Les Vignes folles (1860), in Poésies, 14.

40 Letter to Henri Cazalis, September 25, 1862; Corr, I, 51.

41 OC, 333. Sainte-Beuve also compares rhyme to wings and kisses at the same time in 'A la Rime' (Joseph Delorme): 'Ah! plutôt, oiseaux charmants, . . . Que ma lyre et ses concerts / Soient couverts / De vos baisers, de vos ailes.' For Banville, in the 'Épilogue' of Idylles prussiennes, rhyme is 'le baiser / Qui joint deux bouches amoureuses'.

42 On images of verticality and rigidity applied to verses, see pp. 116, 132, 203, 206–7 and 240, n. 24.

43 See for example Mauron, Mallarmé l'obscur, 180; Richard, L'Univers imaginaire, 268; Cohn, Toward the Poems, 186–7.

44 Mallarmé et la 'couche suffisante d'intelligibilité', 347.

45 OC, 571–2. (In collaboration with Francis Vielé-Griffin.)

46 Cf. Mallarmé's article, 'The Impressionists and Édouard Manet', Art Monthly Review, September 1876, republished by C.P. Barbier in DSM I (only the English translation exists): 'In extremely civilized epochs . . . , art and thought are obliged to retrace their own footsteps, and to return to their ideal source, which never coincides with their real beginnings.'

47 While Mallarmé was writing his sonnet, Ferdinand Brunetière was drawing a very Mallarmean comparison between the music of Wagner and the painting of Puvis de Chavannes: what Wagner did for music, extracting from it 'ce que la musique a de plus intellectuel, M. Puvis de Chavannes l'a fait dans la peinture contemporaine' (La Renaissance de l'Idéalisme [Firmin-Didot, 1896], 65).

48 P, 327.

49 OC, 333.

50 Mallarmé refers to the shepherd's song in La Musique et les Lettres (OC, 646).

51 Cohn gives this as a possible alternative reading (Toward the Poems, 187).

52 Molière, Le Bourgeois Gentilhomme, IV, 1; quoted by Maurice Grevisse, Le Bon Usage, 10th edn (1975), § 843.

53 'Une fête chez Gautier', *Rimes dorées*, in *Poésies complètes. Les Exilés* (Charpentier, 1899), 251.

54 *Mallarmé et la 'couche suffisante d'intelligibilité'*, 355.

55 'From "Quand l'ombre menaça" to "Au seul souci de voyager": Mallarmé's Debt to Chateaubriand', *The Modern Language Review* L, 4 (October 1955), 414–32.

56 'Le Pâle Vasco', *Revue d'histoire littéraire de la France* LVIII, 4 (October–December 1958), 510–21.

57 L. Cellier, 'Le Pâle Vasco', 516, quoting 'Les Mages', part 10 (*Les Contemplations*, VI).

58 OC, 333.

59 OC, 366. Mallarmé was perhaps remembering those 'remarques si fines de Joubert' applied by Gautier to Banville, whose words surround the idea 'comme un bracelet de pierreries': 'Les mots s'illuminent quand le doigt du poète y fait passer son phosphore.' (Preface to the Lemerre edition of *Les Exilés*, extracted from *Les Progrès de la poésie française depuis 1830*.) Gautier's preface is visibly 'inspired' by Baudelaire's essay on Banville, which comes after Gautier's in the Lemerre edition . . .

60 OC, 386.

61 OC, 366.

62 Letter to Catulle Mendès (?), Winter 1872; *Corr*, XI, 25. See also, ibid., note 4 on Mallarmé's reasons for ending with a masculine rhyme (Lloyd Austin, quoting Mendès's plan for *Le Tombeau de Théophile Gautier*).

63 OC, 333. A passage in Balzac's *Séraphîta* suggests the possibility of combining both senses of 'gisement': 'Souvent . . . , il faisait une légère déviation pour éviter un précipice, un arbre, un quartier de roche qu'il semblait voir sous la neige, comme certains marins habitués à l'Océan en devinent les écueils à la couleur, au remous, au gisement des eaux.' (*La Comédie humaine*, ed. P.-G. Castex, XI, 746–7.) One might think

also of the *topos* of gems buried in the ocean (e.g. the stanza of Gray's *Elegy* imitated by Baudelaire in 'Le Guignon').

64 Cf., in *Salut*, a similar nautical sequence: 'Solitude, récif, étoile'.

65 This is Mallarmé's description of the first lithograph in Odilon Redon's *Hommage à Goya* (letter to Redon, February 2, 1885, *Corr*, II, 280; quoted in this connection by L. Cellier, 'Le Pâle Vasco'). See also Mallarmé's letter to Cazalis, April 1866: 'la matière . . . s'élançant forcenément dans le rêve qu'elle sait n'être pas' (*Corr*, I, 207).

7 *Le doute du Jeu suprême*

1 *Oeufs de Pâques*, IV; *P*, 634.

2 OC, 870.

3 OC, 647.

4 OC, 332.

5 *Toward the Poems of Mallarmé*, 177.

6 OC, 541.

7 OC, 367; and see Julia Kristeva, *La Révolution du langage poétique*, especially p. 229. On the 'architectural' properties of music according to Mallarmé, see Suzanne Bernard, *Mallarmé et la musique* (Nizet, 1959), 43–9.

8 OC, 645.

9 Letter to Joséphin Péladan, October 4, 1890; *Corr*, XI, 57.

10 Letter to Joséphin Péladan, December 6, 1891; *Corr*, XI, 68.

11 *Oeuvres complètes*, I, 183. This part of Baudelaire's abortive preface for *Les Fleurs du Mal* first appeared in Charles Asselineau's biography in 1868.

12 February 17, 1886; *Corr*, XI, 36.

13 On Mallarmé's usual view of poetry and its superiority to music, see the texts quoted in this connection by Gardner Davies: *Les 'Tombeaux' de Mallarmé: Essai d'exégèse raisonné* (Corti, 1950), 132–4 and, below, p. 117.

14 *La Poésie de Stéphane Mallarmé*, 307.

15 '"Le principal pilier": Mallarmé, Vic-

tor Hugo et Richard Wagner', *Revue d'histoire littéraire de la France* (April–June 1951), 154–80. See p. 174.

16 OC, 542.

17 Peter Hambly, 'Deux sonnets de Mallarmé: "Le vierge, le vivace . . ." et "Hommage" (à Wagner)', *Australian Journal of French Studies* XXV, 1 (January–April 1988), 5–28. See p. 23.

18 *Toward the Poems of Mallarmé*, 177.

19 *Corr*, II, 294, n. 2.

20 Gardner Davies, *Les 'Tombeaux' de Mallarmé*, 131–63. Guy Michaud, *Mallarmé*, nouvelle édition (Hatier, 'Connaissance des Lettres', 1971), 139.

21 OC, 361.

22 OC, 360.

23 OC, 856.

24 *Les 'Tombeaux' de Mallarmé*, 141.

25 Letter to René Ghil, March 7, 1885; *Corr*, II, 286.

26 OC, 333; my emphasis.

27 OC, 364 and 365.

28 Charles Chadwick, *Mallarmé, sa pensée dans sa poésie* (Corti, 1962), 110–11.

29 OC, 419 and 500.

30 'Le vers, au pli pur' (letter to Charles-Henry Hirsh, June 4, 1895; published by Lloyd Austin in *French Studies* XL, 1 [January 1986], 17).

31 *P*, 666.

32 OC, 418.

33 *P*, 380. See also, on 'Une dentelle s'abolit . . .', pp. 137–9.

34 OC, 379.

35 *P*, 672.

36 Baudelaire, 'Le Squelette laboureur'.

37 Cf. Marceline's famous line, 'Prisonnière en ce livre une âme est renfermée!', quoted by Baudelaire in his essay on Marceline Desbordes-Valmore (*Oeuvres complètes*, II, 148).

38 For example in *Étalages*: 'Feuillets de hollande ancien ou en japon, ornement de consoles, en l'ombre' (OC, 377), and *Igitur*: 'un livre ouvert que présente la table' (OC, 435).

39 OC, 379.

40 OC, 381 and 372.

41 On the newspaper as an *immeuble* with 'columns', see OC, 381 and, below, p. 117. Cf. Gautier's 'Après le feuilleton' in *Émaux et Camées*: 'Mes colonnes sont alignées / Au portique du feuilleton', etc. In 'Théodore de Banville': 'Ce cri de pierre [la Poésie] s'unifie vers le ciel en les piliers interrompus' (OC, 521).

42 Cf. the 'fulgurante console' of 'Tout Orgueil . . .' (see p. 139), and the 'consoles' or 'crédences' of the *sonnet en yx* which support no 'ptyx' – fold or writing tablet (see p. 63).

43 OC, 385.

44 OC, 542.

45 For example, 'Un solitaire tacite concert se donne, par la lecture' (OC, 380); 'L'écrit, envol tacite d'abstraction' (OC, 385); and *Corr*, III, 177, quoted below, p. 117; and 'Le Vers et tout écrit . . . doit se montrer à même de subir l'épreuve orale . . ., au lieu qu'effectivement il a lieu au delà du silence que traversent se raréfiant en musiques mentales ses éléments' (OC, 855).

46 OC, 366.

47 Letter to Camille Mauclair, October 9, 1897; *Corr*, IX, 289.

48 Mallarmé's comments on a play by François Coppée, recorded in 1895 by André Fontainas; quoted in *Corr*, VII, 156.

49 OC, 367.

50 OC, 644–5.

51 Letter to Georges Rodenbach, March 25, 1888, on his book of poems, *Du silence*; *Corr*, III, 177.

52 B. Marchal, ed., *Poésies* (Gallimard, NRF, 1992), 248. See especially B. Marchal's *La Religion de Mallarmé* (Corti, 1988), 191–201.

53 OC, 649.

54 On this use of 'ébat', see OC, 386 (applied to language) or OC, 375 (to verse).

55 Ernest Prarond, 'Un poète' (of the Lamartinean school), dated 1854 in *A la chute du jour: Vers anciens et nouveaux, 1847–1876* (Lemerre, 1876), 297.

56 In *Le Parnasse contemporain*; quoted by P. Hambly, 'Deux sonnets de Mallarmé', 23. See also Ferdinand Fabre, 'Révérence', in *Feuilles de lierre* (Charpentier, 1853): 'Car je gage / Que malgré / Mon langage / Mesuré, / Dans l'armoire / La plus noire / Je pourris, / Loin du monde / Proie immonde / Des souris.'

57 Édélestand du Méril, *Essai philosophique sur le principe et les formes de la versification* (Brockhaus et Avenarius; Joubert, 1841).

58 *La Poésie de Stéphane Mallarmé*, 307.

59 OC, 332.

60 OC, 263. See also *Le Tombeau de Charles Baudelaire*: 'avec frissons / Celle son Ombre même', if 'Celle' refers to Poetry (see p. 231, n. 26).

61 OC, 261.

62 Mallarmé likes to point out that writers work with a stock of twenty or so letters. See also his remarks on the size of different vocabularies (OC, 1047).

63 Cf. letter to Paul Hervieu, February 1895, on a chapter of his book, *L'Armature*: 'une banque s'écroule, vraiment d'un fracas exact, sans le fastidieux entassement de détails préalable amoncelé toujours par les romans' (*Corr*, VII, 146). 'Fracas' could also be used to support the theatrical reading: 'Il se dit, dans les compositions littéraires, et surtout dans les pièces de théâtre, de ce qui frappe l'oreille et l'esprit comme fait le fracas' (Littré).

64 OC, 546 and 544.

65 OC, 648.

66 Letter to Charles Guérin, November 7, 1894; *Corr*, VII, 93.

67 Letter to Edmund Gosse, January 10, 1893; *Corr*, VI, 26. See also Mallarmé's letter to Albert Mockel, September 28, 1891 (*Corr*, IV, 310): 'une sorte de silence qui est la vraie spiritualité. Peut-être y a-t-il, et certainement, supériorité sur l'emploi des réels moyens: cuivre, bois, etc., puisque c'en est mentalement la raréfaction.'

68 *Journal*, ed. R. Ricatte, III, 800

(February 23, 1893); quoted in *Corr*, VI, 50, n. 5.

69 Notable exceptions: a chapter on *Petit Air II* in Gardner Davies' *Mallarmé et la 'couche suffisante d'intelligibilité'*, first published in *Synthèses* (Brussels, 1968); a peremptory analysis in Charles Mauron's *Mallarmé l'obscur*; lucid commentaries by J.-P. Richard in *L'Univers imaginaire de Mallarmé* (Seuil, 1961) and Paul Bénichou, 'Sur un sonnet de Mallarmé', in *Du romantisme au surnaturalisme: Hommage à Claude Pichois* (Neuchâtel: La Baconnière, 1985).

70 Cf. the Goncourts' *Journal*, ed. R. Ricatte, II, 632 (March 3, 1875): 'le nébuleux Mallarmé, qui professe qu'on ne doit pas commencer une phrase par un monosyllabe'.

71 Letter to Henri Cazalis, April 25, 1864; *Corr*, I, 117. See also the file of notes published by Jacques Scherer under the title, *Le 'Livre' de Mallarmé*, nouvelle édition (Gallimard, NRF, 1977), 181 (A): 'un livre ne commence ni ne finit: tout au plus fait-il semblant.'

72 OC, 653.

73 P, 8. See also pp. 12 and 19.

74 Ronsard, *Sonets et Madrigals pour Astrée*, I.

75 OC, 283.

76 A 'oiseleur' catches birds; a 'oiselier' breeds and sells them.

77 'Critique des *Poèmes saturniens*' (1890), *Oeuvres en prose complètes*, ed. Jacques Borel (Pléiade, 1972), 721.

78 See also 'A Théophile Gautier' in *Les Exilés*: 'Aux oiseleurs pareil, / Tu fis monter les Odes au vol d'aigle / Vers le rouge soleil.'

79 Gustave Le Vavasseur, 'Satire', *Poésies fugitives* (Dentu, 1846): 'Puis le collet tendu, complice de maint crime, / Cette trompeuse glu des poètes, la Rime, / Happe les rossignols ainsi que les moineaux.'

80 Nicarchus, in the Greek Anthology (II, 186): commentary by Norman Douglas in *Birds and Beasts of the*

Greek Anthology (Florence, privately
printed, 1927), 109–10. Thanks to
Gregory Hutchinson and Geoffrey
Neate.

81 'Sur un sonnet de Mallarmé', 276.

82 Letter to Rodolphe Darzens, March
25, 1888; Corr, V, 285–6.

83 Letter to Edmund Gosse, January 10,
1893; Corr, VI, 27.

84 On this subject, see Austin Gill,
'Mallarmé's Use of Christian
Imagery for Post-Christian Con-
cepts', in Order and Adventure in
Post-Romantic French Poetry: Essays
Presented to C.A. Hackett (Oxford:
Blackwell, 1973).

85 OC, 368.

86 Letter to Edmund Gosse, January 10,
1893; Corr, VI, 26.

87 OC, 368.

88 Mallarmé et la 'couche suffisante
d'intelligibilité', 327.

89 'Sur un sonnet de Mallarmé', 280.

90 Term used in the Petit traité de versification (1923) of Jules Romains and
Georges Chennevière to designate
rhymes like machine-niche. Mallarmé
uses a similar 'rhyme' – a variation
on the rime fraternisée – in Le Pitre
châtié: 'Qui pure s'exhala de ma
fraîcheur de nacre, / Rance nuit de la
peau. . . .' See also p. 240, n. 23, and,
on the 'inverse' rhymes of Salut, p.
191.

91 Quelques mots à quelques-uns (P,
84).

92 In Les Mots anglais, the letter d is said
to express 'la stagnation, la lourdeur
morale et l'obscurité' (OC, 950).

93 P, 471.

94 OC, 320.

95 Letter to Edmund Gosse, January 10,
1893; Corr, VI, 26.

96 Letter to Albert Giraud, April 3,
1891; Corr, IV, 215; French Studies
XLVIII, 1 (January 1994), 18.

97 'Sur un sonnet de Mallarmé', 277.

98 L'Univers imaginaire de Mallarmé,
307–8.

99 Allusions to the great project at this
stage are either extremely vague or
pessimistic: for example, the 'rêve
secret déçu' in a letter to Henri de

Régnier, December 5, 1891 (Corr,
IV, 345). On the habit of situating
Mallarmé's notion of writing at the
limit rather than along the asymp-
tote of his teleology: Barbara
Johnson, A World of Difference (Bal-
timore and London: The Johns
Hopkins University Press, 1987),
58.

100 On the verb 'abdiquer' in Prose pour
des Esseintes, see p. 173.

101 OC, 366.

102 OC, 396.

103 OC, 647.

104 OC, 367.

105 OC, 647.

106 This and the following definitions
are from Littré.

107 La Musique et les Lettres (Perrin,
1895), 43; and OC, 646.

108 Yves Bonnefoy proposes two corrections to the original edition, one
confirmed by Mallarmé in Divagations: Igitur, Divagations, Un coup
de Dés (Gallimard, NRF, 'Poésie',
1976; 1993), 434.

109 OC, 326.

110 On falconry as a literary image, see
Baudouin van den Abeele, La
Fauconnerie dans les lettres françaises
du XIIᵉ au XIVᵉ siècle (Leuven University Press, 1990).

111 OC, 395.

112 Letter to Émile Verhaeren, February
1895; Corr, VII, 149; my emphasis.

113 OC, 379.

114 Art. cit., 279, n. 7.

115 Y.-A. Favre, ed., Oeuvres, 513.

116 OC, 364.

117 OC, 364.

118 Letter to G. Albert Aurier, December 20, 1889: '[L'Oeuvre maudit]
laisse je ne sais quelle vibration de
silence furieux!' (Corr, III, 373).

119 Letter to Francis Vielé-Griffin,
October 9, 1893; Corr, VI, 172.

120 Letter to Henri Vandeputte, June
1898; Corr, X, 216.

121 Unpublished diary of Henri de
Régnier, quoted by Lloyd Austin in
Corr, VII, 38, n. 1.

122 Gardner Davies, Mallarmé et le drame
solaire: Essai d'exégèse raisonnée

(Corti, 1959), 227. See, however, the rich, cake-like analysis by R.G. Cohn, *Toward the Poems of Mallarmé*, especially 208 ff.

123 Émilie Noulet, *Dix poèmes de Stéphane Mallarmé* (Giard; Droz, 1948).

124 *L'Univers imaginaire de Mallarmé*, 263.

125 OC, 370.

126 Letter to Théodore Aubanel, July 28, 1866; *Corr*, I, 225.

127 Interview quoted in *L'Amitié de Stéphane Mallarmé et de Georges Rodenbach*, 119.

128 OC, 990.

129 OC, 327 and 867.

130 OC, 390.

131 OC, 360; my emphasis.

132 Letter to Méry Laurent, May 14, 1898; *Corr*, X, 188; my emphasis.

133 OC, 367.

134 Cf. Francis Ponge's 'Pluie' in *Le Parti pris des choses*: 'Au centre c'est un fin rideau (ou réseau) discontinu . . . elle ruisselle en nappe très mince, moirée à cause de courants très variés.'

135 See a similar sequence in notes published by J. Scherer: *Le 'Livre' de Mallarmé*, 39 (A) (*suite*).

136 See Mallarmé's letter to Léon Dierx, June 1894: 'ce petit livre ou temple' (*Corr*, VI, 275). Mallarmé also refers to his own work as a 'Temple' (letter to Armand Renaud, December 20, 1866; *Corr*, XI, 22).

137 *La Vie de Jean-Arthur Rimbaud* is described as an 'abrupt et dur basalte de conscience, le monument, dû à Rimbaud' (letter to Paterne Berrichon, December 1897; *Corr*, X, 45).

138 OC, 333.

139 OC, 367.

140 OC, 381.

141 OC, 647. Cf. OC, 229: Poe's *Philosophy of Composition* is described as 'un examen quasi sacrilège de chaque effet'.

142 First version of 'De l'orient passé des temps . . .' (*P*, 224–5). On the important corrections to be made to the text of *P* (verses 7 and 8 reversed; an extra syllable in line 4), see the review by Eileen Souffrin in *French Studies* (1984), 477–8. On *rimes homonymes*, see also, above, pp. 35 and 171.

143 OC, 503.

144 OC, 481.

145 OC, 333 and 860.

146 OC, 417.

147 Just as Mallarmé sometimes confuses himself with his work: for example, in a letter to Aubanel, July 28, 1866: '[le] centre de moi-même [replacing 'de mon oeuvre'], où je me tiens comme une araignée sacrée' (*Corr*, I, 225 and n. 1).

148 P, 419.

149 Letter to Victor Margueritte, August 29, 1886; *Corr*, III, 50.

150 *Mallarmé et le drame solaire*, 235.

151 OC, 368.

152 OC, 370.

153 OC, 481.

8 Un subtil mensonge

1 OC, 367.

2 OC, 511 (concerning Verlaine).

3 The earliest known version appeared in *La Revue critique*, April 6, 1884.

4 Letter to Rodolphe Darzens, March 25, 1888; *Corr*, V, 286.

5 Letter to Eugène de Roberty, November 1893; *Corr*, VI, 180.

6 *L'Univers imaginaire de Mallarmé*, 314.

7 Image borrowed from 'La Fausse entrée des sorcières dans *Macbeth*' (OC, 351).

8 Littré. Used in this sense by Mallarmé in a letter to Verhaeren, April 1898 (*Corr*, X, 133).

9 OC, 374. See also OC, 318 – 'l'écran de feuillets imprimés' – and a letter to André Ruÿters (April 15, 1898): 'je suis sous le charme laissé par *les Mains gantées et Pieds nus* volume comme un éventail, digne de la toilette d'une âme récente, entr'ouvrant cinq feuilles si variées et balançant presque un même souffle

de vie intense et de sourire' (*Corr*, X, 140–41).

10 Cf., in the Vers de circonstance, 'Bel éventail que je mets en émoi / De mon *séjour* chez une blonde fée' (*P*, 552).

11 For this use of 'subtil', see p. 151 and note 39 below.

12 OC, 366.

13 OC, 365.

14 OC, 374.

15 Ibid.

16 A. Eude-Dugaillon, 'Le Boa', in *Fiel et miel, poésies* (Paris: Paulin; Nancy: Mlle Gonet, 1839). See also Glatigny's 'Pour une comédienne' in *Les Vignes folles* (1860); *Poésies* (Lemerre, 1870), 19: 'une douce nonchalante / Faite à manier l'éventail, / Et laissant, de sa bouche lente, / Tomber quelques mots en détail'.

17 OC, 365.

18 Curiously, Roger Fry translates 'Vertige! voici que frissonne / L'espace' as 'Vastness! See how thrills / Space', and Mallarmé's 'aigrette de vertige' in *Un coup de Dés* is Brian Coffey's 'aigrette of vastness' in *Dice Thrown Never Will Annul Chance* (Dublin: The Dolmen Press, 1965).

19 Cf., in the *Finale* of *Hérodiade*: 'vertige / Ensuite pour couler tout le long de ma tige / Vers'.

20 OC, 318.

21 See the *Éventail* for Mme Madier de Montjau (*P*, 552): 'Aile quels paradis élire', etc.

22 OC, 653.

23 'The Traditional Element in Mallarmé's "Autre éventail de Mademoiselle Mallarmé"', *French Studies Bulletin* XLVI (Spring 1993), 11–15 – was Mallarmé the only poet to use fans as images of poems?

24 For a description of the fan, see *P*, 297.

25 OC, 286.

26 OC, 374.

27 OC, 921.

28 *P*, 555. See also Lloyd Austin's note

in *French Studies* XLIV, 2 (April 1990), 193–4.

29 P, 552.

30 Les Fenêtres, 'M'introduire dans ton histoire . . .', *Dons de fruits glacés*, XXXI.

31 P, 670: *temple* rhymes only with *exemple*, *ample* and *contemple* (very strictly speaking a derivative rhyme); *pompe* ('pomp') rhymes only with *rompe* (and compounds), *trompe*, *estompe* and *pompe* ('pump'). See also the fourth *Éventail* (*P*, 552), where 'Simple' at the beginning of verse 1 is picked up by 'Semble' at the beginning of verse 4 (cf., *supra*, p. 47: *ensemble-exemple*).

32 Words, 'comme une virtuelle traînée de feux' (OC, 366); 'une réciprocité de feux distante' (OC, 386); assonance, 'dans son feu plus nu presque plus précieuse que la rime' (OC, 858). Also the 'feux vils' of 'Quand l'ombre menaça . . .' and the images of 'foudre' and 'fulguration' (pp. 67, 171, 192 and 209).

33 Letter to Émile Verhaeren, January 6, 1892; *Corr*, V, 29.

34 OC, 648.

35 Cf. OC, 499–500: 'les morceaux d'étoffes d'Orient . . . amortissent [le mur] en crépuscules doux.'

36 OC, 380.

37 Letter to Charles Valentino, February 15, 1896; published by Lloyd Austin in *French Studies* XL, 1 (January 1986), 18.

38 OC, 311.

39 OC, 285, and another example of an etymological 'subtil' in a letter to François Coppée, May 18, 1887: 'un courant subtil et supérieur de rêverie ou de sentiments' (*Corr*, III, 113).

9 Un jeu qui confirme la fiction

1 OC, 420.

2 For the date of *Prose*, see Appendix II. The variants given in *P* are unreliable, as the manuscript reproduced in the same edition opposite page

334 reveals: 'Je le maintiens' should have a small *j*; 'de paysage' should be followed by a full-stop instead of a comma; and the last words of line 10 are 'les tiens!', not 'les siens!' For an accurate transcription, see the editions of *Poésies* by L.J. Austin (Flammarion, GF, 1989) or B. Marchal (Gallimard, NRF, 'Poésie', 1992). For a facsimile of the Gualdo copy: *DSM I*, 15–16.

3   For critical bibliographies of *Prose* studies: Lloyd Austin, in *Revue d'histoire littéraire de la France*, 1954, 146–61, and Marshall Olds, *Desire Seeking Expression: Mallarmé's 'Prose pour des Esseintes'* (Lexington, KY, French Forum, 1983), 84–110.

4   *A Rebours*, chapters 15 and 14.

5   Some idea of the needless difficulties created by a traditional approach can be found in Paul Bénichou's sensitive and detailed commentary, 'La *Prose pour des Esseintes*', *Saggi e Ricerche di letteratura francese* XXVII (1988), 51–2: 'Je n'ai considéré la *Prose pour des Esseintes* que du point de vue du sens, m'abstenant . . . de vouloir y éclaircir les voies et moyens de la réussite poétique . . . considérant comme hasardeux d'expliquer les beautés d'un poème avant d'en avoir compris la signification.' The exact opposite was more likely to succeed.

6   *OC*, 420.

7   Cohn, *Toward the Poems of Mallarmé*, 241.

8   This and the following quotations from Edmond Bonniot's preface to *Igitur* (*OC*, 427).

9   *OC*, 428.

10 Ancient Greek unit of measurement for dry goods.

11 *OC*, 646 ('ingéniosité' should be changed to 'ingénuité').

12 *OC*, 855.

13 *OC*, 645.

14 *OC*, 850.

15 *OC*, 921.

16 *OC*, 333.

17 *OC*, 400.

18 Chadwick points out that in the earlier version of the penultimate stanza, 'Elle' can only be attached to 'soeur' since the 'enfant' is not mentioned. 'Soeur' and 'enfant' must therefore be the same (*Revue d'histoire littéraire de la France* LXVIII, 1 [January–February, 1968], 87).

19 *Mallarmé and the Art of Being Difficult*, 33.

20 *Toward the Poems of Mallarmé*, 245.

21 *OC*, 367.

22 *OC*, 374 and line 16 of *Prose*.

23 *Oeuvres complètes*, II, 108; Baudelaire's emphasis.

24 *OC*, 333.

25 *OC*, 365.

26 *OC*, 366.

27 *OC*, 345.

28 *OC*, 363.

29 *Oraison funèbre d'Henriette d'Angleterre*; my emphasis.

30 Ecclesiastes 6:4–5. Lemaître de Sacy translation.

31 Revelation 13:8; 17:8; 20:15.

32 See Austin Gill, art. cit., p. 235, n. 84.

33 A. Desplaces review of Ténint's *Prosodie* in *Revue de Paris*, 1844, p. 190; Sainte-Beuve, 'A la Rime', in *Joseph Delorme*; Banville, 'Épilogue', *Idylles prussiennes*.

34 *OC*, 264. Cf. Hugo: 'Mes deux rimes sont deux cymbales' (*Dernière gerbe*, no. 82).

35 *OC*, 368.

36 *OC*, 327.

37 *OC*, 333.

38 *OC*, 663. See also 'le devoir / Idéal' in *Toast funèbre*; *Richard Wagner* ('[les] poëtes dont il usurpe le devoir'; *OC*, 541); 'quelque devoir de tout recréer' (*OC*, 481); and Mallarmé's letter to Cazalis: '[le bonheur] est le faux but de la vie: le vrai est le Devoir. Le Devoir, qu'il s'appelle l'art, la lutte, comme on veut' (April 27, 1863; *Corr*, I, 88).

39 *OC*, 850.

40 *Pas-pas* is a *rime homonyme*; *sais-tu-vêtu* is a potential *rime riche*; for *rie-Pulchérie*, see p. 176.

41 Letter to Huysmans, May 18, 1884; *Corr*, II, 261.

42 *L'Art poétique*, III, 173–6.

43 Cohn, *Toward the Poems of Mallarmé*, 249.

44 *Jean-Louis* (1822), chapter 18. *L'Oeuvre de Balzac*, ed. Albert Béguin (Formes et Reflets, 1953), XV, 664.

45 Letter to François Coppée, December 5, 1866; *Corr*, I, 234.

46 OC, 851.

47 'Épilogue', *Idylles prussiennes*. For the image of crying, see also the opening lines of Valéry's *La Jeune Parque*.

48 Cf. *L'Après-midi d'un faune*, where the 'jonc jumeau' produces a 'solo long' and, between, the rhyme *joue-joue*.

49 Cf. Mallarmé's comments on free verse in *Le Figaro*, August 3, 1895: 'Les occasions sont rares qui exigent toute l'ampleur du Verbe, tout le chatoiement de la parole, toute la symphonie des mots.' (Quoted in *P*, 432.) On 'ampleur' as a positive aesthetic quality: J.-P. Richard, *L'Univers imaginaire de Mallarmé*, 332–3; and on the dangers of too much 'ampleur': 305.

50 *Desire Seeking Expression: Mallarmé's 'Prose pour des Esseintes'*, 47.

51 Paul Bénichou, 'La *Prose pour des Esseintes*', 48–9.

52 *Le Symbolisme de Mallarmé* (Nizet, 1950), 42.

53 OC, 403.

54 B. Marchal, ed., *Poésies*, 227.

55 Cf. Brunetto Latini, *Le Livre du Trésor*, quoted by Littré ('Rime'): 'Li sentiers de rime est plus estroiz et plus fors.'

56 OC, 648.

57 Cohn, *Toward the Poems of Mallarmé*, 260, n. 11.

58 A.R. Chisholm, *Mallarmé's 'Grand Oeuvre'* (Manchester University Press, 1962), 51.

59 Letter to Henri Cazalis, 1864; *Corr*, I, 137.

60 OC, 853.

61 *Mallarmé and the Art of Being Difficult*, 57–8.

62 Alfred Ernout, *Recueil de textes latins archaïques* (Klincksieck, 1947),

no. 133. Thanks to Gregory Hutchinson.

63 Bowie, *Mallarmé and the Art of Being Difficult*, 69.

64 Ibid., 78.

65 OC, 362.

66 *Illusions perdues*, *La Comédie humaine*, V, 204.

67 OC, 481.

68 OC, 530.

69 The same pun occurred to Balzac in his *Conte drolatique*, 'D'ung paoure qui avoit nom le Vieulx-par-chemins' ('pourceque il estoit iaune et secq comme velin, ains pourceque il estoyt touiours par voyes et routes, monts et vaulx').

70 Bowie, *Mallarmé and the Art of Being Difficult*, 58.

71 OC, 368; my emphasis.

72 OC, 380.

73 OC, 851.

74 According to Edmond Bonniot (OC, 429).

75 OC, 655.

76 OC, 868.

77 OC, 492.

78 OC, 875.

79 OC, 395.

80 OC, 336. For a third (but obviously not the only) nuance of 'terme' ('Beauté' or the definitive, impersonal poem), see J. Lawler, 'Vers le "terme" mallarméen', *L'Age nouveau* I (1987), 18–26.

81 OC, 335–6.

10 Conclusion: Tangage

1 Letter to Emmanuel Delbousquet, June 29, 1895; *Corr*, VII, 233.

2 Huysmans, letter to Émile Zola, quoted in *Corr*, II, 262, n. 1.

3 Letter to Octave Mirbeau, September 10, 1888; *Corr*, III, 260.

4 OC, 664.

5 Letter to Zola on *Son Excellence Eugène Rougon*, March 18, 1876; *Corr*, II, 107.

6 For a more generalizing and – despite appearances – subjective approach to the self-referentiality of *Hérodiade*,

see H. Ishida, 'Le *rythme-sujet* des poèmes mallarméens', *Études de langue et littérature françaises* 54 (March 1989), 35–52.

7 Émilie Noulet, *Dix poèmes*, 147.

8 For example, Cohn, who assumes, however, that the 'vague littérature' is also Mallarmé's (*Toward the Poems of Mallarmé*, 190).

9 Quoted in *P*, 433.

10 Letter to Léon Dierx, June 1894; *Corr*, VI, 275.

11 March 25, 1895; quoted in *Corr*, VII, 185, n. 2.

12 June 7, 1887; *Corr*, III, 120.

13 *Stéphane Mallarmé in English Verse* (Cape, 1927), 151.

14 *The Penguin Book of French Verse* (Penguin, 1975), 439.

15 Letter to Rodolphe Darzens, March 25, 1888; *Corr*, V, 285.

16 Letter to Edmund Gosse, January 10, 1893; *Corr*, VI, 27.

17 February 1895; *Corr*, VII, 159.

18 Cohn, *Toward the Poems of Mallarmé*, 33.

19 Letter to Jean Moréas, May 24, 1886; *Corr*, III, 33.

20 *Le Symbolisme de Mallarmé*, 107–8.

21 *OC*, 408. Sirens are also associated with ideas in *Planches et Feuillets* and *Crise de vers* (*OC*, 328 and 367).

22 Acrostically. Cf. the last quatrain of 'Une négresse par le démon secouée . . .' –

E
L
A
Pâle

See also Mallarmé's letter to Félicien Champsaur, May 12, 1890: 'Je ne vous hais qu'en raison de la majuscule ôtée au vers, la lettre d'attaque y a, selon moi, la même importance que la rime et on ne saurait assez fastueusement la marquer' (*Corr*, IV, 105); and a similar comment in a letter to Charles Guérin, October 25, 1895: 'ô joie, la majuscule est restituée au vers' (*Corr*, VII, 278). The principal idea is that the initial

letter of the verse is its 'clé allitérative' (*OC*, 654).

23 Cf. *L'Après-midi d'un faune*, vv. 60–62: 'avide / D'ivresse [. . .] divers'; 'Le vierge, le vivace . . .': 'vierge', 'givre'; 'vivre', 'hiver'; *Le Pitre châtié*: 'nacre / Rance'; etc. (See also p. 128)

24 See p. 231, n. 42. Dujardin's irregular verses are described as flower-stalks, 'les unes à hauteur du pied, sous la main les autres, vos vers' (May 5, 1891; *Corr*, IV, 230–31). The seemingly irrelevant length of verses (i.e. their actual length on the page rather than the number of syllables) is alluded to in Verlaine's 'Dans la grotte' (*Fêtes galantes*), where alexandrines are visually 'concealed' among the octosyllabic lines.

25 Letter to Léopold Dauphin, August 1898; *Corr*, X, 245.

26 On Mallarmé's allusions to English words – 'se délivre', 'grief', 'ignoré', 'legs', etc. – see G. Robb, 'Mallarmé's False Friends', *French Studies Bulletin* 49 (Winter 1993), 13–15. For representative complaints that Mallarmé thought in English, see the texts cited by Scherer in the first section of *L'Expression littéraire dans l'oeuvre de Mallarmé* (Droz, 1947): 'L'Influence anglaise.'

27 *Toward the Poems of Mallarmé*, 35. As in Boileau's prescription for the *idylle*: 'Son tour simple et naïf n'a rien de fastueux / Et n'aime point l'orgueil d'un vers présomptueux.' (*L'Art poétique*, II, 7–8.)

28 B. Marchal, ed., *Poésies*, 179.

29 F.C. St Aubyn, *Stéphane Mallarmé*, updated edition (Twayne, 1989), 99.

30 *OC*, 332.

Epilogue

1 *Un coup de Dés.*

2 *OC*, 860.

3 Letter to Henri Cazalis, July 1866; *Corr*, I, 220.

4 *OC*, 333–4.

5 *OC*, 881.

6 Examples of typographical devices announcing *Un coup de Dés* are given

by Jacques Scherer in *L'Expression littéraire dans l'oeuvre de Mallarmé*, 206.

7 For example, in 'A la nue accablante . . .', 'faute', at the rhyme, refers to the absence of any hubristic 'faute' that might have brought about 'perdition'.

8 See M. Bowie, *Mallarmé and the Art of Being Difficult*, 118.

9 'Septentrion' can also designate Ursa Major.

10 Letter to André Gide, May 14, 1897; *Corr*, IX, 172. See also Mallarmé's letter to Camille Mauclair, October 8, 1897; *Corr*, IX, 288.

11 OC, 386.

12 Letter to Charles Morice, October 27, 1892; *Corr*, V, 140.

13 For example in the edition of *Un coup de Dés* by Mitsou Ronat and Tibor Papp (Change errant / d'atelier, 1980): see comments by Cohn in *Vues sur Mallarmé* (Nizet, 1991), 269–71. The same edition contains a similar set of *rapprochements* to those which follow in Jacques Roubaud's typographical reconstruction of the poem. According to M. Ronat's introduction, J. Roubaud shows *Un coup de Dés* narrating the death of the alexandrine and the advent of free verse: Victor Hugo as the 'maniaque chenu', the dozen of the dice and the alexandrine, the 'voile alternative' of the Page, 'ais' as a typographical term, the silence of the mute 'e', 'quelque point dernier' as rhyme, etc.

14 *Traité de poétique supérieure* (Neuchâtel: H. Messeiller, 1956), 367–8.

15 Cohn identifies writing as a 'second level of imagery' in *Un coup de Dés*. 'Intermittent' imagery, but which 'dictates in great part the general wave-pattern of the Poem: each Page begins with a crest and ends with a trough, *aliter* inflated versions of the squiggles constituting man's most characteristic activity.' He also notes 'a gigantic pen and ink-well' on page three and the leaning of the writing pen on pages seven and ten

(*Mallarmé's 'Un coup de Dés'*, 28). The 'isotopy' of writing is also mentioned by G. Montbertrand (art. cit., p. 231, n. 37).

16 *La Religion de Mallarmé*, 366–72.

17 OC, 866–7.

18 OC, 645.

19 *A Short History of French Literature* (Penguin, 1954).

20 In *What is Art?* There are similar remarks in Benedetto Croce's 'Il "Segreto" di Mallarmé', *Quaderni della 'Critica'* V, 14 (1949), 91–7, with nine errors in the transcription of the sonnet.

21 See p. 236, n. 137.

22 Letter to Émile Verhaeren, April 14, 1891; *Corr*, IV, 223–4.

23 Letter to Maurice de Faramond, January 1898; published by Lloyd Austin in *French Studies* XLIV, 2 (April 1990), 184–5.

24 On the contested ambiguity of 'plume', see examples given by Cohn in *Mallarmé's Masterwork. New Findings* (The Hague and Paris: Mouton & Co., 1966), 67, and Derrida's *La Dissémination* (1972), trans. Barbara Johnson (London: The Athlone Press, 1981), 274–5.

25 OC, 387.

26 An analogy might be drawn with the deliberately 'flat', two-dimensional murals of contemporary painters like Puvis de Chavannes and, generally, with their suspicious, intellectualizing approach to perspective and the other traditional means of painting.

27 OC, 870.

28 OC, 647; see also OC, 400: 'Évoquer, dans une ombre exprès, l'objet tu, par des mots allusifs, jamais directs, se réduisant à du silence égal, comporte tentative proche de créer.'

29 Obliteration is built into the text itself. Along with the familiar problem of 'obscurity', there is the more severe one of transmission. To reproduce *Un coup de Dés* accurately would require an enormous amount of data, and no perfect edition has ever existed. On editions, see Vir-

ginia La Charité, *The Dynamics of Space: Mallarmé's 'Un coup de Dés jamais n'abolira le Hasard'* (Lexington, KY: French Forum, 1987), chapter 2.

30   On different possible sequences, according to size and order of appearance, see V. La Charité, *The Dynamics of Space*, 90 ff.

31   Gardner Davies, *Vers une explication rationnelle du coup de Dés*, 79.

32   In his preface, Mallarmé claims that the irregular form of the poem is appropriate for 'tels sujets d'imagination pure et complexe ou intellect'.

33   *OC*, 375.

34   On the possibility that 'où' in 'où la manoeuvre avec l'âge oubliée' should be 'ou', see Gardner Davies, *Vers une explication rationnelle du coup de Dés*, 95.

35   Not 'passe', as in *OC*.

36   *OC*, 645.

37   *OC*, 364.

38   *OC*, 362.

39   Boileau, *L'Art poétique*, I, 173.

40   *OC*, 362.

41   *OC*, 363, 362, 361 and 512.

42   *OC*, 644.

43   *OC*, 365.

44   *OC*, 386.

45   *OC*, 367.

46   *OC*, 850.

47   *OC*, 646.

48   *OC*, 366.

49   *OC*, 647.

50   *OC*, 867.

51   *OC*, 367.

52   *OC*, 367.

53   *Arts Magazine*, January 26, 1965; quoted in OED, 2nd edn ('Minimal').

54   April 7, 1891 and July 21, 1896; *Corr*, IV, 219 and VIII, 203.

55   'Ces fâcheux . . . par le fait de feuillets entre-bâillés pénètrent, émanent, s'insinuent' (*OC*, 375).

56   *OC*, 364.

57   *OC*, 369–70.

58   *OC*, 481.

59   The words 'de vertige' should be on the same line as 'aigrette' and the following lines should also be raised (cf. *OC*, 470–71).

60   *OC*, 333.

61   *OC*, 364.

62   *La Religion de Mallarmé*, 490.

63   See Peter Dayan, 'Poetry Dies Again', in *Poetry in France: Metamorphoses of a Muse*, ed. Keith Aspley and Peter France (Edinburgh University Press, 1992), 183.

64   See the 'Bibliographie' of *Divagations* (dated November 1896): 'un poète qui par habitude ne pratique pas le vers libre'.

Appendix I: Rhyme Lists

1   Letter to Henry Coutant on the subject of bicycles, May 20, 1896; *Corr*, VIII, 155.

Appendix II: The Date of Prose pour des Esseintes

1   Huysmans first told Mallarmé of his idea for *A Rebours* in October 1882 (*Corr*, II, 234, n. 1).

2   With minor exceptions, the 1885 version is the same as later versions in *Poésies* (édition photolithographiée) and *Vers et Prose*.

3   Most recently in his edition of *Poésies* (GF, 1989).

4   *DSM* I, 9–39.

5   Letter to Huysmans, May 18, 1884, alluding to chapter 8 of *A Rebours*; *Corr*, II, 261.

6   *OC*, 664.

Index of Names and Works

Index of Works by Mallarmé